Families, Schools, and Communities

Families, Schools, and Communities
Building Partnerships for Educating Children

Chandler Barbour
Towson State University

Nita H. Barbour
University of Maryland, Baltimore County

Merrill,
an imprint of Prentice Hall
Upper Saddle River, New Jersey   Columbus, Ohio

Library of Congress Cataloging-in-Publication Data
Barbour, Chandler.
    Families, schools, and communities : building
partnerships for educating children / Chandler
Barbour, Nita H. Barbour.
        p.   cm.
    Includes bibliographical references and index.
    ISBN 0-02-305861-7 (paper)
    1. Home and school—United States.
2. Community and school—United States.
3. School environment—United States.
4. Students—United States—Social conditions.
5. Education—United States—Curricula.
6. Child development—United States.
I. Barbour, Nita.   II. Title.
    LC225.3.B27   1997
    370.19′3—dc20   95-51298
                                                            CIP

Cover image: © Robert Mayo
Editor: Ann Castel Davis
Production Editor: Louise N. Sette
Copy Editor: Robert L. Marcum
Photo Editor: Dawn Garrott
Design Coordinator: Jill E. Bonar
Text Designer: Susan E. Frankenberry
Cover Designer: Brian Deep
Production Manager: Laura Messerly

This book was set in Adobe New Caledonia by The
Clarinda Company and was printed and bound by
Quebecor Printing/Book Press. The cover was printed
by Phoenix Color Corp.

© 1997 by Prentice-Hall, Inc.
Simon & Schuster/A Viacom Company
Upper Saddle River, New Jersey 07458

Photo credits: The Bettmann Archive, pp. 23, 30, 37,
39; Ben Chandler/Merrill/Prentice Hall, p. 18; Scott
Cunningham/Merrill/Prentice Hall, pp. 11, 59, 74, 88,
107, 146, 153, 200, 205, 239, 243, 246, 266; Dan
Floss/Merrill/Prentice Hall, pp. 141, 202; Scott
Haskell/Bangor Daily News, pp. 1, 15, 132, 137, 165,
270; Courtesy of IBM, p. 129; Bruce
Johnson/Merrill/Prentice Hall, pp. 123, 171, 275;
Lloyd Lemmerman/Merrill/Prentice Hall, p. 228;
Anthony Magnacca/Merrill/Prentice Hall, pp. 43, 48,
49, 61, 119, 121, 176, 179, 226, 267; Mary Jane
Porterfield, p. 160; Barbara Schwartz/Merrill/Prentice
Hall, pp. 105, 196, 223, 259; Anne
Vega/Merrill/Prentice Hall, pp. 5, 12, 31, 40, 53, 71,
83, 93, 96, 99, 115, 148, 169, 182, 190, 220, 235, 253;
Tom Watson/Merrill/Prentice Hall, p. 187; and Todd
Yarrington/Merrill/Prentice Hall, pp. 67, 78, 178, 213,
217.

Printed in the United States of America

10 9 8 7 6 5 4 3 2

ISBN: 0-02-305861-7

Prentice-Hall International (UK) Limited, *London*
Prentice-Hall of Australia Pty. Limited, *Sydney*
Prentice-Hall of Canada, Inc., *Toronto*
Prentice-Hall Hispanoamericana, S. A., *Mexico*
Prentice-Hall of India Private Limited, *New Delhi*
Prentice-Hall of Japan, Inc., *Tokyo*
Simon & Schuster Asia Pte. Ltd., *Singapore*
Editora Prentice-Hall do Brasil, Ltda., *Rio de Janeiro*

DEDICATION

We dedicate this book to the fascinating families with which we are connected, to the many challenging schools we have served and from which we have learned, and to the many satisfying communities we have been welcomed into and that have provided good settings for our own networks and for our aspirations.

Preface

Children start their formal schooling with four to five years of an extensive education already in place, and they continue to encounter educational experiences—in places other than classrooms—throughout their school lives. But in spite of this increasing bombardment of outside stimuli on children, schools in the United States too often continue to struggle with traditional academic content and skills while ignoring the other educative forces in children's lives. The results are overlapping efforts between school and home, incomplete schooling, missed opportunities, schools accused of irrelevance, and certainly confusion about the direction children's formal eduction should take.

Today, new and sobering challenges face our postindustrial society. Cultural and ethnic diversity is expanding rapidly in the United States, and special needs grow each year. An increasing amount of poverty cries out for resolution. The face of the world will never be the same again, and requirements for citizens in the twenty-first century will be very different than they are today. It is paramount that we develop education programs aimed at blending interests, using cooperation to the fullest, and identifying all resources possible for addressing children's educational needs.

Fear of being overwhelmed in the international marketplace stirs anxiety in many quarters as we approach the beginning of a new century, and fed-eral and state governments have refocused interest on upgrading the quality of education in the the United States. The 1994 Goals 2000: Educate America Act resulted from political recognition that education must be the responsibility of all citizens, not just teachers. Business and commercial establishments in the United States are becoming attuned to the imperatives of a well-educated populace, and many businesses now seek connections with schools. Most authorities agree that major changes in the procedures, the curriculum, and the formats of U.S. schools are needed as never before. For many, the greatest changes focus on drawing more partners into the management of formal education.

A basic tenet of *Families, Schools, and Communities: Building Partnerships for Educating Children* is that schools will always be a primary venue for educating the young child. However, to accomplish the task at hand, all communities must develop vibrant partnerships—uniting parents and community members with teachers in educating tomorrow's citizens. School personnel must be in the forefront of this endeavor, and must become the brokers for establishing collaborative relationships.

Significant steps for improving children's education through collaboration are already at work in different schools and communities across the United States. These beginning ventures provide intriguing evidence and guides for others to follow. We do not need to reconceptualize our curriculums and our teaching practices. The big job now is to study and adapt the amazing examples that now exist.

ORGANIZATION OF THIS TEXT

We feel it vital for preservice teachers, as well as inservice teachers, to understand the myriad influences on children's lives and how the structures of homes, schools, and communities affect their learning. By acknowledging this broader scope of curriculum, teachers in training will recognize the family and the community as crucial educative forces.

We begin with an overview of influences surrounding young children. We identify the three primary social settings of home, school, and community, and discuss how they interact to affect children's lives. Society does change, of course, and some situations influencing children have intensified in recent years. We categorize these influence patterns to gain a perspective of what exists in the United States today.

Chapter 2 focuses on how responsibilities for children's education have emerged over time, and how different ethnic groups in the United States have been affected over three centuries. We look particularly at the uneven progress of collaborations in schoolwork.

The next two chapters present information on U.S. family life, reviewing various family patterns and recognizing the different ways that families function. Prospective teachers will grasp the range of situations professionals encounter as they work with children in a diverse society, and may comprehend the logic for establishing collaborations in light of this diversity.

Chapter 5 examines the responsibilities of each of the three social settings for educating children. We point out the various educational assignments and expectations each setting places on the others.

Chapters 6, 7, and 8 deal with curriculum in the three social settings. Curriculum surrounds children, and much of what children learn comes from the world outside classrooms. Readers should recognize that all citizens are educators, and that when teachers acknowledge this there is even greater potential for learning.

The last four chapters focus on the possibilities for collaboration among the three social settings. In Chapter 9, we discuss traditional as well as new ways for teachers, parents, and others to work together. Chapter 10 reviews current model programs that demonstrate partnerships working beneficially. Chapter 11 highlights effective social settings and extends ideas about the ingredients for developing partnerships. Chapter 12 examines the difficult process of getting together. In this last chapter, we review the steps required to establish a partnership. We then use idealized rural and urban school districts to demonstrate how two communities are struggling toward collaboration, exploring the typical problems they encounter, and evaluating their progress.

SPECIAL FEATURES

To assist instructors and students using this text, we have included several pedagogical aids.

Chapter objectives and summaries. Concise statements of each chapter's main ideas serve as advanced organizers for the content that follows. Chapter summaries review the highlights in the content.

Vignettes. Depictions of real-life events clarify many concepts throughout the text. These will encourage readers to reflect on their own experiences and will make the information more meaningful.

Suggested activities and questions. Each chapter ends with questions and activities that give instructors a means to make the text applicable to their own classrooms. For students, the activities will help apply learning and stimulate reflection on experience.

Recommended readings. In addition to the extensive references, which serve as background and base for the text, we list particular titles at the end of each chapter. These selections allow for a more thorough examination of the chapter content.

Annotated bibliography of children's literature. This annotated bibliography provides instructors as well as preservice teachers with curriculum material. In addition, the selections depict valuable examples of children in different family arrangements learning in a variety of settings.

Glossary. Because the text draws from sociology, psychology, human development, and anthropology, as well as from pedagogy and curriculum content, we include a glossary to help readers with specialized terms.

ACKNOWLEDGMENTS

Many people assisted in the writing of this text. We would like to acknowledge particularly the following individuals: Audrey Jewett for research on materials; Stevie Hoffman for reading and commenting on manuscript drafts; and Christine Fowler for basic research on children's literature. Library personnel at the University of Maine and the University of Maryland have been patient, helpful, and supportive in filling numerous requests and supplying materials in a very timely fashion. We also wish to thank Louise Sette, our production editor at Prentice Hall, and freelance copyeditor Robert L. Marcum for their many valuable contributions. Many individuals reviewed this text, and we thank them here: Linda G. Aiken, Southwestern Community College; Dorothy W. Hewes, San Diego State University; Janie H. Humphries, Louisiana Tech University; Ruth McBride, Colorado State University; and Donna S. Quick, University of Kentucky.

Contents

CHAPTER 4

Parenting the Child   67

CHAPTER 5

Responsibility for Educating Children 93

CHAPTER 6

Curriculum of the Home   115

CHAPTER 7

Curriculum of the School 141

CHAPTER 8

Curriculum of the Community 165

CHAPTER 9

Traditional and Innovative Strategies for Working Together 187

Home, School, and Community Influences on Children's Lives

There was a child went forth every day, And the first object he looked upon and received with wonder or pity or love or dread, that object he became, And that object became part of him for the day or a certain part of the day . . . or for many years or stretching cycles of years.

(Whitman, 1855, p. 90)

This chapter highlights the many ways in which young children's learning, behaviors, viewpoints, and habits are affected by family members, by school personnel, and by members of the immediate and larger community. In reading this chapter you will learn:

1. How the three social settings—home, school, and community—affect children's perceptions and attitudes about learning and schooling.

2. How these three social settings have greater or lesser impact depending on the child's age and stage of development.

3. How various forms of media, plus the entertainment industry, exert influence on children and how that influence affects their learning and behavior.

4. What the impact of special interest groups is on children's learning and behavior.

Zach was waiting at the child care center for his mother to pick him up. He donned his Power Ranger™ helmet, a gift from his father during their last visit. Zach picked up his Power Ranger™ toy from his cubbie where he had left it on arriving at the center, and approached Kelsey, also waiting for her mother. "I'm warning you, if you don't tell me where you planted the bomb, I'm going to drill a hole in ya," he said in his deepest voice. He pushed his toy at Kelsey. "No, I won't tell. We'll all blow up," giggled Kelsey, entering into the play and holding up her fists to Zach. The children lunged at each other growling and hissing until Zach accidentally struck Kelsey, and she began to cry. At that moment, Zach's mother and the teacher entered the room. The teacher, calming Kelsey, said to Zach's mother, "We don't allow aggressive play here at the center. I really wish you wouldn't let Zach bring toys like that."

In spite of Zach's attempt to explain what happened, his tired mother informed him he couldn't watch television while she got ready to go out. But while he waited for his father to pick him up, he could read a book, quietly. *When they reached home she let Zach select* Three Billy Goats Gruff *and* Max's Dragon Shirt. *When Tom, Zach's mother's boyfriend, arrived, Zach asked him to read. As Tom got to the first little goat crossing the bridge, Zach exclaimed, "Oh, let me read the troll* part," and pulling the book closer, asked, "Is this where the troll speaks?"

"How did you know?" Tom exclaimed.

Zach replied, "Dad told me," then, in a gruff, "pretend read" voice, demanded, "Who's that tramping on my bridge?" At each goat's passing his voice got gruffer, and he clenched his fist as he told the goats he was going to eat them up. When the third goat passed, Tom, in character, gave Zach a gentle push, hugging and tickling him, as the "goat" pushed the troll into the river. Zach giggled and said, "Let's read it again, and I'll be the goats this time." When Zach got to the third goat part he butted Tom, who gently pulled Zach off the couch with him, "falling into the river." A bit of horseplay ensued. Zach then got up and said, "Let's read Max's Dragon Shirt. I'm going to ask my Dad to buy me a Dragon shirt like that. Isn't it wild?"

....

All children are constantly developing. Developmental processes and influences from the environment do not cease when adults stop instruction or leave the scene. Experiences of one kind or another bombard the perceptual field of any child, constantly influencing learning and development, for better or worse. Zach's feelings and attitudes toward aggressive behavior, as well as his reading habits, are influenced by his interactions at school, at home, and in his community, and by what he witnesses through the media.

The messages children receive from their surroundings aren't always consistent, but all still influence attitudes and values. One can't be sure, for example, exactly what Zach is internalizing. It appears his attitude toward reading is positive and that he is getting similar messages from those close to him. Reading appears to be fun, people answer his questions about text, and respond to his reactions to the story. Though his mother denied him television that day, she allowed him to select favorite books to entertain himself.

The messages Zach receives about aggression, though, may not be as consistent. Zach's father buys him toys, such as his Power Rangers™ toy and helmet, that represent aggression, but the child care center bans them. The mother attempts to reinforce the school's nonaggressive policy by forbidding television temporarily, and by suggesting a more passive activity. Still, Zach finds acceptance for his need to express aggression by reenacting a story with his mother's friend and engaging in mild horseplay.

Children's learning is greatly affected by the attitudes, values, and actions emanating from homes, schools, and communities, but of course the impact varies according to children's stages of development and their amount of contact with these social settings. Children's learning is also extensively influenced by their immediate neighborhood, and perhaps even more so by their extended community as communicated to them through the media and the entertainment industry. Special interest groups will influence policies of schools and community endeavors, and thus will have an impact on children's learning. Graham (1993) points out that the school can actually be less effective in educating children than can the cumulative influences of other forces. This is especially true when school messages contradict the impressions children receive from community, home, and television or other media.

As a teacher, you cannot ensure that all the influences children receive are positive for their learning, but you must be sensitive to the idea that children's learning will be affected, both positively and negatively, by many factors beyond your control. You must also be attuned to your own feelings and reactions, as these, too, affect children's growth.

As you identify the strengths of family, media, and community influences, you should strive to build on these qualities. When outside influences or your own disposition adversely affect children's learning, attempt to counter some of the dissonance and the negative effects. Figure 1.1 shows the relative influence on children of their home, school, and community experiences.

FIGURE 1.1
Social setting influences according to age.
Source: Adapted from Berns, 1993; Belskey, Lerner, & Spanier, 1984; Owens, 1993; Schiamberg, 1988.

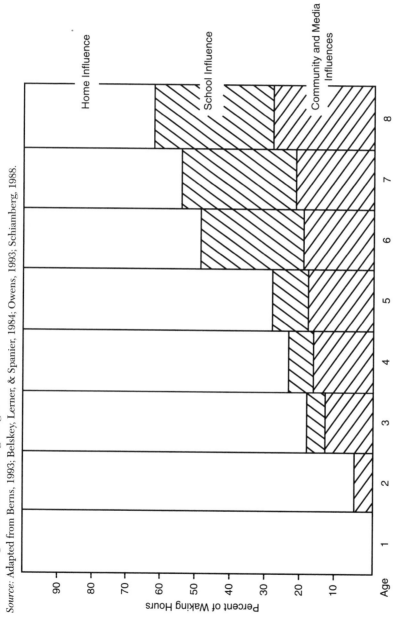

Note: Percentages show the waking hours experience of composite American children. The increasing influence of school and community relates to other factors in addition to age, e.g., stage of development, location, family SES, and extent of contact. Day care is included with home influence.

CHILD ATTITUDES

Attitudes determine what individuals attend to in a situation, how they perceive the situation, and even their response to the event. Children acquire certain attitudes by hearing words, observing actions, and surmising the feelings of significant adults in their environment. These attitudes then become more firm when children are reinforced for expressing such beliefs.

Adult attitudes result from perceptions sustained over years. Attitudes change, of course, but those demonstrated at any one time affect those children exposed to them. How parents or teachers view their roles will affect the socialization and learning of children under their supervision (Ecksel, 1992). For example, children are aware at early ages of their family's and community's attitudes regarding education, other cultures, racial or religious groups, and roles that males and females play in society (Coleman, 1987).

The impact of parental behaviors and attitudes is not linear with regard to children's development. In infancy, parents begin by responding to

the child's perceived level of ability, but as bonding intensifies, parents affect the child's abilities by the interaction patterns they establish (Bradley, Caldwell, & Elardo, 1979; Sigel, 1982). Over time, both parent and child attitudes and behaviors change, and these influences and interactions affect the child's intellectual ability. Clearly, children's early experiences form a foundation for helping them cope with change (Sigel, Dreyer, & McGillicuddy-DeLisi, 1984).

Home Influence on Attitudes

Children's attitudes develop early from home influences. Families communicate to even very young children how they feel about themselves and their neighbors, and about their schools and community.

....

Mrs. Kohl was astonished when her 3-year-old, Brittany, spat at elderly Mrs. Foster. Mrs. Kohl didn't remember that yesterday, when Mrs. Foster knocked at the apartment door, she had told her

Parents affect their children's abilities through the interaction patterns they establish.

husband not to answer, saying, "I'm tired of the old hag coming around, nosing in our business, and always borrowing something. Sometimes I feel like spitting, she annoys me so." When Brittany's mother took her to her room as punishment, the child said defiantly, "I spit, she old hag."

At this point, it may be just Mrs. Foster that Brittany has antipathy for, but continued negative attitudes expressed by her parents towards elderly persons will affect the child's acceptance and attitude towards older persons' presence, interactions, and authority.

Parental attitudes and feelings will influence their children's feelings about school in similar ways. The annual Gallup/Phi Delta Kappan polls (Elam, Rose, & Gallup, 1993) over the last quarter century show that on the whole Americans value their local schools and have confidence in them. But we find vast differences throughout the country in the faith that individuals have in schooling. Parents communicate this faith, or lack thereof, to their children, and thus influence how they react to their teachers, to their learning experiences, and even to attending school.

A few years later, Mrs. Kohl and her neighbor, Mrs. Reed, received letters stating their daughters would be in Mrs. Owens's first-grade class. Reactions in the two households differed, and each affected the children's feelings about first grade. Mrs. Reed was delighted. Turning to her daughter, she said. "Oh, Samm, you're going to love school! Mrs. Owens was my teacher, and you'll just love all the fun things you'll do in class."

Mrs. Kohl, on the other hand, felt quite different. She expressed her thoughts to her husband in her daughter's presence, "Rats, Brittany has that old Mrs. Owens. I was hoping she'd get the new young teacher." It was no wonder the two children reacted differently about taking the bus on the first day of school. Both mothers and daughters met at

the bus stop. Samm jumped up and down and grabbed Brittany's hand as she ran toward the stopped bus, saying, "Oh, we're going to have so much fun." But Brittany pushed her away and refused to get on the bus. No amount of cajoling from the adults could convince her that she should get on. Mrs. Kohl was forced to drive Brittany to school for several days before the child would take the bus with her friend.

Parental attitudes, interests, and involvement regarding such things as home organization, disposition toward work, or attitude toward reading provide models for children's interests and involvement. Because young children learn by manipulating their environment, we can see that how parents and caregivers organize their surroundings affects children's intellectual development. Researchers have found strong positive correlations between higher IQ scores and child interaction in environments rich with appropriate materials and space (Sigel et al., 1984). Coleman (1991) points out that children whose parents stress the importance of good work habits, punctuality, and task completion carry these traits over into their schoolwork and have greater academic success.

Since Durkin's (1966) classic study of the commonality of influences for early readers, other studies, on the effect of home environment and parent perceptions of literacy development, indicate that parental attitudes and modeling regarding reading with young children are factors in later reading achievement (Walberg & Tsai, 1985; Walker & Kuerbitz, 1979). Adults engage in literacy events in nearly all homes (Heath, 1983; Teale, 1986; Wells, 1986), but there are considerable differences in adults' attitudes towards the importance of these events in children's lives (Fitzgerald, Spiegel, & Cunningham, 1991), and thus in the amount of literacy interaction between adults and children. Children respond more positively to books when they engage in a greater amount of literacy interaction with adults and when the adults believe in the importance of these interactions (Adams, 1990).

School Influences on Attitudes

Parental attitudes affect children's learning and acceptance of school. In turn, school personnel attitudes affect how children learn. Research by the Institute for Responsive Education, regarding educators' attitudes toward low-income parents, shows that many of these individuals didn't expect low-income parents to be productive participants in their children's education, and, in turn, those parents felt that their participation wouldn't have much effect, and therefore often had negative attitudes toward the schools (Heleen, 1990). Children internalize these attitudes of mutual disrespect. Children's self-worth is diminished or enhanced as they sense how school personnel view the lifestyle and culture of their families, and these attitudes can breed tolerance or intolerance for others.

....

Camille and Helen arrived at their homes distressed over a comment their bus driver had made. There were empty cans on the bus, and the driver said to the children, "Don't touch them cans. I just drove a bunch of black kids on a trip, and they aren't clean." Camille exclaimed to her mother, "But, I ride the bus every day. Does he think I'm not clean 'cause I'm black?"

Helen's distress was similar, but from a different perspective. "We had to ride the bus after a bunch of black kids today and they left it dirty. Ugh!" Both Camille and Helen could have misinterpreted the bus driver's words, but their attitudes about self and others were affected by the driver's careless speech.

....

Rosenthal and Jacobson (1968) advance the notion that teachers' expectations of children result in self-fulfilling prophecies, and children whom teachers perceive as capable and intelligent will do much better than those children teachers do not perceive to be capable. In this classic study, first and second graders appeared to be most subjected to their teachers' attitudes. More recently, Good and Brophy (1972) and Proctor (1984) also found that teachers treated children differently according to their perceptions of children's abilities, garnered from sources such as children's background, personality, gender, and physical attractiveness. The children studied tended to react both behaviorally and academically according to their teachers' expectations of them.

In grade school, girls are likely to do better academically than boys (Tittle, 1986), but by the time students graduate from high school, boys score higher on SAT tests (Sadker & Sadker, 1985). Some researchers suggest that the reason for this is that teachers treat boys and girls differently. Researchers have noted that, as early as preschool, girls are inclined to select activities with more rules, guidelines, and suggestions for accomplishing the task, while boys tend to select activities allowing for more open-ended behavior. Being rewarded for such behavior, girls tend to become more compliant, and boys become more assertive (Sprafkin, Serbin, Dernier, & Conner, 1983; Tittle, 1986). As children progress through school these reinforced behaviors get boys more attention, more opportunities for classroom discussion, and more specific guidelines as to the correctness of their responses. Girls are called on less often than are boys, are asked to raise their hands, are given less feedback on their responses, and are encouraged to listen rather than to participate. Girls tend to be praised for their neatness, while boys receive praise for academic contributions. Consequently, girls get the message that their academic responses are not important (Sadker & Sadker, 1994). Because in elementary school achievement is often measured on tasks that require skill mastery, girls, reinforced for obeying the rules, can be expected to do better than boys, but as children progress and school success depends more on problem solving and assertiveness, boys, having been reinforced for more aggressive behavior, can be expected to outperform girls (Tittle, 1986).

Teachers also may discriminate against children of different ethnic and ability groups by treating them differently—due to their expectations for different children's performance. Teachers are likely to give high achievers and majority-culture children more opportunities to respond, more praise, and more time to formulate a response. Teachers who perceive minority children to be low achievers do not expect them to know answers, and do not give them as many opportunities or as much encouragement to respond (Minuchin & Shapiro, 1983). Such differential treatment over time lowers children's involvement in school and may prevent their developing confidence in their abilities (Leacock, 1969).

Community Influence on Attitudes

Community influence on children's attitudes varies due to the different perspectives held by the organizations within a community, as well as to the interactions of individual citizens. Bronfenbrenner (1986) points out that a community's influence on children's growth and development will be from both formal and informal community structures. Influence from formal structures comes from political and social systems, health and recreational services, business enterprises, entertainment, and educational services. The informal structures are the personal social networks that each family establishes with people outside the home. Members of some communities hold attitudes in common toward their local schools, as evidenced by communitywide political support for various activities, in linkages established with other community organizations, and in news coverage by local media.

It is difficult to measure the actual effect of community attitudes on student achievement, but children quickly assimilate attitudes expressed by adults around them. Research suggests that a community's social climate and the personal relationships that children form within the community influence their attitudes about learning (Hoffer & Coleman, 1990). For example, if school sports activities receive thorough media coverage and the teams get money for trips, but the school librarian can't buy good children's literature for the library, then children soon get the message that being a good athlete is more important than being a good reader. When a community paper publishes the poems, stories, and artwork of local primary school children, then children understand that the community values their academic achievements. Primary-age children are less likely to make such direct connections to community attitudes toward their schools, but they get excited about winning a pizza for reading a certain number of books. Eventually they get a message that reading is important.

Businesspeople often provide support for various school programs. Sometimes children witness that support and learn that important people value learning. When children hear the local grocer, businessperson, or politician comment on the positive qualities of teachers, they learn that others value the learning experiences these teachers provide.

As a teacher acting alone, you have minimal opportunity to change the attitudes, feelings, and biases of others that impinge on your classroom. You can, however, become alert to your own attitudes and how they affect the children with whom you work. You can reinforce the positive attitudes of community and home toward children's learning. And while you cannot change all of the negative aspects of children's environment, you can provide a supportive school or child care environment. By providing curriculum and activities that take into account the attitudes and feelings of children's families and community, you help create coherent learning experiences for your students.

AGE LEVELS AND INFLUENCE

Community, home, and school exert a greater or a lesser influence on children's learning depending on the age of children concerned. Theorists have described the stages of children's development from dependency to independence, as well as theorizing how children do learn. See Table 1.1 for a review of selected theories. In practice parents, teachers, and community people do not necessarily subscribe to one particular theory, but the decisions they make about children's learning will reflect a stronger belief in one viewpoint. As you develop strategies to promote partnerships for children's education, it is helpful to keep in mind that others may have a different perspective of development than your own.

The Early Years—Strong Home Influence

Maslow (1970), Erikson (1963), and Piaget (1967) all emphasize the strong need for attachment and environmental support of infants and toddlers. Developing children require a physically and emotionally supportive environment for their basic needs to be met. Infants must first develop trust in others so they can venture out and explore their surroundings. According to Piaget, it is this exploration that enables them to construct knowledge about themselves and about their world. He states that "the period that extends from birth to the acquisition of language is marked by an extraordinary development of the mind" (Piaget, 1967, p. 8).

The type of housing, the presence of caregivers, and the lifestyles associated with different homes influence children's lives in profound and dramatic ways. Some environments are extremely supportive and nurturing, while others are dominating, negligent, and even dysfunctional. For example, consistent practices, organized schedules, and high-quality nourishment bring support and security to young children. But the trials of homelessness, highly mobile families, and absentee parents provide children with very different, unsupportive backgrounds. Schaimberg (1988) lists functions that any family, regardless of configuration, performs in society: economic support, psychological support and socialization, family status and role expectations, and emotional support and intimacy. Nurturing families are those that sustain their infants and toddlers in these major areas. In contrast, negligent or dysfunctional families rarely provide the help in these areas that is crucial for children's positive development.

Economic Support

The dependent infant relies on its mother and significant others for food, clothing, and shelter, all of which require a basic economic foundation. Inadequate nutrition in the early years naturally affects children physically, emotionally, and cognitively. Too little nutrition results in children not growing properly. In many cases they become unresponsive to adults. When this happens, mothers, in turn, may alter their attitude toward the child, and vital interactions for healthy emotional and intellectual growth become impaired (Owens, 1993). Longitudinal studies of inadequate nutrition indicate that malnutrition results in poor cognitive functioning that persists throughout the child's schooling years (Physicians Task Force on Hunger in America, 1985; Salt, Galler, & Ramsey, 1988). Erikson (1963) summarizes the primary features of economic support, stating that when basic needs are met, children develop a sense of trust that enables them to venture forth and explore their environment.

Psychological and Socialization Support

Infants and toddlers begin their socialization process in a family structure when they begin to communicate their needs and respond to their primary caregiver. As their actions are reinforced or rejected, infants and toddlers come to understand what is appropriate social behavior in dealing with others. Infants coo, cry, and gurgle, and nearby adults respond to these sounds as if the

TABLE 1.1
Major Theories of Young Child Development

	Nativism	Behaviorist	Psychoanalytical (Psychosocial)	Interactionist
Basic Premise	Genetics or internal mechanisms as primary force in child's development.	Environment as primary force in child's development.	Sexual energy within humans as force for personality development.	Both internal mechanisms and environment are forces for child development.
Major Contributors	Arnold Gesell (1880–1961)	J. B. Watson (1878–1958) B. F. Skinner (1904–1991)	Sigmund Freud (1856–1939) / Erik Erikson (1902–1994)	Jean Piaget (1896–1980)
Stages of Development	Developed sequences of characteristic behavior. Maturational readiness means that child must develop to an appropriate point before training or teaching has an effect.	No stages. Learning happens as a result of conditioning. Classical conditioning and unconditional stimuli result in reflex response, which later becomes a learned response. Operant conditioning. Child learns as a result of receiving positive reinforcers or a reward.	Three structures: Id—Instinctive Ego—Rational Superego—Moral. Oral stage (birth–1 yr) need for gratification from mouth. Anal stage (2–3 yrs) need for gratification from the anal area. Phallic stage (4–5 yrs) need for gratification from the genitals. Latency stage (middle years) repression of sexuality. / Expanded on Freud's theories. Basic trust (birth–1 yr) development of sense of inner goodness. Autonomy (2–3 yrs) development of sense of self and pride of achievement. Initiative (3–5 yrs) takes charge of own activities. Industry (6 yrs to puberty) becomes producer and user of things.	Children develop by assimilating external stimuli and accommodating new stimuli to already existing structures. Sensorimotor stage (birth–2 yrs) use of senses. Preoperational stage (2–7 yrs) use of mental imagery. Concrete operations stage (7–11 yrs) logical thinking occurs.
Meaning for Parents and Educators	Adult supports development, observes outward behaviors that would indicate readiness for learning.	Adult determines desired behavior and sets up strategies for reinforcing children when behaviors occur.	Adults provide the needed support so children's instincts are satisfied, but not so much that children do not move appropriately from one stage to the next.	Adults provide a rich and stimulating environment assisting children to interact with that environment as they construct their own knowledge.

baby is trying to communicate (Meadows, 1986). As adults respond and babies' needs are satisfied, babies begin to differentiate the sounds they make based both on intent and on expected response. As they do so, their caregivers adjust their own responses to the sounds they hear, conforming them to what they both understand and desire them to mean.

....

Sarah was confident in dealing with her new baby. She maintained she could tell what he needed when he cried, because he cried differently when he was hungry, was wet, or was bored and wanted company. Not only did she inform anyone present of her knowledge, but she also told her infant as she provided whatever "he was asking for." Whether the infant really understood may be debatable, but Sarah and the baby were establishing communication links.

....

Early infant-mother attachment is an important factor in how children develop the socialization skills that enable them to function effectively with peers and in schools.

Family Status and Role Expectations

Because infants and toddlers are extremely dependent on all aspects of their environment, their status and role within the family and community are not clearly defined. They gradually begin to understand that an important relationship exists between themselves and other members of the family. This developing understanding will later enable them to function in the larger society.

....

Susan, 18 months old, was accustomed to her mother feeding her juice. Sometimes, when her mother wasn't available, she would accept help from her older sister, calling her "li-ul mamma." The first time Susan was left with her aunt's fam-

Infants begin their socialization when they communicate their needs and respond to their primary care giver.

ily, she expected similar treatment, referring to her aunt as "aunt-mamma." When her uncle tried to feed her her juice, she balked at the idea, asking for "aunt-mamma." When that strategy didn't work, Susan looked about in vain, searching for her "li-ul mamma."

Susan, even by 18 months, had clearly defined specific roles to her mother and to her older sister. She clearly maintained her status with a "new family environment" by indicating her "new parents" carry on her view of their roles.

Emotional Support and a Sense of Intimacy

Infants and toddlers require emotional support and a sense of intimacy. When significant adults in the baby's environment express joy and delight in them as social beings, babies develop a sense of well-being, and respond. As they grow older, this basic emotional security leads to a desire to share their feelings and emotions with loved ones. Ecksel (1992), summarizing several studies, states that infants who formed secure attachments to their mothers were more socially competent later in school than were children whose mothers were unable to give their infants a warm, supportive surrounding.

Some families lack the emotional or social ability to provide adequate emotional nurturance. We find some households with problems so great that adults lack the inner resources to manage an infant's many needs. Other families with deficits, however, have support systems to rely on, or may know how to use community support systems, such as day care and health and human services,

Quality preschool programs have lasting effects on children's development.

to supplement their own meager resources. Schools and day care providers should always assist needy parents by informing them of available services. Teachers must help by reinforcing parents' positive attempts at meeting their children's basic needs.

Preschool/Kindergarten Years— Increasing School Influence

Children developing a sense of autonomy need to learn the boundaries they can operate within, and must learn to identify new ones they will encounter as they separate from home. As parents give their children necessary support, they must also give them freedom to try things on their own. For preschoolers and kindergarteners, the significant others in their home setting continue to influence their development as they move from basic trust to autonomy and independence. Their sense of self first develops in the home; at school, the teacher and their peers begin to alter or reinforce this sense. Children modify their behavior in school in response to different rules and regulations, and in response to perceived teacher and peer expectations.

Some children have school-like experiences in their preschool years. For other children, school as a culture first comes into focus when they enter formal public or private schooling. In the preschool years, children may encounter several different types of school-like experiences. Head Start programs, child care centers, nursery schools, and play schools all demonstrate somewhat different philosophical orientations. Some programs provide rich experiences for children; others provide only custodial care. It is difficult to conduct rigorous studies to determine the influence different programs have on developing children, and such research is always confounded by socioeconomic factors, community support systems, types of curriculum, and parental interaction styles. However, we have evidence that quality preschool programs do have lasting positive effects on children's academic growth and on subsequent life skill development (Levin, 1991; Schweinhart & Weikart, 1993).

Primary Years—Growing Community Influence

The impact of the community appears early in children's lives and progresses steadily as children mature, emerging through the effect the community has on the family. The nature of that effect is not simple, but derives from the many subsystems within the community (Bronfenbrenner, Moen, & Garbarino, 1984). For example, the family may live in a neighborhood that provides moral and physical support, or in a neighborhood where parents are afraid to go out or to take their children out.

All families need quality social and health services, and such agencies' ability to help families in need affects children's well-being. Positive interactions between community and family give a sense of security and well-being to all, so that families are better able to provide the nurturing children need. Children raised in communities where there is a great deal of violence can be affected adversely due to stress the violence causes. Inattentiveness to schoolwork and hyperactivity are but two of the results that stress has on academic achievement (Groves, Zuckerman, & Marans, 1993).

As children expand their horizons, the living conditions of the neighborhood and community give them experiences on which to build their linguistic, kinesthetic, artistic, spatial, and interpersonal skills. Children who can visit zoos, museums, libraries, business establishments, and parks and other natural settings are better equipped (than children who can't) to deal with the many mathematical, scientific, social, and language concepts discussed in schools.

Primary-age children are becoming independent and are moving from the preoperational to the concrete operational stage of intellectual development. Traditions, cultural values, community mores, opportunities for recreation, and other social and cultural activities play a part in children's development. Experiences interacting with adults in clubs, in sports, and in art and music activities open up to children differences in communication styles and offer them a range of experiences. Coleman (1991) calls this type of involvement with adults a child's *social capital,* and stresses that this capital is as important as financial capital in determining school performance. Heath and MacLaughlin (1989) point out how these experiences interacting with different adults give participating children greater opportunities to practice their negotiating, problem-solving, and intellectual skills.

Steven, in second grade, had joined a riding club but was unhappy because the instructor was "always criticizing" what he did. "I don't even know what I do wrong," he told his mother.

"And what do you do, when he tells you something?" she asked.

"I get so mad, I just glare and ride away."

"Are you sure he never compliments you?"

"Hardly ever," pouted Steven.

"Well, why not try an experiment?" his mother suggested. "The next time he even suggests something is good, smile at him and say, 'Oh, that really helps me know what I should do,' and just ignore the criticisms." Steven reluctantly agreed to give it a try.

Two weeks later a jubilant Steven returned from riding club, saying, "Hey mom, he really does tell me lots about what I'm doing good!" Whether Steven or the riding instructor changed behavior patterns isn't clear, but certainly Steven was learning new ways of working with adults so he could profit from their instruction.

Adults in some communities do a better job in reaching large numbers of children than do those in others. Community tolerance for gangs, for illicit activities, or for sexual encounters will have unhealthy and negative influences on the growth and experiences of children. Violence in the streets limits everyone's sense of security. Any opportunity for positive interactions, or for the use of community resources to expand children's skills, is lessened in disruptive communities.

Peer Group Influence

In ways similar to the community, the peer group becomes an agency of enculturation and development. Even very young children develop a sense of self from their perceptions of important people in their surroundings, including relatives, teachers, and peers. Socioeconomic status, ethnic identity, and the type of work parents undertake affect how families view themselves and the process by which they socialize their children (Hoffman, 1984). Later, as children leave the home setting, their self-perception and socializing skills become influenced by how their peers view them.

Peer groups begin to form early or late depending on a child's experiences and availability of playmates, and on her personality and sociability (Parke, 1990). When children move out from the family into child care centers, school, and the community at large they begin to form attachments, and real friendships emerge later through their play. These relationships influence behavior. Even young infants and toddlers have been noted to react to other infants by touching them, by crying when others cry, and later by offering nurturance or comfort. It is not until around the age of 3, however, that early friendships begin to form and children's peers begin to have a more lasting influence (Parke, 1990).

Peer influence on behavior gradually becomes more dominant. Children discover that others can share their feelings or attitudes, or may have quite different ones. The perspectives of others affect how children feel about their own families. Children usually have a "family" view of their own and of other cultures. When confronted with other perspectives, they often need to rethink their own viewpoints. It is often difficult for children to adjust to the idea that other families may function radically differently from their own and yet may hold many of the same attitudes and beliefs and be equally nurturing and secure. The peer group serves as a barometer for children examining themselves and their feelings about self and family.

The peer group also influences development of children's socializing skills. It is from these early friendships that children learn how to negotiate and relate to others in addition to their siblings and other family members. They learn from peers how to cooperate and socialize according to *group norms,* group-sanctioned modes of behavior and thought. The peer group can influence what the child values, knows, wears, eats, and learns. The extent of this influence, however, depends on other situational constraints, such as the age and personality of children and the nature of the group (Hartup, 1983). In its most acceptable form, the group is a healthy coming-of-age arbiter where children grasp negotiating skills, learn to deal with hostility, and learn to solve problems in

Children learn from peers how to cooperate and socialize according to group norms.

a social context. In its most destructive mode, the peer group can demand blind obedience to a group norm, which can result in socially alienated gangs with pathological outlooks (Perry, 1987).

MEDIA INFLUENCE

All members of our society are influenced both directly and indirectly by powerful media vehicles, including print, television, sound recordings, cinema, and computer CD-ROMs. People have at some point used all of these media to advocate what people should wear, what they should eat, and what values they should hold. Vivid colors and language tell us both what is happening in the world and how to react to the events shown. While our society's media vehicles seem to be dominated by social interaction, aggression, and violence, they are also sources of education, humor, and nonviolent entertainment.

The different forms of media may be used for information, education, and entertainment. We here discuss what we broadly term the *entertainment industry* in its role as a general societywide influence on young children. We first discuss two of its primary forms, print and television, then treat other current media under the rubric of the industry in general.

Print media—such as books, magazines, and newspapers—present content using words and static images. Though both pictures and language convey a message, printed materials do require greater reliance on readers' language development and life experiences to be understood. As children decode words from the printed page, thoughts generated by these words serve to create images, thus requiring children to rely on their imaginations and interpretations (Singer & Singer, 1990). Generally, this is helpful to children's developing minds.

Of all media forms, television appears to have the most impact in terms of memory recall. Input is presented using both sound and moving pictures, and the active images assist children in remembering familiar content. Though viewers might be required to interpret some messages, television basically does little to stimulate children's imagination. Families can control what children see by selecting programs, but most homes exert less control over television than over printed media.

When Meringoff (1980) compared children's reactions to stories presented through television, books, and radio, children seemed to view television events as something not directly associated with themselves, but appeared to personalize the events in books. Berns (1993) surmises that, because the reader is more intimately involved in the book, it is a stronger socializing agent. However, the stronger personal influence of printed materials over television also could reflect the manner in which the two are presented to children (Neuman, 1991). Young children first know about books because someone reads to them and interacts with them about the story, whereas more often than not children are left to watch television by themselves. Perhaps children are socialized on how to react to books, thus getting more personal meaning from them as they become readers themselves. Some researchers suggest that when parents or other adults interact with children viewing television, those children develop better interactive and processing skills (Neuman, 1991).

The entertainment industry, a powerful influence in life in the United States, engulfs society through print, television, radio, sound recordings, computer games and networks, and live performances (Figure 1.2). The entertainment industry influences the actions, dress codes, and values of many adults, and captures and holds children's interests for a large part of each day. As a teacher, you must understand that the entertainment industry's influence on children both enhances and inhibits their growth as human beings. You should not underestimate the effect of this influence, but rather should work to incorporate it into your teaching, helping children to assimilate it in context with the rest of their education.

Print

Print materials reach the child indirectly, through parents and other caregivers, and directly, such as when children participate in a presentation or interact personally with particular publications. Newspapers, magazines, books, and other print media normally portray different ideas, actions and activities, and subsequent consequences or reactions. What print is available implies the values and philosophy of the community, and can influence all areas of education.

Physical Development

Print media affect children's physical, emotional, and intellectual development indirectly, through the parents or other significant adults. Books and magazines inform adults how to lead healthy and productive lives, and proclaim the dangers of unhealthy practices. Mothers whose reading persuades them to quit smoking, acquire healthy eating habits, and avoid drugs and alcohol during pregnancy produce for the most part healthier babies. In contrast, parents who believe that teaching young children to play sports gives them a head start on athletic participation may exert pressure too early. This expectation pushes their children to learn tasks for which they may be physically unprepared.

Social Development

Advertising, from both print media and television, affects the type of clothes, food, and, especially, toys bought for children. Some toys engage children's imagination and are designed for groups of children playing together. Other toys are more suitable for children playing alone. Children's potential for social development is affected by which type of toy adults are influenced to buy. According to Piagetian theory of development, children construct knowledge about their world by interacting with materials in their surroundings. A flexible environment that has opportunities for imaginative play and group interaction enhances children's potential for social development. Environ-

FIGURE 1.2
Media influence on children.

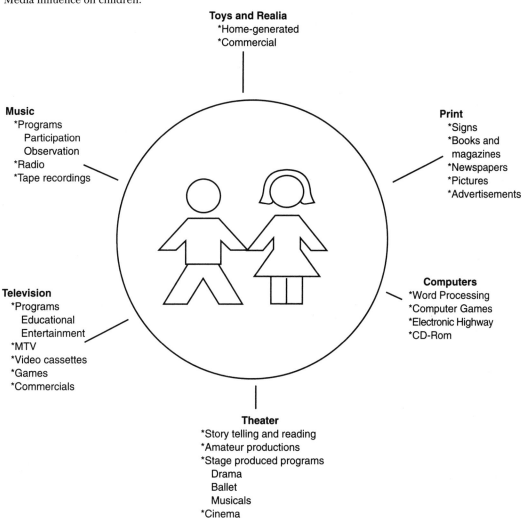

Toys and Realia
*Home-generated
*Commercial

Music
*Programs
 Participation
 Observation
*Radio
*Tape recordings

Print
*Signs
*Books and
 magazines
*Newspapers
*Pictures
*Advertisements

Computers
*Word Processing
*Computer Games
*Electronic Highway
*CD-Rom

Television
*Programs
 Educational
 Entertainment
*MTV
*Video cassettes
*Games
*Commercials

Theater
*Story telling and reading
*Amateur productions
*Stage produced programs
 Drama
 Ballet
 Musicals
*Cinema

ments with fewer opportunities inhibit such development.

Intellectual Development
The toys children acquire affect their intellectual as well as their social development. Some toys have multiple uses and engage children's imagination; other toys have only one use, resulting in less creative play. Thus, adults' choice of toys may en-hance or inhibit children's intellectual development.

Print media also affect children's literacy development. Studies on early literacy indicate that the amount and types of printed materials that adults have in the home, as well as how adults interact with these materials around children, affect the children's interest and literacy achievement (Adams, 1990; Durkin, 1966; Smith, 1990; Teale,

Television can exert more influence on children than can the school.

time tells only part of the story, for some children spend as much as 75 hours per week watching television. According to Postman (1983), between the ages of 6 and 18, many children spend more time viewing television (16,000 hours) than they do going to school (13,000).

Television influences children in direct proportion to both time spent viewing and the overall effect of what is viewed (American Academy of Pediatrics, 1990). Television can exert more influence on children than can the school. Certainly eating habits, family interactions, and use of leisure time are considerably influenced by television (Leibert & Sprafkin, 1988). Commercials take up twelve to fourteen minutes (or more) of every hour of television, and in that time, advertisers try to influence viewers about all types of consumerism. Notar (1989) points out how advertisers use the power of imagery to hook both children and adults to their products. "Advertisers view training of children's imagery as all important. Once children are trained to view life in terms of commodities, they have many more years of productive consumption" (p. 67). The results of this influence can be positive or negative depending on the degree to which parents and children respond to the lure of advertising or program content (Huston et al., 1992).

Advertising, of course, is not the only way television influences viewers. Two major concerns about effects of television are the amount of violence, in both commercials and programs, and the amount of time children's television watching takes away from more creative and intellectual pursuits.

In summarizing the amount of violence on television, the National Association for the Education of Young Children (1990) points out that there is evidence that violence in programs has increased since the Federal Communication Commission's deregulation of children's programming in 1982. The fascination for more violent programs may be due to children's needs to express their own sense of powerlessness and to work out aggressive feelings (Carlsson-Paige & Levin, 1987).

1986). From the books that adults read to children, children internalize attitudes, feelings, biases, and perspectives about their own and other cultures. Zach, in the chapter's opening vignette, had a chance to express aggression in acceptable ways through *Three Billy Goats Gruff.* He was influenced in the kind of clothes he wanted by the story, *Max's Dragon Shirt.*

The kind of books that children read and have read to them influence and support their emotional, social, and intellectual development both directly and indirectly. Sutherland and Arbuthnot (1991) point out that "to function successfully in society, children must learn to know themselves, to achieve self identity, . . . [to] learn about social interaction and recognize ways in which they are alike as well as different from others" (p. 20). Books, like peers, provide children with a vision of their world that sometimes reaffirms their own lives and sometimes challenges their perspectives.

Television

Television's substantial impact on all growing children began in the 1950s. Today, nearly every household in America contains at least one television set. Preschool children watch an average of 4 hours of television per day, and primary-age children average 3 hours (Nielsen, 1990). But the

Gerbner and Signorelli (1990) summarized twenty years of research on the effect of television violence on children's behavior, and report that it is difficult to make direct linkages between television watching and aggressive behavior in children due to the difficulty of isolating television's influence from other violent events in children's lives. There does seem to be fairly strong accumulated evidence that television violence affects behavior—heavy viewing, without adult mediating effects, results in greater child aggression and in acceptance of violence as a viable reaction to life's situations.

Of course, not all television programming is violent, and we have some evidence of positive effects. Some researchers indicate that programs depicting positive and altruistic actions also influence children, so they prize this behavior and act in more positive ways toward their peers (Comstock & Paik, 1991).

Research on the impact of television viewing on academic achievement indicates that such influence is complex in nature. Television viewing takes time away from important social interactions, such as conversations, storytelling, imaginative play, and, for primary-age children, leisure reading that promotes literacy. Children who are heavy viewers of television have less practice conversing and reading, but the amount of viewing and kind of programs watched as well as IQ and socioeconomic status are all factors that affect children's achievement. In studies on television viewing, children of low socioeconomic-status (SES) families tended to do better academically if they watched up to four hours a day and watched more educational programs. However, achievement scores from high-SES children tended to decline from heavy viewing (Singer & Singer, 1980; Truglio, Huston, & Wright, 1988; Williams, Haertel, Haertel, & Walberg, 1982).

Some suggest that television viewing is an easier mental task than reading. Therefore, those who have difficulty in school are apt to find television viewing more comfortable than reading. There is also concern that too much television viewing makes children passive learners who are less creative in their thinking. Reading requires children to translate the printed word into visual imagery, and requires concentration. Television, on the other hand, provides instant visual and auditory messages, requiring little mental activity or analytical thinking (Singer & Singer, 1990). Given such considerations as our society's growing need for a work force with developed analytical and creative skills, parents, teachers, and the larger community must take seriously, and must not underestimate, television's influence and impact.

The Entertainment Industry

Most school-age children in the United States are daily exposed to entertainment and education delivered through other media in addition to print and television. Films (in theaters and on videotape), radio, sound recordings on compact disc and audiocassette, and computers (most now equipped with CD-ROM players) have great influence on American society. Whereas relatively few movie stars, musicians, and sports figures provided role models for generations earlier in the twentieth century, the new media—cable television, with its special programming and music television, videocassettes, video games, compact discs, CD-ROM, and high-profile concerts—present myriad role influences for young children today. Visual and auditory stimuli bombard most homes and communities. Some of this exposure is educational, positive, and directed at an appropriate level for young children. But much current fare is violent in nature and is presented in ways unsuitable for children's level of maturity. With the emerging electronic "information highway," young people will be exposed more than ever to both good and bad influences.

Producers and advertisers market successful films and television shows in various ways, such as by urging the purchase of associated toys, clothing, soundtrack CDs, and videocassettes. Video games, computer games, and other types of interactive media provide new forms of entertainment and new marketing avenues. These new forms influence individuals' values, compete for children's attention, and reduce the amount of reflection and interaction time children have with both adults and peers.

Although video and computer games provide players with interaction and choice by allowing them to select different paths that events can take, again aggression, sex, and violence seem to dominate the choices. While some maintain that such games are opportunities for children to let off steam, others insist there are better ways of achieving this goal. Preliminary research suggests such games make children both more aggressive and more tolerant of aggression. For example, children pulled away from games containing such violent actions as kickboxing have been observed afterward kickboxing in their play yard (Elmer-Dewitt, 1993).

As when watching television, children often are engaged with video games without adult supervision or guidance, and thus are left to interpret the game's messages on their own. Such games, too, take time from activities that require more physical, intellectual, imaginative, creative, or problem-solving strategies such as playing outdoors, reading, interacting with peers, or engaging in musical or artistic endeavors. (Although, to be fair, we must note that some games do require players to demonstrate sophisticated problem-solving skills.)

When parents watch videotapes or television programs with their children, the children benefit more from these programs and the parents learn more about their children. Parents discover what their children know and what interests or bores them, and may act to enhance their learning. Parents may introduce children to the original stories from which the programs were adapted, helping them to learn to make comparisons and develop better discrimination skills about stories and presentations. For children to be engaged in positive learning, it seems urgent that schools, parents, teachers, and other concerned individuals develop partnerships for interpreting and dealing with the products of both currently available media sources and those soon to appear in their communities.

SPECIAL INTEREST GROUP INFLUENCE

In recent years, the United States has witnessed a steady increase in the number and potency of special interest groups, such as the National Association of Christian Educators, Literature Review Council, Action for Children's Television, and the various pro-choice and pro-life groups, organized to affect everything from legislative matters to informal controls on curriculum topics. These groups can have both direct and indirect, and positive and negative influence on children's learning, depending on family, school, and community reactions to their efforts and objectives.

A special interest group usually has a single objective (though some are quite broadly conceived). Many groups have had considerable success in meeting their objective. Many groups have been formed by parents concerned about an educational issue in the lives of their children. For instance, in 1968, Peggy Charren, concerned with the amount of violence in children's programs, organized a group of parents to form Action for Children's Television (ACT). This group lobbies for improved television programming and advertising during children's viewing time and works to educate the public regarding television's positive and negative influences.

Grassroots efforts by special interest groups have resulted in legislation for improving education for all children. In the 1960s, local groups of parents, concerned about the lack of appropriate education for their children with disabilities, gained first local and then national attention. Civil rights organizations, local and national organizations for citizens with mental retardation, and the Children's Defense Fund joined the original groups in a battle that resulted in legislation assuring the "right of handicapped children to a free and appropriate education" (Children's Defense Fund, 1981, p. 3). As children with special needs were mainstreamed into regular classrooms, curriculum, classroom environments, and learning for all children expanded as particular disabilities were taken into account.

The influence of special interest groups is not always viewed as positive. Schott (1989, p. 61) warns of the danger of groups, such as the National Association of Christian Educators, who wish to "gain control" of schools to eliminate the influence of "secular humanism." He notes that such groups seek to effect legislation that would permit censoring of books and dictating of particular elements in curricula. In many communities, both schools and libraries have been forced to remove certain books, deemed outstanding literature by literary critics, because of the views of special interest groups. One teacher was dismissed for teaching such poems as Langston Hughes's "Dreams," material that a special interest group deemed inappropriate (Kozol, 1991).

At the local level, some religious groups have succeeded in banning Halloween activities and even traditional fairytales that include supernatural events and characters. Other groups have successfully changed units of study in schools about Christmas, Hanukkah, and Easter holidays. Special interest groups have positive influence when they act to initiate dialogue among parents and teachers as to the appropriateness of materials in schools. Their influence is negative when they seek to restrict children's access to humanity's best artistic, philosophical, and intellectual efforts, and attempt to deny children learning experiences about different ethnic and cultural groups and other historical periods.

CONCLUSION

Children become well or poorly educated depending on many factors that both directly and indirectly influence what they learn and how they

learn it. The attitudes, values, and interests that homes, schools, and communities have regarding children's learning can be in concert or in conflict. Young children are usually more strongly influenced by immediate or extended family attitudes, and primary-age children begin to be influenced by peer groups, media, and community mores and traditions. Teachers in many instances have no control over these factors, and must study about and be alert to their influence in order to provide appropriate education for children in their classrooms.

According to Coleman (1990), children need many types of support systems to grow into functioning adults. They need what he calls human, financial, and social capital, which provide the nurturing and physical environment in which children learn to cope with their world. Children with little financial capital may still succeed if sufficient social and human resources are available to them. We find that families can compensate somewhat for lack of effective community and school influences on their children, and community and school personnel can exert influence and extend resources to compensate for missing family social resources. However, schools are far more effective in educating children when families, schools, and communities unite their efforts. When these three social settings recognize the influences on children's experience and work together in resolving conflicting issues undermining child development, the best possible circumstances result.

SUGGESTED ACTIVITIES AND QUESTIONS

1. List what you consider the major influences that guided your education. Are they different from those we have noted in this chapter? What influences did your classmates list? Discuss.
2. Interview a friend, regarding her or his feelings about kindergarten, high school, and finally college. Ask what parents, friends, teachers, and neighbors thought of the different schools. From

this discussion, state how you think those home and community influences affected your friend's attitudes toward schooling.

3. Watch at least two samples of the following different types of television programs: news, situation comedy, soap operas, and cartoons. Chart the incidence of violence in each program. Identify what you believe could be the effect of this televised violence on primary-age children. Discuss your conclusions with your classmates.

4. Interview a teacher or a principal in a local primary school and determine (if possible) which, if any, special interest groups influence the decisions this person makes with regard to curriculum. Do some groups exert positive pressure? If so, how does the person view these pressures as benefiting children's learning? Do some exert negative pressures? If so, how does the person view these pressures as limitations for children's learning?

5. Interview a primary-age child and ask her or him to give you a list of favorite books, movies, television shows, and entertainers. Ask what the child likes or finds important about these choices. Ask if the child wants to be like any of these people or characters, and why? Attempt to determine how the media the child routinely is exposed to has influenced these choices.

RECOMMENDED READINGS

Coleman, J. S. (1990). *Foundations of social theory.* Cambridge, MA: Harvard University Press.

Haveman, R., & Wolfe, B. (1994). *Succeeding generations: On the effect of investments in children.* New York: Russell Sage Foundation.

Heath, S. B. (1983). *Ways with words. Language, life, and work in communities and classrooms.* New York: Cambridge University Press.

Kozol, J. (1991). *Savage inequalities: Children in America's schools.* New York: Crown.

Parke, R. D. (Ed.). (1984). *Review of child development research: Vol. 7. The family.* Chicago: University of Chicago Press.

Piaget, J. (1967). *Six psychological studies.* New York: Random House.

Singer, J. L., & Singer, D. G. (1980). *Television, imagination, and aggression: A study of preschoolers.* Hillsdale, NJ: Lawrence Erlbaum Associates.

Teale, W. H., & Sulzby, E. (Eds.). (1986). *Emergent literacy: Writing and reading.* Norwood, NJ: ABLEX.

C H A P T E R 2

Historical Perspectives

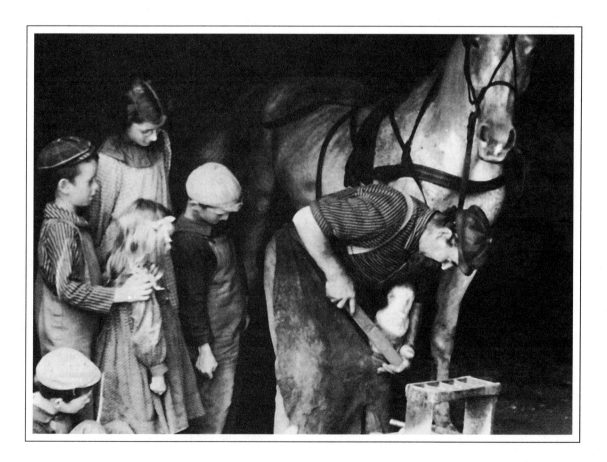

All experience is an arch to build upon.

(Adams, 1907, p. 177)

The intent of this chapter is to examine the evolution of roles played in children's education by the home, the school, and the community. In reading this chapter you will learn that:

1. Historically, the family and the community have always played significant roles in children's education, but at different periods each has had a more dominant role, with the school assuming leadership at the beginning of the twentieth century.

2. Although *partnerships for educating children* is a relatively new phrase, parents, teachers, and community members have always worked together to some degree for children's benefit.

3. The federal government, in fostering equal educational opportunities, has required more parental involvement in children's education during recent decades.

4. Programs for poor children, children with special needs, and children of differing ethnic orientation have focused on the importance of parents as an educating force.

5. Although Anglo-European culture has dominated in shaping American schools, other cultures gradually exerted enough influence to stimulate a multicultural emphasis for most curricula of the 1990s.

6. In the 1980s and 1990s a multicultural perspective in a school has meant changes in attitudes, staffing arrangements, content, and interaction patterns.

Partnerships among homes, schools, and communities for children's education is a term of the 1980s and 1990s, yet throughout the history of the United States we find connections among the roles of these three social settings. At different times each, as an institution, has occupied a dominant role in children's education, while acknowledging the others as important forces helping children to succeed in society.

In colonial times, the family was the major force for educating children, although the community exerted pressure on families not conforming to local codes of conduct. Later, as towns and villages developed, community leaders recognized that some families were not willing or able to educate their children successfully. Taking command in the later colonial period, community leaders gave needed support to families, started to develop laws concerning education, and eventually formed public schools to ensure that children met the goals and objectives of the community.

In the late 1800s, as public schools developed into bureaucracies, professional educators moved to the forefront and took responsibility for overseeing schools and curricula. But, at the same time, the public mandated a more diverse curriculum, so teachers were required not only to teach academic skills but also to provide programs designed to help children develop socially, physically, morally, and emotionally. At this time, when more blue collar jobs required technical skills, schools became responsible for teaching vocational skills as well. In the twentieth century, when only a part of the school population succeeded in these extended schools, questions began to arise. Parents and communities became perplexed, displeased, and often alienated from their schools.

In the 1990s a new trend for developing collaborations (stimulated by researchers and professional educators) became a focus for parents, community leaders, and teachers. In this way, many people came to appreciate the truth in the African proverb, "It takes an entire village to educate a child." As you review this brief historical overview of relationships among parents, communities, and schools, consider what happens to children as society changes.

In this chapter, we trace the changes and forces that have shaped the current condition in the United States with respect to roles played in childhood education by families, communities, and schools from the dominant culture. We also consider attitudes that have changed over the three centuries toward special populations, such as children with disabilities, children in poverty, and children from minority cultures. All changes have affected the roles and responsibilities of the three institutions for the education of all children. Table 2.1 lists major American events affecting family–community–school relationships.

FAMILY AS A SIGNIFICANT EDUCATIONAL FORCE

From primitive cultures to modern society, the family was and is the most important social setting for educating the child. In all societies children must learn skills of survival, the rules and regulations of the society in which they live, and the values by which their society functions. Children learn by following their elders' examples, through direct teaching of important skills by their elders, and by oral telling of traditions, lore, attitudes, beliefs, and values (Frost, 1966).

In the original English colonies, the family was the prime educator, though the community exerted pressure on the family to teach what that society deemed important. The education that children received in the colonial period depended on economic status, ethnic (racial) background, child gender, and to some extent (due to dominant religious groups) on the section of the country the child lived in.

Early settlers for the most part were able to form cohesive family units, depending on each other for survival. Towns and villages, particularly in New England, were initially established around particular religious groups migrating from Europe. With their religious heritage, early colonists believed that children needed to learn not only the vocational skills necessary for survival but also particular codes of behavior and moral integrity. The more economically advantaged also valued reading and writing for their own children. It was a patriarchal society, and in most cases teaching was the responsibility of the home, with the father the dominant force. Parents, grandparents, and older siblings were the primary instructors. Fathers taught the sons skills needed to carry on the family vocation; mothers taught their daughters homemaking skills. In the intact homes children had a profound appreciation and sense of family. They tended to understand who they were and how they were a part of the larger community (Zelizer, 1985).

Puritans in New England were adamant about the necessity for reading and writing, and stressed the importance of reading the Bible. Parents assumed this responsibility. In addition, certain women, who became more skilled in teaching, gathered in their homes children whose parents were unable to teach reading and writing. This practice resulted in the creation of Dame schools, precursors of our current primary schools.

In the Southern colonies, wealthy settlers hired tutors to teach their children academic skills plus the behaviors befitting a plantation owner. But poor parents were responsible for educating their children as best they could. For the most part, African Americans were forbidden an education, and because of slavery, black families were often torn apart so even parental teaching of basics was hampered (Travers & Rebore, 1995).

TABLE 2.1
Events Affecting Family–Community–School Relationships

1600s	**Families Responsible for Children's Education (Community Responsibility)**
1642	Massachusetts Act requiring all families to teach children to read Bible and laws of the land
1647	"Old Deluder Satan" Law requiring every community of 100 or more to establish schools
1700s	**Community Responsible for Children's Education (National Influence—State Responsibility)**
1779	South Carolina outlaws education for black children
1785–1787	Northwest Ordinances reserved sections of land in the Midwest for the support of schools
1789	Constitution of the United States—no mention of education, assuming it to be states' responsibility
1800s	**Education Establishment Responsible for Children's Education**
1815	First parent program in Portland, Maine
1835	Massachusetts establishes first state board of education
1852	Massachusetts first to establish compulsory education law
1867	U.S. Office of Education established
1873	First public school kindergarten founded in St. Louis
1888	Federation for Child Study founded
1889	G. Stanley Hall established first child study center at Clark University for studying children and disseminating information to parents about childrearing practices
1896	*Plessy v. Ferguson* decision supporting segregation
1897	National Congress of Mothers founded (later became Parent-Teacher Association)

When colonial boys needed to learn skills the family was unable to provide, apprenticeships were sought, and boys, as young as 7, were sent to live with a master craftsman. They could be apprenticed until age 21. Apprenticeships were the precursors of our later grammar schools, for in many colonies the masters were expected to teach reading and writing as well as the skills of their trade (Webb, Metha, & Jordan, 1996).

In the English colonies, basic formal education was available to established families, but children of slaves and Native Americans were considered unworthy for teaching. There were, however, notable exceptions to this trend. The Church of England in the South and Quakers in the middle colonies provided educational opportunities for a few African Americans, some Native Americans, and some poor Anglo colonists.

COMMUNITY AS A SIGNIFICANT EDUCATIONAL FORCE

As townships in the colonies became more established in the late 1600s and the 1700s, religious leaders became more dominant in determining the education of children within the community.

1900s	**Education Establishment Responsible for Educating Parents as well as Children**
1909	First White House Conference on Care of Dependent Children
1912	Children's Bureau established in Washington, DC
1916	First parent cooperative founded at University of Chicago
Mid 1900s	**Parent and Community Involvement in School Policies**
1954	*Brown v. Topeka Board of Education* opened the way for desegregation of schools
1956	Ford Foundation grant to New York City to train volunteers to work with teachers
1964	Civil Rights Act mandating desegregation of schools paved way for compensatory education acts, which required parental involvement in schools
1965	Elementary and Secondary Education Act; Project Head Start; Title I/Chapter I
1965	First Bilingual Education Act
1967	Economic Opportunity Act Follow Through programs
1972	Home Start programs
1975	Public Law 94–142: Education for all Handicapped Children Act (now the Individuals with Disabilities Education Act)
1984	First national symposium on partnerships in education sponsored by President's Advisory Council
1986	Federal Preschool and Early Intervention Program Act (PL 99–457) extends PL 94–142 to infants and toddlers
1986	Handicapped Children's Protection Act (PL 99–372) passed
1988	National Association of Partners in Education formed
1988	Educational Partnerships Act Title VI passed
1992	Head Start Improvement Act passed
1994	Goals 2000: Educate America Act signed into law

Thus began the American heritage, extant today, that a community oversees its schools and determines school policy and curriculum.

The Puritans are credited with establishing the foundation of public education in this country, because of their belief that all children, no matter their economic status, needed to be educated. They believed that every child in the land should learn the rigid codes of behavior for a religious society and the "meaning of salvation" from Bible reading. As early as 1642, a Massachusetts law required all parents and master craftsmen to teach reading and writing to children in their care to ensure that children attained "religious understanding and civic responsibility" (Travers & Rebore, 1995, p. 42). There was, however, difficulty in enforcing such a mandate because of widespread illiteracy in the adult population. Consequently, in 1647 the "Old Deluder Satan Law" was passed, which required that townships with 50 or more households provide a teacher of reading and writing for young children in the community. Townships that had more than 100 households were also to provide a Latin grammar school to prepare boys for university study (Cohen, 1974).

Though these laws were not easy to enforce, they were important in establishing a precedent for education as the young nation expanded. First and foremost, the family had primary responsibility for educating a child, but the laws also laid a foundation for community responsibility in assisting families in educating the young. Since communities hired the teachers, they also taxed families on their property so as to have funds to pay teachers (Cohen, 1974).

In the late 1700s and early 1800s, political and economic factors in the young United States again affected the relationships of families and communities in educating children. The advent of the Industrial Revolution meant that families moved from an economy dependent on farming to one increasingly dependent on manufacturing. This meant the family was no longer a tight economic unit relying on each family member assuming a responsibility for producing food and clothing. Now fathers, and sometimes mothers, left home to earn a living, and naturally there was little opportunity to teach children vocational skills or reading and writing in the home. An urban population began to arise and many families became more isolated from their kin. Thus, the changed circumstances demanded a new response to the country's needs.

The Republic was coming into being at the end of the eighteenth century, and as it unified the strong influence of religious communities was replaced by the notion of nonsectarian education. Political leaders such as Benjamin Franklin and Thomas Jefferson believed that the new nation needed a literate populace, and that it was not sufficient to educate only the wealthy and the strongly religious. Education, they felt, needed to be available to children from different social and economic classes and needed to be more functional. Merchants added their voices to that of politicians, for business interests realized the nation needed workers with more than rudimentary literacy skills and more practical skills than those provided in Latin grammar schools (Sadker & Sadker, 1991).

If wider schooling opportunities were to be available, then something needed to be done to help communities establish schools. The new government responded and significant pieces of legislation, such as the Land Ordinance Act of 1785 and the Northwest Ordinance Act of 1787, were passed by the Continental Congress. These acts encouraged settlers to move to the midwest and to set aside land to support schools. Such acts indicated the new nation's faith in education, even though in writing the Constitution the founding fathers did leave the responsibility for education to individual states.

The ideas and practices of European philosophers and educators, such as Comenius (1592–1670), Rousseau (1712–1778), Pestalozzi (1746–1827), and Froebel (1782–1852), influenced educational thought in the United States. These new ideas, however, regarding who was to be educated, and where and how, did not immediately change American children's education. Community sentiment first had to endorse any practice. Even today, in a general sense, community standards, mores, and expectations are among the strongest determinants of social behavior and participation. We find that community validation continues to be necessary for any substantial change or redirection to take place in children's educational opportunities.

SCHOOL AS A SIGNIFICANT EDUCATIONAL FORCE

The mission of formal schools and support for public education have increased gradually over the more than two centuries of the United States as a nation. In spite of our founding fathers expressing a need for universal, free, and secular education, it has taken a long time to achieve such a goal for all children.

Even in the early 1800s, the prevailing view was that education was the family's responsibility; any education beyond a family's immediate capacity to give was a luxury. Some communities at that time maintained public schools for their children, and some charity schools existed for the poor. In addition, religious sects continued to provide schooling in some areas for all children, and of course there were private schools for the wealthy (Cremin, 1982). But universal education was not yet supported in the United States of the early 1800s.

It was the mid 1800s before the political and economic climate provided fertile ground for the establishment of free, open, secular schools in the United States. On one front, new immigrants were voicing dissatisfaction in not being a part of the political process. Trade unions were forming, and unionists believed the path to success was through educating their children. Also, humanists and educators, such as Horace Mann (1796–1859) and Henry Barnard (1811–1900), wrote and lectured about benefits of universal and secular education. In addition, population movement from rural to urban areas meant many families lacked the resources to educate children at home. The time for public education had arrived.

States at this time urged local communities to begin taxing themselves in order to provide public schools for their citizenry. States also started the practice of giving aid to communities needing support. In 1852, Massachusetts began to require compulsory attendance, but it wasn't until 1918 that the last state in the union, Mississippi, enacted legislation requiring children to attend school (Cremin, 1961). With such enactments, parents began to relinquish to schools the responsibilities for educating their children; however, home and community continued to influence many educational trends.

As schools became the major force in educating American children, a professional education establishment emerged that influenced parents as well as local and state government about curriculum. Some collaborations between schools and homes resulted, but other parents and communities were at odds about the specifics of children's education.

As compulsory education took hold in the late 1800s, it became apparent that many children in the United States were not being reared in the manner the dominant culture felt necessary. Poor children in urban communities were often viewed as neglected, and new immigrants from southern and eastern Europe, unable to speak English, had different values and views on childrearing. It became clear that schools, with their prevalent Puritan ethic, did not meet the needs of many children. Something needed to be done, and parent organizations with strong female advocates were formed to press for action on more comprehensive schools. Schools were urged to provide hot lunches for needy children, and immigrants were taught English so they could be assimilated into American society (Kagan, 1987).

Philosophical swings in education, from conservative and academic to more liberal progressivism, have resulted from what the American public has perceived as needed in different periods. For example, with new immigrants and a growing urban, industrialized society, a movement emerged in the 1920s and 1930s for more openness in education—with schooling tailored to the needs, interests, and abilities of children. Then, in the 1950s, as the "space race" captured people's imaginations, United States citizens became concerned with the lack of strong academic focus, and a swing to a more rigorous academic curriculum followed. Following the civil rights movement, social issues were of great concern and again schools were pressured to change to a more responsive curriculum to serve all children. In the 1990s, Japanese economic successes had people worried that American graduates could not compete with their Japanese counterparts. So, again pressure from parent groups and communities was on schools to promote greater academic achievements.

Parent Involvement in Schools

At the turn of the twentieth century, as society brought pressure on schools to change ways of operating, similar forces were directed at parents. No longer were parents viewed as knowing the best way to rear their children. Psychology as a science came into its own at this time, and young children quickly became a focus of study. Many theories were advanced on child development and the best ways to rear children. In 1815 the first parent education program was held in Portland, Maine to instruct parents in proper childrearing practices. Through the efforts of Elizabeth Peabody (1804–1894), a follower

In the twentieth century, schools have become a more significant force in children's lives.

of Froebelian programs, kindergartens were established, first by church societies and settlement homes, and later as part of public schools. Besides providing moral and religious training and a safe and healthy environment for children, the kindergarten was also a way to reach immigrant families and influence them in rearing children according to the beliefs of mainstream society (Weber, 1969).

Early parent involvement meant educating parents as well as involving them in supporting school activities. The National Association of Parents and Teachers, later to become The Parent-Teachers Association (PTA), was established in 1897 for this very purpose. Community involvement in parent education came in the form of

women's organizations, such as the Society for the Study of Child Nature (1888), the American Association of University Women (1882), and The National Association of Colored Women (1887). These organizations sponsored lectures and conferences and published magazines promoting parent education and stressing the importance of parents taking an active role in children's education (Schlossman, 1976).

Child study in the late 1800s became a focus at colleges and universities due to the work of G. Stanley Hall (1844–1929). Many universities established laboratory schools for preschool age children, where educational theories and childrearing practices could be tested. Supported by federal and private funds, these universities and colleges provided courses in child development and parent education and practice for teachers and researchers, and disseminated information on their research (Schlossman, 1976).

Perhaps the zenith of early parent involvement came with the founding of parent cooperatives at the University of Chicago in 1916. Founded by twelve faculty wives to provide quality care for their children and parent education for themselves, these programs were modeled after the nursery school program in England founded by Margaret McMillan (1860–1931). Though McMillan founded her school for the poor, nursery schools and the first parent cooperatives were adopted in the United States by middle-class parents, and parent involvement became entrenched. An open, play-oriented curriculum was emphasized in both nursery schools and parent cooperative programs as they developed. However, not all the newer nursery school programs were committed to total parent involvement as were the parent cooperative programs. Parents of children in cooperative programs were decision makers for the schools. They hired teachers, approved the type of program, served as assistants in the classroom, and planned the parent education programs (Taylor, 1981).

During the first half of the 1900s, parent education became viewed as vital to the welfare of society, and professional educators began to feel responsible for providing this service. Parents, even though no longer considered experts in child upbringing, were still viewed as essential components for children's success in school and later in life. And experts felt parents needed help in seeing how they could support their children's learning and thus benefit society (Taylor, 1981).

Federal Government Involvement

Following the establishment of the U.S. Office of Education in 1867, the federal government took particular interest in families. The first White House Conference on Care of Dependent Chil-

The notion of parent cooperatives continues to be important in nursery school programs today.

dren in 1909 sparked interest in child welfare throughout the nation, and in 1912 the Children's Bureau was established as a followup. Following that period, educational opportunities abounded through university courses, lectures and conferences, school programs for parents, magazine articles, and books. Later, television programs were developed instructing parents on how to educate their children. Benjamin Spock's book, *The Common Sense Book of Baby and Child Care* (first published in 1946), and Burton White's *The First Three Years of Life* became popular guides in childrearing practices, especially for the middle class (Schlossman, 1976).

As society has become increasingly urban, decision making regarding children's education has become more complex. The federal government has become influential by granting monies for projects, or by withholding the same from states not complying with federal mandates. State educational offices have also developed curricula and issued mandates regarding what should be taught in schools. Also, to qualify to receive state monies, local school authorities in recent years have begun to dictate certain educational requirements, and teachers have felt obligated to respond. At times, strong parent and advocacy groups also have attempted to influence what should be taught. Occasionally, the myriad forces have worked together in harmony, but more often we observe conflicting sets of interests.

Goals 2000

The Goals 2000: Educate America Act, signed into law on 31 March 1994, signaled a change in federal involvement in educational practice. Goals 2000 was presented as a new face for the federal government—where the federal role is to be one of support and facilitation to improve schools for all children. The act establishes very general goals as incentives and then gives support to states and communities as they work to meet those standards and objectives established locally to effect the goals (Riley, 1995). The legislation incorporates the six national education goals developed in 1990 by the Bush administration, expanding them to include partnerships for federal–state–local cooperation in improving children's learning. The act provides for financial support for states and communities working to improve their schools, and offers waivers for some federal regulations, when needed.

The expectation implicit in Goals 2000 is that the United States educational system will meet the 1990 national educational goals by the beginning of the twenty-first century. The 1990 goals are stated as follows (National Education Goals, 1993):

1. All children in the United States will start school ready to learn.
2. The high school graduation rate will increase to at least 90 percent.
3. U.S. students will leave grades four, eight, and twelve having demonstrated competency in challenging subject matter, including English, mathematics, science, history, and geography, and every school in the United States will ensure that all students learn to use their minds well, so they may be prepared for responsible citizenship, further learning, and productive employment in the modern economy.
4. U.S. students will be first in the world in science and mathematics achievement.
5. Every adult American will be literate, and will possess the knowledge and skills necessary to compete in a global economy and to exercise the rights and responsibilities of citizenship.
6. Every school in the United States will be free of drugs and violence and will offer a disciplined environment conducive to learning.

Partnerships and Collaborations

Partnerships in education is not a new concept, if we consider the various groups and interests that have worked together with our schools. As we have pointed out, families and community leaders have great input into the functioning of schools. The question arises as to how these would-be partners for the professional education establishment view their roles and how they assume responsibility and leadership.

In the 1950s and 1960s the American public, for the most part, viewed all education as the responsibility of schools, and parents were expected to support teachers and their programs. However, the community school movement also developed at this time, and for those subscribing to the movement, the purpose of schools was more comprehensive. As well as serving young children, community school advocates felt schools could serve the larger community by providing various resources for the public within the school facility (Kagan, 1987).

Educators took an active and strong role at this time, often advising parents on their roles and responsibilities. There was prosperity in the United States, and a belief that through education the United States could provide equal opportunities for all citizens.

Schools needed support to meet this goal, and volunteer programs sprang up as a result. In 1956, the Ford Foundation granted money to the Public Education Association in New York City to recruit and train volunteers to teach reading and to assist children who did not speak English fluently. In the beginning, these volunteers were primarily nonworking mothers. But as these programs expanded and spread to other areas, retirees, college students, and businesspeople also began providing volunteer services (Merenda, 1989).

Parent, school, and community relations found a new impetus for collaboration in the 1980s, as businesses became concerned with the quality of education in the United States. Some government officials recognized that educational problems could not be solved by the public sector alone. Thus, an Educational Partnerships Program was established under the Educational Partnership Act of 1988. The purpose of the act was to encourage community organizations, including businesses, to form alliances to encourage excellence in education (Danzberger & Gruskin, 1993).

Partnerships no longer involve just the basics of establishing good relationships with parents and using the resources that a community provides. Businesses have become involved in schools in a variety of ways. Partnership arrangements have grown to include such supports as volunteers for the classroom, incentives for children to improve skills, internships for teachers, mentors and tutors for particular areas of study, visiting a business enterprise, special projects sponsored by businesses, providing new technology for classrooms, and assistance in shaping school policy. The "business for education" movement grew from 17 percent involvement in 1983 to include around 40 percent of all schools by 1989 (Heaverside & Farris, 1989). Such partnerships have provided greater educational opportunities for children in schools, and they also have given businesspeople and community leaders means to directly learn about today's educational challenges.

CHILDREN WITH SPECIAL NEEDS

Political movements in the 1960s resulted in sweeping changes in American education, and in the corresponding roles of parents, schools, and communities. The civil rights movement resulted in the Civil Rights Act of 1964, which acknowledged that children in segregated schools received an inferior education. Whereas middle-class white parents have generally felt themselves a part of their children's educational process, many parents in various minority and low-SES groups felt disenfranchised prior to the landmark legislation of the 1960s. Parental involvement for all, regardless of heritage and economics, became highlighted in this era, and continues to be an important issue.

Children in Poverty

In 1965, President Lyndon Johnson launched the War on Poverty. Children raised in poverty were now to be given equal access to education and thus to greater chances at success in society. The Elementary and Secondary Education Act of 1965 (PL 89–10) was the largest grant ever made by the federal government to aid education. Educational programs such as Chapter I (originally called Title I), Head Start, Home Start, and Project Follow Through were designed under this act to compensate for the lack of early education by children living in poverty. The Head Start project was perhaps the most comprehensive. In addition to educational experiences, children and families were provided with health, nutritional, and psychological services. Parents also were to play important roles as volunteers, paid aides, and instructors in their children's education. Parents became a part of Head Start advisory boards, helping to make decisions regarding the educational opportunities provided under the project (Lazar, 1977).

Children with Disabilities

As the federally supported programs developed, parents realized they had more power in determining their rights to educational opportunities for their children. A group of parents in Missouri, concerned about how their children with disabilities were being treated, united with a civil rights organization to begin the focus on rights for disabled children. Thus the Education for All Handicapped Children Act (PL 94–142, later renamed the Individuals with Disabilities Education Act) emerged in 1975 because of the groundswell of initiatives that parents of children with disabilities mounted (Children's Defense Fund, 1981). This act insured a free and appropriate education to all children with disabilities, and in 1986 the Federal Preschool and Early Intervention Program Act (PL 99–457) extended rights and services to infants, toddlers, and other preschool children. In keeping with this legislation, the Head Start Act was amended in 1992 by the Head Start Improvement Act.

Under the above acts, parents are given rights of due process. They have the right to be involved in the entire process of their child's evaluation,

placement, and educational objectives. Children placed in special education programs now must receive an individualized education program (IEP) prepared by a school team, including parents. Parents have the right to accept or challenge any school decision and the right to examine all records the school keeps on their children. Parent involvement is assured in these procedures, and the acts have actually had the effect of forcing parents and educators into partnership relations.

In many instances, parents and educators have collaborated successfully in educating children with special needs. They have also used the resources of the community in different ways, including having volunteers work one to one with children. However, not all school personnel and parents have agreed on the most appropriate education for particular children. Since the laws have been enacted, the number of children classified as having disabling conditions has risen steadily (Webb et al., 1996). Half of these identified children are now classified as learning disabled, and a disproportionate number are African American and Hispanic children. Concerns about inappropriate placements or mislabeling children have appeared as the number of children classified as learning disabled has risen. It is understandable that some parents have used their due process rights to sue schools for inappropriate placement. With the passage in 1986 of the Handicapped Children's Protection Act (PL 99–372), whereby parents can be awarded legal fees if their suit is successful, schools find themselves under attack from more dissatisfied parents. With such pressures, it becomes vital for schools to find new ways to work successfully with parents and to use community resources for improving education for all children.

Minority Populations

The history of parent–community–school involvement has taken a different course for other families. Some individuals of diverse racial and ethnic backgrounds have integrated, through education and employment, into mainstream American culture, and have gained greater educational opportunities and material benefits. Others, reluctant to forego their own culture, have unfortunately sustained problems in opportunity. Still, for many groups, assimilated or not, discrimination and denied opportunities for equal education are continuing problems.

The history of the United States is a story of waves of immigration. In the 1600s and 1700s, West Europeans came to colonize different parts of the United States—crowding out Native Americans and bringing slaves from Africa. In the 1800s, as a result of famine in northern Europe and with the acquisition of Mexican lands by the United States, new minority groups became a part of the American fabric. Then, in the early 1900s, many people from central and southern Europe and Asia came to the United States seeking new opportunity. In the later part of the 1900s, as other countries sustained internal strife, a large number of immigrants came from Latin America, Asia, and the Caribbean seeking refuge from conflict and persecution (Kellogg, 1988). All immigrant groups have had an impact on American culture, but the dominant culture has remained Anglo-European.

Over the years, minority groups have been assimilated in accordance with how much they were able or willing to adapt to the majority culture. This (usually) worked for Europeans but rarely with other ethnically different populations. Today Native Americans, African Americans, and Hispanics comprise large ethnic groups in the United States (O'Hare, 1992), but parent–school– community relationships integrating these groups into the American mainstream have been difficult to establish. Throughout the history of the United States, these particular groups have been denied easy and equal access to quality education. They have been subjected to severe discrimination that ranked them as inferior and less worthy of quality education (J. M. Rich, 1992).

Minority Populations and Families

During the colonial period, the two major non-white cultures were Native American and African American. For these two groups, the family in conjunction with its ethnic community was the primary means for educating children.

A communal ethic has always prevailed in Native American communities. Historically, community groups have helped parents educate children and teach them economic skills, their cultural heritage, and spiritual awareness. The community expected all women to teach necessary homemaking skills, and boys as they matured were taught by various elders to hunt, survive, and fight. Through rituals, ceremonies, and oral traditions, the tribal elders passed on the religious beliefs and cultural heritage to young Native Americans (Szasz, 1988).

African Americans have lived in the United States since 1619, when the first individuals appeared as indentured servants at Jamestown. By the 1700s, most African Americans were slaves, and plantation owners exercised complete control over them. Though there were few opportunities for formal education in slavery, African Americans formed a distinct culture. It was the family and the members of the small community within each plantation that taught the children values, community behaviors, and as much of their native customs as possible. In some instances, the children learned reading and writing as they played with their owners' children (J. M. Rich, 1992). But during these early years, the sanctioned education for African American children was limited to the necessary skills for working and living within the plantation community.

Minorities and the Community

As the colonists encroached more and more on frontier lands, conflicts arose regarding the education of non-Anglo persons. Some colonists believed that Native Americans should be annihilated, and that African Americans should be kept from getting an education in order to avoid revolts. Others, from religious zeal or from practical considerations, maintained it was necessary to acculturate minority children about Anglo-European culture through education. In different parts of the country, religious groups established schools and missions to convert Native Americans. They found that they had to teach reading and writing before they could teach Christianity. In the Southwest, priests and nuns taught Native Americans farming practices, vocational skills, and the Spanish language (Kidwell & Swift, 1976). Still, the major emphasis at that time was that all groups should accept the Caucasian conqueror's religious teachings and behavior codes.

In the South, despite laws forbidding education for African Americans, some plantation owners did teach the children of slaves to read and write in order for them to become skilled workers and to read the Bible. Later, some of those literate African Americans formed their own clandestine schools (Weinberg, 1977).

Despite these modest efforts to provide education, the majority community made no effort to work with Native American and African American children. The Euro-American community dictated the rules of conduct irrespective of the values and culture of other groups. For many minority groups these early practices were the beginnings of alienation between schools and families.

Minorities and the Schools

In the 1800s, as schools became the major force for educating children of the dominant culture, so schools were seen as the way of melding the increasing number of immigrants in American society into one cultural group. But Mexican Americans and Asian Americans migrated to the United States in increasing numbers in the 1800s, and these groups created more variety in ethnic grouping and therefore more controversy. Differences that existed in earlier periods regarding how society provided schools for minority groups reappeared in the 1800s. Unfortunately, the controversies continue in some areas today.

Native Americans. To ensure better acculturation of Native Americans, boarding schools were established in the late 1800s and children were taken from their families and tribes. Some schools were established on reservations, but the Bureau of Indian Affairs, not the tribe itself, was in charge

of them. Anglo-American–style schools were established to teach Christianity, English, basic skills, and some vocational training to young Native Americans. No sense of partnership on education existed, and each Native American community was expected to submit to the type of education provided by the majority culture (Szasz, 1977).

African Americans. The aftermath of the Civil War offered greater chances for formal education for many African Americans. "Freedman schools" were established in the South where former slaves and their children, along with some impoverished white children, were taught the curriculum of the New England common schools. Reading, writing, math, geography, moral development, and industrial education became the curriculum so that these students would be ready for the labor force (Gutek, 1986). There was, however, so much resistance from Southern whites after Reconstruction that, until 1954, African American children were educated in segregated schools. The landmark case of *Brown v. Topeka Board of Education* (1954) precipitated action by African American leaders and some whites that led to the Civil Rights Act of 1964 forcing school desegregation (Bullock, 1967).

Hispanic Americans. Family, school, and community attempts at partnerships have had a history more of alienation than cooperation for the Hispanic American population. When America gained possession of the northern half of Mexico in 1848, the Spanish-Mexican-Indian population was expected to become American. But attitudes of most Americans at that time were that Mexican Americans were inferior and could be denied their rights (J. M. Rich, 1992). In spite of negative attitudes and unequal treatment throughout the era, migration of Mexican Americans to the United States has continued to the present.

Other Hispanic groups from Central America and the Caribbean have migrated to the United States, especially since the 1960s. Some new emigres were affluent and had few economic and educational hardships, but this situation did not ex-

The aftermath of the Civil War offered greater chances for formal education for many African Americans.

ist for the great majority. Presently, over 60 percent of Hispanic Americans in this country are Mexican American, and together with Puerto Ricans experience the most discrimination (Sadker & Sadker, 1991).

From the beginning, the concept of assimilation in American public schools created great conflicts with Mexican American populations. English was the language of instruction, and newly enrolled children were expected to abandon Spanish. They were to learn the culture of the schools and to negate their own culture if they were to succeed. During the late 1800s, most school districts believed that minimal skills in reading and writing were needed for Hispanic children, and there was more emphasis on vocational education and qualities that make a "good worker" by Anglo standards (Carter & Sequra, 1979). Though no legal segregation existed for Hispanic Americans, "de facto" segregation did, and most Mexican Americans over the years attended separate and inferior schools or were placed in separate classes. They usually had less well-prepared teachers and less monies were spent on their education. Classrooms were monocultural—reflecting Anglo traditions, learning styles, and value systems.

These circumstances often alienated Hispanic parents, who saw no purpose in education that destroyed their family lifestyles (Weinberg, 1977), even though early political leaders in the Hispanic community urged assimilation to avoid troubles. During the civil rights movement of the 1960s, new leadership appeared for Mexican Americans. Parents and political leaders joined forces in making demands for better schools and more equal treatment. Some gains came in a curriculum more responsive to their cultural heritage, instruction in Spanish, and culture-free IQ tests (Weinberg, 1977). The Bilingual Act of 1968 and subsequent acts have provided non-English–speaking children with instruction in both their native language and English. Even though the changes have been positive, controversy continues over the best type of instruction for Hispanic students.

Asian Americans. Asian Americans, an extremely varied group, are relatively late arrivals to this country. Chinese workers first came to the western United States in the nineteenth century in connection with railroad building. The first Japanese came at the beginning of the twentieth century, and Southeast Asians immigrated in the 1970s and 1980s as they fled their wartorn countries. Though Asians have been discriminated against and have experienced hardships adjusting to living in the United States, they have been, as a group, more academically and economically successful. However, like other emigres, Asian Americans have been expected to put aside their languages, cultural mores, and customs and adjust to Anglo-European culture. Because there are many different Asian languages, schools struggle to find the best types of bilingual education programs for Asian children. As with other minority groups, Asian American parents have often been alienated or confused by school expectations and by mainstream American culture. This problem makes good parent–school–community relations difficult to maintain.

Compensatory Education

Because parents and political leaders from different ethnic groups have struggled to gain educational opportunities for their children, the federal government has over the years funded compensatory education programs. Head Start, Follow Through, Chapter I (now Title I), and various bilingual education programs (discussed earlier) are aimed at children living in poverty and in non-English–speaking communities. All were designed to provide comprehensive programs allowing for academic experiences, as well as nutritional and health needs. Initiators of these programs recognized that, to be successful, they must involve parents and the leaders in the community where these children live.

One positive outcome for these programs implementing federal guidelines was providing an early model for family–school–community involvement. In Head Start programs, for example, parents inherited decision-making powers by sitting on the boards that hired teachers and made curriculum decisions. Teachers in these same programs were expected to make home visits and the curriculum used was expected to reflect both the experiences and the cultural heritage of the diverse children.

MULTICULTURAL EMPHASIS

Adjustments for minority groups with regard to educational opportunity has changed dramatically in the last half of the twentieth century. As federal legislation has guaranteed educational opportunities for all children regardless of race, color, or national origin and has given a voice to parents, a change in attitude towards cultural diversity has also taken place. From an earlier "melting pot" thesis, American schools and communities in general have moved in recent decades to a position of valuing multicultural education. As this type of education gains dominance, we find parent and community involvement more prominent in schools. Multicultural education requires change—in attitude, staffing patterns, curriculum and materials, and interaction patterns—from the techniques of the monocultural curriculum that has always dominated education in the United States.

Like other emigres, Asian Americans have been expected to adjust to Anglo-American culture.

Attitude Change

At the beginning of the twentieth century, the dominant attitude in the United States held that minority groups and new immigrants should be assimilated. The children from different groups were to learn behavior codes, values, and the cultural expectations of the majority culture. This attitude of assimilation continued into the 1950s and 1960s, making the tacit assumption that "something was wrong with the other culture" that assimilation could fix. *Cultural deprivation* was the term used during the War on Poverty and in the initial bilingual programs. Officials believed that children needed compensatory programs to make up for this deprivation (Stein, 1986). The

healthy dimension in the legislation of this period was that parents became included as decision makers. This important step required teachers and parents to communicate and work together, thus affording all a chance to grow.

As parent–home–community partnerships became established in the 1980s and 1990s, attitudes gradually changed toward ethnic groups and people of different heritages. Instead of the monocultural curriculum, multicultural education has been implemented in many American schools. In schools adhering to principles of true cultural pluralism, attitudes have changed so that children of diverse cultures and their parents are viewed as having strengths that contribute to and expand the education of all children.

Staff diversity is important in demonstrating positive role models for children from different ethnic groups.

Staffing Patterns

Historically, American thinking has been if children were to be acculturated, then it was important that teachers and administrators be from the majority culture so that children would have "proper" role models. In earlier periods, when teachers were recruited from minority groups, they were always sent to training schools that would educate them for the dominant culture (Gutek, 1986), thus continuing the ideas of monoculturalism.

As multicultural education gained ground, it became apparent that the staff in any school needed to have members representing different cultures. Such diversity of staff is important, as it provides positive role models for children from different ethnic groups. All teachers can emphasize their own cultural heritage, as they invite parents and members of diverse cultures and backgrounds to collaborate in providing richer classroom experiences. Using their own experiences, teachers from different minority groups can now help others understand different nonverbal behaviors and learning patterns.

Curriculum and Teaching Materials

Early publications and all curriculum materials were based on an Anglo-European worldview. White children were the main characters in stories where people lived in pleasant homes surrounded by grassy yards. There were two parents, the father working hard and the mother tending the children lovingly. Extended families were rarely depicted. Individuals with different lifestyles were often portrayed as somehow wrong, to be pitied, or quaint (Stein, 1986). Moral lessons, based on Puritan ethics, were often taught along with reading and writing. History and geography were taught from the Anglo-European viewpoint, and the contributions of other cultures to society's development were largely ignored (Garcia, 1993).

Our newer multicultural curriculum presents materials from several perspectives. People of all cultures are viewed in a variety of situations, and children study the major contributions to the United States of numerous cultural groups. Customs, rituals, and traditions of different cultures are explored, so that students may appreciate both similarities and differences. Teachers can now begin to view minority-group parents as a vital link in communicating aspects of culture to all children.

Interaction Patterns

When minority-group children were first educated in public schools, it was assumed they learned in the same manner as children from the dominant culture. If they responded in an unfamiliar way, the teacher assumed they were being impolite or were not very bright (Stein, 1986). Parents who taught their children in different ways were assumed to be wrong. Official America had a correct way to rear children, and minority-group parents were expected to learn these ways or doom their children to failure. Competitive, individualistic, and aggressive learning styles have always been rewarded in traditional American schools, and cooperative learning, until recently, was seen as cheating.

Schools that now sponsor multicultural education recognize different learning styles, and understand the need to employ different strategies to accommodate different children. In multicultural classrooms, children learn about these different patterns, and learn to accept these differences. One can see that the family becomes an important part in providing a bridge from the family's cultural patterns to the more diverse patterns found in a multiethnic and multicultural society. With proper opportunities, we find all children can learn to be conversant with more than one culture (Banks, 1993b; Garcia, 1993).

SUMMARY

Parents, communities, and schools have always assumed significant roles and responsibilities for the education of children in any society. At different times in American history, each of the three social settings assumed greater leadership and responsibility than did the other two. And in most periods, we find some instances of parent–school–community cooperation and collaboration. At other times conflicts appeared, when one institution seemed to dominate the way children were educated.

In colonial times, the family was responsible for educating children. The Puritans of New England are credited with the notion that the community at large should oversee education, and early laws in that colony regulated the teaching of academics, behavior codes, and moral development. By the 1800s, with universal education a political rallying cry, communities became the strong voice in organizing schools, hiring teachers, and taxing themselves to support these schools. Professional educators gained dominance over curriculum decisions in the twentieth century.

Parents, communities, and schools have, of course, collaborated from time to time. But not until recently have we seen any significant joining of forces. By the 1980s it became clear that strong parent–school–community relationships were necessary for schools to be responsible for educating all children. Various partnerships for educating children have been formed since then.

Though free and compulsory education has been a tenet of American educational theory for many years, most communities still have not extended equal opportunity to all cultural groups. From the 1800s to the mid 1900s, most minority-group children attended segregated schools or de facto segregated classrooms with fewer educational opportunities. As desegregation became more prevalent in the 1950s and 1960s, federal programs provided compensatory programs for children living in poverty, and many minority-group parents acquired decision-making powers over their children's education—a situation that had been absent for generations.

In the 1990s, Americans began to realize the importance of multicultural education for all children. Attitudes continue to change, school staffs have become diverse, and curriculum materials now present topics from a multicultural viewpoint. Many educators have started to value differences, and in the process include parents as valuable partners in the curriculum.

SUGGESTED ACTIVITIES AND QUESTIONS

1. Interview a senior citizen and determine whether and how he or she thinks family influence patterns

have changed from his or her childhood to the present.

2. Read one of the following juvenile historical books (or another of your choosing that reflects children being enculturated): *The Ox Cart Man*, by Donald Hall; *Sarah, Plain and Tall*, by Patricia MacLachlan; *The Little House in the Big Woods*, by Laura Ingalls Wilder; or *The Friendship*, by Mildred Taylor. What forces in the families and communities described affect the education of the child characters? Discuss, with classmates who selected other books, the role of the dominant culture in the educational process. Compare similarities and differences in the various characters' experiences.

3. Divide your class into teams of between three and six students each. Each team is to identify three areas of federal law affecting education in the United States. Each team member selects one statute from each identified area and interviews a teacher, a parent, and a local businessperson to assess their feelings about the statutes. Compare your findings with your other team members. As a group, draw conclusions about how and why the interview subjects felt as they did about the given laws. Each team then presents to the class.

4. Visit a primary school classroom in your area. Interview the teacher to determine the amount of parental involvement the teacher feels he or she has at present. Ask the teacher whether this level of involvement has changed over his or her career. To what does the teacher attribute the change (or lack thereof)?

5. Examine a primary-grade curriculum guide (or textbook) from the 1950s. Compare the amount of multicultural material you find with that found in a current guide (or textbook). Make a chart or list of these changes.

RECOMMENDED READINGS

Berger, E. H. (1995). *Parents as partners in education: The school and home working together* (4th ed.). Englewood Cliffs, NJ: Merrill/Prentice Hall.

Cremin, L. A. (1970). *American education: The colonial experience, 1607–1783.* New York: Harper & Row.

Cremin, L. A. (1982). *American education: The national experience, 1783–1876.* New York: Harper & Row.

Gutek, G. L. (1986). *Education in the United States.* Englewood Cliffs, NJ: Prentice Hall.

Schlossman, S. (1976). Before Home Start: Notes towards a history of parent education in America, 1897–1929. *Harvard Educational Review, 46*(3), 436–467.

Stein, C. B., Jr. (1986). *Sink or swim: The politics of bilingual education.* New York: Praeger.

Taylor, K. W. (1981). *Parents and children learn together.* New York: Teachers College Press.

Weinberg, M. (1977). *A chance to learn: A history of race and education in the United States.* New York: Cambridge University Press.

Zelizer, V. A. (1985). *Pricing the priceless child: The changing social value of children.* Princeton, NJ: Princeton University Press.

Viewing Family Diversity

> *The American Family does not exist. Rather, we are creating many American families of diverse styles and shapes.*
>
> *(J. K. Footlick, quoted in McCarthy, 1992, p. 3)*

Chapter 3 focuses on the demographics and the diverse nature of families in the United States today. In reading this chapter you will learn that:

1. American children are reared in many different types of households and family groupings.
2. Many social and economic factors affect family life.
3. Racial, ethnic, and language differences affect the structure, status, and functioning of families.
4. Religious factors, cultural expectations, and conditions of disability also have an impact on family life.
5. Families are always in a process of change from one stage or condition to another.

Five-year-old Jana had just entered Mrs. Thompson's multi-age classroom. Mrs. Thompson found her a happy child who came from a "nice family." As did other mothers in the neighborhood, Jana's mother walked her to kindergarten. At noon her mother met her again, and they walked to Gramma's to tell about Jana's day at school. In the evening Jana bubbled away at the dinner table, telling her father and older brother all about her day. Jana was secure and snug in her world where love abounded. But Jana's world was about to change.

Her mother became very ill that fall and was often hospitalized. Gramma came to take Jana to school on most days, though the child sometimes was angry with her and didn't want her there. Then she became worried and frightened that Gramma would not be close by.

Jana's mother died within the year, and the following year Jana's life was filled with adjustments. But Gramma and Grampa came to live at her house and take care of her and that helped. She sometimes missed her mother taking her to school, for now she had to go school with her older brother, who wanted to be with his friends, not with her. Her dad, always involved in his work, just didn't seem to be there every evening as she would like. Jana, however, worked hard in school and enjoyed the consistent routine Mrs. Thompson provided over the three years Jana was in her class.

At age 8, Jana's world shifted again. Her father remarried, and now she had an extra older brother and an older sister. Her own older brother became a "pain," when he looked after her while her father and stepmother were out. Sometimes when that responsibility was shared by her stepbrother, the two boys quarreled, and it was awful. Jana tried to tell her side of the story, but it seemed to her that her stepmother became angry and unresponsive. Jana's father tried to comfort her in her room in the evening, but he felt she should cooperate and help become a part of this new life. Jana's stepsister was away at school, but helped Jana when she came home, and they exchanged consoling letters. Gramma and Grandpa had moved away, which seemed to delight Jana's stepmother, who felt they interfered.

When Jana was 10, a new baby was born into the family. At times Jana enjoyed the delightful baby, but she became jealous when the baby got a lot of attention. Jana did begin to develop a more accepting, although shaky, relationship with her stepmother—they especially enjoyed cooking together and taking special packages to neighbors who were sick or in need.

....

What is a family? Family can mean different things at different times. Jana, in the opening vignette, was always part of a family, but the configuration changed several times in her growing-up years.

The term *family* describes particular household groupings that occur in all human societies. Historically, the designation indicated a specific home grouping, but in today's world, sociologists argue that "family" denotes a variety of clustered adults and children (Fine, 1993). For some families the cluster remains relatively constant; others, like Jana's, evolve into different arrangements over the years. Whatever the cluster, the family is a dynamic and ever-changing force in a child's life. As anthropologists demonstrate, the family is a social system, and the human race requires something like family to provide support levels needed for survival of the young (Hallpike, 1986).

Though family composition may not have actually changed a great deal over the years, cultural concepts of what constitutes a "proper family" and the percentages of different family clusters have altered considerably. In the late nineteenth century, Victorian society in Britain and the United States idealized the family as consisting of two doting and proper parents with several adoring and capable children at their knees. Of course this was far from universal even then, but through literature and folklore, people accepted this picture of what should and ought to be the situation in their towns, cities, and neighborhoods.

Changes in family composition and arrangement in the latter part of the twentieth century have certainly been dramatic, and we now have many variations in family structures before us, resulting from recent significant social, economic, and political upheavals. Traditional and idealized American family forms are obviously diminishing and other arrangements grow more commonplace. While the total number of family households expanded 11 percent between 1980 and 1993, the nuclear family (with two parents plus their biological children) decreased from 31 percent of household families to only 26 percent, and in the same time period single-parent families increased 26 percent (U.S. Bureau of the Census, 1994). Toffler and others point out that change in families will increase in the years ahead, and more "forms" will be present in the next century (as cited in Kelly, 1993).

While there may be distinct advantages to the traditional nuclear family, labeling it as the only "good" or "positive" family form is risky, to say the least. Many other family arrangements have proved coherent and viable. Human service professionals need to be aware of subtle and unsubtle prejudices toward nontraditional families. It is all too easy for teachers to value or feel comfortable with only those configurations that approximate their ideal family unit. The important thing to remember is that many arrangements work quite well, and most young children will experience changes in their family structure. As you learn about interacting with families, be sensitive to differences and carefully search out ways to support, value, and work with all the differing types you encounter (Fine, 1993).

The family is the organizational arrangement recognized by society as foremost in protecting, nurturing, supporting, and mediating for children in their growing years. The term *family* in Western culture connotes married adults. Our definition in this text does not require marriage. Many stable and prospering family units involve unmarried adults. And while some partners have been married to others, they have reconstituted a family singly or with a new partner without the formality of marriage.

In the 1990s, recognized family groups in the United States are very different than and vary more from traditional arrangements than ever before. It is important to remember that one-half of all families in the United States do not have children. Statistics on family makeup cited in this text are based on families with children in the household.

Most families, like Jana's in the chapter's opening vignette, are dynamic. Family structure is never permanent; members form a particular configuration for only a brief time. For example, when Jana was in eighth grade, her teacher asked her to draw and label two pictures: one of her family when she was in kindergarten and another of her family now.

In her kindergarten picture, Jana drew and labeled, "my real mom, my dad, my brother, and me." In her eighth-grade picture she drew herself in the center with other people in clusters around her. Closest to her were figures labeled, "dad and my older brother." On the other side but distanced from her were four people labeled, "my stepsister, my stepmom, my stepbrother, and my little sister." In the right corner she had drawn a circle for four people and wrote, "my aunt, my uncle, me, and my cousin." When her teacher asked her to explain her pictures, she said, "This first picture is me and my family before Mom died. Dad remarried, so now I have a stepmom and a brother and sister and a little sister. These people," she added, pointing to the encircled, "aren't really my family, but I stay with them a lot so sometimes they feel like my family."

Public schools in the United States must (at least initially) accept all children in a community, with whatever orientations and experiences they have. This means that any one classroom teacher relates to and interacts with representatives from several different family types. The backgrounds, values, and experiences vary from one child to the next, and teachers and other community workers must accept and value all families as they communicate and work to enhance programs. Sensitive and responsive interactions are the only base for healthy home–school–community relations.

In any description of family lifestyles it is impossible to include all configurations, but as a prospective teacher or community worker you will need to ascertain the makeup of homes in your community and assess how they function. We discuss family functioning in depth in Chapter 4.

DIFFERENT TYPES OF FAMILIES

Nuclear Families

From shortly after World War II through the early 1970s, media producers in the United States presented what they considered to be the typical American family. That image, the nuclear family, was viewed by and throughout the United States as the all-American, *Leave It to Beaver* model family. It appeared in the cinema, on television, in books and magazines, and in product advertisements of all types.

This model, two-parent home with children usually was presented as stable, thrifty, economically secure, and very happy. Of course, individual situations varied with regard to health, social status, and problems encountered for the sake of the plot or to meet current marketing needs. The archetype has been part of American (and British, and, to a lesser degree, continental European) culture for generations.

A *nuclear* family is one in which the parents are first-time married, the children living with them are their biological children, and no other adults or children live in the home. A minor variation is the home where the children are legally adopted rather than being biological offspring.

Once a common pattern for families with children in the United States, the nuclear family is much less predominant today. In fact, a few years ago Bronfenbrenner (1986) opined that the traditional family was probably a thing of the past. Role redefinitions for males and females, social pressures, changing economics and law, and reconsidered family functions have all affected the nuclear family's dominance. The Center for the Study of Social Policy (1992) stated that in 1990, only 26 percent of children in the United States lived in a two-parent "Leave It to Beaver" family with a breadwinner and a homemaker, and that this group constituted less than 7 percent of all American families (Braverman, 1989). This significant demographic change for this type of household implies concurrent changes in regard to other types. Figure 3.1 shows this demographic distribution as of 1993.

FIGURE 3.1
Where American children, birth to 8 years, lived in 1993.
Source: Adapted from 1993 census figures, from U.S. Bureau of the Census, 1994.

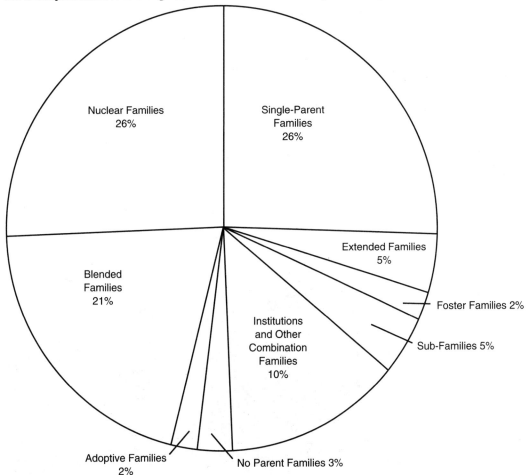

Extended Families

The multigenerational family unit resembles the nuclear family but with additions, usually adult relatives. The identifying feature of an *extended* family is that the reference person, head of household, or wage earner is the adult with young children. Older relatives or other adults are appended to this nucleus.

The extended family arrangement is typical for agrarian societies. Many farms in such communities have three generations of a family living together. In the United States, many individuals who were born near the beginning of the twentieth century can remember living as part of an extended family. Intergenerational families have advantages over nuclear ones—the "extra" adults can provide care and nurturing for the young, to say nothing of helping with farm chores. The extended family was common in Europe in the nineteenth century, and immigrants to the United States brought the practice with them when resettling (Bailyn et al., 1992).

Extended families survived in urban areas for different reasons than they did in rural areas—the practice fitted the need to economize, the cottage industries, and the social situations in which newcomers found themselves. Extended families became less common in American culture after industrialization, but the configuration has been retained in many minority-group homes (Webb et al., 1996), and sometimes temporarily in single-parent homes, as in the case of Jana in our vignette. Economics alone can dictate a need for sharing a dwelling when families are pressed. Heritage, the need for security, and the sharing of materials all combine to make the extended family a logical arrangement for many groups.

An extended family can occur in any of a number of combinations. Typical are the following:

1. Mother and father with children, plus one or more grandparents.
2. Mother and father with children, plus one or more unmarried siblings of the parents or other relatives.
3. A divorced or separated mother or father with children, plus grandparents or siblings or other relatives.
4. Combinations of the above.

It is easy to see that extended families can be quite large, often including several related adults and children. But the decline in number of extended families continues. Gestwicki (1991) estimates that less than 5 percent of U.S. families now fall into this category.

Single-Parent Families

Single-parent families, one parent living with her or his children, have always been present. The death of a spouse was not uncommon as a disrupter in the lives of our ancestors. Surviving

The multigenerational family unit resembles the nuclear family but has extra adult relatives.

spouses in earlier periods often remarried soon after the death of partners, creating stepfamilies. However, in the late twentieth century in the United States, divorce and separation, rather than death, has precipitated the increasingly large number of single-parent families. The rising number of out-of-wedlock births creates even more (Eitzen, 1992).

For a variety of reasons, the single-parent family is becoming one of the most common family groupings in the United States today. Census statistics for 1993 show 26 percent of families with children are now single-parent. This contrasts with 1970, when there were 11 percent (U.S. Bureau of the Census, 1994). Projections also show that between 50 percent and 60 percent of all children born after 1987 will spend part of their minor years in a single-parent family (Hodgkinson, 1987; Bianchi, 1990; Eitzen, 1992). Currently over 60 percent of all African American children live in female-headed households (Anthony, Wiedeman, & Chin, 1990).

The single-parent family has several structural variations:

1. Single mothers, divorced, widowed, or never married, living alone with their biological children.

The single-parent family is becoming the most common family grouping in the United States today.

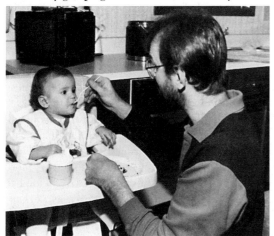

2. Single fathers, divorced or widowed, living alone with their biological children.
3. Single parents (male or female) divorced or never married living alone with adopted children.
4. Male or female parent living alone with children and spouse incarcerated, deserted, or moved away.

Single-mother families are by far the most common (87%) of one-parent families, but fathers raising their children alone are found much more often today than only a few decades ago.

Blended Families

Most divorced and widowed persons remarry, and different kinds of family units emerge from remarriages. Single adults join already existing single-parent families to form stepfamilies, and in others, adults with their own children join a partner with children to form *blended* or reconstituted families. Each year about one-half million children in the United States experience a remarriage of their custodial parents (Reid & Crisafulli, 1990). Though statistics are not kept on these families, studies indicate that 19 percent of married couples with children include one or more stepchildren, and one demographer estimates that one out of every three Americans is now a stepparent, stepchild, stepsibling or some other member of a stepfamily (Ahlburg & DeVita, 1992). The following are typical arrangements in blended families:

1. Parent with children remarries a single adult to produce a stepfamily for the new partner.
2. Two parents, each with children, remarry to produce stepchildren for each other and stepsiblings for the children. At least one half of such new marriages produce children who are half-siblings for the existing children (Kantrowitz & Wingert, 1990).
3. Common-law families, which are similar to numbers 1 and 2, but without marriage.

Not all parents seek marriages when realigning their living arrangements. Blended families can easily be formed without marriage, functioning exactly as married blends would. The Census Bureau in 1993 revealed that of the 3,513,000 unmarried couples sharing a household, over one-third have children under 15 years of age (U.S. Bureau of Census, 1994).

Adoptive Families

Most *adoptive* families function as nuclear ones, except that some of the family's children are not biological issue of either parent (though they may be related to one parent). Many families include both biological and adopted children. Adoptive families can also be single-parent—divorce occurs in adoptive families, and sometimes a single adult chooses to adopt children while foregoing marriage. In addition, some single-sex (gay and lesbian partners) families adopt children. In 1987, about 2 percent of married couples with children fell into the adopted family category (Ahlburg & DeVita, 1992).

Sub-Families

Though certainly not a new phenomenon, some family groupings, referred to as *sub-families,* reside in other households for economic or protective reasons. Perhaps the most common is the unwed mother who takes up residence with her parents or other family members. The condition is much like the extended family, except that the parent(s) with young children is appended to and is not the central family figure in the household. We also find communal arrangements, in which two or more family groups choose to live together for economic and other support reasons (Cohen, 1992; Center for the Study of Social Policy, 1989).

Foster Families

Families with *foster* children have been in existence for centuries. Dickens and other novelists allude (frequently in poignant terms) to foster home arrangements. The arrangements, both legal and informal, exist today in the United States and are increasing in many urban areas as social welfare agencies try to find suitable living quar-

ters for unwanted, abused, and neglected children. While sources vary in numbers of foster children, the Children's Defense Fund (1993) records 406,000 children in foster care. At times, childless couples elect to become foster parents for children, but more frequently it is the nuclear family that decides to extend itself to accommodate additional children. Arrangements for foster care are most often financial contracts by which a family agrees with a state agency to accept one or more state wards for a stated remuneration. Time elements vary from several weeks for newborns, who will be placed for adoption, up to 18 years for other children. In the nineteenth century, foster care was often without remuneration and families accepted children for humanitarian reasons as well as economic objectives, such as for securing help for farms or households.

Other Family Groupings

As noted, the family types discussed here occur in many specific configurations. It is also true that some children, as Figure 3.1 shows, have no organized family, living in institutions or boarding facilities that serve as a family substitute. Less common family groupings involve children living in homes not headed by a parent. Significant numbers of young children live with grandparents, aunts, uncles, cousins, and even nonrelated adults. Census Bureau figures show that in 1993, 3 percent of American children were in such arrangements (U.S. Bureau of the Census, 1994). Other informal living arrangements involve runaways and abandoned children who have escaped social agency notice and have adapted to temporary homes that provide the basics. These arrangements are always fragile and extralegal.

The family types discussed in this chapter all exist to some degree across the United States, and while quality of childrearing varies with individuals, all family structures can be viable. It is more than likely that you know people who belong to several of the above noted patterns, as perhaps you do yourself. Economics and social pressures in our country ensure that diversity in family arrangements continues, and transformations from one type of family to another occur daily in thousands of homes, as in our opening vignette. One positive result of this continuing transformation is the acceptance now found in our society for a "multiplicity of forms," which was not present a generation ago. But diversity also is a challenge for professionals working with families. As an educator, you must come prepared with knowledge, communication and interaction skills, and an ability to accept differences. Think of how you will work for consensus with myriad groupings as you help your community educate its children.

SOCIAL FACTORS RELATING TO FAMILIES

Ethnic and Cultural Factors

Physical characteristics, language, and cultural factors distinguish some families from mainstream culture in the United States, and may give them a different identity. Though "racial awareness" has a long history in our nation, "race" labels are often unproductive, inaccurate, and meaningless (indeed, the very existence of "race" itself has come to be questioned by some). The Census Bureau still uses four "racial" categories (plus "Other"), but in 1990, when respondents had a write-in blank for "race" available, they wrote nearly 300 different ethnic group labels! (O'Hare, 1992). This clearly suggests that current labels provide inadequate information, but with continued reliance on census-based formulas for distributing federal aid, ensuring minority election districts, and expanding affirmative action, the United States seems destined to use them for some time yet.

In this text, we use the term *ethnic* to refer to the general complex of cultural and physical individual and group characteristics, and use the term *cultural* to refer specifically to that complex of created, linguistic and societal, nonphysical characteristics that distinguish societies and groups. We

feel that reflecting on ethnic identification instead of focusing on "racial" lines and characteristics is more productive, because it more accurately reflects the wide demographic palette in the United States. This focus is certainly more helpful for educators and community workers whose task is to support all children's development.

Until the 1980s, American schools and communities operated mostly on the basis of assimilating different cultural and ethnic minorities and language groups into the mainstream Anglo-American culture (Tiedt & Tiedt, 1989). Since the 1980s, the concept of "cultural pluralism," as suggested in Chapter 2, has taken root. A large number of schools and communities currently subscribe to the idea of recognizing the positive contributions and qualities of the numerous cultural groups in the United States and using these to build a stronger society. Most professionals accept the notion that diversity can produce strength.

Applying this acceptance notion in communities and schools means emphasizing a multicultural curriculum that promotes positive multiethnic relationships among children, school personnel, parents, and community. As a teacher, you must be prepared to occasionally alter your curriculum to accomodate special cultural characteristics and qualities, and to make adjustments in discussions and interactions with parents. Among these are minority versus majority ethnic/cultural status, and the presence in your class of children belonging to bilingual and interethnic families.

Minority Status

The United States, whose population was once predominantly of West European Caucasian (white) ethnic derivation, has expanded swiftly in the last century to include numerous ethnic and cultural groups. At the beginning of the colonial era, the Eastern seaboard colonists were mostly Europeans, with a tiny minority of African Americans. A large group of Native Americans, indige-

TABLE 3.1
U.S. Population by Race and Ethnicity in 1992

Total U.S.	254,992,000
Non-Hispanic Caucasian	190,604,000
African American	30,372,000
Asian & Pacific Islander	7,937,000
Native American & Eskimo	1,873,000
Hispanic	24,136,000

Source: U.S. Bureau of the Census, *Current Population Reports*, P-25, No. 1092 (1992), table 2.

nous to the continent, existed as a separate and parallel cultural complex. The United States now has a large minority population, and minority families are common in all but a few of the 50 states. As Table 3.1 shows, in 1992, minority populations represented 25 percent of the total U.S. population (Estrada, 1993). Both African American and Hispanic minorities are growing much faster than is the Caucasian population. Minorities currently account for 30 percent of the total school population, and 22 of the 25 largest city school systems have over 50 percent minority students (Quality Education for Minorities Project, 1990). Estrada (1993) estimates that, within a few years, the group of minority, schoolage children will increase three times as fast as the white group will (Figure 3.2). We will soon need a descriptive term to replace *minority*.

The concentration of minorities across the United States is very different. Hispanic, Native American, and Asian families are concentrated more heavily in the western and southwestern U.S.; African Americans are concentrated in the southern U.S. and in urban areas nationwide. Six states now record 50 percent or more minority population (O'Hare, 1992), which means Euro-Americans are nearing minority status in some parts of our country.

Educational orientations, expectations, and learning styles vary within all families, and many

FIGURE 3.2
Projected ethnic composition of the U.S. population for years 1990–2050.
Source: From "The Census Bureau's New Projections of the U.S. Population" by D. A. Ahlburg, 1993, *Population and Development Review, 19*(1), 167. Reproduced by permission.

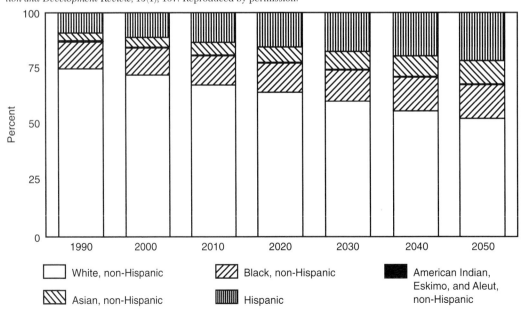

minority families have favored and even encouraged different *learning strategies* (Webb et al., 1996). Schools and communities must recognize that people have different ways of knowing, and acknowledge that some differences are beneficial. As a teacher, you must accommodate these different cognitive styles. (See Chapter 6 for more on different learning styles.)

Bilingual Families

Bilingualism and linguistic differences are far more common for American children than is generally perceived. Over 30 million people in the United States speak a language other than English at home, and over 13 million "do not speak English well" (U.S. Bureau of the Census, 1991). Bilingual school programs have been developed in response to the growing numbers of linguistically different children. In recent years bilingual education has been most closely associated with teaching Hispanic minorities, but programs exist for over 90 other minority groups in U.S. schools (McNeil, 1990).

Approximately 3.6 million students in the United States show a need for special linguistic assistance in order to participate in a public school curriculum. But less than 10 percent of that figure actually are in bilingual programs (McNeil, 1990). These statistics are significant for communities and schools where concentrations of non-English–speaking families live and work. Particular problems in communication and general acceptance do appear, and since English is the language of instruction in most schools, children with less than full fluency are in some ways handicapped. One of your challenges will be to support children and families with different language backgrounds. This challenge forms another basis for school–home–community discussion and action.

Interethnic Families

Since interethnic and intercultural marriages are becoming more common (Estrada, 1993; Smolowe, 1993), more children with parents of different ethnic backgrounds attend American schools today. *Population Bulletin* reported about 3 percent of births nationally as "mixed race," and much higher rates for Asian and Hispanic groups (O'Hare, 1992). "The New Face of America," a special issue of *Time* (1993), highlights the changing racial diversity in the United States, and indi-

As the U. S. becomes more culturally diverse, professionals need a stronger grasp of multicultural interests.

cates a gradual homogenizing of our American population.

Since different ethnic groups generally hold differing cultural expectations, interethnic families will have different perceptions about culture and their child's participation in school and community. Through adoptions, some families are rearing children from a different culture than that of the parents, and many of those parents are interested in preserving features of the adopted child's heritage. Other families will have a multiethnic makeup due to remarriage or combinations of parent and child ethnicity.

Culture and ethnicity are family characteristics. As the United States becomes more culturally and ethnically diverse, professionals need a stronger grasp of the range of multicultural interests. The history of "race relations" in the United States has seldom been positive, and most minority-group children have felt the stings of racism and ethnocentrism. If children from our various ethnic groups are to succeed, they need to know and feel that schools and communities want them to succeed.

SOCIOECONOMIC STATUS OF FAMILIES

While the United States is reputed to be a classless society, most sociologists point out that indeed we do have a several-tiered system in our country that defines a social class structure closely related to socioeconomic status (SES). Social classes are not easily portrayed because there are overlaps, but in general, class standing is based on the occupation, income, education, and values of the parents in a family. Figure 3.3 diagrams the social classes generally used to show the organization of American society.

FIGURE 3.3
Social class structure in the United States.

Source: From *Society and Education* (8th ed.) (p. 7) by D. U. Levine and R. J. Havighurst, 1992, Boston: Allyn & Bacon. Reproduced by permission.

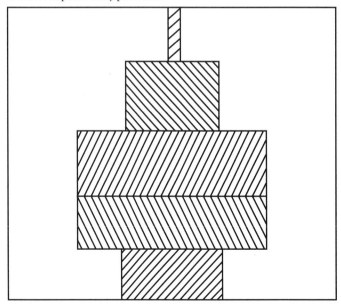

Upper	2%
Upper-Middle	16%
Lower-Middle	32%
Upper-Working	32%
Lower-Working	18%

Historic Class Descriptions

The upper class in the United States parallels the aristocracy in other societies. These families have inherited wealth and a close-knit circle of friends, family, and colleagues. Children from upper-class families normally attend exclusive private schools and prepare for careers in a family enterprise or in public service, such as in politics or with social help organizations. Family heritage and "proper rearing" are very important in this class, and children are expected to conform to established standards of behavior, etiquette, and education.

Middle-class families have arrived at their status through vigorous pursuit of education and industry. Upper middle-class American families are affluent, hardworking, and achievement oriented. They are often the community's leaders, physicians, lawyers, and successful businesspersons. A defining quality for these families is the practice of "delayed gratification"; children are reared from an early age to exercise self-discipline, to avoid conflict, and to wait for rewards. Families are often nuclear and closely knit. Middle- and lower middle-class families are much the same as those of the upper middle class in expectations and desires. Less highly paid professionals are in this category, as are many successful businesspersons. This is "middle America," which enjoys many social advantages and good-quality living standards.

Upper working-class families represent skilled tradespersons, factory workers, and other hourly wage earners. Members of this class emphasize hard work, but hold education to be less important than do members of the middle and upper classes. Working-class children are encouraged to expect a life of wage earning. Economic ups and downs often affect working-class families, and they are more likely to deplete their available resources. Child raising is more direct, and parents often dominate their children and frequently use physical punishments. Archie Bunker in the 1970s television series *All in the Family* made stereotypical behavior attributed to this class well known to the rest of the viewing public.

The lower working class is made up generally of unskilled laborers, who are susceptible to layoffs and at times must depend on welfare for subsistence. Male and female roles are definitely shaped in this section of the scale, and males dominate most family decisions. Families in this class will often live in substandard housing, and have poorer diets and marginal health practices. Children of lower working-class parents are expected at an early age to develop responsibilities for care of their siblings and doing chores. Cramped living quarters is a trademark of those living in cities. The class is most at risk in an economy of the future, since the emerging Information Age has only minimal opportunities for people with manual and nontransferable skills.

The Underclass—A New Dimension

Although not represented in the classic diagram, sociologists and demographers now recognize an expanding group, previously merged with the lower working class, that occupies the lower margin of our economic and social scales (Morgenthau, 1989). The *underclass* is comprised of individuals and families locked into a debilitating cycle of poverty and despair from which they can find little escape. Underclass families subsist primarily on welfare or other government assistance, live in inferior housing or on the streets, and face lives racked by crime, deprivation, and abuse. Most individuals in this class possess little education and limited experiences, so the culture of poverty spirals onward. This perpetuation of economic and social dislocation gives individuals and families little chance for working out of the chain of burdens.

Many at-risk children are in the underclass, which means nutrition and health care are minimal, and illness, disease, and abuse are common. Minority families are highly represented in this expanding group (Children's Defense Fund, 1992). As a social dilemma, the underclass is perhaps the greatest challenge we face in our efforts to eradicate poverty.

We have considerable evidence that persons move from one socioeconomic or social class group to another via education, personal improvement efforts, or fortunate investments. While upward movement for middle-class Americans seems almost assured, options for the underclass seem far less promising in the future—education levels and minimal experiences as well as the neglect of mainstream America represent a fixed ceiling for them.

Economics and American Families

The economic base of a family is extremely important for its members. It determines the family's quality of life, health care, nutrition, and living conditions as well as level of self-esteem and ability to function in a community. While a majority of U.S. families maintain a high standard of living compared with the rest of the world, we find increasing numbers of families in poverty. Industrial jobs are being eliminated rapidly in the late twentieth century and are being replaced by lower-paying service employment. The effect is that real wages for most families fell 14 percent between 1973 and 1986 (Eitzen, 1992). "Downward mobility," rather than upward movement, has become the pattern for more Americans in this generation.

Affluence in the United States has risen for a few sections of the electorate, but on the whole most Americans have less buying power in 1990 than they had in 1970 (Eitzen,1992). Attempting to ward off declining living standards, more nuclear families now have both parents working. This condition has negative implications for quality of life in these families as well as for their participation in their schools and communities.

Middle-Income Families

The "American dream" is to achieve a middle-class style of life. The middle class are supposed to enjoy full employment and the esteem that society places on the engine that propels the nation.

For many, this scenario is true. In 1991, over 30 million families, or about 48 percent of all American households, enjoyed an income above the median, one that permitted them to enjoy a better-than-average lifestyle (U.S. Bureau of the Census, 1992b). However, we must remember that real earnings slipped badly in the 1970s and 1980s, so to remain in the middle class, many of these families have moved to the "dual-income plan" in order to maintain the features of suburban living, recreational opportunity, and college education for their children (Huston, 1991).

Middle-income families often hold to traditional values. Child raising practices are in line with status, featuring reasoning with children in lieu of direct punishment. Communication is valued. Middle-income families are more easily involved in school and community activities, and the parents' education level usually makes communication easier. Their volunteer work can be considerable, and since their participation has a history, minimal instruction or organization is necessary. Members of this group can make valuable contributions to a school program, in sharing talents, giving presentations, or managing projects. But time may be scarce with middle-income parents, and new demands—especially with dual-income families—can place time constraints.

Working-Class Families

Values in working-class families often differ from those presented in schools. While we need to draw all families into school and community service, professionals need to be prepared for communicating and interacting with people who want productive lives for their children, but do not always understand school and agency strategies or objectives.

Working-class families fit well into "previously arranged" school and community programs. Family members here consider themselves as "doers" and normally are willing to work avidly on projects or other means to support a school or agency.

Underclass Families

As discussed, the United States has for generations contained an underclass of families with limited education, limited employment, and a history of subsisting on government assistance. In addition, financial reversals and economic deterioration in some locations have resulted in poverty for previously working-class American families. In the closing years of the twentieth century, the number of families in the United States at or below the subsistence level is growing. In 1992, statistics showed 14.5 percent of the population as "officially poor" and included 21 percent of all children (U.S. Bureau of the Census, 1994). This figure does not count the numbers in welfare-directed agencies or groups. The Center for the Study of Social Policy (1989) estimates that one in every four young children live in poverty. Minority children under the age of 6 have the highest rate of poverty, with figures ranging up to 46 percent (National Center for Children in Poverty, 1990) (Figure 3.4).

Poverty is a risk factor associated with numerous negative outcomes—particularly for children. In the 1980s and 1990s poverty has become more permanent because of difficulties individuals have in breaking out of menial task jobs. The United States has a permanent underclass now, and two expanding groups at this level are homeless and itinerant families.

Homeless families. Some families suffering economic hardships must surrender their homes, others have a history of wandering from state to state, and changes in mental health regulations in many states have resulted in previously institutionalized persons being left to their own devices. These persons and their families make up our homeless population.

Because they have no permanent address, homeless families spend increasing amounts of time in shelters, in automobiles, or on the street. Whereas the typical media image of the homeless person is the unemployed male who abuses substances and wanders streets, statistics show that over 25 percent of the homeless in 1990 were family persons and two-thirds of that number were small children (Blau, 1992; Nichelason, 1994). Numbers of homeless are difficult to ascertain and estimates differ sharply; however, conservative figures show that nearly 200,000 American children are homeless in the course of a year (Blau, 1992; Ahlburg & DeVita, 1992). Many of the parents in homeless situations are employed, but work in low-end jobs that pay insufficiently for housing. Some children from homeless situations manage to attend school, although usually only parttime. Clearly, these circumstances offer a challenge to communities and schools working together to produce basic health and nutrition services for our neediest children.

Itinerant families. Some families are highly mobile because of erratic work availability and the unsettled lifestyles of the parents. Living conditions for families in this category are normally poor and many suffer from serious health problems (Educational Research Service, 1992).

Migrant workers constitute a significant block of both U.S. citizens and resident aliens who move up and down the continent during harvesting seasons. Many families are without a permanent home—children are in one location for several weeks and then move to another. Life for these children has little security, health care, or stability. This situation poses a particular problem for schools and teachers. Children are forced to move into a new situation every few weeks, so have little continuity in school or community experiences. The progress in cognitive growth for migrant children is often minimal, and they frequently become socially alienated simply because they cannot feel a part of any school or community (National Commission on Migrant Children, 1992).

Effects of Economics

The economic foundation of a society governs in large part the socioeconomic status (SES) of individuals within that society. Financial resources for

FIGURE 3.4

American children under 18 in poverty, 1960–1990.

Source: National Center for Education Statistics, 1992, *The Condition of Education: 1992* (Stock no. 065-000-00-505-1) (p. 39), Washington, DC: Author.

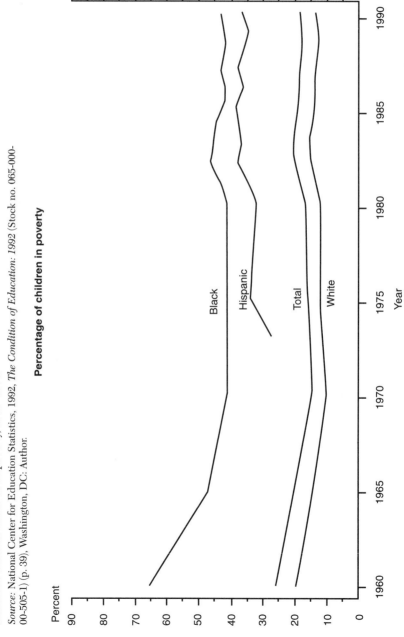

Percentage of children in poverty

Frequent moves produce unsettled lifestyles for families, making children's care and schooling difficult.

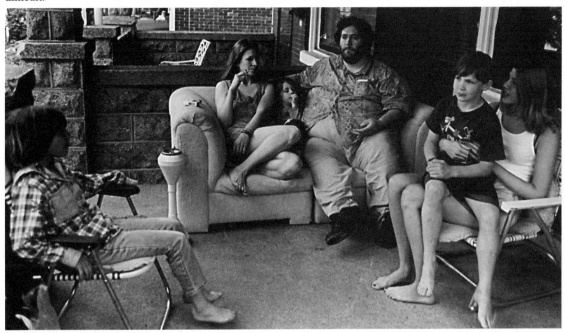

families become the most important variable in determining class status and opportunity; money governs diet, place of residence, access to health care, and chances for the future. Naturally, children's achievement in school is affected tremendously by these factors.

Early studies by Coleman (1966) showed a strong correlation between family SES and children's cognitive development and achievement. More recent studies qualify those findings. Graue, Weinstein, and Walberg (1983) point out the importance of the psychological environment at home for child learning, and Clark (1983) shows that the parents' childrearing style determines children's success. Iverson and Walberg (1982) find a similar pattern, noting that parental behaviors toward children are more strongly predictive of cognitive growth than are SES variables. So we may hope to keep alive the chance for upward mobility and improvement for economically disadvantaged populations, if we can deliver to these

families intervention in the form of educational programs. If parent attitudes and behaviors represent those characteristics that can be affected by education and training (Walberg, 1984), then schools and communities have the best chance for engaging parents in the process of educating their children.

FAMILIES WITH DISABLED CHILDREN

Special education, or, as it is now known, education of children with disabilities, involves a large number of diverse families with children whose disabilities range from mild to severe. But in spite of a generation living under PL 94–142, disabled persons frequently encounter conditions of discrimination and segregation.

During the 1990–1991 school year, 4,817,503 children and youth from birth through age 21 were served under federal programs for children with disabilities (Educational Research Service, 1992). This is a significant population (7.5% of children and youth in that age bracket, according to U.S. Census Bureau statistics) and places considerable challenge and pressure on available assistive time and resources. When you work with schools and communities, you need to understand not only particular disabilities, but also those problems and pressures that affect both the family and the child. Professionals must be both sensitive and supportive when working with families of children with disabilities. (Note the legacy recounted in Chapter 2.)

Families with special needs are a part of all communities, and since disabilities cut across all socioeconomic groups, affected children will be present in most schools. Diversity is always a challenge for education professionals, but often the special-needs families require more school–home–community planning to realize the most positive outcomes. While major disabilities are evenly distributed across SES groups, milder disabilities (called *school identified* disabilities) occur much more frequently in poor and disadvantaged families (Educational Research Service, 1992). Lacks in health care and particularly prenatal care are responsible in large part (Argulewicz, 1983; Brantlinger, 1991) for the milder disabilities.

RELIGIOUS ORIENTATION

Ethnic origin, SES, and the presence of disabilities are demographically identifying family characteristics. The family's religion is another. In their attempt to follow the letter of the constitutional requirement of "separation of church and state" in the United States, schools often try to ignore or to deliberately overlook the religious affiliation of children and their families. However, religious affiliation affects how children feel about school activities, rules, and the behavior of others. Religious practices may affect interaction and participation, holiday observances, foods eaten, and gender roles. It is important that school and community professionals know and respect the tenets of the different religions represented in community families. Their ability to accommodate different religious practices directly affects whether their work with children, their families, and particular communities will be successful.

The major faiths represented in the United States are Christian, which includes Protestants, Catholics, and Mormons; Jewish; and Islamic. Small representations of Hinduism, Buddhism, Taoism, and other beliefs are found in major U.S. cities. All major faiths are divided into smaller sects and denominations, which vary considerably. For example, within the Protestant Christian faith are dozens of denominations, ranging socially and politically from liberal to conservative. Catholic subgroups include Roman Catholic, Greek Orthodox, and Russian Orthodox. Jewish groups range from conservative Hassidic sects to liberal Reform synagogues.

Religion helps many persons find purpose and meaning in their lives. And while socioeconomic success does not seem to be linked with any particular faith, some researchers indicate a correlation between religious commitment and moral behavior (Gorsuch, 1976). This statistic should be comforting, considering that 90 percent of Americans profess to having a religious attachment! However, attendance at religious services rarely exceeds 20 percent of the population in any one community.

The *Yearbook of American and Canadian Churches, 1993* (Bedell, 1993) catalogs the religious affiliation of approximately 158 million persons in the United States indicating a religious connection. Of that figure, the membership percentage for the predominant groups is as follows:

Protestant Christians	63%
Catholic Christians	30%
Jews	3%
Muslims	3%

These figures affirm a dominant Protestant religious heritage in most areas of the United States. This stems from a strong Protestant affiliation in the United States's colonial era.

Religion directly influences how families rear children, as well as how they conduct their affairs and relate to a community. And even though the U.S. Constitution carefully separates church and state, one finds a great deal in legal codes and the common law of the United States resting firmly on a Protestant ethic (Uphoff, 1993).

Applications of Religion

All religions deem sacred certain ideas, objects, or aspects of the natural world, and these dictates have implications for observance within those groups. Even though many children are only casually acquainted with the practice of their religion, it is still a background feature in their lives, and their behaviors and reactions will demonstrate that. The following are points to consider as you collaborate with parents and community members in educating children.

Observance of holidays. Most religions have selected, faith-specific holidays. Christians celebrate Easter and Christmas holidays; Jews celebrate Rosh Hashanah, Yom Kippur, and others; Muslims celebrate Ramadan and other holidays.

Codes. Religious groups have codes relating to sexual behavior as well as to the observance of marriages, births, and deaths. Many religions have dietary laws, and children will seek or avoid specific foods at certain times or during particular occasions.

All religions have a moral code, and when we compare religious practices around the world, many aspects of the different codes resemble one another. Differences are in such features as locus of control. For example, Protestant groups hold that human beings are individually responsible for their behavior, but other groups teach that it is loyalty to the group that counts and that individuals must adhere to acceptable practice as defined by the religion or its authorities.

Educators must remember the following points regarding religion (Uphoff, 1993):

1. Ascertain the religious affiliations of associates, clients, schoolchildren, and community members.

All religions have ideas, objects, and rituals that are deemed sacred, and the religious practices form a background for children's lives.

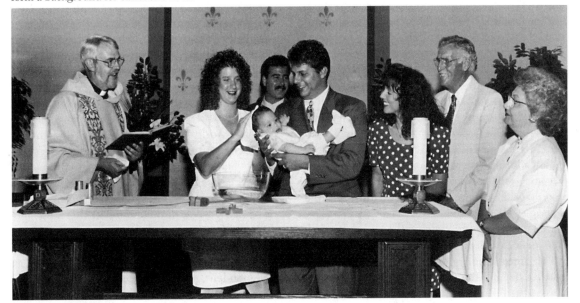

2. Learn to value all religious practice and encourage people to share information about their faiths.
3. Learn about the larger community endeavors that focus on religion or feature religious holidays.
4. Learn how to use the various religious links in the school and community to educate children and to help them develop tolerance for others.

CHANGES IN CONTEMPORARY FAMILIES

Even though the concept of family has been with humanity for millennia, we find gradual changes in form and function of this basic unit. The focus of this text is on families in the United States in the late twentieth century, but here we consider family evolution over the past two centuries. The comparisons will help explain how we arrived at our present situation, and will provide some insight for what may follow in the future.

From its inception to the mid 1800s the United States was primarily an agrarian economy and its population was mainly rural. This circumstance produced a typical farming family structure across the United States. This land-based family was often extended, and often included three generations of members. Children were considered valuable assets to families at this time, since farm work involved numerous and plentiful tasks calling for extra hands.

With the advent of the Industrial Revolution in the late 1700s and early 1800s, American economy and social structure changed rapidly. Urban centers expanded and whole new classes of jobs in manufacturing, merchandising, and commerce became available. Changes in the economic situation brought changes to families also. A large working class emerged. A whole new ethic was injected into family life. Roles in the home changed. The need for many hands in the home diminished, since children of factory workers did not participate in the work of parents. Homes changed from places where childrearing was linked with acquiring adult skills to environments where childrearing only took place. Education was no longer passed from older to younger family members, but became something taught in "schools" as children's need for literacy and calculation skills moved beyond parental expertise.

At the beginning of the nineteenth century, the urbanization of the United States was well underway. Industrial and commercial development continued in rapid strides until World War II. Following the westward expansion movement in the 1880s and the general availability of railroad transport, relocation became relatively common for American families, especially after the early 1900s. Some families became isolated from relatives as they tried to establish roots in other communities and regions (Bailyn et al., 1992). It is during this period that the extended family diminished, and the classic model of the nuclear family, typified by the smaller family of children living with their parents in an individual house with mother as homemaker and father as breadwinner, became more prominent. After World War II, mobility intensified as large groups moved to different parts of the country to find better living conditions. This activity and reorganization increased the prevalence of nuclear family features.

Of course there were many exceptions in early twentieth-century households. Death often left single-parent families in its wake. Single parents clearly had a difficult task, so remarriages and, consequently, stepfamilies occurred frequently. Divorce was rare in this time, but foster care was not.

With World War II, new shifts in economics, a rise in minority populations, and changes in social habits had great impact on families in the United States. These changes included increasing numbers of women in the work force, instability in marriages, a rise in divorce rates, increased mobility for families, and the rise of a peer group culture (Bailyn et al., 1992).

Women joining the work force became more independent, redefined family roles, and changed attitudes for both males and females. Many couples chose separation, remarriage, and different styles of living when they found they now held different expectations of family life. Female heads of households became more common and there were fewer adults in a family unit (Figure 3.5). One drawback to this phenomenon was the loss of what Coleman (1991) calls "social capital" in families—meaning adults' attention to and involvement with children's learning at home and in the neighborhood.

After a decade of legislation and social challenge with the Civil Rights movement, American social behavior took an even greater turn in the 1960s and 1970s. Younger Americans challenged an older order and experimented with different types of living arrangements. The more informal relationships, more flexible marriage and living arrangements, and new lifestyles of the 1990s are outgrowths from this period.

The postindustrial era arising in the United States at the end of the twentieth century brings new directions and implications for families. The rise of massive service and communications industries shows that the importance of physical labor, as known to previous generations, has lessened considerably (Naisbitt & Aburdene, 1990). In lieu of high-energy occupations, more U.S. workers now direct their attention to service of equipment, service of living conditions, and transmittal of information and processes. More and more employees work at home, and in a variety of different locations (Naisbitt & Aburdene, 1990). Thus the notion of a constant skill for employment or an established work place diminishes.

At the same time that the Information Age and the service industry blossom in the United States, we have a more noticeable differentiation in economic "haves" and "have nots." Blue-collar workers are finding physical labor less in demand. Automation and robotics increasingly replace manufacturing jobs, and large segments of our skilled labor forces are witnessing the end of their vocations. Younger members of this force find themselves inheriting a minimum number of available jobs, while others are moved to depend

FIGURE 3.5

American families in the labor force, 1940–1990.

Source: From "Family Members in the Work Force" by H. V. Hayghe, 1990, *Monthly Labor Review, 113*(3), 16. Reproduced by permission.

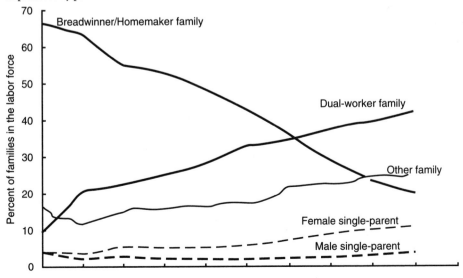

on welfare. While the Information Age has brought acceptance of different lifestyles, it has produced abrupt economic demands that leave Americans scurrying to find new ways to cope. All of these changes have immense implications for family and home situations.

As we approach the end of the twentieth century, new attitudes concerning sexual behavior have also emerged, and cohabitation without marriage has become socially acceptable. Interethnic marriages are more common, and out-of-wedlock births appear less controversial. Communal living arrangements are more accepted, as are gay partnerships and gay adoptions. Though flexibility and tolerance are key requirements for new lifestyles, educators must appreciate the need for a far more sophisticated education of all younger people. The demand on literacy, problem-solving, and negotiating skills is higher for youngsters who as adults will be very mobile and less constrained in living arrangement, and who will face frequent job changes and must constantly learn new methods for accomplishing things.

In the midst of all these changes in conditions and societal attitudes, children from various families will continue to arrive at schools and to participate in communities. The new conditions and family configurations may be very stable and supportive for young children, or may precipitate difficulty. As in all family and community changes, children are expected to adapt to new circumstances. They usually do, but they can also suffer. Living arrangements affect children's academic participation. Teachers and other service personnel need to acknowledge such conditions and circumstances when planning for the next steps in each child's educational endeavor.

SUMMARY

Family, though undergoing radical change in many communities, is still the primary building block of the United States. Families vary in cultural, ethnic, reli-

gious, economic, and educational features, but all parents contribute in some way to their communities and to the schools where their children seek instruction, guidance, and direction.

The diversity of American families is said to be its strength. That fact can be generally interpreted as meaning that different heritages, values, work styles, and habits give a character to the American landscape that is both stimulating and an incentive for production. However, members of some of these diverse groups are in dire need of help and special support services.

Families have changed over the history of the United States, and will continue to change. Ethnic proportions are constantly changing, mobility will change, values will change, and even socioeconomic status will change. In the past, each generation has had its special problems and its particular successes. With this dynamic base, schools and communities must shape programs that can involve all participants fully and productively. Indeed, we find that many have already begun.

SUGGESTED ACTIVITIES AND QUESTIONS

1. Discuss with several colleagues the family structures in your homes. Have these changed over time or have they remained constant during your and their lifetimes?
2. Do a quick survey of the cultural and ethnic demographics in your school or center neighborhood. How do your results compare with the overall U.S. population?
3. Estimate the socioeconomic status of 10 children in a day care center or school with which you are familiar. Then determine if records or interviews confirm your estimates.
4. Have the children in one group draw pictures of their families and then tell you about the persons they portray. How much information do you receive about the types of families these children have?
5. Find out why children that you meet in your field work are identified as *disabled*. Was a school or center involved in referrals? Did diagnosis come through a clinic, a family physician, or another source?

RECOMMENDED READINGS

Banks, J. A., & McGee-Banks, C. A. (Eds.). (1993). *Multicultural education: Issues and perspectives* (2nd ed.). Boston: Allyn & Bacon.

Blau, J. (1992). *The visible poor: Homelessness in the United States.* New York: Oxford University Press.

Hodgkinson, H. (1987). *All one system: Demographics of education—kindergarten through graduate school.* Washington, DC: Institute for Educational Statistics.

Kaplan, L. (Ed.). (1992). *Education and the family.* Boston: Allyn & Bacon.

Levine, D. U., & Havighurst, R. J. (1989). *Society and education* (7th ed.). Boston: Allyn & Bacon.

Morgenthau, T. (1995, February 13). What color is black? *Newsweek, 125,* 63–65.

Naisbitt, J., & Aburdene, P. (1990). *Megatrends 2000.* New York: William Morrow.

National Commission on Migrant Children. (1992). *Invisible children: A portrait of migrant education in the United States* (Stock No. 022-003-01173-1, Supt. of Documents). Washington, DC: Author.

Parenting the Child

*I think that parenting is the most important job in this society,
and the one that has been neglected most.*

President Bill Clinton, Time, *13 Dec. 1993*

Differences in customs, modes of interaction, parenting styles, and outside influences affect the nurturing practices in all family situations. In Chapter 4, we discuss how these qualities and conditions affect the parent role and the outcomes of parent practices. In reading this chapter you will learn that:

1. Parents are key persons in providing the nurturance needs of young children.

2. Parents assume particular roles in children's upbringing and that these roles have changed in recent years.

3. Although there are commonalities in parenting practices childrearing varies in different ethnic communities in the United States.

4. Researchers have determined that there are different parenting styles among parents, and that these styles affect children's participation in school and community life.

5. Some forms of stress affect childrearing practices, and in the late twentieth century new and intensified stressors have impact on families in the United States.

All families, irrespective of the ways they are constituted, share in community life and in school life, and most of the diverse household arrangements are workable settings. Although some arrangements may be more vulnerable or sensitive, when considered against the dynamics of a particular community, each family can make positive contributions to children's development.

When we consider how families function, we find different customs, different priorities, and even somewhat different values. Of course, the differences signal the unique arrangements in our diverse society, but at the same time those very different elements fuse in most families to provide coherence and stability for members in the household.

In spite of the differences, however, we find some constants that exist in all families with children. The first constant, nurturance of children, precedes all others. Nurturance is followed by defined family roles, cultural patterns, interaction styles, and family experiences. Additional characteristics, such as child care arrangements, poverty, or divorce, can emerge as stressors that have an impact on the parenting quality of some family units.

NURTURANCE IN FAMILIES

Generally, *nurturance* means providing the basic necessities of life for children, but in a wider sense it denotes general support and cultivation for the growing child. In other words, nurturance is "parenting."

Few adults are actually trained for nurturing roles, but our society anticipates certain minimums of support and effectiveness as parents rear children. The assumption is that nurturance in its general and wider sense has been modeled by our forebears, and is refined by an individual's experience and participation in society. But do these qualities exist in all U.S. homes? The range is wide indeed.

Range of Childrearing

The nurturer accepts responsibilities not only for basic physiological care, guidance, and valuing children, but also for stimulating their investigations of the world. The nurturing parent is one who is grounded in humane practice and who has a vision of what children can become.

Abusive behavior in families moves parenting toward the antithesis of nurturing. While few parents are so disordered in outlook to carry out destructive acts with children, a significant number suffer lapses in judgment and vision that result in psychological and physical abuse. But even families with less desirable childrearing habits frequently have positive qualities, such that through education, counseling, and network support, these families can learn to modify detrimental practices.

Indifferent child care practices, which become a different form of abuse, stem from self-centered and impersonal temperaments. We find these qualities in persons who lack a vision and sensitivity about human relationships and who do not or cannot sense their responsibility.

These categories represent a wide span, and within each domain we find various levels of nurturing competence. This text does not focus on the pathologies that accompany abuse and indifference; rather, we have chosen to consider the range of positive nurturance, which is featured in the great majority of U.S. families. In spite of highly publicized accounts of dysfunctional family situations, the norm in all communities is that parents are nurturing and concerned for the welfare of their youngsters.

Communities and schools inherit the parenting or nurturing practices occurring in their localities, including the differences that exist within them. All families are linked with particular cultural groups, and each group will possess particular values and mores. In a community with two or more cultural groups, we find somewhat different viewpoints and probably different practices. Just because a community contains different cultural groups, however, does not mean antagonism is present. On the contrary, quite different child raising patterns can easily coexist and interact positively.

Features of Positive Nurturance

Maslow (1970) provided a paradigm (Figure 4.1) that shows, in ascending fashion, the scale of human needs. When related to the lives of young children, the levels of the pyramid clearly imply the need for positive nurturance. It is easy to associate the early nurturing practices of parents—and these are almost universal—to the hierarchy developed by Maslow.

Addressing Physiological Needs

Food, warmth, and shelter are bare necessities for survival, and all parents provide these except in rare cases when families are caught in physical distress, dislocation, or mental illnesses. In spite of positive intentions, some financially stressed families find difficulty in providing these basics. Cold or hungry children cannot respond to any educational program. On the other hand, improper food choices lead to obesity and other nutritional problems, and unhealthy living climates lead to reduced functioning. Teachers and other service providers must be alert to problems and deficiences.

Ensuring Physical Safety

The next level of Maslow's hierarchy involves safety. Ensuring children's safety is almost instinctive with parents, and we expect this attention to be provided carefully and lovingly. While most parents are alert to dangers from natural disas-

FIGURE 4.1
Maslow's hierarchy of needs.

Source: From *Psychology of Teaching* (6th ed.) (p. 270) by G. R. LeFrancois, 1988, Belmont, CA: Wadsworth. Reprinted by permission.

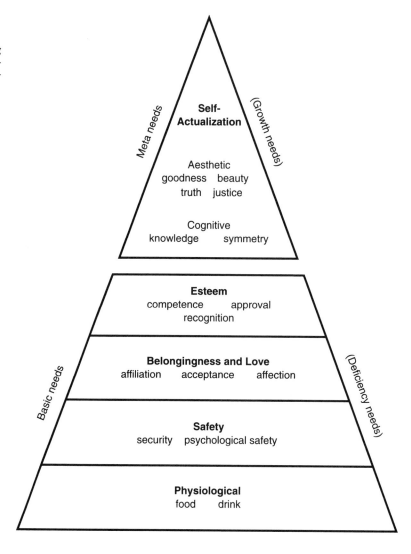

ters (earthquakes, storms, and such), it is all to easy to overlook hidden dangers such as leaded paint, polluted areas, and unsafe objects and locations.

Providing Love

Giving emotional support and providing love are features of nurturance that occur naturally in typical families. Families express these feelings in different ways. Expressions of love range from nonverbal signals and understated expressions to effusive expressions of affection. Differences in discipline practices are linked with this area of nurturance, as well. Some families use physical punishments while others depend on verbal reprimands and discussions or explanations to rechannel behavior. All practices can be effective under particular circumstances. Occasionally parents overdo their support role and encourage dependency and immaturity in their child. Overcon-

Families foster children's sense of responsibility, sharing, and problem solving.

cern and hovering often have undesirable consequences.

Promoting Esteem, Success, and Achievement
Families vary greatly in how they foster esteem and support the achievements of their children. Some parents campaign vigorously with and for their children in action or at work, while others gently encourage or deliberately withhold praise until the end of a task or game. Parents sometimes hold children to adult standards in playing games, conversing, or socializing. This expectation can be unfortunate if children do not succeed, for their aspirations may be deflated. Adult encouragement and delight in partial success normally provide a foundation for children to lift their levels of aspiration.

Self-Actualization
The final level in Maslow's hierarchy is an adult level of competence, but families foster readiness for self-actualization by supporting children's growing independence and sense of responsibility, and by encouraging problem solving and decision making at children's appropriate levels of growth.

FAMILY ROLES

The family in the 1990s has certain roles to perform. Society evolves, and these roles vary from those of a century ago. Lifestyles are different now, circumstances have changed, and new expectations have emerged. However, certain basics and constants of family roles do remain, such as providing economic support, rendering emotional support, arranging socializing influences, and supplying educational underpinnings for later life.

Fulfilling these functions varies from family to family depending on circumstance. When parents fail, other persons and agencies may assume these family capacities and duties. In all cases, the family roles are complemented by the efforts of teachers and various community agencies.

Economic Support

We recognized in Chapter 3 that some families in the United States live on a few thousand dollars per year while others enjoy extraordinarily high incomes. This variable determines the type of shelter and quality of food and clothing the family acquires, as well as other family living conditions.

Even though one or more family members are employed, we find in the 1990s some families challenged to meet economic minimums who must depend on government assistance and private charities to supplement the basics. Remember that nearly 25 percent of U.S. children under the age of 6 live in families with incomes below the poverty line (Educational Research Service, 1993).

Almost all families do manage their economic responsibility, marginal as it may be at times. Athough an increasing number of U.S. families are subsidized, most do have adequate shelter, food, and clothing . Most families also have reasonable choices in how they allot their finances. But poverty is exacerbated for families struggling to make appropriate choices, and even with meager resources some choose fads, get manipulated into credit buying, and fail to recycle goods. In other words, the economics of parent education is not solidified. A more desperate circumstance emerges for the underclass, where the basic levels of the Maslow hierarchy are often threatened.

Social agencies are established in communities for the purpose of guaranteeing economic basics for all families. The success rate is reasonable, but communities must pursue even more aggressively the task of monitoring and guiding basic economic practices. Parent education is a first step in guaranteeing better living conditions, and it is a focus that integrates well with collaborations among communities, schools, and families.

Emotional Support

Even though most parents have little training or instruction in psychological support roles, emotional nurturance for offspring appears to be a natural response. Emotional support begins with the bonding between mother and child at birth and continues as both parents seek to ensure happiness and security for their child. Most new parents emulate the parenting skills they observed and experienced in their own childhood. A growing problem with our present generation is that smaller families, dual-income families, and, especially, single-parent families provide noticeably less modeling of parenting behavior for their growing children. Where, for example, do children in a single-mother-only home observe fathering behaviors?

Parenting classes and clinics are available (and needed) for young mothers who are skeptical and anxious about ways to nurture their new children. Again, community policies must ensure availability of the resource, and stimulate the use of the same.

Socialization

While many agents, such as the school, the peer group, the church, and the media, are involved in socializing children, the family has the primary responsibility for beginning the process. Socialization involves values, beliefs, attitudes, family ethnic and religious identity, and gender roles. And though most families carry out this function quite readily in the preschool years, competition for the child's perception and attention becomes more intense once school and community life become significant (Berns, 1993).

Parental impact on children's socialization was more significant in earlier periods of history. More isolated communities, less mobility, and the virtual dominance of parent figures helped values, beliefs, and attitudes become quickly inculcated in children through example and statement. In addition, earlier communities in the United States were highly idealistic in orientation, and role expectations were similar for everyone in the more restricted venues.

Patterns differ today. We have less general agreement in the United States on social mores, due to the heterogenous communities in which we live. Families must work harder to establish the socialization roles for their children. One mother determined that her children would have a better life than she had as a child. Later, explaining her success, she declared that the television show, *Leave it to Beaver,* was her salvation. "I watched those shows and figured out how to manage and help my two girls." Although today we might view these shows as less than realistic, this woman recognized her need to find acceptable ways to socialize her children for middle-class interactions.

Values, Beliefs, and Attitudes

Parents rarely plan to teach about values and beliefs. They do, however, model via their behavior what they value and prize, and what they are willing to accept. This practice has both positive and negative aspects. If a parent rushes to help a stumbling neighbor, the idea is passed on to children; if a parent models lying, that habit, too, is passed on. Recall that one part of Jana's story, in the opening vignette in Chapter 3, was the way her stepmother modeled "helping neighbors." Today, Jana is raising her own children and responds to neighborhood difficulties by making and bestowing food.

In today's world, with virtually all homes bombarded by television and other forms of entertainment, many beliefs and values accrue to children just from viewing such programs (Singer & Singer, 1990). Parents, of course, can monitor and watch programs to discuss actions and make comments, but few take the time or show an inclination to do this. As noted in Chapter 1, the risk is the effect that influence peddlers may have on family values.

Gender Roles

Inculcating gender role is more complex in our modern age. Both gender and parenting roles in today's society are quite different than those for earlier generations. But while gender-related expectations are less rigid in many U.S. homes, most parents do seek to steer their children toward gender-appropriate behaviors.

Fathers are still, in most U.S. families, the primary economic mainstay, but that role is changing. Today, 60 percent of mothers with children under 6 are in the labor force, and 75 percent of mothers with children between 6 and 17 are employed (Center for the Study of Social Policy, 1992). In many dual-income homes, mothers and fathers contribute equally to the economic support. In addition, mothers are the breadwinners in most single-parent homes. Thus the notion of associating economic support with one parent is an ambiguous one for many children.

Beyond economic dimensions is the changing character of family duties in the household. Historically, roles were that mother was cook and general homemaker, while father was in the field or away at work. In the modern home, duties are not as clearly defined. It is still a small percentage, but some fathers now have major responsibilities for meal preparation and cleaning in addition to child monitoring. Fathers now attend childbirth and parenting classes along with their wives, and take responsibility for infant care. Attempts to eliminate sexism in the late twentieth century have surely recast gender roles for U.S. society. Many quality children's books, noted in the Appendix, now portray up-to-date gender roles.

All roles are disrupted when a family separation occurs. Gender roles realign when one parent or the other (or both) has custody of children. Single-parent families function in very different

Fathers are taking more responsibility for nurturing their children.

ways—which can be confusing for children who travel between homes periodically—and again gender role becomes more ambiguous.

Ethnic and Cultural Identity

Children become aware of cultural and ethnic differences by age 3 or 4 (Katz, 1976), when they encounter differences in their communities, but family is the primary source of information. Preserving cultural heritage and learning about one's ethnic identity are very much on the minds of most minority parents today (Banks, 1993b).

Disparagement of a minority heritage typically is initiated by the dominant culture. Such disparagement leads, as in U.S history, to many minority families denigrating their own heritage. For exam-

ple, Butler (1976), in reviewing ethnic preference in literature, found that, up through the 1960s, African American children across social and geographical settings preferred white dolls and white playmates. Since 1970, however, research findings have changed, and African American children now show preference for black characters in most studies (Butler, 1976). Ethnic identity and validation are clearly in the province of the family, and feelings about self depend on accurate information and sensitive guidance (Black, Puckett, & Bell, 1992). Some minority homes provide support and foster pride in the family culture and give training on how to overcome derogatory messages. But responsibility for enhancing heritage goes beyond family efforts. It must be supported throughout the community.

A positive feature of multicultural education efforts now practiced is that cultural and ethnic heritages are featured in schools, in communities, in museums, and in the mass media. Families celebrate differences now, and few are opposed to sharing stories about their cultural background and traditions in schools or in community programs.

Much of a family's cultural history comes in the form of stories shared and passed down through generations. A fine example in adult literature is *Roots*, by Alex Haley (1976). Another is *Daughters of the Dust*, by Julie Dash (1992), a story of Gullah families in Georgia's outer islands. Children's literature has many examples as well (see Appendix).

Educational Underpinnings

As noted in Chapter 2, parents in previous centuries assumed a major role in all aspects of educating their children. Even in the 1800s, many families still attended to basic lessons for living and preparation of vocations for their children. As the 1800s became the 1900s, however, schools expanded rapidly in scope and assumed most of the role for educating children in literary skills, calculation, and sciences. They even acquired the job of developing work habits; moral training and health education were added quickly thereafter. Today's school has expanded to include sex education, health and recreation training, vocational training, and other educational aspects formerly a family's responsibility. It appears that only the early educative tasks are retained by families in the modern United States.

The unfortunate outcome of this transfer of educative roles is that most parents have lost a perspective, as well as participation, in role directing for their children about essential responsibilities. We realize that demands on today's homes are immense, but parents are still answerable for 75 percent of their children's waking hours during the typical school week. This figure on parent supervision carries a responsibility for educating, in the broad sense, that is too often overlooked.

Families can provide the support, the critical demonstrations, and followup for a child's learning opportunities, if they are mindful of (1) the parents' logical status as guide, (2) their intimate knowledge of the learner, (3) the influence parental status provides, and (4) the many chances for translating text material to everyday life. In fact, many parents are doing just that by "home schooling" their children. Chapter 6 provides more detail on home learning and on home schooling.

Changes in Functions for the 1990s

As noted earlier, U.S. families are diverse and will continue so. Roles for family members in the Information Age are still evolving, and certainly changes will continue to appear. One can only guess how different the typical family roles will be in another decade.

Some changes in the 1990s that show increased momentum are that fathers are more involved in early education, and this benefits children; mothers are more involved in sports and recreational activities, and this benefits children; but extended families continue to decrease in contact and impact, and this does not benefit chil-

dren (Hoffer & Coleman, 1990). Single parenting, while normally less advantageous for children, is likely to continue at a similar pace. School responsibilities are still increasing, but efforts to share and exchange responsibilities are more in evidence (see Chapter 10 for particular models of cooperation).

Children of the 1990s face a very different socializing environment than in previous generations. Less constancy is found in family matters, and more and different adults are involved with their experiences. Peer-group influences have expanded, to say nothing of the explosion in influence of the media and entertainment industries. All human service personnel must work for more joint efforts between homes, schools, and communities, where well-reasoned decisions about roles will enable families to produce quality experiences and opportunities for their children.

CULTURAL PATTERNS AND FAMILY FUNCTIONS

We are made up of increasingly different ethnic backgrounds in the United States, and we find differences in the ways groups perform tasks, establish values, and relate to one another. Different ethnic groups frequently have varying cultural features, but also, we find multiple cultures within the various groups (Bullivant, 1993). This makes for an interesting cultural mix in our nation, and one that professionals must study and reflect on.

Ethnic background refers to the national origin or "race" of individuals, whereas *cultural* background refers to the attitudes, traditions, and customs of a certain group of people. Simply stated, culture is how a group survives in the overall society (Bullivant, 1993). Ethnicity and cultural identity frequently overlap; for example, many Native Americans continue to identify themselves by ethnic background, and, culturally, these people are separate from mainstream U.S. culture. We also find groups of people with similar ethnic backgrounds who differ culturally. For example, in English-speaking regions, Appalachian Americans are very different from Oregonian ranchers or Connecticut commuters, even though they have similar roots. Their traditions, values, and attitudes place them in different cultural groups.

Considerable differences in cultural orientations exist within any ethnic group, and we will discuss these from time to time. For simplification, we differentiate in this text among the Euro-American (white), English-speaking majority, and the main minorities in the U.S., even though each contains more than one ethnic group. Table 4.1 presents the proportions of these primary ethnic groups as of 1990. While census charts include Hispanic Americans in other totals, our figure divides the population into Hispanic and non-Hispanic, then calculates totals from those two categories to avoid counting Hispanic Americans twice.

Different ethnic groups have different patterns and different ways of communicating. It is important for professionals to examine and learn about these patterns to help when conducting discussions, when planning, and when making decisions for children.

Cultural groups are far more wide ranging than are ethnic groups, and, of course, cultures overlap. In this section, we use examples to suggest different patterns in parenting (Table 4.2). We urge readers to investigate specific cultural situations occurring in their communities.

In addition to the basics of childrearing, other variables enter into cultural parenting. Gender roles will be important in the practices of some groups, and social class will have an effect on all parenting. Because occupations influence the actions and goal aspirations of most groups, this feature also affects parenting activities.

The values of any culture are transmitted primarily through adult modeling, directions and instructions given to children, pressures from the cultural group, and reinforcements for certain serendipitous actions that each child displays.

Parenting Features in Various Cultures

Child raising practices in the United States have changed during the twentieth century. We find great variation from one cultural group to another within the society as a whole. And the socioeconomic status (SES) of different families within one cultural group indicates that other differences exist.

For Euro-American groups, behaviorism was valued in the early years of the twentieth century, and many parents at that time valued the principles of reinforcement and extinction popularized by psychologists. A "child-centered" phase bloomed in the middle years of the century. At present the swing is toward a middle ground. Most minority cultures have retained their traditional child raising practices much more than have Euro-American families, but the proliferation of ideas in the mass media has altered some of their practice, as well.

The following lists enumerate general parenting tendencies that sociologists and anthropologists have determined exist, to some degree, within selected ethnic groups. These are examples only; you could easily find a family in one of the groups displaying few of the features noted for that group (adapted from Janosik & Green, 1992; Sadker & Sadker, 1991; Berns, 1993).

TABLE 4.1
Major Ethnic Groups in the United States (1990)

Ethnic Group	Percent of Population
African American	11.0
American Indian/ Alaskan	0.8
Asian & Pacific Islands	2.6
Euro-American	73.0
Hispanic Americans	9.0
Other ethnic groups	3.5

Note: Persons of Hispanic origin, regardless of ethnic origin, are separated from other groups for this table.
Source: Interpolated from U.S. Bureau of the Census, press release CB91-216, and Census of Population and Housing Data (CPH-L-74), 1992.

TABLE 4.2
Cultural Differences in Parenting

Group	Physical Contact	Authority	Infant Care	Family Interaction
Euro-American	Less intimacy, aggressive play encouraged.	Shared between mother/father	Babies held less. Allowed to cry it out.	Independence prized. Child does challenge. Distance from nuclear group.
Mexican American	Accepting of contact. Use of physical punishment.	Father	Babies kept close to mothers.	Solidarity with family. Feel obligated to family.
African American	Contact is encouraged. Lots of physical handling.	Mother	Babies fed on demand.	Nonverbal, minimal words used. Extended family focus.
Asian American	Restrained contact.	Father	Babies fed on demand. Constant mother/child contact.	Respect of elders. Care for family.
Native American	Close contact. No physical punishments.	Father	Continuing contact for mother and child.	Nonverbal signals. Distance is valued.

Mexican American

Solidarity and importance of family is primary.

Children play with siblings rather than with peers.

Mother is the primary caretaker and affection source.

Displayed affection is frequent and prized.

Father is the authority figure, and is dominative.

Children adapt to conditions around them.

Children are accepting of others' wishes.

Family is close to extended family members.

Children feel obligated to family.

Children are obedient and respectful to parents.

Cooperation is emphasized, rather than independence.

Gender role is important.

Physical punishments are used more than reprimands.

Parents emphasize appropriate behavior.

Children learn by observing others, and through reaction of others to own efforts.

African American

Babies are normally fed on demand.

Children relate to numerous people of household.

Closeness of family relationship is emphasized.

More emphasis is placed on involvement with people than with things.

Body contact is expected and encouraged.

Mothers are physically close to children.

Nonverbal communication with young is common.

Mothers communicate directions with few words. Tasks are broken into small units with brief instructions for each.

Vigorous physical movement and activity encouraged.

Excitement and enjoyment are encouraged.

Signals, head movements, and laughs are all meaningful communication.

Mother frequently is a dominant force in the family.

Time elements (schedules, engagements, deadlines) are flexible.

Asian American

Child raising has a permissive quality.

Infants are seldom allowed to cry.

Mother has constant contact with child in early years.

Babies are fed on demand and are weaned late.

Children often sleep with parents.

Nonverbal communication is often used.

Verbal communication is not as strong in early as in later years.

Affection is indirect—love is shown in ways such as an adult's sacrifices for child.

Discipline in later childhood is more strict.

Child actions are known to reflect on the home.

Father is the family disciplinarian.

Respect for older members in family is emphasized.

Native American

Children are socialized by extended as well as nuclear family.

Great respect is given to elders.

Strong bonds exist between family members.

Brotherhood, sharing, spirituality, and personal integrity are emphasized with children.

Respect is taught by example as well as by instruction.

Cooperation is highly valued.

Competition is rarely viewed as positive.

Modesty and moderation are stressed: children are encouraged not to boast or to show emotion.

Children are not expected to be perfect, only to do what they are capable of.

Failure is not a valued concept.

Approval given through smiles, pleasant tone of voice, or a pat.

Child is corrected by parent lowering voice.

No physical punishment, no verbal praise.

Frowns, shaming, withdrawal of affection are controls.

Group pressure is effectively used.

Time elements (schedules, engagements, deadlines) are flexible.

Strong bonds exist among family members in Native American families.

Euro-American

(Overall, contemporary Euro-Americans are quite susceptible to beliefs of current theorists and depend less on folklore and tradition than they did in prior generations. Thus, cultural child raising practices vary considerably over time. However, the following are observed in most Euro-American homes.)

Parents prize independence in children. A low profile, downcast demeanor, and shrinking behavior are criticized.

Aggressive and dominating behaviors are commended.

Parents are eager for child to make a first step.

Parents prize taking turns, and being fair, but also prize winning.

Children are encouraged to challenge situations and overcome problems of environment or situation.

Parents encourage children to move out, to go beyond family, to make other friends.

Gender roles are more merged; fewer gender-specific tasks or play situations are seen.

Mothers and fathers share more roles in family raising.

Emotional distance and private space are prized.

Less intimacy is found between parents and children.

Babies are not held as much and are allowed to "cry it out."

Time elements are crucial. Heavy emphasis on speed and being on time.

Parents value verbal skills and explanations.

Parents talk through situations rather than use physical action.

You can see the differences that exist among ethnic groups. These differences lead to behavioral expectations that adults form for their children. You will see many of these expectations in action as you work with different cultures.

Parenting is complex, and often factors other than a family's general orientation can influence childrearing behaviors or any one outcome. Birth order of children, the child's age or gender, parental experiences, and parent temperament will all make an impact. All parents use a mixture of childrearing practices, and impressions and information from other sources influence their behavior. In general, the higher the education level of parents, the more variation in practice you will find.

"Parenting involves a continuous process of interaction that affects both parents and children" (Berns, 1993, p. 138). The requirements are not always easy to meet. The numerous decisions parents must make regarding the conflicting forces that surround all homes—media, entertainment, peer culture, and other attractions—increase their responsibilities.

INTERACTION STYLES WITHIN FAMILIES

Research tells us about patterns of child behavior. We also find that childrearing practices pertain to children's behavior as we observe it in schools and communities. The studies discussed in this section demonstrate connections between parenting and observed behavior.

Baumrind's Classification

In Baumrind's (1968, 1971) classification, parenting styles are placed along a three-part continuum.

Parent Behaviors

1. Authoritative (democratic). Controlling, demanding, but warm. Rational and receptive to child's communication.
2. Permissive (child centered). Noncontrolling, nondemanding, and relatively warm.

3. Authoritarian (autocratic). Detached, controlling, somewhat less warm.

In her classic study, Baumrind (1968) found that most children of authoritative parents showed independence and were socially responsible. These parents took into account their child's needs, as well as their own, before dealing with situations. The parents respected children's need to make their own decisions, yet they exerted control. They reasoned with their children and explained things more often than did other parents.

On the other hand, Baumrind found that children of permissive parents frequently lacked social responsibility and often were not independent. She concluded that parents who looked at all behavior as natural and refreshing had unrealistic beliefs about young children's growth and socialization.

Baumrind found that children of authoritarian parents also showed little independence and were only fairly socially responsible. Such parents feel children need restraint and need to develop respect for authority, for work, and for traditional structure.

Baumrind's summary (noted in Berns, 1993), indicates that the following adult behaviors foster socially responsible and independent behavior:

1. Serve as responsible and self-assertive models.
2. Set standards of behavior where responsible behavior is rewarded and unacceptable behavior is punished.
3. Are committed to child in a way that is neither overprotective nor rejecting.
4. Have high demands for achievement and conformity but are receptive to child's rational demands.
5. Provide secure but challenging and stimulating environments for creative and rational thinking.

Maccoby and Martin (1983) reviewed literature on parenting styles and in general supported the findings of Baumrind. Clark (1983) also produced similar findings. His "sponsored independence" style is consistent with Baumrind's authoritative style.

One caveat is needed concerning this research. Baumrind used white, middle-class parents in her study. But later, Maccoby and Martin (1983) in their replication studies found that Baumrind's conclusions did not always translate directly for other groups, such as poor, minority, and single-parent families. However, Clark (1983) found that the authoritative or sponsored independence behaviors in Mexican American and African American homes often made the difference between success and failure for minority children in schools.

White's Study

White (1971), in his Harvard Preschool project, investigated the development of competence in children and then related his findings to their parents. White categorized the children in his study as A, B, or C according to competence:

1. A's knew how to hold adult attention, how to use adult resources, and how to express affection and hostility. They got along with others, were proud of achieving, and wanted to be grown up. They used language well and understood other points of view. They were able to concentrate on tasks and plan out activities.
2. B's were less competent than A's in all the skills.
3. C's were deficient in the social and work skills, even lacking ability to anticipate consequences.

When White and Watts (1973) looked at the homes of the subjects, they found notable differences between the behaviors of the parents of A's and C's. White concluded that, as early as ages 1 and 2, a parent's style of childrearing registered an effect.

The main differences White and Watts found among parents were in interaction, attitudes, and attending to environment. The "A" mothers made themselves available to children, were eager and enthused about helping children, and were tolerant of messes. They set limits and were firm and consistent. "C" mothers were not as involved, even when they were in contact with children. Some were disorganized and overwhelmed by home tasks, and most restricted their children by using playpens (White & Watts, 1973).

Bernstein's Work

Language is a primary avenue through which a child learns to understand and function in the world. Children tend to develop language on a predictable developmental scale, but different parental language styles and interactions affect children's socialization and literacy development. In Bernstein's (1972) classic study of family language patterns, he describes two general linguistic codes used in homes, which he terms *restricted* and *elaborated*. The codes reflect two quite different styles: the position-oriented family and the person-oriented family.

Position-oriented families use a restricted code, and the family role system is positional or object oriented and present oriented. In contrast, person-oriented families use an elaborated code, and the family role system is personal or person oriented and future oriented. The following example will illustrate.

In the space of two minutes, two attractive family groups approached a traffic light-controlled crosswalk at a busy intersection. One mother and son approached hand in hand, talking freely. Within a few feet of the crosswalk, the mother leaned toward her son and said, "See, the light there, it's red and we have to stop. See the cars still coming this way? We need to stay right back here, 'til we get the flashing walk light, OK? You watch and tell me when to go."

The second family, a mother, father, and little girl, approached the crosswalk and stopped. Suddenly, the mother noticed the child, who was slightly ahead, starting toward the crosswalk, and yelled, "Stay here!" The girl continued to advance, and the mother screamed again, "Stay here, I said!" The father leaped and yanked the girl back beside him. "Just stand!" the mother said, and the family waited silently for the signal to change— bodies rigid, holding tightly to the child.

The second family here is position oriented, and has a prescribed role system. Members have little choice, and roles are assigned according to family position. According to Bernstein, their communication is object oriented and present oriented. Aspects of restricted language code appear, characterized by syntactically simple sentences and concrete meanings. The parents communicate one thing only to the daughter—to obey, a single command. There is no explanation, and sentences are simple and direct.

The open quality of the mother and son in the person-oriented family, on the other hand, permits discretion in learner performance. Communication in the open system includes judgments and reasons, and children learn to cope with abstractions and ambiguity. The elaborated language code accommodates this type of content. The mother chats with her son about the crosswalk, explaining what is happening. She engages the child in the decision making.

Teachers must know that children from a closed or position-oriented family must depend on the school and the larger community to help them in acquiring elaborated language. As a teacher, you can become a vital communication model for children from families using restricted codes, as can other children. Older children may often help their teacher communicate with new children not familiar with school language and culture.

Ms. Dansky, a white teacher, wasn't successful in getting Philip, an African American 5-year-old just entering school, to join other children in a circle. She had used a polite invitation to call all the children. When Philip didn't move, she gave a more stern and specific command to Philip. Then Greg, a seasoned African American 8-year-old, raised his hand and asked quietly, "You want me to get him for you?" Upon receiving a polite "Yes, thank you," he yelled to Philip, "Boy, get yo'r butt over here, yu' hear!" When Philip came immediately to sit beside Greg, Greg leaned to him and continued, "When she say, 'Boys and girls join me,' she mean 'come here.' And when she say, 'Philip, it's time for circle!' she mean, 'Get yo'r butt here (pats a spot beside himself) NOW!'" (Seefeldt & Barbour, p. 337)

Greg had learned not only the correct language patterns of the school but also the politeness rules. He used language and tonal patterns familiar to Philip, and he skillfully switched between the two patterns to explain what the teacher's words meant. One can appreciate the advantages that elaborated codes have in the broadening requirements of the Information Age. All teachers and other service personnel must be sensitive to the increasing requirements for skilled language use.

Even families that use more elaborated code systems have cause for alarm if the amount of substantive interaction does not happen (Fitzpatrick & Vangelisti, 1995). With the busy work schedules in many homes and the amount of television viewing by the entire family, substantive dialogue—which does not include directions, commands, or reprimands—between parents and children is becoming rare. Some dramatic and startling figures command our attention. Schwartz (1995) points out that in far too many homes fathers average only 8 minutes per weekday in meaningful conversation with their offspring, and working mothers only 11 minutes! Weekend interactions aren't much better (Richards & Duckett, 1994).

Teachers alone cannot compensate for important adult-child interactions. But, as you work to establish strong home and school partnerships, you can help parents become aware of this necessary area for skill development.

No two families are exactly alike, and parents have diverse ways of managing. The various features of parenting make family behaviors very complex and difficult to understand. However, we may examine general patterns of parenting, and we can relate these patterns to children's behavior. Investigators find that neither extreme of the parenting pattern, referred to respectively as *permissive* and *dominative*, is ideal. Some combination or modification appears more beneficial.

Parenting styles are influenced by more than basic orientation. Professionals will be alert to the major influence of family size, family SES, and levels of stress in the home, and of different community characteristics.

EXPERIENCES OF FAMILIES

The life experiences of children establish a background for their performance and their contributions in their school and community. What children see, do, and sense creates a foundation for their communication patterns, perceptual styles, and modes of thinking. Children learn within the context of learning about life to comprehend messages or understand objects within the environment (Elgin, 1990). Likewise, children's understanding of encountered images frequently depends on explanations and connections made by nearby adults.

Culture and experiential background make a significant difference in how a child learns, communicates, and participates, as will economic status. In addition to basic nurturing, family histories of interactions, experiences, and practices will enhance or detract from children's development potential. When stress or problems arise, some families are resilient, and display an ability to explain changes and modify problems; others are ill equipped and cannot cope (Werner & Smith, 1982). Some adults even lean on their own children for support (Garbarino, Dubrow, Kostelny, & Pardo, 1992). Such resilience or its lack derives from many aspects of family experience, including skill levels and the type and degree of family mobility.

What children do and sense creates a foundation for their perceptions and ways of thinking.

Skill Levels and Experience

All parents and other caregivers have knowledge about their world—how to operate within society and how to evaluate their surroundings. Adults in families always pass some bits of this wisdom to their children, some in particularly beneficial and productive ways.

Homemakers know their living quarters and what it takes to live in a particular home. Parents have experiences in food shopping, preparation, and serving, and some have added skills with nutrition and food presentation. Involving children in food management can be realized easily in all homes and contributes a basic foundation for healthy living.

Using tools to build or repair household objects is common in many homes. Some parents have woodworking or other skills, and perhaps have home workbenches. Almost all parents have interesting experiences involving tools, and many take pleasure in their use. Adults may easily transfer these skills to interested children through demonstration (Voss, 1993) or by children's books, such as *How Things Work* (Macaulay, 1988).

Some families invest a great deal of time in gardening for relaxation or for summer vegetable acquisition. The growing of green things fascinates many youngsters. It is the beginning of a basic science children will encounter during their school years. A child's home is a nice place to meet gardening, and any growing project provides a healthy venue for discussion and interaction.

Many games feature family interactions, and by using games as entertainment parents can provide children with involvement in group activities, experience in strategy development and planning, positive use of aggressiveness, and practice in cooperative activies. Games are fundamentally simulations of life experiences, and children with extensive experience with various games internalize approaches for living and considerable amounts of strategy for facing interactive situations (Jones, 1988).

Storytelling plays an important part in children's growth. A large part of language development comes through stories. In families where stories are used for recreating family history, for entertainment or as examples, listeners grow in appreciation of language and also in appreciation of their culture, and of their family's experiences and identity. One very important manifestation is the story in book form. In a book, the story belongs to someone else, but it gives much the same satisfaction to the young child.

Parents' skill levels in these and many other aspects of life can and should be passed on to children in the family. All community life and school programs must reinforce these practices. Given the right conditions, home management and repair, gardening projects, game playing, storytelling, and other family-oriented experiences represent marvelous resources and a worthy heritage for parents to relay to their children. Classroom teaching is a complex and demanding job, but we must remember that teaching itself is only a small part of that total responsibility. Most parents are not skilled instructors, but may be very successful in teaching home activities and projects. When a caregiver is engaged with a single child on a topic of mutual interest, then most classroom "teaching" demands are not present. Instructor and student can go directly to the task of transferring a particular skill to the learner. Most parents can be successful at this natural process, and most yearn to pass on their culture when an opportunity presents itself.

Mobility of Families

Another feature of experience that may greatly affect children's emotional and academic progress is the mobility that families have in and around their community and further afield. For families, mobility comes in two forms: forced and voluntary.

Forced mobility for families produces images of migrant work, homelessness, coping with unemployment, and escaping hostile actions or trouble. Forced mobility (apart from job-related transfers) is always a reaction to undesirable conditions and contributes to erratic lifestyles for parents and their children. Isolation is implied, for forced mobility signifies that a family lacks connections or community linkages that could provide help. Whatever the conditions, a family's forced move

to a new environment gives different but rarely positive learning experiences for children. Little pleasure comes with a transfer from one area to another under duress.

On the other hand, voluntary travel, local or distant, frequently connotes vacation time or fun activities for recreation. The important distinction is that voluntary travel involves the positive expectation of new encounters and all family members view it as a learning experience.

Local travel can mean short trips to the country for scenic views, snow sports, or the sea shore, or trips to a museum or zoo. Arranging for the travel is a learning experience too, for families can involve everyone in preparations. Getting to a destination involves a certain amount of investigation, map reading, negotiating local conditions, such as driving requirements or bus schedules, and anticipating difficulties. Family members learn together, and these social and educational values are important.

Long-distance travel, while involving many of the same skills, joys, and learnings, has another level of enrichment that is hard to duplicate locally. Transnational or international travel brings a family in touch with other cultures. Travelers need to adapt to new conditions, different foods, and a different sense of space. Such travel is expansive, and families gain psychic income and social capital.

The ways that families exploit surroundings, relationships, agencies, and even challenges show facets of their childrearing practices and socializing acumen. Some families use their experience with great facility, while others do not. Such use of experience may be a function of SES, as economically privileged families have the means to do more nurturing of this type (Coleman, 1966; Jencks et al., 1972). However, we find instances of modestly endowed families enriching their children's lives through carefully developed experiences (Clark, 1983), and some affluent families neglect needs for family interaction and experience (Metz, 1993).

OTHER INFLUENCES ON PARENTING

Parenting needs to be examined and analyzed in the context of culture and community. As noted earlier, numerous variables affect family life, and may be external factors of community and environment as well as internal factors of cultural background, family demographics, and economics. Following is a brief discussion of some of these other dimensions.

Child Care Arrangements

Much has happened in child care arrangements during recent decades in the United States, and a huge number of families must cope with requirements for temporary care. At one time, when most mothers were homemakers, child care was a consequence of the family condition. Mothers attended their preschool-age children, welcomed children home from school, and supervised most at-home hours. In the 1990s, with increasing day care requirements and fewer extended families at home, the situation is far different. In 1992, 60 percent of mothers with children under 6 were in the work force (Center for the Study of Social Policy, 1992). This means a huge number of young children, whether from single-parent or dual-income homes, are in some type of child care arrangement for part of every work day. It is also not uncommon for very young children to be watched over during the day by babysitters, in day care programs and in other arrangements. Some are cared for by slightly older siblings.

Preschool day care and afterschool care for young children in the 1990s are facts of life for most communities, and will intensify as programs nationwide seek to push more welfare families into the work force. Most day care programs have waiting lists for children who need this service; added requests will intensify the problem. A number of schools now operate their own afterschool care programs to meet some needs.

Though some day care can be less than desirable, for many children the situation is more dire. Some children return after school to empty homes, to wait unsupervised for several hours until parents return from work. These "latchkey" children are a feature of the 1990s family, and while some situations work reasonably well when older siblings monitor activities, this group of children is at risk. Abuse, accidents, and social deviance are physical and safety problems resulting all too often from latchkey children being left on their own. The social and emotional endangerment that results from no adult interaction and direction is, or should be, obvious.

Elaborate child care plans are stressful, restricting, and even frustrating for parents, but teachers and community workers must also expect the challenges and the fallout from "tightrope" balancing of care arrangements. Professionals working with children must expect tightly scheduled and harried parents, children with dramatic shifts in schedule, and a general lowering of priorities for school functions or recreation. We find parents in dual-income homes often lead busier, more frenetic lives and are less involved in the school and community matters of their children than are parents in single-income households.

Stress in Families

Adversity creeps into all families; it is a condition of living in a social matrix. Some stressors resulting from adversity are more damaging than others, but some families, through coping skills and resources, are better able to handle problems than others. While a few stressors are self-inflicted, many are unavoidable or are developed through conflicts and economic pressures and through racist, elitist, and sexist practices. The accumulation of stressors leads to at-risk situations, and policy makers, educators, and others must be mindful of this possibility. The effects of risk on the intelligence measurements of preschool children

(Sameroff, Seifer, Barocas, Zax, & Greenspan, 1987) are instructive (Figure 4.2). As the figure shows, most children can cope with low levels of risk but an accumulation of more than two risk factors jeopardizes their mental development. The message is clear: we must either prevent or compensate for accumulated risk factors.

Before ending our discussion of family functioning, we review frequent concerns and risk factors that affect families. Strategies exist to deflect or accommodate stress arising from these factors.

Divorce

As noted earlier, divorce has become common for U.S. families in the latter half of the twentieth century, and becomes more accepted with each passing year. In the 1980s, between 11 and 12 percent of U.S. children under 18 experienced a divorce or separation in their families each year (Hetherington & Camara, 1984). That rate has continued to hold steady.

Liberalization of divorce laws in most states permits couples to separate more easily and more amicably. Most family members cope reasonably well with separations, but the situation does invite risk factors. Whenever divorce comes about, parents must make many adjustments, particularly when children are involved. Separation changes all roles in a family and alters the way a family functions. Responsibilities for the custodial parent increase dramatically, particularly with regard to child care arrangements. There are more household tasks to care for, and financial obligations are heavier than before.

Financial aspects of divorce. Mothers are most often given custody of children in a divorce, but this often has dire consequences for the resulting single-parent family. Bianchi (1990) notes that children in mother-only families have a one in two chance of living in poverty, contrasted with a less than one in ten chance for children living with two parents. It is a fact in the United States that women in the work force earn less than men do. And even though child support judgments are made in divorce cases, fathers may not pay, and mothers must seek employment and suffer even greater management problems. Weitzman (1985) stresses the financial problems for women after divorce: divorce improves the economic position of husbands but reduces that of women and children left with their mothers. Fathers with custody of children do better financially.

Other consequences of divorce. After separation or divorce, roles change for all family members and responsibilities grow. For custodial parents,

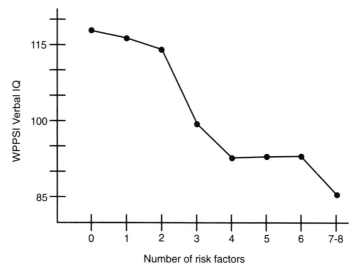

FIGURE 4.2

Effects of multiple risks on preschool intelligence.

Source: From "Intelligence Quotient on Scores of 4-Year-Old Children: Social-Environmental Risk Factors" by A. Sameroff, R. Seifer, R. Barocas, M. Zax, and S. Greenspan, 1987, *Pediatrics, 79,* p. 347. Copyright 1987 by the American Academy of Pediatrics. Reproduced by permission.

extensive new responsibilities in managing and maintaining a household emerge. Increased work hours and decreased social interaction often result, and this means less parenting (Emery, 1988). Children will face increased responsibilities and less time with either parent, and less emotional support. A serious long range effect that divorce can bring about is that it removes the marriage models for children affected.

Behavioral changes for youngsters often result from divorce and separation. A considerable amount of research shows the negative effects for children of divorce are sadness, fear, aggressiveness, and disobedience (Hetherington, 1988; Wallerstein, Corbin, & Lewis, 1988). But Olson and Haynes (1993) point out that many studies are slanted toward "what's wrong with single-parent families" (p. 260). Olson and Haynes go on to demonstrate that single parenting can be successful and that strengths do exist in single-parent homes when compared to a predivorce situation: happier environments, better custodial parent-child relationships, more commitment to a wider community, and better-run households.

Negative stereotypes continue to affect single parents and their children (Fuller 1986). For example, teachers have a tendency to assume that problems in school are related to the single-parent home. A large number of young and schoolage children will experience their parents' separation or divorce; therefore, school personnel and community workers must find ways to accommodate the extra needs these individuals will have. Divorce will remain a part of U.S. society, and professionals must look for the positive factors and make the best of the developments.

Support groups are available to help families through the period of adjustment, which is always one or more years. Children's literature, when sensitively read and discussed, can also help children who are caught in a family upheaval. See the Appendix for recommended titles.

Dual-Income Families

Management of household life in the dual-income home produces stress at times. While the double income enables a family to enjoy a higher standard of living than it would obtain with only one, there are drawbacks, such as less time for family interaction, tighter schedules, increased dependence on child care, and fewer choices in recreation. Statistics show that 62 percent of children living with both parents have mothers and fathers in the work force, and the trend increases each year (Center for the Study of Social Policy, 1992). In addition, over 6 percent of American working men and women hold two or more jobs (U.S. Bureau of the Census, 1994), a total of four jobs for some dual-income families. Time for family interactions is minimal in these situations.

Poverty

Poverty restricts many positive experiences for children and their families, because financial resources dictate quality of housing, diet, clothing, and amount of health care, to say nothing of entertainment and recreation. Most of all, poverty lays a veil of despair on families, and aspirations and a sense of self-worth become hard to elevate. Of all the stressors present in U.S. families, poverty is perhaps the greatest, and it is growing in the United States (refer again to Figure 3.4 in Chapter 3).

Children's Defense Fund (1993) shows that in 1992 over 13 million, or 21 percent, of U.S. children were living below the poverty line. In addition, the record demonstrates a steady increase in the amount of poverty in the United States during the 10-year period ending in 1992. Other figures show that Hispanic and African American minorities dip even deeper into poverty—one-third of the U.S. black population lives below the poverty line (U.S. Bureau of the Census, 1994).

Poor families are burdened with the need to survive, and their lives are punctuated with stress brought on by lack of money. Family members are frequently ill, they sustain injury more often, and they encounter hostility from numerous sources.

Lives become saturated with despair, and each new plight adds to family discouragement (Kozol, 1988; Shames, 1991; Polakow, 1993).

The buildup of stress in poor families is extensive. Housing that is affordable to families below the poverty line tends to be in crime- and drug-ridden areas where children and many adults lead lives of sheer terror (Kotlowitz, 1991). Cramped living and meager diets result in illnesses that precipitate even more stress. Reversing the state of poverty in the United States requires strong community action and large investments in fed-eral, state, and private aid to provide job training, child care, adequate housing, and health facilities to help rebuild families in besieged areas of society. Recommendations outlined in *S.O.S. America* (Children's Defense Fund, 1990) serve as a beginning.

Abuse and Illness

Abuse and illness are associated with, although not limited to, the condition of poverty. Because families in poverty are in dire straits and services are meager, abuse rises in concert with the frus-

Poverty lays a veil of despair on families, where aspirations and a sense of self-worth become hard to elevate.

trations and anxieties of needy families (Gersten, 1992). Most abuse occurs where conditions are unpleasant and where frustrated parents and youth are in frequent conflict with individuals, agencies, and conditions around them (Barth, 1983; Children's Defense Fund, 1991).

Abuse occurs at higher SES levels, too; it is not restricted to the poor. Physical and sexual abuse occur at all levels of society, and although more often disguised in middle-class families, it is no less a source of stress to family members. Abuse is insidious and continues in the fabric of families for generations—abused children become abusive adults or the victims of other abusers later in their lives (Groves et al., 1993). Abuse is an infection coloring the feelings and attitudes of families, and it destroys normal relationships for the entire family.

Illness also is a stressor in families. When a family member becomes injured or ill, numerous interaction patterns must cease or be modified. The amount of family communication can be limited, and attention to those who are not ill becomes restricted. Realignment of the priorities in family functioning is a consequence of long-term illness. Illness of a wage earner has even greater consequences for the family. And if inadequate health care is the cause (which is the situation for one-seventh of the nation's population), then this particular stress gives rise to others.

Family Size

The size of a family can actually be a stressor for the family. Children are considered a boon for most families; many mothers and fathers anticipate them eagerly. However, having too many children has the opposite effect, and an unwanted pregnancy becomes a source of frustration and contention in some families.

Large families can provide for increased peer contacts and more extensive interaction, but at the same time the parents have fewer interactions with each child. Competition among children occurs frequently in large families, and household relations can suffer (Belmont & Marolla, 1973).

Children and families all are resilient to some degree. We find situations that appear depressing and even disastrous, but children survive intact and view the traumatic events in their lives, such as deaths, divorce, and hardship, with objectivity (Comer, 1988) and even with humor at later periods (Buchwald, 1994). This demonstrates that most children are not so fragile and impressionable that they must succumb to their problems. As a teacher, you must be mindful that, as long as reasonably positive experiences and interventions punctuate the lives of developing children, their outlook and perspective can be ultimately optimistic.

COMPETENT FAMILIES

Families function in a variety of ways and possess different attributes. If permitted to pursue their individual courses, most families, given reasonable conditions, develop along healthy lines and rear children who respect a home culture and get ready to meet the world. Though most are competent, many need the help and support of friends, community, and other services.

At times, stresses are too great and a combination of cultural differences, poverty, and family problems causes family dysfunction. If this occurs, then professional aid via the community is the first level of response. It may be possible that school professionals can help by advocating for the family, talking with family members, counseling the family, and listening to family members to show support.

Teachers need to know their students' families as well as their situations, for teachers are in a unique position to explain community to families and vice versa. It is imperative for school personnel to take time to learn about family functioning, to find out about values, ways of doing, and methods of care that work for them. If you obtain this information, you may then find ways of integrating schoolwork with the home situation.

What is a competent family? The competent family does not require affluence, extensive education, any particular culture, or a particular setting. It will, however, display most of the following characteristics:

1. Understand cultural background and values that produce a heritage.
2. View children as persons with valuable contributions, and encourage them to participate.
3. Value open and ongoing communication.
4. Clearly establish standards, values, and expectations.
5. Value experience, and explain and teach using everyday projects and tasks.
6. Confront and minimize stress.
7. Monitor children's use of time, space, and material.
8. Maintain adequate child care.
9. Maintain a "sponsored independence" style for children.
10. Manage financial resources to be above the poverty line.
11. Show involvement and interest in children's work and activity.
12. Praise all family members' achievements and successes.

SUMMARY

U.S. families are diverse in cultural and ethnic orientation. Rather than being a problem, diversity provides a richness for society and produces numerous benefits. The United States is an unusual nation today, for nowhere else on the planet do such diverse ethnic and cultural groups work together so productively. Ethnic relations, though far from perfect, are certainly well beyond the horrific contests seen elsewhere in the world.

Different styles of interaction exist for all families. Research shows that the authoritative parent style usually produces better results for most parents and their children than does a permissive or authoritarian pattern.

Experience defines a family's quality of life, and some families show greater command over their environment than do others. All families pass on their culture and attempt to instruct children in profitable ways. Some families have natural gifts for instructing the young about tasks, thereby giving them added command of their lives. Mobility is one avenue for enhancing experience; another is manual work skill.

Handling stress is a mark of a family's ability to cope with surroundings. All families encounter stress, but processing and managing it are hallmarks of well-adjusted families.

Unified support and collaborations among homes, schools, and communities pay large dividends when cooperative spirits are willing to work together.

SUGGESTED ACTIVITIES AND QUESTIONS

1. Name three basic responsibilities that parents have for their children. Speculate about how you see those manifested in one child with whom you work.
2. Consider the home environments of children appearing in the vignettes in the text to this point. Deduce the parenting style of each family. Give reasons for your deductions.
3. Reflect on the parenting you received as a child. Was it authoritative, authoritarian, or permissive in style? If you feel comfortable, exchange ideas with one or two colleagues and compare experiences.
4. Select two families represented in your classroom or community setting. What appear to be the social and cultural influences affecting them? Are there differences? What do you infer about the education of children in these families?
5. Observe a parent interacting with his or her child in a library. Observe a similar situation in a supermarket. Are the interactions different? What circumstances do you think account for any differences you see?

RECOMMENDED READINGS

Blankenhorn, D. (1995). *Fatherless America: Confronting our most urgent social problem.* New York: Basic Books.

Curran, D. (1983). *Traits of a healthy family.* Minneapolis, MN: Winston.

Gestwicki, C. (1991). *Home, school, and community relations: A guide to working with parents* (2nd ed.). Albany, NY: Delmar.

Kagan, S. L., Powell, D. R., Weissbourd, B., & Zigler, E. F. (Eds.). (1987). *America's family support programs: Perspectives and prospects.* New Haven: Yale University Press.

Kotlowitz, A. (1991). *There are no children here: The story of two boys growing up in the other America.* New York: Doubleday.

Parke, R. D., & Slaby, R. G. (1983). The development of aggression. In P. H. Mussen (Ed.), *Handbook of child psychology: Vol. 4. Socialization, personality, and social development* (pp. 547–642). New York: Wiley.

Scarf, M. (1995). *Intimate worlds: Life inside the family.* New York, Random House.

Werner, E. E., & Smith, R. S. (1982). *Vulnerable but invincible: A longitudinal study of resilient children and youth.* New York: McGraw-Hill.

Responsibility for Educating Children

Across this nation, we must cultivate communities where children can learn. . . . Where the school is a living center of a community, where people care—people care for each other and their futures. Not just in the school but in the neighborhood. Not just in the classroom, but in the home.

President George Bush, 18 April 1991 address announcing
America 2000: A National Education Strategy

In Chapter 5, we consider the obligations for educating the United States's children and which people and agencies bear responsibilities for carrying these out. In reading this chapter you will learn that:

1. Societal traditions convey responsibilities to families, schools, and communities for educating the young.

2. Legal requirements exist for all social settings, and these hold families, schools, and communities accountable for providing different aspects of education for children.

3. Society in general expects the informal or nonacademic curriculum to be arranged and fulfilled by homes and communities.

4. The formal academic curriculum, though overseen by the community, is largely the responsibility of school personnel.

5. Overlaps and even disagreements occur regarding responsibilities and obligations for some aspects of children's experience.

6. The impact of one social setting on children's education can run counter to the expectations of another.

7. Even with conflicts, partnerships among homes, schools, and communities are the best means for providing meaningful experiences for children.

Maria had been annoyed with her son's school for a month. Tony kept bringing from his second-grade class paper after paper with instructions for Maria to go over and practice with him. Maria felt the teacher couldn't be doing her job, because Tony never seemed to understand what the assignments were all about. One day when Tony brought home a math paper, a reading paper, and a social studies assignment, Maria had enough. She stopped working on the meal she was preparing for her six children and gathered up a basket of jeans and sweatshirts that needed laundering and mending. With the pile of laundry and Tony she marched the three blocks to school. Maria entered Ms. Srichan's classroom and plunked her basket on the teacher's table. "You expect me to do your work? I think you should help with mine," she remarked angrily, and then marched off with Tony in tow.

Whose responsibility is it to see that Tony learns his math, reading, and social studies concepts? In our opening vignette, the teacher and parent obviously are not in agreement, and probably are not communicating at all.

In Chapter 1, we assert that young children become what their world provides, and that they learn skills to the degree that surroundings guide, entice, or motivate them. The influences and forces affecting children in the late twentieth century are numerous and constant. Children encounter them in all three of our fundamental social settings: family, school, and community. As you prepare for a career in teaching it is important for you to identify and understand where and how persons in each setting assume responsibility for children's learning. You also must understand that each institution can work in tandem or in conflict with the other two, as seems to be happening in Tony's case.

Societal expectations in the United States imply that family, schools, and communities have responsibilities for both formal and informal education and enculturation of children. Responsibilities range from instructing in basic social skills and hygiene practices to teaching the skilled manipulation of equipment to awakening children's aesthetic appreciation and reasoning ability.

Surrounding each child is a formal and an informal curriculum propelled and moderated by and through the three social settings. Responsibility for accomplishing the objectives will overlap at times, and representatives in each setting may contend concerning whose prerogative it is to accomplish such and such. However, a greater danger to children is when persons in one setting see what another agency is doing or should be doing, but at the same time fail to acknowledge their own responsibility.

In this chapter, we examine the educational responsibilities associated with each of the three social settings. We view them both from a legal standpoint and as traditional and cultural practices found in communities in the United States. We discuss the following: (1) who determines appropriate content and experience for children's learning, (2) where we find nurturance and support for that curriculum, and (3) who governs, coordinates, and evaluates children's education.

YOUNG CHILDREN'S LEARNING

Schools provide an academic curriculum for all enrolled children, whether in private or public schools. Preschool programs are plentiful, as well. A school's academic curriculum is constantly affirmed by school personnel as well as by laypersons, and its purpose is, in general, to help children accumulate knowledge and skill. However, much of what children learn actually comes from the experiences, associations, and interactions they have outside and beyond scheduled school activities. This is the unplanned, the informal, or hidden curriculum that teachers and parents often forget about or overlook. This second curriculum is a dominant part of any child's life, and it must be related to the formal curriculum as prepared and implemented by schools (Dreeben, 1970; Apple, 1979; Giroux, 1978).

Children's interests and stage of development determine what is meaningful for them, and the stimuli and experiences that result in learning come from many forces within each child's life (Bronfenbrenner & Weiss, 1983). When we consider who is responsible for children's education, we must ascertain who has the most substantial and direct access to children's time, minds, and interests. We must take into account all of the forces bombarding children with information and experience. For example, a definite curriculum of the home exists, although we do not label it as such. It starts at birth and continues to be dominated by primary caregivers for children's earliest years. The community begins to affect children by the time they are toddlers; these stimuli increase dramatically through early childhood. School programs will begin as early as age 3 for some children and by age 5 almost all children are involved with school curricula. Williams (1992) summarizes by pointing out that a child's knowledge comes from her observation of society and through playful imitation of the life she sees around her.

Children's knowledge comes from observation and through physical imitation of life activities.

While much of the informal curriculum is random and incidental, following normal living patterns in particular homes and communities, we find cases where some parents impose an almost academic curriculum, with definite ideas on what their children are to be exposed to and how. For instance, some parents obtain materials for teaching their children letter recognition at age 2, have prescribed reading-to-baby times, program all play with "educationally valuable" toys, and arrange selected private lessons with specialists in the arts. While the extreme of this idea invites comparisons to laboratory conditions, the underlying attitude is very much the orientation of some middle-class parents wishing to "prepare" their children for formal schooling. Without intending to stimulate the "super home," the first goal of *America 2000* (now called *Goals 2000*), which states, "All children will enter school ready to learn," actually does risk inciting parents in this category to push even further (see Chapter 2).

Some of the informal curriculum takes place within a community, and may include children's playmates, neighborhood visits and activities, community agency activities, media involvement, and recreational areas. Haberman (1992), a spe-

cialist in urban schools, presents the case for understanding communities before attempting any school curriculum reform. He notes, "The greatest indirect [impact] of communities on both education and schooling may be the influence exerted by community forces on inner city families and peer networks" (p. 31).

In addition, the larger community creates an impression on all citizens, one that children feel and internalize. Communities control children's learning by (1) providing (or disallowing) opportunities in sports facilities, recreation arenas, museums and arts areas, clinics and other health facilities, and (2) supporting or challenging particular attitudes, lifestyles, and mobility patterns. The "way of doing things here" is the community ethos, and therefore part of children's informal curriculum. Minority children, for example, are still very young when they encounter the attitudes and mores of the dominant cultural group, whether these be positive or negative (Lightfoot, 1978).

Components of Home Responsibility

Parents and caregivers bear great responsibility for children's early learning, and for the genesis of and support for the curriculum that children will use for their entire lives. Parents also have a significant role in nurturing the academic work children experience after entering school. In Chapter 6, we discuss opportunities for learning in the home and outline the process for selecting suitable materials.

No formal or legal requirements exist that require parents to instruct their children. However, common cultural assumptions regarding child-rearing infer that parents will guide and prepare children for life in a community. Also, statutes concerning neglect have emerged over the years, and parents parsimonious in nurturing and guiding their child risk citations of neglect and its consequences (Seefeldt & Barbour, 1994). It is tradition, by and large, that forces parents and homes to provide the basics or beginnings of instruction. As we noted in Chapter 1, American society (considered in the abstract) has, through media, health and medical advisements, and social service agencies, tried to influence families about educating and rearing children since the 1800s.

Most societies do little to formally prepare parents for rearing children, and the United States is no exception. When extended families were more common, child raising was probably more coherent. Advice was more available, community standards were more constant, and families were far less mobile (Hoffer & Coleman, 1990). In today's society, with its matrix of ever-increasing forces producing stress, mobility, and differing home styles, child raising practice has become less consistent and more pressured (Elkind, 1981). Daily lives now are more frenetic, and all too often families come close to abandoning responsibilities for a home curriculum in favor of that offered by the entertainment industry—a community force that is not always appropriate.

Nonetheless, expectations exist, and persons in other social settings anticipate that families will provide beginning experiences as children grow and move into the conventional school environment and the neighborhood. Goals for *Goals 2000* will certainly not be realized without significant family and community input.

What are the responsibilities of homes for curriculum and content? We describe some representative areas here.

Early Socialization Skills

Except in cases of severe neglect, parents and other family members automatically instill in their children the basics of socialization. Children early and naturally learn to greet and respond to others, recognize acquaintances, play games with siblings, and mimic and follow each other. In addition, many parents recognize the importance of educational toys and playmates in controlled situations (Smilansky & Shefatya, 1990).

Language

Communication skills start before age 1 and expand rapidly because of planned and unplanned family interactions and experiences. Parents echo their infant's vocalizations, indulge in naming or labeling things, and direct attention to objects. Later literacy development includes listening to and sharing stories, practicing reading, and modeling more elaborate speech (Dworetsky, 1990; Schiamberg, 1988).

Exploration

Beginning experiments with natural phenomena are common family experiences. Children's experiments with toys and use of or play with materials and substances in the home are all logical, natural, and typical.

Interaction and Negotiating Skills

Imparting basic wisdom about human relationships must begin in the home. It is the family's responsibility to develop children's initial interaction and negotiating skills. Teaching about sensitivity to others, the logic of cooperative action and taking turns, and the need to respect others and to share materials has its place in the social life of growing children (Black et al., 1992).

Aesthetic Appreciation and Value Development

Early aesthetic development is normal for preschool children. Experimenting with music, graphic arts, and movement leads to pleasant associations with these art forms. Parents validating these experiments, participating in the action, and demonstrating possibilities help young children form values and develop appreciation (Seefeldt & Barbour, 1994). In the arena of social values, Seefeldt and Barbour state, "The democracy of an early childhood program supports and fosters the attitudes and values of equality and respect for others" (p. 567).

Health Education and Sex Education

Eating habits, such as interest in nutritious food, brushing teeth, and caring for bodily functions (some care centers exclude children who are not toilet trained) are skills normally accepted as part of the home curriculum. Sex education is a controversial topic. We advocate that families can and should take responsibility for children's sex education. At the minimum, families should focus on attention to gender differences, attention to privacy and knowledge of "good touching" and "bad touching," and respect and appreciation for one's own body (Calderone & Ramey, 1982).

Components of School Responsibility

A formal curriculum starts with "schooling"—no matter how young the child. Schooling, whether it be at nursery school, day care (including infant/toddler programs), or public or private school, will begin where some parts of the formal and informal home curriculum have paused. The word *curriculum*, used constantly in organized schools, serves as an organizer for all school programs. Different conceptions of curriculum do exist, and the philosophical orientation of a particular school's staff members will determine the extent and the quality of children's learning there. In some schools, curriculum will be an outline of content and skills to be presented, while in others it will be a constantly changing set of experiences that children and teachers decide to pursue in satisfying their interests (Doll, 1989). All gradations between these two are found in schools in the United States. As a beginning professional, you should anticipate the definition of *curriculum* as

the formal and informal content and processes used by and for learners in gaining skills, knowledge, and appreciations (McNeil, 1990).

We discuss school curriculum more fully in Chapter 7. Basic education for preschool and primary school-age children will involve extending skills, mostly those begun in the home:

1. Literacy skills: reading, writing, literature, speaking, and listening competencies
2. Math competencies: numeration skills, calculating, measuring, spatial relations, and problem solving
3. Physical and natural science competencies: observing phenomena, drawing conclusions, experimenting with plant growth, animal care, and chemical combinations
4. Social skills: study of human relationships, increased and intensified as children grow
5. Health education, sex education, recreation skills: extension of skills and habits begun in the home
6. Aesthetic education: appreciation of crafts and fine arts
7. Negotiating skills: procedures for planning activities, arranging teams, and developing assessments (mostly in the informal curriculum)
8. Attitudes and values: social, ethical, and moral judgment, respect for and cooperation with others

By expanding and building on the curriculum started in the home, partnerships between school and home assure continuity of children's learning. Whenever one enhances the objectives of the other the result is enriched experience for children.

Components of Community Responsibility

All communities have multiple facets, and the impact of different agencies and enterprises is pervasive in the lives of children. While it is true that the youngest children have limited contacts beyond the home, primary school-age children will

Basic education for preschool and primary school-age children extends skills learning begun in the home.

experience, at some level, almost as much community conditioning, pressure, and influence as do adults.

Responsibility accrues to the community, as an institution, for supporting its citizens, families, and schools and for furnishing a "curriculum" of experiences and opportunities. No laws or mandates require this involvement, and few would enumerate the particular services of a community as features of curriculum. But in formal and informal ways, each community provides a way of life, bits of knowledge, chances for skill development, values and moral education, aesthetic validations, and an array of opportunities that will affect children's perceptions and promote attitudes (Haberman,1992; Heath, 1983).

Formal and informal learning opportunities are found in various places maintained in and by the typical community:

- City services: police, health, fire, sanitation, and so on
- Religious: churches, synagogues, mosques, and other places of worship
- Community education: workshops and classes on various topics held in schools, clinics, community centers, and so on

- Recreational: parks, natural areas, sports fields, play centers
- Civic organizations: Rotary, business clubs, scouts, 4H, and so on
- Aesthetic channels: museums, galleries, theaters, concerts
- News and information: publishing houses, newspapers, television, magazines, bookstores

In terms of Bloom's taxonomy (Bloom, Englehart, Furst, Hill, & Krathwohl, 1956), a community's impact on its children occurs primarily within the cognitive and affective domains. Three community elements with great influence on children are peer groups, entertainment facilities, and religious institutions.

Cognitive Impact

Each community supplies news and information through publishing, television, and radio outlets that provide children specific bits of knowledge. Sports and recreational areas promote physical skills, exercise, and knowledge about recreation. Parks, zoos, museums, and theaters all provide information and aesthetic appreciation to benefit the growing child. Community service offices all have informational outlets to promote health, safety, and good parenting practices. These social organizations, religious institutions, and educational outlets interrelate with and expand the home and school curricula to promote skills, knowledge, and attitudes on various subjects. Figure 5.1 illustrates how the three social settings interrelate to develop and reinforce one cognitive area, mathematic ability.

Affective Impact

In the affective domain, communities and neighborhoods provide children with a sense of se-curity, well-being, and identity. The kinds of protective services available, and the attitudes and values modeled by citizens and leaders, send children clear messages about community values and concerns. For example, citizens can demonstrate and support fair play in games and sports. By playing fairly and rewarding all players, as opposed to emphasizing and rewarding only winners, sports directors and spectators communicate pride in striving and participating instead of in winning at any cost.

FIGURE 5.1

Children's Math Development Interrelated in Three Social Settings.

	HOME	SCHOOL	COMMUNITY
Age 1	Exploring nearby space		
Age 2	Rote counting, comparing objects for size		Sensing larger spaces
Age 3	Contrasting sizes More counting	Nursery rhymes of counting	Rote counting experiences
Age 4	Seriation, placing objects in sequence, acquiring number sense Grasp of time	Distinguishing geometric shapes Determining more & less, basics of adding & subtraction	Applying number sense to the larger world Counting games
Age 5	Ordering objects, grasp of money Sense of measurement in cooking and home projects	Making one-to-one correspondence Grasp of rational numbers Starts to understand time	Noting sizes of larger & less; notes geometric shapes
Age 6	Using knowledge of time; using grasp of number in home to calculate	Addition algorithm, subtraction algorithm Measurement study Geometric study	Applying knowledge of money for purchases
Age 7	Application of measurement to projects and hobbies Estimating quantities, distances, etc.	Continuing practice of number facts Estimation problems	Figuring how far to throw a ball Sensing how long to walk to friends' homes
Age 8		Multiplication algorithm	Using math concepts to solve problems in play, etc.

Community services and functions do not fall easily into categories of formal and informal learning, of course, but they do in differing ways show children the range of human response—from sensitive and reasonable to greedy and malicious. Lessons emerge as children sense their community at work and at play, when celebrating, and when struggling economically and politically or with natural disasters.

Peer Groups

As we noted in Chapter 1, peer groups exert a strong influence in any community. Peer groups are social in nature, and inculcate a curriculum of experience in those involved. Constructively, peer groups provide children's all-important coming-of-age experiences, where they encounter manifestations of folklore and rituals, and begin developing competitive skills (Asher & Coie, 1991). Peer groups also provide early experience in social interaction and cooperation. Destructively, peer groups may evolve into alienated gangs that commit acts of violence and hostility.

Peer groups begin to form early in children's lives, and exist in most homes, schools, and communities. A community has a responsibility regarding the formation of peer groups and their assorted actions. Some parents assume responsibility for monitoring, evaluating, and imposing codes of acceptable behavior for the peer groups they encounter. Consider the following vignette.

Tina and her mother walked next door to welcome to their southern California community the new family who had just arrived from Hawaii. The two new girls, Terry and Adrianne, came to Tina's yard to play. They taught Tina a new form of hopscotch, and while they were playing, the neighborhood "gang" appeared at the yard and told Terry and Adrianne they had to leave because "We don't play with Chinese kids." Tina's mother, witnessing the scene, went out to the yard and asked the two new neighbors to stay. "All children are welcome in this yard, as long as you play well together. I saw the fun you two had yesterday showing Tina that new

hopscotch. Perhaps you can teach these other children how to play it?" Tina's mother tended her shrubs and observed for awhile, but as all the children got involved in play, she left them to negotiate on their own.

Tina's mother warded off hostility toward the new children in the neighborhood by suggesting and guiding a constructive experience. Teachers in schools as well as family members have a responsibility to monitor and guide children's peer interactions.

Entertainment Facilities

The entertainment industry is a part of the greater community, and is probably the most pervasive force in children's lives today. From earliest times, societies have recognized a need for activities that lift spirits and that entertain. A community sanctions and supports entertainment for its citizens; few persons would disagree with that objective.

Communities have planned occasions and established recreational facilities that provide for entertainment—sports areas, natural areas, parks, and so on—and parades, community fairs, and other celebrations are typical. In addition, a whole private industry has grown up in most communities for the purpose of entertainment on command, day or night. The following are typical entertainment formats:

- Radio, tape, CD players
- Cable and broadcast television, videocassette films
- Theaters, cinemas, arcades
- Theme parks
- Computer games

While much of the entertainment industry's offerings are consonant with typical community endeavors, the time and expense allotted to them can intrude on family's and children's schedules, personal objectives, creativity, schoolwork, and socializing. The challenge that parents and school have is that entertainment may be overdone in proportion to other aspects of curriculum in the home and at school (Singer & Singer, 1990).

What is the community responsibility for expanding or limiting its entertainment opportunities? Communities have legal responsibility to protect children from inappropriate situations, but assume little responsibility for children's overexposure to sanctioned entertainment forms. Responsibility in guiding children's choices rests primarily with families and primary caregivers; some cannot manage this well (Singer & Singer, 1990). When schools collaborate with parents and community leaders, it is possible to provide guidance to children regarding entertainment when parents have difficulty monitoring children's exposure.

Religious Institutions

Another private part of community learning experiences lies with organized religious groups, and occurs in mosques, synagogues, churches, and other places of worship and study. The curriculum in religious locations is directed primarily toward participants' spiritual and moral growth, but includes academic, philosophical, and theological knowledge, concepts, and interpretations. While endorsed on the whole by the larger community, religious establishments are selective in membership and orientation. They represent particular neighborhoods for children to experience fellowship and associations that promote social, emotional, and intellectual growth. In the past, community traditions gave religious institutions formal responsibility for moral training, expecting the inculcation of religious faith and the development in children of moral character and appropriate attitudes and practices. The situation today is much more ambiguous.

No state has statutes requiring religious practice, but all have laws insisting on religious freedom. In spite of mandates to separate church and state, cooperative action between some churches and local schools has resulted in appreciation of different religious practices, and also for addressing social issues such as serving at-risk families

and stemming violence in communities (American Association of School Administrators, 1986). Too often, educators, parents, and community agents are confused about laws regarding religion in and around public schools. All professionals in social and educational practice can benefit by obtaining a copy of the concise joint statement regarding religious practices recently developed by 35 organizations spanning the ideological, religious, and political spectrum (American Civil Liberties Union, 1995).

Linking Responsibilities

All communities have established schools within their boundaries to develop children's cognitive and affective skills. In some instances, schools assume responsibility for the total care of children. Laypersons rarely recognize the heavy burdens often placed on present-day schools. With good communication channels, more understanding and cooperation are possible, and the overloads that take place in some schools could be mitigated.

Some skills and attitudes are best enhanced through projects and activities under community sponsorship. We as educators must be alert for collaborations between community agencies and schools that promote children's education and welfare. The following vignette illustrates this point.

....

Life in the small coastal community was quiet. Josh and his friends were restless after a month of summer vacation. Returning from the ball field one day, they pedaled their bikes toward home, throwing trash from their lunches at poles and fences. They seemed intent on marring their community's quiet roadside beauty. At one lovely spot near the ocean, they noticed an artist setting up his easel, and stopped to watch. The painter paused, then asked the boys if they would help him clean up debris near the shoreline, so he could paint the scene without distractions. They did, and then stayed to watch the man work. The boys became fascinated with the artist's rendering, and the artist became aware of how little experience these youngsters had in developing a sense of their surroundings.

A few days later, the artist and a colleague invited Josh, his friends, and their parents to their painting studio to share and talk about their art and its relationship to the world around them. This worked so well that the artists, with the help of a small group of parents, persuaded town officials to budget space and funds to open a modest gallery in the community. Classes in painting and art appreciation are now offered in the gallery, and the artists are helping teachers at the local elementary school integrate "the arts" into their curriculum.

No single agency—home, school, or community—felt a need or responsibility for developing the aesthetic senses of Josh and his friends, but an interested citizen was able to establish a link with this responsibility and provide a needed aspect of curriculum for the youth in that community.

NURTURING EDUCATIONAL OPPORTUNITY

In the 1990s, we find more conflict regarding education. More ambiguity occurs, and we have more to accomplish with fewer resources. At one door, critics are dissatisfied with reduced skill levels and educational outcomes. At another door, intensely involved parents challenge teachers, and push for a greater voice in curriculum. And at no door, but clearly in view, we have more social turmoil, more homeless persons, greater poverty, and more dysfunctional family groups who have given up on schools.

Providing and arranging appropriate educational experiences for children require support, dedication, great interest, and commitment. All three social settings are involved in nurturing and supporting educational programs in some fashion, but less-than-uniform support exists throughout the United States.

New challenges reveal perplexing tasks for all workers in American education. Are there ways to address the issues and restore both credibility in educational objectives and a commitment for moving ahead?

One person working alone seems inadequate. Chris Zajac, as recounted in *Among School Children,* tries hard to meet challenges in her classroom and despairs when one student loses out (Kidder, 1989). In the overall picture, does one individual's effort help that much? The well-focused family is usually successful, but without a followup program in school and community, their work can be sabotaged also. Even in affluent families, nurturing educational opportunity can be accidental at best (Metz, 1993). Quality schools can do only so much to compensate for disadvantaged children. Sustained progress requires a united front.

Do we need a child advocate to run interference for each child? Available resources, time, and human energy are not sufficient. Child advocates note there is little question: Everyone in contact with children should nurture and support children's educational experiences in society. Cooperation among institutions in children's lives is required for full nurturance, and will offer far better opportunities and more continuity of educational experience for children than will any of the alternatives.

Families and Nurturance

It seems natural for families to nurture and promote education and even seek enhanced opportunity for their offspring. Generations of humans have shown a disposition for nudging youngsters up the educational ladder. Only the most callous or indifferent families deny or prevent children from profitable gains in learning; some do better than others.

Much has been written of educational opportunity and social class, which indicates that higher socioeconomic status (SES) groups provide and receive, in general, better quality education

(Coleman, 1966). However, evidence exists to show that it is quality of interaction rather than socioeconomic group environment that makes the difference (Graue et al., 1983).

If we accept a broad definition of *nurturance,* then most families show evidence of capability, at least in children's early years. It is almost natural for new parents to foster their child's growth. What parent does not express pleasure at a baby's beginning language? Parents reinforce almost any verbalization. What parent does not take an active interest in a baby's beginning steps or ability to manipulate toys and games? The active overseeing of these basics, the encouragement, and their deliberate arrangement all speak to the primal and natural nurturing tendencies of family members.

Parents and other family members normally show pleasure at later educational gains. Opportunities for literary accomplishment, artistic endeavors, skill in crafts and sports, and social encounters are normally greeted with enthusiasm. Note that single parents, as well as two-parent families, are often successful in these endeavors (Olson & Haynes, 1993). Ironically, some affluent children are at risk (Metz, 1993).

After children are in school, parental nurturance may be less evident. This is due to confusion about the family responsibility for directing educational experiences, and to incursions in children's life by school, media, peers, and entertainment. However, an underlying principle for most families is that the objective of supporting their child's growth and education is paramount. Some families almost "live for their children."

Extreme evidence of the motivation to nurture is seen when a family elects to introduce a program of home schooling for their schoolage children. Of course, in this way the parents continue to be the dominant force in children's educational lives, as they assume both parental and school prerogatives. This can be ambitious and even arrogant at times (Van Galen & Pitman, 1991; Guterson, 1992). Another example of extraordinary motivation is the willingness of modest-

income parents to sacrifice in order to send children to a private school or to a specialized program in the arts.

In general, a nurturing family has the following characteristics:

1. Monitors and provides for children's basic needs.
2. Interacts with children in kind and pleasant manner.
3. Provides reasonable problems and challenges for children to confront.
4. Models, extends, and enriches language.
5. Highlights successes and supports self-esteem.
6. Helps children acquire basic skills to function in home, school, and community.
7. Plans recreational activities, games, and excursions.
8. Models productive work habits and organizing strategies.
9. Provides consistent guidelines and places limits for social behavior.
10. Supports and extends aesthetic encounters.

Family nurturance and support are evidenced by accepting responsibility for "helping" children integrate with community and school, whether preschool, day care, or regular public school. Parents support the school program, help out at school, and follow regulations (even when they are confusing) for enabling and supporting schooling endeavors.

Parents in some cases lack the background or insight to make the best choices. They become confused about priorities, and fail to anticipate unhealthy outcomes of a school procedure or activity. Children are then caught in the middle. Education is impeded when parents and teachers are unable to communicate and negotiate. However, temporary confusion or perplexity does not alter these parents' basic motivation to support and enhance their children's experiences. Sometimes this type of problem precipitates school reform and positive outcomes result (Bloom, 1992; Comer, 1980).

Children's artistic endeavors are greeted with enthusiasm.

Other families provide minimal support for their children's education. Some provide the basics of primary care—food, shelter and safety—but little else. These families assume the "system" will provide all other nurturance. They do not grasp the basics of educational practice and how learning comes about. Parent education can make a difference for minimally supportive families. It is quite possible to assist parents in rethinking this commitment for nurturance.

Marginalized families cannot or will not provide even basic family support. This special class of family has extensive need for social intervention and rehabilitation (Wagstaff & Gallagher, 1990). Some rehabilitation has been successful. When schools are able to bring marginalized families into planning sessions and management teams, there is substantial evidence that these families' self-concept and levels of achievement, and the motivations of at-risk children, are raised (Haberman, 1992; Comer, 1980).

Schools and Nurturance

All schools provide a curriculum of experience. That is, of course, the main business of schools in the twentieth century, as it was in earlier times. But nurturance goes beyond the basic curriculum to include the social and emotional enhancements of children's lives. If the school nurtures, it demonstrates a special concern for individual children, parents, and teachers.

Teachers choose to teach presumably because they wish to facilitate children's educational attainment and growth. But nurturing teachers move beyond academics to find ways to link experience with children's learning style and modes of behavior. Such teachers are in many preschools and primary schools today. However, we find procedures in some schools that appear to serve teachers more than children. Approximately 30 years ago, books such as *Death at an Early Age* (Kozol, 1967) and *How Children Fail* (Holt, 1964) detailed the unproductive and nonnurturing dimensions of some schools. Unfortunately, some of these situations continue.

Nurturing educational objectives means teachers not only carefully plan, facilitate, and promote educational opportunity, but also carry out focused stimulation. We find this situation in many schools. In fact, many school administrators and teachers have assumed "substitute parent" roles in promoting the aspirations of particular children. But as noted earlier, schools can not do this alone. Haberman (1992) pleads that "special attention must be given to schools that transcend traditional distinctions between learning in and out of school, between schooling as a traditional process limited in time and place to the institution of school, and education as a continued life process occurring in a variety of community contexts" (p. 35).

A nurturing school displays the following characteristics:

1. Has a broad and up-to-date curriculum related to and guided by a philosophy that teachers and administrators support.
2. Is a welcoming place for children, parents, and others.
3. Thinks of children as individuals instead of as classes or groups.
4. Has a rich source of materials and supplies.
5. Is linked with parents, volunteers, and community agencies.
6. Works to heighten the self-esteem of all involved persons.
7. Provides a safe and healthy environment for children that allows them to develop diverse positive values and attitudes.
8. Is organized and serious about its mission.
9. Provides opportunities for children to develop concrete and abstract concepts and to use knowledge as a basis for reasoning.
10. Supports recreational and aesthetic encounters and includes them in its program.

Communities and Nurturance

Community commitment for enhancing children's educational opportunities undergirds family and school endeavors in nurturance. Children who live in an educationally nurturing community are indeed fortunate.

In many communities, pride and care for schools are evident to visitors and newcomers. A groundswell of support for promoting education, however, does not just happen; it means that committees, groups, and leaders have been active in establishing goals and lobbying for better conditions. Administrators know the easiest means of obtaining financial support for new ventures is to label them as "educational." The electorate and community decision makers are almost always motivated to lean over backward to support increased educational opportunities—particularly for young children.

A community that is nurturing education is doing many things, including the following:

1. Planning new schools and community recreational centers.
2. Raising scholarship money.
3. Subsidizing or endowing programs such as libraries, museums, and galleries for children, as well as for adults and senior citizens.
4. Supporting and funding bond issues for educational plant and equipment.
5. Funding grants for school or community educational experiments.
6. Showing interest in participating as a partner in school activities.
7. Displaying schoolwork and highlighting children's achievements throughout the community.
8. Actively exploring education programs.

A nurturing school welcomes parents and children.

9. Supporting all school and club activities (scouting, 4-H, sports groups).

Interestingly enough, community leaders and agencies normally consider the larger context of curriculum when analyzing programs and raising support for schools. Arts programs, as well as sports and recreation, are often heralded first by community agencies, though it may begin with a strong initiative by an individual, as was the case of the artist in the vignette in this chapter. Community members often anticipate better than teachers the outcomes of particular educational projects for promoting healthier attitudes and better opportunities for children.

Unfortunately, some communities do not facilitate and nurture children's education. Some references in this text portray conditions of despair, despondency, and social crisis in too many U.S. communities (Zinsmeister, 1990; Kotlowitz, 1991; Garbarino et al., 1992; Morgenthau, 1989). Exten-

sive social remediation is needed in all these locations. The community context affects and controls family and school settings to a huge extent. And when economic, social, and political crises arise, community problems always detract from school programs and other educational objectives. Controversy often results in minimal nurturing, and too often it prevents the community from making changes that have been initiated in schools and elsewhere.

GOVERNANCE OF EDUCATION

Governance for educational opportunity is, like nurturance and curriculum, a shared responsibility for the institutions involved with children's welfare. Governance involves the management, coordination, and evaluation of children's educational opportunities, and frequently the factors are summed up by the word *administration*. Legal requirements as well as traditions relate to these responsibilities. While governance in education would seem, in today's world, to be a basic function of schools, some features of governance devolve to homes and to the community setting.

The community at large must be the general overseer for educational practice, opportunity, and development. Direct administration and supervision are assumed by the local community school board. Of course, state and national versions of "community" school boards exist also, and these also have authority over education in the United States.

Legal Requirements

Tradition, to some extent, plus laws and mandates to a major extent, are the means by which the several institutions focus on educational opportunity. It is impossible to discuss governance without considering the large volume of local, state, and national laws, mandates, and regulations that affect all homes, schools, and communities.

Most people believe that the United States, from the federal government to the local community, is laden with laws and requirements. In fact, the American legal system is conceptualized on the principle of "minimum restraint to be imposed on individuals to achieve an acceptable level of social orderliness" (O'Reilly & Green, 1992, p. l). And when viewed objectively, we find that U.S. citizens make most decisions by themselves. This "minimum restraint" stems from centuries of precedent in Anglo-American social traditions, and can be detected today in the way Americans operate businesses, schools, assemblies and agencies. To protect citizens' rights, freedoms, and traditions to carry on life, pursue dreams, and educate children, legislatures and other authorities have, in general, enacted laws and regulations that permit people to live their lives with the least amount of interference and conflict.

The federal government, with the U.S. Constitution as a guide, has developed education-related laws (PL 94–142 is an example). Federal laws take precedence over those enacted in all lower jurisdictions. But the federal government is actually a minimal force in education; the tenth amendment to the Constitution relegates education (and many other responsibilities) to the individual states. Because of this, federal law is based on selected parts of the Constitution—those that invoke the government's role as protector of individual rights. The U.S. Supreme Court has done likewise in settling educational disputes referred to it.

The U.S. legal system permits citizens to pursue life as unencumbered as possible, but that system also insists that communities make rules and provisions that effectively serve the citizenry, including development of free schools to "protect people from ignorance" and to facilitate quality of life. So, even though it appears that our educational system is replete with regulation, the organizational arrangement is to protect and maintain the general welfare of citizens.

Legally, then, the bulk of school law comes from state constitutions, statutes, and regulations. These statutes and regulations frequently change due to the changing political processes and conditions extant in the United States today (O'Reilly & Green, 1992). Examples of state responsibility are to provide free public education to all children, to compel students to attend school, and to maintain the "separation of church and state." Each state has established a department of education to oversee matters within that state. One appendage of each education department is the Local Education Agency (LEA) often called the local *school board.* LEAs serve in individual communities to operate the state-required schools.

Local Level Decisions

At the local level, the school board (LEA) operates as an agent for the state, but makes its own rules, regulations, and policies, which in turn serve the community involved. LEAs determine policies and oversee the schools in their jurisdiction, and hire administrators and teachers to carry out the day-to-day operation of the schools.

LEAs, operating within the statutes of state government, are the first and foremost responsible parties. LEAs determine curriculum, develop budgets, hire personnel, and provide guidance for the formal education programs in their communities. State governments, frequently following the example of the federal government, enact laws directed at protecting or helping individuals or groups. Federal law is paramount, state laws not conflicting with federal laws come next, and local education agencies operate in agreement with both.

One other agency involved is the judiciary—the courts. When adjudicating differences of opinion, courts may have much to say about education. Even though courts interpret rather than make laws, it is fair to say they have become extensively involved in education matters in the late twentieth century (Shoop & Dunklee, 1992). Some court decisions have pushed educational requirements in very different directions (Valente, 1994). Examples involve civil rights and free speech issues, the separation of church and state, and definitions of unreasonable search or seizure.

Financial Clout

Even though one agency or institution has direct responsibility for certain objectives, a superior agency can wield a potent force by controlling money for projects desired by the subordinate agency. The federal government, for example, withholds money when it feels lower jurisdictions do not conform or adhere to federal guidelines. States act in similar ways with local municipalities. An example is the loss of special education funds that numerous districts experienced several years ago when their use of classroom aides did not follow guidelines. Federal regulations require classroom aides employed with special education funds to work only with children with special needs. But many districts encouraged these aides to serve in a much broader fashion and work with nondisabled children. When exposed, the non-conforming districts found their federal reim-

bursement for special education aides threatened or withheld.

Home Governance

Various state laws specify parent or guardian responsibilities toward children in their care. These regulations reside in the general welfare statutes, and are minimal. The laws are invoked when neglect is an issue and when local authorities or agencies find families are not providing general safety and support for children in their care (Webb et al., 1996). In addition, all states have laws requiring home responsibility for supervising children and making sure they attend school (Valente, 1994).

The general requirements for home support have come down through the culture and are responsibilities that most families accept without question. It is the family in trouble where negligence becomes an issue. If social welfare agencies are alerted by other parents, schools, or public safety officials then they may initiate legal proceedings to remove children. Still, negligence is the exception to the rule in most communities.

As children mature, home governance practices become more indirect, but laws and traditions require basic support, parental guidance, and family monitoring ("Do you know where your children are tonight?") through young adulthood.

Other Family Governance

All families informally evaluate their schools, teachers, and communities. Without objective criteria for making these highly subjective and personal assessments, families use whatever they have at hand—their own experiences in school, what they have read, seen, or heard, and their own perceptions of what is right for education. Most schools do not have a process installed whereby outsiders may evaluate personnel, programs, or other school undertakings. As a result, feedback from families is often overlooked or neglected.

While rare, there is provision in some school districts for direct family involvement in public school management and governance. We find family involvement most often in early childhood programs, such as in Head Start centers, on boards for child care centers, and in parent cooperatives. One well-known foreign program that actively pursues parent involvement at the primary level is the Reggio Emilia (Italy) plan (Gandini, 1993; Edwards, Gandini, & Forman, 1992), and a few schools in the United States are now modeling their programs on this plan, in which parents and others are elected to hold advisory and even directory roles for school or program functioning.

Because of conflicts or exposed problems, some communities have witnessed parent campaigns for a greater voice and role in school management (Bloom, 1992). Controversy is a normal outcome in situations of this type, and strained relations and misunderstandings often result. But at times productive school–home partnerships have emerged from grassroots campaigns. An example is an alternative school in San Andres (Mexico), which grew out of the frustrations in a community that viewed their school curriculum as irrelevant. Over 600 persons pooled resources and established an education center that develops a curriculum focused on improving social and economic conditions in the community. Building on traditional understanding of cattle raising and agriculture, the adults at the center, including teachers and students, are adapting knowledge to their modern world. Of course, this social reconstruction experiment, while judged successful by citizens, is distressing to the educational bureaucrats that it undermines (McNeil, 1990).

Families are normally disenfranchised in governance of school curriculum, except in the role of followup for schoolwork and minor supporting roles as helpers in the school (Henderson, Marburger, & Ooms, 1986). Most families are quite willing for the school hierarchy—school board, administration, teachers, staff, and specialists—to continue with governance of the academic curriculum. The unfortunate dimension here is that the close working relations with parents that

could come about do not, and a potent resource is overlooked and underused. Schools lose chances to unite community members and develop better programs when they do not seek to involve parents.

School Governance

Schools are a highly visible feature in any society's structure. Although a few citizens in the United States contest schools' viability and purpose, most accept them as necessary for the proper development of educational opportunity for young children. The Phi Delta Kappa/Gallup survey (Elam, Rose, & Gallup, 1994) finds year after year that Americans rate their own local schools highly.

Schools are established for the management, sequencing, and coordination of that formal curriculum we noted earlier, as well as to provide other educational services. In some cases, this responsibility has resulted in bureaucracies with all the trappings of large multifaceted agencies (Figure 5.2). Because of the structure and rigidity in many urban school systems, some communities, in recent years, have argued for decentralization and for site-based management for individual schools. Responsive school situations often result when decentralization is done carefully and with community involvement. The Charter School movement (discussed in Chapter 10) is one recent example of decentralizing.

The above notwithstanding, we have probably no alternative to the school bureaucracy for supporting general education for the masses of schoolage children in a highly technical and work-oriented society. The demands for literacy, for scientific understanding, and for math and social science training, to say nothing of the socializing, recreational, and health needs of children, are immense in the United States today. To accomplish this basic formal curriculum, our society needs carefully organized schools for the majority of the population. One has only to note situations where communities experience extended school strikes

FIGURE 5.2
Governance of local schools.

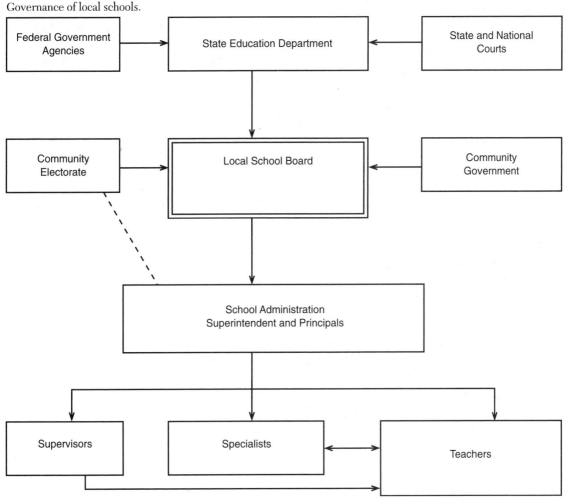

to see the confusion and exasperation that come with trying to fill in the gaps left by school closings.

Teachers Are Central
As agents for the community school board (LEA), administrators and teachers exert the greatest influence and authority over what happens in a community's schools regarding management and coordination of curriculum, time commitments, assessments, and so on.

As part of their governance function, public schools establish grade levels and programs for each age bracket from 5 to 18, and sometimes for younger children. Interpreting their mandate from LEA rulings and state statutes, school leaders develop specific plans for what each grade level is to attend to, experience, and learn, including all processes and strategies for implementation. In addition, school leaders develop assessments to evaluate the educational attainment of groups of children.

At times, schools assume prerogatives where no direction exists, and may develop procedures that serve internal interests rather than community needs. One teacher, for example, insisted that she needed to proceed with "three-group rotation" in her first-grade classroom because the principal required it. When queried, the principal insisted the school system required it, and system personnel insisted the state required it. The state's department of education's reaction was, "We were trying to discourage the use of three-group rotation!" We must be wary of the "myth of mandates" that can appear in a bureaucratic organization.

Community Governance

In theory, all educational governance starts with the community. All states delegate most responsibility to the local community for oversight of public safety, of child welfare, and for developing and operating schools. That community may be a small municipality of a few hundred persons in Vermont, or a huge metropolitan district like New York City or Dade County, Florida.

Most states retain some prerogatives in governing schools, and maintain requirements on licensing of personnel, general prescriptions on curriculum, regulations for special populations, and, frequently, requirements on testing. For these purposes, states establish departments of education, which include offices on teacher education and certification, curriculum and instruction, testing and assessment, special education, media and instructional technology, and others.

Deriving from state mandates, all initiatives in local school governance begin with the community school board (LEA) elected or appointed to oversee schools. The LEA is the policymaking agency and the reviewer of programs in progress. As noted, the LEA delegates authority for administration and implementation. Monies are raised from community taxes to support school programs the LEA has proposed. The school board's central

office hires personnel to carry out these programs, and the board sets general directions for curriculum and considers program evaluations. To a large extent, board members depend on those administrators (superintendent and principals) they have hired to give counsel for board actions and to carry out the day-to-day operation of schools. This means that most of the responsibility for operating or managing schools, interpreting curriculum, and conducting assessments is in the hands of school administrators and teachers. Most citizens think of school administrators as the creators and directors of school programs and strategies, and this image is not often diminished by the responses of school personnel.

Curriculum content for schools is also supposedly determined by the community served, but only in a general way does a community elect what is to be developed in a program, or monitor what unfolds in its schools. Community members most often surrender governance to the school board and its administrators, becoming involved in school matters only when a crisis surfaces in curriculum or in response to political repercussions from nonaccomplishment, such as falling SAT scores.

Considering the anxiety about school programs in the United States and the burgeoning problems in many school districts, it may well be time for more direct community involvement in school life and governance. Shared decision making, more extensive exchange of information between school and community, and alliance among community representatives would produce more thoroughly understood programs, more successful outcomes, and a more supportive constituency.

Communities evaluate their schools in a general way by observing the outward functioning of programs and by noting outcomes. Most citizens have an idea of what schools should do, though the criteria used may be folklore and traditional interpretations as well as well-reasoned standards. We find most persons judge school performance by happiness of children, by tangible outcomes such as report cards, by the later success of students, and by how school is like or unlike what they experienced in their generation. These are valuable criteria, for too often assessments and judgments are based on standardized test results that do not connect with the aspirations of a particular community (Stiggins, in press).

SUMMARY

Many people, agencies, and organizations are responsible for and equipped to deliver education to children. Homes working with schools, which in turn work with communities, result in the best circumstances for enhancing educational opportunities for any child. The three social settings have a shared responsibility for making certain that optimal conditions and arrangements are in place and that model programs are publicized when implemented. Model programs exist today in selected areas (we discuss model programs in Chapter 10).

A curriculum of experience accrues to every child, but children have very different experiences depending on circumstances in the three social settings. The curriculum is divided into two interactive parts, formal or academic and informal or hidden. Traditions and law impose requirements on homes, schools, and communities to fulfill their share in presenting the curriculum. But, overlaps, disagreements, and redundancies are not unusual as children move from one setting to another. Education is most productive where strong cooperation and alliances exist among homes, schools, and communities.

The objective observer can see the unique and vital position of the school in any cooperative endeavor. Parents and communities, of course, have a vested interest in the education of their children. The school is delegated the responsibility of accepting all entrants, organizing a curriculum, executing that curriculum, and generally steering children through the educational process. Because educators are trained professionals with daily contact with children they can best see the places where involvement from parents and the larger community will help. But if the school, as an institution, neglects to engender cooperative action among all social institutions, then the interests and hopes of parents and communities are difficult to realize. We discuss the school as facilitator in Chapter 12.

SUGGESTED ACTIVITIES AND QUESTIONS

1. Consider a new teaching situation in which you must figure out how to build support for several marginalized children. Even though all three social settings bear responsibility, how may you best enhance educational opportunity for these youngsters?
2. Find a copy of your state's legal codes regarding education and identify statutes that hold communities accountable for education of children. Identify two that focus on the school's responsibility for educating children. Is there any statute directed at parent responsibility?
3. What statutes exist in your state's legal code regarding protection of children from abuse and neglect? How is the teacher involved?
4. Construct a chart showing the areas of sex education that you think children normally encounter between ages 1 and 8. Indicate home, school, and community responsibilities at each age level.

	1	2	3	4	5	6	7	8
Home								
School								
Community								

5. Visit a local Head Start center and talk to the director and a teacher about the skills and understandings they feel responsible for developing with the children during this month. Do they feel that the home and community should be involved in these learnings? What do they feel the balance should be?

RECOMMENDED READINGS

Bloom, J. (1992). *Parenting our schools.* Boston: Little, Brown.

Clinton, H.R. (1996). *It takes a village: And other lessons children teach us.* New York: Simon & Schuster.

Edwards, C., Gandini, L., & Forman, G. (Eds.). (1992). *The hundred languages of children: Education for all of the children in Reggio Emilia, Italy.* Norwood, NJ: ABLEX.

Elkind, D. (1981). *The Hurried Child.* Reading, MA: Addison-Wesley.

Hechinger, F. M. (1992). *Fateful choices: Healthy youth for the 21st century.* New York: Carnegie Corporation.

Kidder, T. (1989). *Among school children.* Boston: Houghton Mifflin.

Lightfoot, S. L. (1978). *Worlds apart: Relationships between families and schools.* New York: Basic Books.

Mitchell, B., & Cunningham, L. L. (Eds.). (1990). *Educational leadership and changing contexts of families, communities and schools. Eighty-ninth yearbook of the NSSE, part II.* Chicago: National Society for the Study of Education.

Valente, W. D. (1994). *Law in the schools* (3rd ed.). Englewood Cliffs, NJ: Prentice Hall.

Curriculum of the Home

Every future leader for good or ill starts life with a mother, with a family. This primary experience leaves an imprint that sends ripples into the future of everyone who touches that life.

(Clawson, 1992, p. xix)

The home curriculum is all the experiences that children have while under the direction and influence of their families. In this chapter, we give examples of the many experiences children have at home and of the resulting potential for learning. In reading this chapter, you will learn that:

1. Parents provide an organizational structure for children that teaches them their roles and responsibilities in society, and the values and attitudes that parents exhibit reinforce this learning.
2. The amount of space and the freedom children have in using that space will dictate the extent of children's emotional, intellectual, physical, and creative development.
3. The home curriculum varies for children depending on how the family structures the day.
4. The routines of the day, rituals and traditions, parental talents, and the ways families reach out into the community create a foundation for children's learning in the home.
5. Home schooling, though not a new movement, has had a resurgence in the United States and many families welcome this trend in assuming responsibility for the education of their children.

The educative processes of all homes are important ingredients for society in the United States, for, as Clawson (1992) indicates, how each person develops affects all who relate to that individual. Because of the diversity in U.S. families, we do not find one single home curriculum, but many variations. Too often, educators underestimate the power of the curriculum in the home. When this happens, teachers miscalculate and misjudge the learning that children have acquired outside of school.

Research indicates that, no matter what the ethnic or socioeconomic makeup is of the family, common parental styles and activities support children's growth toward a productive lifestyle (Bernstein, 1972; Clark, 1983; Heath, 1983; Sigel, McGillicuddy-DeLisi, & Goodnow, 1992). Unfortunately, in some family situations, parental styles and habits mitigate against children's natural pursuit of knowledge and positive development.

All families have an organizational structure that defines family members and their roles. Even in homeless families, parents have some kind of organizational structure to provide physical and emotional support. Whatever children's environment, they learn who they are, how to use the space, and what kind of a world they live in. And no matter what family structure exists, home learning will be a consequence of family interactions, use of time and space, routines of the day, sharing of interests and skills, family rituals and traditions, and family outreach to others.

In this chapter, we develop the thesis that parents are children's first and probably most influential teachers. Further, we illustrate that common features of parenting imply a curriculum; some families have specific goals for their children's development, while others' intentions are vague and ill defined. It is impossible to cover all the learning opportunities that even one family provides, and certainly not the range of curricula that diverse families contribute. However, we demonstrate the breadth of home activities and interactions that support children's growth. Vignettes illustrate various situations in the home crucial to education. We also examine the home schooling movement in the United States as an indication that some parents choose to take full responsibility for the education of their children.

LEARNING ROLES AND RESPONSIBILITIES

We discussed the diversity and functions of U.S. families in chapters 3 and 4. We there defined a *family unit* as any two or more persons living together in one household. Children in that household have at least one adult (referred to in this text as a *parent*) who is responsible for them. Siblings, who play an important role in any children's learning, also may be present. Many households have extended family members, who may or may not be living in the home, but who give added support and nurturance. The teaching in any family situation, whether direct or indirect, intentional or accidental, will happen in a context where several things are occurring simultaneously. In all situations, children's learning depends on their readiness for the tasks and experiences they encounter. Figure 6.1 shows the range of children's learning at home and how particular family members are involved.

Parents Foster Roles and Responsibilities

An important part of the home curriculum is for children to learn family values and ever-changing role expectations for themselves toward other members of the family. Children also learn the role expectations of family members toward each other and the extended family. All families have commitments, values, and priorities. Some of these sentiments are explicit and well defined, but often many are only implied (Garbarino & Abramowitz, 1992). Family goals are often expressed as wishes or as, "What we are trying to do." Some are long-range goals; others are planned for a limited period of time. Within the organizational structure of the family, children absorb these goals, and their role in accomplishing them.

Every morning before her children left for school, Mrs. Martinez gathered them at the door and said, "Remember, what you do today reflects on all of us. We are an honest and respected family, and what you do is important in maintaining such an honor." She then asked each child to make a small but important commitment for his or her conduct or learning for the day, frowning on a child who gave the same response each day or copied a sibling's statement. Studying hard, practicing the piano, or getting better at shooting baskets were accepted goals. At dinner one evening, when the family had gathered to share accomplishments and worries, Jose told his family he wasn't going to read with Louie (a Down syndrome child in his class) any more, because he was "just too hard to deal with." The older brothers and sisters sympathized with Jose, but also reminded him of the ways they had read to him when he was little. Mrs. Martinez hugged Jose hard a few days later when he told her, "I'm going to read with Louie. I found out yesterday Louie can read lots of words, if you help and read along with him."

In the Martinez family, goal setting was important, but the entire family had discovered ways to model behavior and support each other in their efforts to "sustain the family honor."

FIGURE 6.1
Different family members nurture the home curriculum.

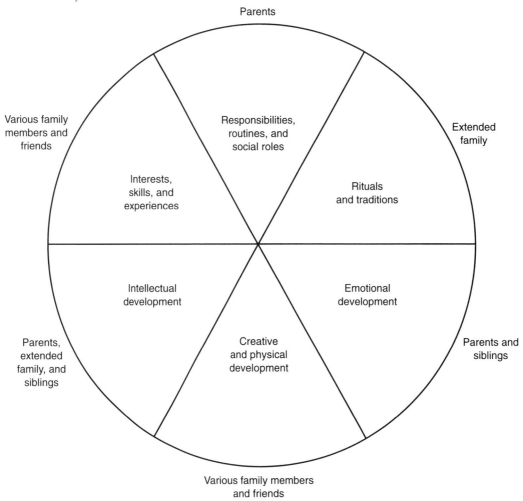

Note: Foundational skills, concepts, attitudes and experiences
are developed in the child's home environment. Some areas are
influenced more strongly by particular family members.

Beth Clawson (1992), 1989 Michigan Mother of the Year, explains how she unconsciously set rules for her family and how important they were to the progress of her children. "Long ago I put a list (titled 'A Cultured Home') on my kitchen bulletin board. It was a reminder to me of some elements that would be valu-

able in helping children. . . . One day I took it down. Before the day had ended, my children wanted to know why it was taken down. I had not realized that the list was a goal statement to them" (pp. xx–xxi). Whether goals are stated each day, written down as reminders, or merely implied, notions of having purpose and

All families have house rules that members are expected to observe.

direction in one's life are modeled and communicated to children.

All families have house rules that members living in the home are expected to observe. Some rules may be explicit and others implicit. They may be communicated in dictatorial fashion, explained reasonably, or expected to be learned through observation. As children learn rules and role expectations, they also form values and attitudes that affect later learning. They learn that some rules are made to be obeyed without question, and that there are good reasons for certain rules. Children's beginning lessons in how to function within their own families provide the groundwork for how to function later in school and in the community.

....

One of the rules in Aaron's home was that each member of the household was responsible for his or her own things. When he finished playing with a toy, Aaron was expected to put that toy away. Whenever Aaron forgot, his mother explained how his toys could get destroyed or lost if he carelessly left them out. As he grew older, she pointed out that one of his responsi-

bilities in the house was to keep his own things picked up.

Penelope's family had different procedures. Rarely were items picked up by any one person. Things appeared to be put away randomly. Occasionally, Penelope's father would rave about the mess in the house and yell at her to put her things away. Penelope usually obeyed him.

In kindergarten Aaron was one of the "helpful" children who always picked up as the teacher announced cleanup time. Penelope attended to housekeeping duties only when the teacher told her explicitly to do so.

In third grade, the orientation was that children should learn to be creative and find ways of expressing this creativity. Penelope found that she had time now to try out all kinds of materials and to "just mess around" by herself without other children interfering. Occasionally the teacher reminded the class there needed to be some order amid the "chaos," and Penelope usually did her share. But Aaron was often frustrated in this class. He had difficulty making sense out of the "stuff" available for creating. He wanted to work with others, but had trouble when they brought more and more materials to a project without "finishing" with the materials at hand.

....

Both Aaron and Penelope learned at home about their certain responsibilities, and they developed attitudes about neatness. At school, Aaron's attitudes and skills were more in agreement with the kindergarten teacher's expectations, and he had an easier time adapting. Third grade, at first, left him in shock, and he had to learn new roles and expectations. Penelope managed in kindergarten, but with difficulty. In third grade, her teacher viewed her knack for creating "her own order" as "creative endeavors."

The attitudes and skills instilled in these families, though different, set the stage for these children as they moved beyond the family circle into school and community life. Depending on your own view of life, you can interpret one set of skills as more "desirable" than another. However, if you are to support the growth of all children in your classroom, you must recognize that children come with different skills and values. It is your responsibility to help them move comfortably into their "new" environment.

Extended Family Fosters Roles and Ritual

In most families, parents garner emotional support from the extended family, and in some cases receive economic support, as well. Members may live close by and be seen regularly, or they may live at some distance but still have strong ties to the parents. This extended family helps to educate children in many ways. Besides teaching about role expectations and hierarchial structures, the extended family helps children absorb the traditions and rituals of the larger group. In some families, both sets of grandparents have equal responsibility, and customs and habits children learn from these members are of equal importance. However, since family structures differ, what children learn from the extended family depends on the extent of influence these relatives have on the nuclear family (Berns, 1993). The extended family expands the home curriculum by interactions, and through the type of gifts or other support given to the family. Because two sets of families with differing values are often joined, children can learn different interaction strategies for solving differences.

....

Elizabeth was an active 6-year-old, who had discovered the rhythms of language early. Her grandmother Dailey, a former English teacher, believed firmly that children should learn to speak correctly and not use "silly phrases" or "special invented terms." But her grandmother Denato delighted in the "discovered" terms Elizabeth used and would often repeat the terms, thus reinforcing that language can be created. At Christmas, Elizabeth received a collection of rocks from her grandmother Denato and books from grandmother Dailey. Her thank you letters to both consisted of drawings of the gift plus a statement. Before sending the letter to grandmother Dailey, Elizabeth asked her mother about Babar, one of the book characters, and with her mother's help carefully copied on her picture the words "I liked the elephant book best." On the picture she sent to grandmother Denato, she wrote by herself "Rnd redrks spkls lgblk rks wjshin ilvu Dne" ("Round red rocks with sparkles long black rocks which shine. I love you Donny"—her pet name for her grandmother).

....

At age 6, Elizabeth has already learned what each grandmother values. In wanting to please each grandmother, she is learning valuable things. For the grandmother who is precise, she learns about story characters, and she has learned to copy a few short words with her mother's help. With her other grandmother she has learned the fun of playing with words and sounds, so is willing to experiment and try out her knowledge of letters and sounds. Elizabeth's mother supports the values of both grandparents by supporting without judgment Elizabeth's efforts.

Siblings Aid in Role Identification

When children grow up with other children, they experience changing role patterns not dependent on age. When a new baby is born or when older siblings start school or leave home, circumstances within the family change for all members and a different "curriculum" emerges. An older sibling who has been a playmate may suddenly become "bossy" after starting school, and younger children must learn new ways of interacting. Older children teach younger siblings "the ways of the world," but what is learned will depend on the younger children's relationships with the older ones.

Much to her mother's surprise, Caitlin learned to spell some words when she was but 3 years old. Her older sister, Jennifer, returning from second grade, often made Caitlin "her pupil" and insisted she "write her letters," giving her words and letters to do. Yet Brad, closer in age to Jennifer, didn't know letters' names until he entered first grade, even though Jennifer at times tried to be his teacher as well. As a baby, Caitlin often called Jennifer her "other" mama, and thus apparently was more receptive to her teaching, whereas Brad and Jennifer were closer in age and Brad resented her "bossiness."

Academic learning is only part of the curriculum children learn from siblings. For example, they may learn physical skills faster and at an earlier age by competing with a more skilled family member. Children learn strategies for convincing others of one's point of view as siblings squabble and solve their differences within the family unit. Even learning how to unite in family loyalty against the outside world gives children important social skills—although not always desirable ones.

PHYSICAL ENVIRONMENTS IN THE HOME

Children's learning is greatly influenced by environmental factors. Amount of space, the kinds of materials found in that space, and the ways in which families allow children to use that space all affect what children learn in the home. Successful

Older children teach young children the "ways of the world."

children from crowded conditions learn a great deal when the family is nurturing and supportive. If children are restricted in their movements or ignored in their environment no matter the amount of space, then learning is lessened. Before children can achieve intellectually, their basic physical and emotional needs have to be met. Clark (1983) found in his study of high and low achievers from poor families that, among other nurturing qualities, high achievers' parents carefully supervised children's use of time and space.

Space Influences Emotional Growth

Great differences occur in the amount and kind of space that children have in their growing years. Of course, as family situations change, so can the amount of available space. Space also can be a factor in the family's ability to support children's physical and mental health. Galle, Gove, and McPherson (1972) report, from a study on the amount of space families had per room, that the greater the density, the more the family was subjected to unhealthy conditions and stresses affecting children's development.

Children learn different things about themselves depending on the amount and quality of space. Hill (1967), in *Evan's Corner*, creates a poignant story of a child's desire for private space.

....

Evan lives with his family in a one-room flat. There is little sense of privacy; even the bathroom is shared with other families in the building. Evan longs for a little bit of space he can call his own. With the help of his mother, he clears a corner of the room which he barricades and furnishes with things he cherishes. Evan's sense of well-being is clearly portrayed as he has the nurturing support of his mother for his own space. However, in the crowded space, Evan also has another lesson to learn. His younger brother wants to come into his space, and it is not without a struggle that Evan learns the joy of choosing to share.

....

As in any home curriculum, children learn many things by accommodating to the space within the home.

Space Influences Intellectual Development

When rooms have different functions, children learn categorization skills for where household items belong and where people do different jobs. When families are crowded, rooms have more than one function and children learn that the same space is used differently. For example, we visited a crowded one-room apartment where two people were sleeping, another was cooking, and two children were playing on the floor most of the day. But across the hall, the same limited space had distinct functions at different times of the day for another family; the room was a living room during the daytime hours, a kitchen/dining room during early morning and evening, and a bedroom at night. Household furniture was rearranged accordingly. The processing skills of children in these families were affected by these situations.

In their classroom, two children, one from each of the above homes, were asked to put household items into categories and place them in appropriate spaces. The child whose home space was haphazard did a random assignment for the items and had no explanation of why he organized the items that way. In fact, when asked to explain his strategies, he began to rearrange the items. The other child had a definite pattern to his selection of items for each category and a clear reason for putting each item where he did.

Space can also be a means of children's developing problem-solving skills.

....

Jack discovered the cookie jar could be reached by shoving a chair next to the cupboard and then climbing up. When his mother put the cookie jar onto the refrigerator further from his reach, it took some experimenting with a chair and different-

sized boxes before Jack was tall enough to reach the forbidden cookies.

Such learning is usually not planned by parents. But when homes are organized so that items for children's use are within easy grasp and other items stored out of reach for various reasons, curious and determined children will try out their ideas, if allowed enough freedom to explore safely.

Children learn concentration skills because of space available to them in the home. Children who have lots of private space and quiet time for activities often develop good study habits. Some skills will carry over to school. Others will have more difficulty sharing space or doing a quiet activity if there are people around them. They have learned to focus on a particular task in quiet and solitude, and a noisy classroom is confusing to them. Still, other children learn to concentrate because they have learned to do so in a large family.

Richard was raised in a family of six children. He read and studied with his older siblings around the large family table. Often the radio or television was on and younger children were playing nearby. As early as kindergarten, Richard displayed concentration skills. He could be found engrossed in a book right next to children playing with blocks. Often Richard didn't realize that it was time to change activities until the noise of the block play ceased. In college, Richard was the only one of his four roommates who could study no matter how many crowded into the dorm room.

Space Influences Physical and Creative Development

Family space and the freedom to explore will assist children in developing physical skills and creative endeavors.

Although Kenisha shared a bedroom with her sisters, and the living area seemed small when the entire family was gathered at the end of the day, outside was a large barn and a yard where Kenisha and her siblings often played. There were trees in the yard and the beams in the barn where she and her friends could climb. Cardboard boxes, old blankets, boards, nails, and hammers enabled

Freedom to explore helps children in developing physical skills and in creative endeavors.

them to create their own fantasy worlds. Kenisha and her friends tied strong ropes to the barn beams, and tested their strength and developed skill in climbing hand over hand up the rope.

Parents who live in crowded cities also have managed to encourage children's imaginative use of space. Rooftop gardens provide additional space where with a few boxes, old boards, and blankets children develop physical dexterity in building as they create their own worlds.

Children thrive in whatever space they live in when adults provide consistent care, nurturing, and support, while guiding their behavior and prizing their creations. Children learn important self-concepts, as they are supported in their endeavors by being praised for successes and by being helped to overcome frustrations at times of failure. When children do not experience such nurturance, the home curriculum is more limited.

HOME LEARNING

In Chapter 4, we defined the areas of home responsibility for children's learning as early socialization skills, language learning, beginning experiments with natural phenomena, interaction and negotiation skills, values and attitudes including aesthetic appreciation, and health and sex education. It should be clear that the home's responsibility is to develop basic skills for preparing children to function successfully in society. But fulfilling these responsibilities is accomplished to differing degrees.

Ethnographers have found ways in which all families provide home learning experiences (Heath, 1983; Clark, 1983; Stinnett & De Frain, 1986). Important skills are taught through daily routines. For example, significant adults transmit the rituals and traditions to the next generation as they share special interests, skills, and aspirations with their children, and as they reach into the community to extend their children's learning.

In these many experiences of the home, the impact on children depends to some degree on the childrearing practices parents evidence (Baumrind, 1968). In Chapter 4, we explicated the different styles and suggested that the authoritative parent rears children better able to cope in society. However, a simple examination of a "successful" childrearing style does not account for the variations in children's growth toward becoming productive adults. Other qualities and the "total constellation of behavioral and attitudinal factors operating in the particular family environment" (Fine & Henry, 1989, p. 7) determine the competent family.

Daily Routines

A broad definition of *curriculum* includes all the experiences children have from the moment of waking to the moment of falling asleep (Doll, 1989). This implies that the home must provide a great deal of children's learning experiences.

When events happen in the home in a timed sequence, children develop a better sense of society's meaning of time. The routine events of the day are those activities that have consistent time and behavior patterns. First is usually the process of getting up and getting ready for school or work. When mealtimes are regular, the second routine involves preparation and a specified mealtime, and a further set of routines revolve around bathing and other toileting procedures. The family reuniting at the end of the day is often another routine event. Bedtime is the final routine, as family members prepare for the night. During these daily events, parents support and encourage or negate and suppress children's physical, emotional, social, and intellectual development.

Preparing for the Day

Children who arise, dress, eat breakfast, and then brush their teeth as a routine morning activity establish a pattern whereby they learn through habit about a sequence of events. Parent–child discussions about these events reinforce parental values and attitudes toward the activities, assist in children's language development, and support children's memory and recall. Varying the routines from time to time with parental questions and explanations about the changes helps children learn to reason, to question, and to adapt to new situations. Establishing routine times and expectations for family events gives children a keener sense of time and a view of rules and role expectations. Children develop a sense of well-being and security when limits are clear and deviations to routines are dealt with in a caring and supportive environment.

Mealtimes

Mealtimes in most families offer many educational opportunities. How events are handled determines the amount and type of learning that takes place. Two examples will serve to support the idea and suggest the degree of variation in family habits.

....

Valerie, at age 3, loved to help her mother get dinner by setting the table. She proudly told her father what a big help she'd been, and he would praise her for such endeavors. At first her mother handed her just enough silverware and plates for each member of the family. After being sure that each place had all the correct utensils was no longer a challenge, Valerie began to get the materials herself. At first she named each member of the family as she got out the materials. Later she began to count the number needed. Eventually she was able to pick up the correct number without counting. When others joined the family she and her mother would figure out how many more pieces they needed.

Casey, too, liked to help her mother. But since the family ate whenever they got in, setting the table meant putting a pile of utensils in the middle of the table. Plates were on the range, as food was served from there. At first Casey would grab a few pieces of each utensil and place them in the middle of the table as she had seen other family members do. Often there were too few, and some member

would have to get up and get a needed fork or knife. Sometimes there were too many and Casey would help put them away after the meal. At each of these occasions, her father would joke, "I see Casey helped you today." Gradually Casey became more and more skilled at getting "the right amount" of silverware on the table.

....

In both instances, children were learning to share in the responsibilities of the household. Valerie learned a sense of self-esteem and pride, and Casey learned that she wasn't quite as accurate as she should be and needed to try harder. Both learned math skills, but Valerie's was a systematic and gradual process of learning through counting and then estimating. Casey learned how to estimate by the physical appearance of the pile.

The entire process of food preparation and mealtime provides children with many learning opportunities:

- Fine motor skills are developed as children help in food preparation, such as when cutting up vegetables.
- Quantity measurement is learned as children help to bake cookies or a cake.
- Following along as the adult reads the recipe develops sequencing skills and other prereading skills.
- Helping to make a grocery list supports writing and spelling skills and language development.
- Observing the change that takes place as liquid jello becomes a solid mass in the refrigerator or as the runny cake dough becomes a solid mass in the oven provides basic scientific understanding of a change process.
- Kinds and varieties of foods children eat during mealtimes communicate the family's values regarding nutrition.

Different parent or sibling involvement in preparation and cleanup after meals teaches children the family attitude toward sex-role responsibilities. In some families, the mother is expected to get meals and clean up afterwards, especially if she stays at home caring for children. In other families we find a sense of shared responsibility, particularly in homes where the mother works outside the home.

Bathing and Toileting

Bathing and toileting in some families is a time when children learn attitudes about their bodies and begin sex education.

....

Stacey, 3 years old, was watching her mother bathing and diapering her 4-month-old brother. She watched with great fascination as her mother sang, splashed water playfully on the baby's arms and tummy, and joined in as her mother sang, "This is the way we wash your arms . . ." The final stage of dressing and diapering Jared was a great revelation to Stacey, as Jared shot urine into the air. Mrs. B. exclaimed, "Whoops, there . . . one less diaper to wash," then quickly began to put on the fresh diaper.

Suddenly, Stacey asked, "When will he lose that?"

Her mother replied "Lose what, Stacey?"

"That!" emphasized Stacey, pointing.

"Oh, his penis," Mrs. B. said. "Why, he won't lose it, Stacey. He's a boy and boys have penises, whereas girls have vaginas."

....

Even as young as 4 months, Jared is beginning to learn about his own body in a positive and enjoyable way. As his mother and sister sing about the parts of his body, he hears terms used in a sensual and pleasing manner. Stacey is beginning to gain new knowledge about basic sexual differences in positive ways, as her mother encourages her to be a part of Jared's daily bath time. She answers Stacey's question directly using correct terminology matter of factly.

Lifelong habits and attitudes towards health are developed in the home by the ways in which parents emphasize cleanliness and proceed with toilet training. Children are naturally great imitators. They enjoy watching their parents do such mundane and routine actions as washing up, shaving, or powdering themselves, and they will imitate the actions. When such modeling is accompanied by occasional explanations for the action, children learn new language and begin to see relationships among actions.

Family Reuniting at the End of Day

When the family's routine is such that each member goes off to work or to school, there is often a routine for coming home. The end of the day can be a stressful time, and both positive and negative lessons are learned.

Members of the family are usually tired and hungry and anxious at day's end, particularly when both parents are wage earners, or if a single parent must do more in meal preparation. Often this will be a time when children begin to learn how to cope in difficult situations. When partners argue and disagree, children are often frightened of the anger and their sense of security is threatened. Nurturing partners resolve their differences and provide models of negotiating behaviors. Partners who lash out, demean each other, or even strike each other are modeling ways to diminish another's self-concept. When parents or partners are able to resolve differences through discussion, apologizing, and coming to agreements, they provide lessons in how to negotiate a peaceful settlement.

Many end-of-the-day routines are pleasant experiences. In some families, children and adults at home share what happened to them during their absence from each other. In such sharing, children learn important socialization skills, such as how to listen, how to take turns talking, and how to explain so someone else can understand, and in some instances learn the skills of "sticking to the topic being discussed." How much understanding and skill children develop in the routine situations of the home depends on a combination of factors such as age, sex of children, socioeconomic factors, children's interest, level of previous understanding, and adult/children interactions (Fine & Henry, 1989).

Bedtime

As children prepare for bed one finds many procedures that assist children's development. As in all routines, regularity and consistency help children develop a sense of time and order of events, and a sense of security.

....

Four-year-old Kevin's parents went out for the evening, and he had a new babysitter, whom he appeared to like very much. She played games with him and read him his very favorite stories. At his regular bedtime she helped him get undressed and brush his teeth. After one last story, she tucked him in, turned out the light, and went downstairs. A little later she heard Kevin crying and went up to see what was the matter. As she calmed Kevin down she finally heard him whimper, "I want Mommy. She says my prayers and you didn't."

....

Kevin derived a great deal of security from a series of routine bedtime activities. Though he apparently forgot a part of the routine, he sensed something wrong and when he remembered became upset. Besides attending to Kevin's sense of security, the episode also demonstrates activities whereby Kevin's parents (or babysitter in their absence) fulfill their educational responsibilities. As Kevin washes and brushes his teeth before retiring, he is learning good health habits. Saying prayers at night or at mealtime can be the beginning of religious training.

Rituals and Traditions

According to Bossard and Boll (1949), *family ritual* is a formal procedure for defining patterns of behavior. Rituals and traditions are important to any society, for it is by such behaviors that individuals show respect for the value system within a

family or clan (Goffman, 1967). Certainly, children learn many social, cognitive, and affective skills that are also learned in other families. Perhaps the most important learnings children gain from rituals are the importance of family structure and the commitment that an individual makes to the solidarity of the group (Levy, 1992). In rituals and traditions, behavior patterns are neither questioned nor examined; the behavior is continued because it is important to the family. As children learn the expected behaviors of the rituals, they learn a sense of identity and self-concept.

Religious ceremonies involve many rituals from which children extend their understanding about the world and their connection to family.

....

At 9 years of age, Jess observed his second brother's bar mitzvah ceremony. At one point he leaned towards his grandmother to whisper, "When will he get the shawl?"

"Soon now, just watch," replied his grandmother.

When the moment arrived, Jess's face lighted. "Oh!" he exclaimed. Afterwards he asked his mother if he'd also receive the shawl.

"Certainly, when your turn comes."

"But I'm the only one who hasn't had it!"

"Yes, but that, too, is important, for now you have the support of your two brothers in helping you understand our faith."

For Jess, the ritual of the shawl had special meaning. Later, when he was 13, he asked the rabbi if his two brothers could place the shawl on his shoulders. At the end of the ceremony he announced to his mother, "There are three of us now, and we are all alike!" The ritual provided Jess with a special connection with his family and religion.

....

Customs, chants, and folklore are often part of rituals and family traditions. Bettelheim (1976) stresses the importance of folklore to children's psychological and emotional development. He maintains that as children hear the old tales they sense deeper meanings and thus find emotional security and comfort. Such stories serve as moral lessons, as well.

Joel frequently yelled in a terrified voice for his mother to hurry and come, only for her to discover that Joel was really not in need of help at all. "Joel, you'll be like the 'Boy Who Cried Wolf' if you yell when you don't really need me."

Joel listened intently as his mother recounted the tale to him. Thoughtfully, he exclaimed, "I remember, the wolf ate him." Several times that week he asked for a repeat of the story and then seemed satisfied. One day a few weeks later his mother was surprised to see Joel suddenly at her side, saying, "I need help tying my shoe." As his mother praised him for coming to find her, he exclaimed, "I only call for help when I really need it. I don't want to be the boy who called wolf."

In addition to providing emotional or moral support, rituals provide intellectual stimulus. Traditional rhymes, chants, and incantations have a language pattern and story structure that supports literacy development. In many families, adults chant or read the rhymes they learned as children, often in the course of playing with children. "This is the Way the Lady Rides," "One, Two, Buckle my Shoe," or "Shoe the Old Horse" provide rhythms and language patterns that form the foundation of children's developing language. Peter and Iona Opie (1969) point out how older children teach younger ones the special games, rituals, and chants of childhood that parents do not attend to. Whether singing traditional songs, writing a letter to Santa Claus, helping count candles on the cake, or learning to read their part for the Seder, parents and older siblings are engaging children in literacy events.

Sharing Interests and Skills

The amount of knowledge that parents transmit to their children varies widely from family to family. The greatest differences in children's special knowledge occur between families who explore their interests together and those who ignore each other. For example, when computer enthusiasts involve their young children in learning rudimentary computer skills, their children often enter kindergarten more adept at using computers than their teachers. Saul (1986) points out how important parents are in interesting their children in science. When researchers asked winners of Westinghouse's Science Talent Search how they became interested in science, most claimed it was their parents who got them interested.

A young mother on a remote island is a skilled violinist and instructs and interests her children and their friends in musical endeavors. Families may also share interest in the arts, as the following vignette shows.

When Mrs. Jacobs placed a Seurat print in her third-grade classroom, Roberto explained to the class that Seurat used a special technique called pointillism. He and his artist father had experimented with the technique after a visit to their nearby museum. Roberto had been fascinated with the Seurat paintings, and Roberto's father extended that interest as the two explored the technique together through art books and in the studio.

Children's curiosity leads them to ask many questions. Parents respond differently depending on their own interests, knowledge, and style of interaction. Children's learning and continued interest depend greatly on the response they elicit.

Eager adults can turn off children's interest as well as expand it. For example, children may learn different things from the simple question, "Where does the wind come from?" One parent may reply, "Gee, I don't know!" Given that answer too many

Interested parents transmit their knowledge and skills to their children.

times, children learn that their questions are not important, or to not bother trying to find answers. Another parent may respond, "From the east" and point in the direction the wind is now blowing from. If that is the end of the conversation, children may learn where east is or that the wind's origin is east, and/or that adults know things and you can get information from them. Another parent may expand on this answer by pointing and then adding, "See, you can tell by how the trees are swaying." Children's knowledge is expanded to finding out something about how one determines direction of the wind. Another parent, whose own knowledge about wind and directionality is limited, may answer, "I'm not sure exactly, let's see if we can find out." When parent and children together pursue an answer, children learn

about the importance of questioning and new ways of knowing.

Besides learning the "rules of the game," children's games teach many academic skills. For example, a game like Candyland® reinforces skills of following directions, color concepts, counting, reading pictures, and matching. Watching television together provides opportunities for parents and children to develop a sense of shared enjoyment. Parents who share programs with their children, both in deciding what to watch and in discussing them afterwards, enable their children to extend their knowledge. Children's appreciation of different types of programs, their ability to select an appropriate program, and even their ability to argue for their point of view are all good skills. Reading to children and listening to children read is the strongest home factor that relates to children's reading achievement in school (Hewison & Tizard, 1980; Teale, 1986; Adams, 1990). When children have favorite stories and parents respond to their requests to read and reread it, children develop an appreciation of language. The sounds and patterns for language are reinforced. When stories and pictures are discussed, children learn much about the framework of stories and how words and text go together (Applebee, 1978).

Gardner (1983) discusses various intelligences that result because of children's different learning styles. These styles may be innate, but parents also support, reinforce, or even squelch their children's natural learning style by their ways of responding. Linguistically oriented parents tend to teach their children through explanations and expressive use of language. Parents with strong logical-mathematical orientations enjoy math and strategy games and encourage orderly and logical thinking in arriving at solutions. Spatially and kinesthetically oriented parents help their children move through space and use their bodies as they figure out how the world functions. And artistic parents expand their children's knowledge through imagining and creating. These responses reflect not only the parents' orientations, but also communicate different ways of knowing.

Children whose parents reinforce their ways of knowing succeed better in school. But when learning styles of home and school are too disparate, children are at a disadvantage. However, teachers who try to understand what and how children have learned at home can create classroom opportunities for supporting and expanding children's skills and knowledge.

As a teacher-researcher, Voss (1993) points out how she discovered a student's learning style by visiting his home and watching as his father taught him how to build. Eric could never explain in class how he did something, other than using his hands and saying, "I first did this and then this and then this." No amount of questioning and attempts at expanding his language worked; expressing himself orally and reading were painful for him. He enjoyed school only when the class worked on projects, and he spent hours figuring out how something went together. Upon visiting the home and getting to know the parents, Voss discovered Eric had a special relationship with his father and was allowed to work on the projects his father did as a business or around the house. His father rarely explained what he was doing, but when asked by the child how he was doing something, he would slow down his activity to demonstrate. Realizing how kinesthetically oriented the child was, the teacher was able to adjust the classroom learning to accommodate Eric's way of knowing and to expand his ability in other areas.

Family Outreach

The home curriculum is enriched or limited in the ways families engage in various activities in and out of the home. The amount of learning varies due to many factors, including economics and personal preferences. Even though parents living on a limited income can provide their children with many and varied learning opportunities, poverty does have a debilitating effect and reduces family choices and energies for learning opportunities (Clark, 1983).

Affluent parents have the means to provide a rich array of toys and reading materials in the home. Children may have their own televisions and computers. These homes arrange trips for their children, as well as a variety of entertainment events, cultural activities, and recreational opportunities.

On the other hand, poverty limits children's experiences with travel and equipment as well as opportunities for scheduled outside activities such as music lessons, horseback riding, little league, scouting, and club experiences. Although poverty is limiting, it does not mean that poor families are not committed to their children's education. We find many do make wise choices enriching their children's experiences with toys, books, family outings, and even scheduled home lessons.

Parental opinions of the importance of different activities vary considerably, and commitments change depending on children's ages. For example, in one study (National Center for Educational Statistics, 1992b) regarding parents' involvement with children's reading, art activities, sports, and educational television viewing, the percentage of parents involved with their children decreased as children entered school and continued to decline as children progressed through third grade. This is understandable, as children become more involved with peers. However, in spite of this decline, at the end of third grade a larger percentage of parents were still involved with their children in sports and games than in any other activity.

Learning opportunities for children vary with parental involvement, but also because of how parents interact with their children during these activities. The vignette in Chapter 1 of Steven's riding lessons demonstrates that curriculum provided by structured lessons is not limited to the skills being taught. In that example Steven, encouraged by suggestions from his mother, was also learning important social interaction skills with adults.

Two other examples of the family outreach curriculum are toys and games, and travel.

Toys and Games

The types of toys parents buy reflect their value structure and extend development in different ways.

....

On the birth of her daughter, Suzanna, Mrs. Williams bought a complete set of unit blocks. When Suzanna was old enough to sit and stack things, Mrs. Williams would take out a few blocks for Suzanna to play with. The blocks were always stored on shelves according to their unit size and gradually Suzanna became involved in restoring them to their correct place on the shelf as she expanded her use of the blocks. Over time other materials were added, such as play animals, toy trucks and cars, pieces of cloth, paper and crayons

for signs. At times Suzanna's father would join her in playing blocks and building towers or complicated structures.

Ashley's father, delighting in his new daughter, bought her a huge toy panda. He would sit holding his infant on the floor beside the panda as he fed her or played with her. As she grew older, Panda became an important source of comfort and a wonderful place to sit while hearing a story or watching television. Ashley had many small toys that entertained her, and she punched them, turned them over, and examined them when playing.

....

Both children experience a curriculum provided through the toys they received. In selecting blocks as the most important toy for her daughter, Mrs. Williams established a highly cognitive curriculum that expanded with Suzanna's growth and development. Ashley's father's first gift reflected his wish to provide a warm cozy support system to be supplemented with random selections of fun toys. Both children are prized and cherished, and their parents are teaching important self-concept and academic skills that will help them as they enter school. But each parent provides a different curriculum. How these two children progress in school will depend on many factors, among which are the stability and continued support of adults in their lives and how well teachers are able to support and extend each child's home learning.

Travel

Most families take trips together, some to the grocery store or to visit local relatives, others lengthy vacations traveling throughout the United States or abroad. Local trips provide rich learning experiences, when parents extend the experience with observations about the scenery and what has changed in the familiar environment, or discussions about what is to be bought, why, and where they will find it. Such involvement helps children learn about their natural environment and become keen observers of change. Among other things, they learn the give and take of

Parents extend children's knowledge when they make observations about the environment.

discussion, reasons for doing things, and classification skills.

For extended travel, parents usually make plans, buy travel guides and maps, and make reservations. If travel is to a foreign country, then passports are procured and currency exchanged. The curriculum of such trips is extensive and the learning depends on how much children are interested in and involved with the plans. Social studies, science, math, language, literature, the arts, cultural differences, social relationships, and problem-solving skills are integrated into such trips.

Camping across the country, the Hi family discovered that temperatures varied considerably when they awoke in the morning. Mai Lin never seemed to dress right for the day. She was either too hot or too cold as they hiked or drove. Without saying anything to anyone, she began to solve her problem by sticking her hand out of the tent each morning to "test" the weather. As the trip progressed, she began to get better at "sensing" what the day's weather would be like, and became a much happier traveler. She also learned how to dress, by observing her parents and from their discussions on what they were going to wear that day. She discovered how to adapt to the abrupt changes in temperatures that sometimes occurred within a few hours as the family traveled through snow in the mountains to the hot desert valleys below. In addition to learning about geography and its effect on changes in climate, Mai Lin learned during the trip to figure out how to make herself more comfortable.

The Hi family never traveled without their children's favorite books and puzzles, plus lots of paper, crayons, and pencils. When the children got restless, everyone read favorite stories or poems aloud to each other. Both children and adults introduced various games they had learned. Some were counting games about the things they were seeing out the window; others were guessing games that required remembering what they had done on the trip or stories they had read together. Rules were made and remade so all could "win" at something. Paper and pencils were used to write down things they wanted to remember. Crayons helped in drawing scenes they'd seen. Besides the literary, math, and memory skills children learned, they were also learning about rule making, adapting activities so the youngest "could have fun," and learning to compromise.

When school programs build on children's experiences and teachers encourage experimentation in class projects, all children benefit. The following vignette portrays a productive outcome in a multi-age group of children.

Eight-year-old Manny and his classmates were creating a story that included a volcano eruption.

The children interrupted their story to build a "pretend" volcano in their classroom sandbox. As Manny watched the simulated lava roll down the sides of the "volcano," he shared his experiences of visiting a live volcano in Hawaii. Struggling to explain what he had seen, he remembered a book the teacher had added to the classroom collection that contained pictures of an erupting volcano. Manny's limited explanations of the hot lava, the students' experiments in building a volcano, and the pictures helped the other students give a more vivid description of an erupting volcano when they continued their story.

All families educate their children to some level of functioning in society. Although we have dysfunctional families, where children's learning is hampered or even distorted, most families provide varied educational opportunities for their children through daily routines and ongoing family activities. The best outcomes occur when families assume their share of responsibility for the education of their children and work with schools and communities to assist in the process. In Chapter 11, we discuss more aspects of family functioning and delineate the characteristics of competent families where positive learning takes place.

Families that assume total responsibility for their children's education often opt to educate their children at home, at least for part of their schooling years.

HOME SCHOOLING

Home schooling is not a new concept, but has gained popularity in recent years. The term is used to define academic learning that occurs as a result of activities provided in the home (or extensions of the home) with the parents acting as teachers/facilitators. Home-schooled children are engaged, often with other siblings, in different activities that are geared to children's interests and abilities (Van Galen & Pitman, 1991). The definition is made more clear by Kerman's (1990) description of a typical day of home schooling, summarized here:

Their day starts with the family eating breakfast. Then the 9-year-old daughter leaves with her father for the library, where she will engage in some preplanned library study, as well as carrying out some errands for the family. At home, the mother provides unscheduled activities for the two preschoolers that relate to children's interests, to household needs, and to events that happen in the neighborhood. They read several stories, wash dishes, make play dough, do "dress-up" and dramatic play, and then walk down the road to watch when they notice a fire truck putting out a fire.

History of Home Schooling

Home schooling was the norm for most families during the early years of the United States's development. In Chapter 2, we described the role of the home in U.S. education during those years. In the late nineteenth and early twentieth centuries, with the advent of compulsory education, home schooling diminished and was confined mostly to remote areas, for children whose parents traveled abroad, or for children in homes with strong religious beliefs (Van Galen & Pitman, 1991). Since the 1980s interest in home schooling has increased, and some of the reasons seem associated with the failure of the alternative school movement of the 1960s (Guterson, 1992). In the late 1970s, John Holt became a strong advocate of home schooling, and parents, disenchanted with their local schools, found support for their efforts in his writings and especially from his newsletter, *Growing Without Schooling* (Gorder, 1990).

Mayberry, Knowles, Ray, and Marlow (1995) contend that in the last three decades we can identify four chronological phases for home schooling. The first phase of renewed interest in home schooling, in the late 1960s, was marked with a period of contention, fueled by school reformers, such as Kozol, Holt, Kohl, and Illich. Some parents decided that "the public school experience would harm their children in some way, or that the parents could provide a superior learning environment" (Knowles, 1989, p. 400).

The second phase, peaking in the 1970s, was marked by confrontations with the courts (Guterson, 1992; Knowles, 1989). School officials, concerned about the quality of education that homes could provide and alarmed by the loss of state funds when children were home schooled, began litigation over parent rights to home school their children. Although confrontations with public officials continue, landmark cases have provided parents with precedents for educating their children at home. *Wisconsin v. Yoder* (1972) established the right of parents to home school their children because of their religious beliefs. And, through rights to privacy, parents gained the right to choose alternative forms of education, according to *Perchemlides v. Frizzle* in 1978 (Bumstead, 1979). In addition, parents won the right to home school their children based on the free exercise clause of the First Amendment (Richardson & Zirkel, 1991). For example, Michigan officials were adamant that children be taught by certified teachers, but in *the People v. DeJonge* (1993) the Michigan Supreme Court ruled that school officials had not shown that certified teachers provided a better education for students than noncertified ones (Mayberry et al., 1995). In many states, as litigation costs have risen, educators have become more reluctant to prosecute home schoolers.

Cooperation, which defines phase three for home schoolers, is a result of changes in attitudes. Some state officials have begun to change regulations regarding education policies, especially as home-school parents become more open and vocal in seeking cooperation with local schools. Kerman (1990) relates how she armed herself with knowledge of local and state laws in Michigan as she prepared for home schooling her children. By dealing in an open and friendly way with local schools, she was able to get support so that her daughter could attend school parttime when her needs and interests were best suited to the school setting.

As more parents select home schooling and schools become more receptive in giving additional support, the fourth phase is becoming apparent. Increased networking among home schoolers has provided such benefits as organizational support, publications, workshops for parents, and improvement of materials and curriculum programs (Knowles, 1989). This consolidation of gains in influence and support systems is marked by a greater public acceptance of home schooling as a viable alternative to public education. In some school districts educators are joining parents in a team effort and allowing children dual enrollment—attending some classes, participating in extracurricular activities, and using school's special services (Terpstra, 1994).

Motivations for Home Schooling

Reasons parents home school their children are probably as varied as the number of parents who have decided on this option. Presently two distinct groups—the ideologues and the pedagogues—appear in home-schooling decisions, and both groups disagree with what is happening in schools today (Van Galen & Pitman, 1991; Groover & Endsley, 1988). Ideologues disagree with the values and belief systems presented by teachers or by children's peers. Since schools do not permit religious education to be taught, these parents choose to home school, so the family's religious values are what their children learn.

The growing group of pedagogues, troubled by their perceptions of school curriculum, feel their children can receive a more personalized and better education if taught at home. Some choose to home school because they fear their children being exposed to problems such as violence, drugs, teenage pregnancy, and disruptive behavior. Others disagree with the instructional and managerial styles of teachers and school administrators. Some

are concerned with the inability of teachers to meet all the individual needs, interests, and learning styles of their children, and are concerned that school will turn their children off to the excitement of learning. And some have had unpleasant experiences in their own schooling and wish to prevent that for their children. Still other parents decide to home school because their children experience difficulty in school, and they find school personnel unresponsive and or even punitive when addressing problems (Gorder, 1990; Jeub, 1994; Nelson, 1986; Van Galen, 1988).

Who Does Home Schooling

Getting accurate statistics on parents who home school is difficult, partially because some parents fear litigation if their practices are revealed. However, Lines (1991) estimated that 250 to 350 thousand children in the U.S. are home schooled. His estimate is based from state departments of education, home school leaders, and curriculum suppliers for home schoolers. This number has steadily grown since the late 1970s, when John Holt estimated that there were 10 thousand home schoolers.

If the reasons for home schooling are varied, the largest number of home schoolers are amazingly alike demographically. The typical home schooling family has two parents, an income near the U.S. median, and is Caucasian and Protestant. Parents tend to have some college education, are professional or skilled workers, and come mostly from rural areas, although some are suburban. Home schoolers appear to be conservative and law abiding, but also individualistic and very child centered (Van Galen & Pitman, 1991; Gorder, 1990; Lines, 1991).

Teaching Methods in Home Schooling

Curriculum and methods for home schooling depend on the home, but most methods fall into three categories: fixed curriculum, units of study, and unstructured learning events (Farenga, 1990). The fixed curriculum consists of guides with specific lessons, suggestions on how to teach, and evaluation techniques. This satisfies parents who are unsure of what to teach and who find comfort in a fixed schedule and prescribed curriculum. Correspondence schools, in which some parents enroll their children, meet this need and provide a structure and routine for home schooling.

Home-school organizations, as well as regular publishing companies, have curriculum guides and suggestions for units of study. In these, the teaching/learning is more flexible, and children move through specific units at their own pace and as their interests dictate.

The instructional learning events consist of the things children are interested in, and development of skills takes place as children experience various aspects of adult life. Each child's curriculum will be very different when parents follow this outlook. Parents, using the "unschooled method," often write about the many ways they enable their children to be successfully schooled. Some read to their children a great deal and provide a range of quality materials. For these families, books of all sorts, including reference materials, are always available.

Children schooled at home are normally included in all family work activities, such as washing dishes, doing laundry, fixing plumbing, or building the extra room on the house, as well as family recreational/educational activities, such as visiting libraries and museums. Some families write plays and poems together, and some share their musical talents. Math skills are developed as parents involve children in building, using money, and figuring out family finances. Many children and parents explore their natural environment together, learning science concepts as they follow their interests.

As children grow older and their interests expand beyond their parents' expertise, some parents apprentice their children to artists, naturalists, and even sheepherders. One parent said that she made a list of people she met who had special interests or hobbies, so when her child showed an interest, she found she had resources to draw on

(Barker, 1990). Parents also see it as their responsibility to extend their children's interest and enthusiasm, especially at moments when "boredom" seems to be setting in.

Even within a single family, the routine and methods followed by home schoolers will vary from year to year as children develop skills, new interests, and the ability to pursue their own learning. The common element is that children's interests are always paramount, and drill or practice is done at the pace they set. In most home-schooled families, projects become a major motivating factor and parents encourage their children's pursuit of these activities (Wallace, 1990).

As children grow older, some parents allow them to select whether to continue home schooling or to go to a public school. In some states home schoolers are permitted to take part in certain school activities and even attend school for specific courses or for a part of the day (Priesnitz, 1990). Some families even alternate between sending their children to school one year and keeping them home the next, depending upon which avenue they feel provides the best education for their children (Nelson, 1986).

Legal Aspects of Home Schooling

The laws concerning home schooling vary among the states, and as home schooling has gained momentum, some states are changing statutes. All 50 states have compulsory attendance laws, and home schoolers encounter legal problems depending on how states interpret these laws. Court and state offices use the following four issues in deciding the legality of home schooling:

1. Parental rights of choice regarding their children's welfare
2. Equivalency of education
3. Home schools defined as private schools
4. Need for certified teachers

Some states mandate that home schooling must provide an equivalent education to what the

Home-schooling parents explore their natural environment with their children to focus on science concepts.

public school provides, and many states define these terms conservatively. Determined home schoolers in these states must provide required curriculum outlines and have their children take required state tests to show that children's education is not being neglected. Incidentally, parents normally win the legal battles rising from equivalency cases.

Other states are more supportive of home schoolers and even cooperate with parents in their efforts to provide what they consider the best possible education for their children. For example, Wisconsin, Missouri, and Wyoming are favorable toward home schooling requests. They do require submission of a curriculum plan, but test-

ing, certification, and "proof of equivalency" are not required. Other states are much more strict in their regulations (Figure 6.2). The three most rigorously regulated states are Michigan, Iowa, and North Dakota. All three require a curriculum plan that has "proof of equivalency" filed with the local superintendent, and "home teachers" must either be certified or be supervised by a certified teacher. In addition, North Dakota requires a list of "courses" taken, and annual tests, and children who fall below the 13th percentile must be professionally evaluated. The remaining states fall between these extremes in terms of their openness to home schooling (Gorder, 1990; Lines, 1991; Miller & Campbell, 1990).

FIGURE 6.2
State support for home schooling.

Source: From *Home Schools: An Alternative* (p. 119) by C. Gorder, 1990, Tempe, AZ: Blue Bird Publishing. Reprinted by permission.

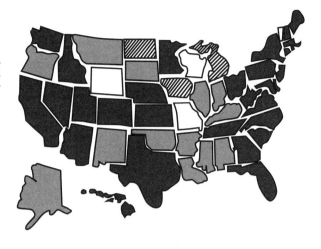

Legal climate for
home schools

☐ 1. Ideal states for home schooling.

▨ 2. States where home schoolers have generally
     been treated well.

■ 3. States that have numerous and/or some strict
     regulations regarding home schooling.

▨ 4. States that are very very strict regarding
     home school regulations.

Criticisms and Successes of Home Schools

As the home schooling movement has grown, some states have registered concern. Some observers maintain the alarm means officials are concerned over loss of tax monies to districts because of lower enrollment figures and because they view home schooling as strong criticism of public school systems (Van Galen & Pitman, 1991). Publicized successes of some home schoolers can, of course, be taken as a refutation of public efforts. The following criticisms are often leveled at home schoolers:

1. Children will not develop important socialization skills or be able to function in the real world.

2. Parents do not have the knowledge and skills to teach a broad curriculum.

3. Parents are unable to provide sufficient equipment to study different subjects, especially science.

4. Parents often ignore drill and practice necessary to acquire basic skills.

Little data have been collected to support or to refute these criticisms of home schooling, but in those states requiring standardized tests, home schoolers score as well academically, if not better, than their counterparts in public schools (Calvery, Bell, & Vaupal, 1992; Frost, 1988; Van Galen & Pitman, 1991). Studies also indicate no significant relationship exists between home schoolers' achievements and parental education level (Van Galen & Pitman, 1991). This appears to counter the argument that parents lack the skills to teach a variety of subjects. The criticism that home schoolers are not being as well socialized to society is harder to support or refute, because we lack studies examining the differences.

Examining the individual success stories of home-schooled children, we find evidence that some home schoolers do well academically and socially when they return to public school, find jobs in the community, or gain acceptance to college (Colfax & Colfax, 1992; Farenga, 1990). But communities and authorities do have an obligation to all children under their jurisdiction, and educators recognize that home schooling is not for all parents or for all children. The reported successes are probably due to parents who wish to be an integral part of their children's learning and are willing to devote the hard work and commitment it requires. Certainly not all parents have the time, inclination, patience, or ability to sustain such nourishment on a long-term basis. We must remember, teachers are key personnel in many phases of children's education, including those children being home schooled. Therefore, communication with homes where children are home schooled is vital. As a teacher, you need to give support and keep communication lines open. The situation must be analogous to the home–school–community partnership.

SUMMARY

Children receive a great deal of education outside the classroom walls. Whether intentional or accidental, parents provide a rich and varied curriculum in the home. Although great differences appear in quantity and quality of home curricula, all parents, as well as other family members, provide emotional, social, physical, and intellectual stimuli for children's development. Children learn role expectations and responsibilities as the family carries out routines and rituals. Parental interaction styles, as well as the physical environment in which children are raised, affect their learning.

Children's home curriculum is an accumulation of all the experiences they have in the home environment. Thus, each child's curriculum is different, but similarities occur due to the daily routines that exist in most families. Both skills and knowledge about the world are acquired as children participate in preparing for the day, in meal preparation, and in bathing and bedtime rituals. From family traditions and rituals, children gain an understanding of their ethnic and cultural identity and of their place in the world. As parents share their own special interests and talents, children expand their concepts of the world around them.

Parents committed to assuming total responsibility for their children's learning may choose to educate them at home. Although a small group has always believed in education at home, the home schooling movement has grown since the 1960s. While numerous reasons are given, most parents choose this route for religious reasons or because of philosophical differences with schools regarding education. Home-schooling parents, though rather conservative, are individualistic, and most are middle class, Caucasian, and Protestant. Home schooling is not for everybody, and all agree this process requires lots of hard work and a strong commitment to sustain positive outcomes.

SUGGESTED ACTIVITIES AND QUESTIONS

1. Visit a suburban home and a city apartment. Walk around both indoors and outdoors in both homes and compare the amount of space. What differences exist? What are some of the things you think children living in each space would learn about themselves? What opportunities for physical development exist in the two homes?
2. Interview two parents and ask about their routines of the day. What learning do you think their children might gain from what the parents indicated? Were your own growing years similar or different?
3. Compare your interests to those of your parents. What skills do you think your parents helped you to acquire?
4. List the kinds of trips that you took with your family when you were growing. Include items such as shopping, visiting relatives, and local recreation outings, as well as vacation trips. From

your memory of the experiences, what do you think you learned (physically, emotionally, socially, and intellectually) from these trips?

5. If you could afford only one toy for your toddler, what would be your choice? How do you react to the two parents in the toy vignettes in this chapter? What do you think are these parents' values for their children's education? Does your choice reflect the same values?

6. Check with your state's department of education to find out about the legal aspects for home schooling in your state. Discuss with classmates your feelings about parents who choose this route for their children.

RECOMMENDED READINGS

Fine, M. J. (Ed.). (1989). *The second handbook on parent education: Contemporary perspectives.* New York: Academic Press.

Garbarino, J. (Ed.). (1992). *Children and families in the social environment* (2nd ed.). New York: Aldine de Gruyer.

Kaplan, L. (Ed.). (1992). *Education and the family.* Boston: Allyn & Bacon.

Sigel, I. E., McGillicuddy-DeLisi, A. V., & Goodnow, J. J. (Eds.). (1992). *Parental belief systems: The psychological consequences for children* (2nd ed.). Hillsdale NJ: Lawrence Erlbaum Associates.

Stinnett, N., & DeFrain, J. (1986). *Secrets of strong families.* Boston: Little, Brown.

Topping, K. J. (1986). *Parents as educators: Training parents to teach their children.* Cambridge, MA: Brookline.

Van Galen, J. A., & Pitman, M. J. (1991). *Home schooling: Political, historical, and pedagogical perspectives.* Norwood, NJ: ABLEX.

Curriculum of the School

After the family, schools represent the most important developmental unit in modern social systems.

(Comer, 1980, p. 268)

In this chapter, we discuss curriculum experiences in typical schools, and how these relate to children's other experiences. In reading this chapter you will learn that:

1. School programs enhance the cognitive and socialization processes that begin in the home.

2. Staffing, administration, and location of school facilities all affect school programs.

3. Some school environments support children's learning and development better than others.

4. Schools differ in program because educators have differing philosophical orientations.

5. All school programs are enhanced when homes, schools, and communities cooperate and collaborate.

Following the first several years of family life, young children enter school, the other major institution in their lives. At this point, a different world emerges for children as well as for parents.

Schooling extends the cognitive and socialization processes children have begun with their families, so naturally the relationships between home and school are of major importance for children's growth. In addition to providing skills and content, the school affects children's self-concept, molds aspirations, starts the foundation for community participation and future employment, and affects a good deal of preteen socialization. Schools are particularly important for at-risk children, for as Werner and Smith (1992) conclude, "resilient children are able to use the school experience profitably as a refuge from a troubled home environment" (p. 109).

The success of children in school is heavily dependent on the relations that exist between home and school. Conflicts over skills and values, differing views about content, or confusion about roles can erode the effectiveness of schoolwork, confuse the objectives that both homes and schools subscribe to, and detract from children's functioning (Hess & Holloway, 1984). Cooperation and compatibility between the institutions enable both to provide stability for children and engender progress toward healthy development.

Schools are more impersonal than homes, so children there function in a different way. Most schools have a distinct chain of command. Rules and regulations abound, and authority figures are seen everywhere. A prescribed order for the day is established in the vast majority of U.S. schools and freedom for the typical student is lessened considerably. The following vignette dramatizes the situation of a 7-year-old entering a conventional school after being home schooled.

"Jessica, please return to your seat. You shouldn't be wandering out to the hall."

The second grader turned and blurted, "I . . . saw my brother and he needed some help."

"I understand Jessica, but there is a school rule—no leaving the classroom without permission," Ms. Strong said firmly.

When Jessica was 7, she entered school for the first time. Her mother had rejoined the family lumber business, after home schooling Jessica and her 5-year-old brother. Now in second grade, Jessica was just getting used to things that her neighborhood friends had been doing for the last two years. "We get lots of books," Margo had said, and that was true, but they were a lot different from the library books and magazines Jessica's Mom had used in teaching her. "I always liked the number blocks we used last year," Cicely had mentioned. "I hope we get them again." Jessica enjoyed most activities too, but she still found the work easy and had lots of time to look around. She was reprimanded twice in one day for chatting with the two boys in her cluster. Ms. Strong didn't like to have social conversations going on, and visiting anyone else was forbidden. "Mom, she gives us directions all the time. I can't keep track of the things she says. It's lucky Harry showed me where to put the date on my spelling paper."

Curriculum for any child involves what happens to her each day from the time she wakes until she goes to sleep. For children 5 years old and older, the school will have a significant impact on that total life curriculum. Schooling involves a formal curriculum of skills and content, an informal curriculum of habits, practices, and attitudes that all school personnel seek to implement, and a hidden curriculum that unfolds in an unintended way but which nonetheless permeates children's consciousness. Each curriculum will be affected by educators' philosophical orientations, which in turn influence the organizational arrangements and patterns we find in individual school buildings and classrooms. In the following sections, we discuss the typical school curriculum and its impact on children.

OVERALL PROGRAM OF THE SCHOOL

In general, schools are seen as places where "kids grow up," learn to interact more skillfully with other children and adults, and assume new responsibilities. While still nurturers, early childhood educators' role differs from parents'; their attitudes, goals, and procedures also are usually quite different. Everyone knows that a teacher's association with a group of students will be short-lived (usually less than a year), so most parents and teachers feel more formality in relationships is normal. Children, of course, must adjust as they move between home and school.

In most schools, children find themselves in a rule- and ritual-bound environment. Teachers frequently compare children to one another and regularly evaluate their performance. Jessica, in the preceding vignette, was used to more independence, and it was hard for her to learn "the school culture" and to operate in a manner where rules did not always make sense to her.

Consideration or allowances for "what happened prior to this grade" are no longer relevant in most school situations. It is what you know now, what you look like now, and what is going on now that are important for the agenda of most schools. Children in school are expected to be more conforming and less assertive, to accept responsibility for behaviors and achievement, and to be part of a group that they know little about. For most children, school is a very different place, and life is starting over.

In the twentieth century, school has represented one major link to adulthood, and in recent years school experiences seem even more necessary for children to adjust to a postmodern society. And though success is sometimes limited, school aims and objectives are focused on preparing children for later roles in a bureaucratic, industrialized, high-tech society. The advantages or disadvantages that children bring to school will naturally influence their progress in the formal learning environment. Experiences in preschool programs and in community agencies such as church, summer camp, or libraries may help make adjustments and transitions easier. But what of children in the danger zone?

It is imperative for at-risk children to have healthy school experiences. School is frequently the only safe, stable, or consistent environment in at-risk children's lives. Numerous accounts show that endangered children choose to linger at their schools as long as possible to avoid neighborhood conflicts and abuse (Garbarino et al., 1992; Kotlowitz, 1991; Kidder, 1989; Freedman, 1990). The rise in numbers of at-risk children in the United States is sobering—one-fourth of our young are in danger (Comer, 1993; Garbarino et al., 1992; Children's Defense Fund, 1990).

The case is clear for dramatically increased collaboration of all human service institutions to produce better environments and better transitions between home and school. To emphasize the need, a Carnegie Corporation report (Cohen, 1994) calls for educators, communities, and health care providers to incorporate services for even the youngest children (birth to age 3) in plans for twenty-first–century schools.

CURRICULUM ORIENTATIONS

As an educator, you will develop expectations for children's conduct and accomplishments, and these expectations will reflect your philosophical orientation. One character or disposition normally dominates in a particular school building, so we usually find the educators there similar in orientation and outlook. Of course, teachers and administrators attempt to accomplish school expectations using different teaching styles and with varying degrees of success.

Volumes are written about different curriculum orientations, and writers use various ways of labelling and explaining the different perspectives. For this text, the continuum discussed ranges from a traditionalist, teacher-dominated stance on one end to a progressive, child-centered stance on the other (Table 7.1). All curriculum orientations focus on developing children's potential, but how to best do that, and with what tools, define the different perspectives. As in Table 7.1, we can section the continuum into several parts and ascribe to each a philosophical base, authorities, features, and teacher roles.

Five categories or positions that appear consistently in the literature and are supported by curriculum authorities (Doll, 1989; McNeil, 1990; Eisner, 1994) are academic, technologist, cognitive process, social reconstructionist, and personal relevance. Borderlines are ambiguous, categories overlap, and authorities use different terms to describe each perspective.

We describe here a three-section continuum of curriculum orientations condensed from the perspectives in Table 7.1. These three areas represent situations observed in many early childhood classes today:

1. Traditional—combining aspects of academic rationalism and the technologist
2. Constructivist—combining aspects of cognitive process and social reconstructionist
3. Personal relevance—follows the personal relevance orientation for individual exploration

The first two are found in most U.S. schools. Though aspects of the third orientation may occur within the first two, curricula based solely on this perspective are found only in a few private or experimental schools.

TABLE 7.1
Typical Curriculum Orientations

Labels	Academic Rationalism; Humanism	Technologist	Cognitive Process; Constructivist	Social Meliorist or Reconstructionist	Personal Relevance; Individual Fulfillment
Philosophical Bases	Idealism	Realism	Pragmatism, Experimentalism	Experimentalism	Existentialism
Proponents	Adler, Hirsch, Hutchins, Bennett	Bobbitt, Tyler, Hunter, Bloom	Bloom, Taba, Bruner, Piaget, Vygotsky, Dewey	Counts, Apple, Freire	Rousseau, Neill, Holt
Features	Classic studies. Wisdom of the ages. Focus on arts.	High order and discipline. Back to basics. Mastery of here and now.	Learning to learn. Experiencing world and accepting change. Problem solving.	Study of world and improving one's surroundings. Social experiences.	Freedom to choose. Student assisted in exploring personal learning journey.
Teacher Role	Teacher mastery and enthusiasm required. Models the ideal. Lectures and discusses.	Well-planned and detailed objectives. Lectures and demonstrates. Interprets and informs.	Develops projects, stimulates study. Directs attention to levels of analysis and progress.	Suggests explorations supporting learners. Resource person.	Assists learners in explorations. Minimal teacher agenda.

Traditional

Traditional academic and teacher-dominated programs expect children to be conforming, respectful of authority, anxious to learn, and to look to their teachers for guidance and stimulation. Intellectual growth in "worthy subjects" is the agenda, and programs of this kind will be as structured and efficiently organized as the teacher is capable. Classrooms are replete with behavioral objectives, and standardized tests are most often used for assessing because the goal is to develop a particular core of knowledge.

This orientation is known as *traditional schooling*, and it has held sway for generations. Given the right circumstances—well-focused and humane teachers working with interested and organized children—it is extremely successful in promoting basic skills and cultural literacy. The following vignette illustrates a well-functioning traditional classroom.

....

Ms. Washington is noticeable and vibrant in her second-grade classroom. The room purrs with efficiency, and she covers every part of the room dozens of times each day in maintaining control and helping children. They have won the PTA banner for five months running now, and the 7-year-olds eagerly inform visitors that theirs is the best room.

The class is arranged as three reading and two math groups, using textbooks that Ms. Washington occasionally supplements with her own material. Assignments are neatly and clearly presented on a side chalkboard, which children consult periodically. Every student is busy at 9:15—two groups work quietly on skill sheets while Ms. W. conducts a directed reading activity with the third group. While working with the group, she beckons two children from the seated groups to check their progress. She gives frequent signals to class members in response to their raised hands; her eyes sweep across the class like a lighthouse beam on a recurring pattern.

A change in groups is handled like clockwork. In less than two minutes, groups have rotated and are at work once more. Ms. W.'s pleasant voice distributes accolades: "Wonderful work in Jawon's group!" "All papers are completed here too, super!" Ms. W. carefully plans all activities, and is ready to go at 9:00 every morning. Even such activities as science projects that the curriculum guide called for children to do at home, Ms. W. has decided to

have at school where she can monitor and supervise. Her movements are quick and energetic, and the class emulates her.

Ms. Washington is the classic traditional teacher; she has everything down pat. She does all the planning, demonstrating, and guided practice, and anticipates almost every problem. "I work hard at what I do, and I get good results," she notes, and this is demonstrated in her students' yearly achievement test scores.

Teachers in traditionally oriented schools think of themselves as in a means to an end situation, as Ms. Washington does. They see themselves working diligently to overcome obstacles, whether ig-

Traditional classrooms today operate in much the same way as in past generations. Some are very effective.

norance, missing skills, or lack of interest, and devise strategies that will entice learners and build skills to support later education. The curriculum is didactic and teacher centered in nature, focused on structure; such teachers are businesslike, and their "can do" aura permeates the traditional classroom.

In keeping with the industrial model, contract learning, programmed learning, and mastery learning all fit with this design. Time-on-task studies, goal analysis plans, scope and sequence charts, critical paths for learning, and management by objectives all fit here very well too. Accountability is foremost, so norm-referenced testing is appropriate. The expectation is development of literacy, computational, scientific, and social skills. The traditional orientation makes for a socially efficient, skills–outcome based educational system, which is easy to rationalize. A clear goal is in sight and teachers pursue ways to get there.

Traditionalists accept new objectives as these become relevant for contemporary living. Personal living skills, health education, and computer literacy all make sense for primary-age children in today's world, so schools with this orientation assume responsibility for these areas in order to produce students tuned to today's needs.

The traditional program is by far the most dominant orientation in the United States today, and its advocates form a long line. Franklin Bobbitt was an early proponent when, in the early twentieth century, he made the case for a curriculum responsive to the time. Since then, advocates such as Benjamin Bloom, Hilda Taba, Ralph Tyler, and Madeline Hunter have propounded the idea. William Bennett, a recent secretary of education, supports the bases of traditional education, as does John Silber (1989) in his book, *Straight Shooting.*

A school with traditional outlook and academic goals does not always have a successful program. Some schools have evolved this way because that is the heritage for the community. Even when a program has questionable objectives for the population served, and garners unenthusiastic response, school boards often perpetuate it. Many low-achieving schools are of this type; they cling to inappropriate goals while being seen by their communities as irrelevant.

The ongoing popularity of the traditional curriculum assures its continued existence, but the lockstep approach seems deadly for some learners. In addition, teacher-centered programs in preschools seem to hold some risk for increasing the later antisocial behavior of disadvantaged children (Weikart & Schweinhart, 1991).

Certainly the traditionalist plan does not flexibly accommodate different learning levels in the way that constructivist and personal relevance orientations do. However, traditional education appeals to many educators working with marginalized learners. Because programs are carefully structured and are developed in steps, dedicated teachers can provide consistency, predictability, and stability for children who would otherwise not find this pattern in their lives. The success of Distar and other highly structured programs for impoverished children with particular special needs is well established.

Constructivist

Constructivist curricula have social efficiency goals similar to the traditional orientation, but employ quite different strategies, permitting individualized instruction and varied content.

Instead of the traditionalist emphasis on skill sequence, the constructivist works to develop children's thinking skills. Valuing the process rather than the product, the constructivist objective is for children to learn how to learn, so they may adapt knowledge and skill to new situations. Teacher behaviors differ from those of the manager/director stance of the traditionalist, but constructivists maintain a strong teacher presence in their classrooms, to direct projects and anticipate next steps.

Rather than carefully designed skill ladders, scope and sequence charts, and behavioral objectives, constructivists favor problem-centered work. Theme-focused programs, units of study, and other similar programs belong in this camp. Since content is often serendipitous and subject to change, teachers with a constructivist orientation must be very secure in knowledge of content and perspectives on child development. They must keep programs relevant to the age levels of students and move them in the direction of social and cognitive competence.

The constructivist orientation stems from educational theorist John Dewey's (1913, 1975) writing, and the progressive education movement of the 1930s and 1940s was based here. It is supported by Piagetian theory of development, and today we find a resurgence that includes team teaching, cooperative learning, and whole language programs.

Constructivist teacher styles encourage free pupil participation. The school program will be heavily project centered, and teachers think of themselves not as founts of knowledge, but as helpers and guides. We do not find a predetermined knowledge base or a set of learnings such as is found in traditional schools; teachers and students enter into investigations and develop or refine skills as they proceed. Curriculum content often focuses on what is interesting and important to children. For example, since social consciousness begins in the primary grades, a focus on environment and care for the earth may be appealing for second- or third-grade children. Constructivist teachers would move in that direction.

Some teachers will retreat to specific tasks at times, and some do have drills and lectures, but group work dominates and teachers easily move from whole-class to small-group to individual instruction. As in traditional rooms, children in constructivist classrooms are expected to be cooperative, good helpers, willing to share, and anxious to learn. In the following vignette, Mr. Perez conducts his primary program quite differently than he would in a traditional classroom.

Constructivist classrooms are project centered and teachers are helpers and guides for groups working on different activities.

Mr. Perez's third grade is relaxed. Two large rugs cover most of the floor, and well-worn sofas occupy the center of the room. Mr. P. has no desk at all, and uses almost the entire day in conferences with small groups and individuals. Children are at different stages in their writings about people who live in their neighborhoods. Mr. P. suggested the activity more than a week ago, and students approached this in different ways, interviewing people, observing folks at home, and just recalling recent events. Youngsters are working this morning all over the room, trying to get their final drafts ready for presenting to one of the response groups. Two children are sitting with Mr. P. on one sofa discussing their impressions of the custodian. They read each other's papers and nod. One asks about the word, "codruy."

"Maybe it's corduroy?" Mr. P. wonders. "Is that right, Jason?"

"Yup," comes the answer.

"Do you want the dictionary spelling, Tyrone?" Mr. P. smiles. Both say, "Yeah, OK," and he spells it for them. "Well, these papers both make good sense to me," he states several minutes later. "Where do you want to go from here?"

Mr. Perez teaches from a constructivist philosophy. He is casual and relaxed, and corrects indirectly. All children seem happy with the slightly noisy room, and students seldom interfere with each other's projects. One of Mr. P.'s few rules is that everyone sit on the rug near the end of the day to listen to those who have decided to share their projects. Today, Andrea does not wish any reactions or comment to the model neighborhood street she is building; she just wants to talk about it. The other presenter, Shana, does ask for comments on her description of the school principal.

Mr. Perez says, "It's easy to get this group to plow ahead on things like this. I think we're keeping up with reading skills, and I know we are way ahead on writing skills. We'll do fine at the end of the year."

Evaluation in constructivist programs is more likely to be criterion referenced and to involve teacher-developed instruments. In that a common core of knowledge is not the issue, standardized tests are less relevant. Teachers will favor holistic evaluation to determine group progress, and assessment is frequently based on presentations or portfolios (for a thorough discussion of these types of assessment, see Stiggins, in press).

Programs following a cognitive process orientation can be mishandled, of course, by persons with a limited grasp of curriculum. Generally, constructivist teaching is not undertaken unless personnel are confident about their background, are committed to flexibility, and are earnest in developing an experimental design. In its true form, it exists in less than 10 percent of all classrooms in the United States.

Personal Relevance

In the personal relevance, or completely child-centered, program, teachers assume a counseling or resource role. Some would say that the child-centered orientation is rooted firmly in Rousseauian philosophy, but it is more than that. The orientation's basic premise is that children possess natural motivations for learning, and adults help best by making things available, by interacting to guide and stimulate, and by being supportive. The Summerhill program (Neill, 1960) is the prototype for the child-centered program. Presently this orientation is found in a few laboratory schools, in some alternative schools, and in a number of preschool programs. Many home schooling situations also are very much of this order.

Responsibility for all educational progress and work is shifted to the student in these liberal programs, and learners must be proactive to make progress. Children must be interested in exploring, in setting their own agendas, and in working individually. Students are likely to challenge authority, abandon their projects on occasion, and often come up with very different results. These behaviors can be disconcerting for parents and teachers who have firm ideas about what children should learn.

Since motivation and incentive are expected to rise from within, students in personal relevance programs determine where, when, and how to go. These learners are often aggressive and highly individualistic, often going on "work binges." No published curriculum exists, so teachers are responsible for displaying a smorgasbord of materials, ideas, and projects to encourage interests. Children make choices and follow their interests with all that they can muster. Typically, children work by themselves for several weeks exclusively on one study, perhaps of insects, airplanes, or computers.

Some stunning examples of success for the personal relevance orientation are evident when we view programs such as the Sudbury (Vermont) School (Gray & Chanoff, 1984) and those at some alternative schools. At the same time, we can find situations that are disastrous, because students were not oriented to the programs, or because teachers lacked commitment for this pattern.

Completely child-centered programs represent a tiny proportion of all school plans, because they depend on highly committed staff members with dispositions for guiding and nurturing, and require a community favoring this type of education. These conditions are quite foreign to the general American public.

We find combinations and variations for these three curriculum orientations. Different degrees of "purity" exist for all types. How do these orientations relate to marginalized children, to inner-city programs, and to multiethnic situations? The traditional schooling orientation is based on Euro-American values, which do not always make sense to poor and disadvantaged populations. Yet, many would argue that the most structured plan allows marginalized children to learn basic skills. And these skills, some maintain, must be attained before further learning can occur.

On the other hand, the project focus of the constructivist orientation, especially when those programs include social investigation and social relevance aspects, seems logical for improving understandings among culturally and ethnically diverse groups. However, we find such plans are rare in schools for disadvantaged children. The constructivist orientation requires children to acquire patterns of self-control and to assume responsibility for classroom learning. When children are raised with little or no structure or security in their lives, many teachers find their classroom exploration difficult to manage.

Programs with minimal structure, such as the personal relevance program, which depend on individual incentive, also may be difficult to manage with some disadvantaged populations. If children lack experiences in work and study habits, if their world is a confusing one, programs based on personal relevance will likely render minimal value even though they are based on the premise that children's needs are foremost.

ORGANIZING SCHOOLS

All schools have their own culture and circumstances. The orientations discussed in this chapter, the student body, the adults who staff programs, the school's physical arrangement, neighborhood priorities and politics, and funding all contribute significantly to school culture and its characteristics.

Staffing Plans

Staffing involves administrators, teaching personnel of all types (regular teachers, specialists, aides, and volunteers), and the service personnel who come to school each day (secretaries, nurses, custodians, food service personnel, bus drivers, and others). All individuals affect the school program, and the character a school possesses comes largely from the personalities, attitudes, and styles of the people who work there.

Administration

Principals, and, to a lesser extent, supervisors, set the programmatic, social, and emotional tone for schools with which they are associated. We find several administrative styles commonly observed in U.S. schools.

Businesslike administrators who place a premium on efficiency, organization, and discipline inject those qualities in a school building's life. This style fits well for the school with a technologist or academic orientation. Managed with skill and tenacity, these schools show a no-nonsense air of business and urgency. While not always the most friendly or open communities, they are predictable, clean, and usually efficient. Rules and regulations are in evidence, things happen on time, all people know what is expected, and most feel secure. There are no surprises. It is the industrial model brought to school. Opinions vary on the appropriateness of the business or bureaucratic model. Many teachers, parents, and students enjoy the comfort of the organization, the discipline, and the high expectations. Others do not enjoy it, labeling the program as paternalistic, stifling of creativity, and not conducive for teachers exercising professional judgment or for students learning decision-making skills.

Inner-city schools with the right mix of personnel have often followed the businesslike style profitably. The combination of rigorous discipline and personal power has produced highly touted success stories, such as those of Joe Clark at Eastside High in Patterson, NJ in the late 1980s and Dr. Sam Kriftcher at Seward Park School in New York City (Freedman, 1990).

Other schools are run on a more democratic, less stringent, basis. Democracy is the objective in many schools and one finds a partnership tone and an agenda for cooperative action. Principals in these buildings are normally exuberant and accepting, and people thrive in their own way. Naturally, there is considerable movement, activities are encouraged (and these can bring about a high noise level), lots of experimentation, and even friction. It is the playground energy and spirit brought indoors.

Many people find the less directive stance and the accepting tone of the democratic administrative position to be conducive for working at one's pace and own agenda. Teachers with charisma, dramatic flair, and outgoing personalities find this climate suitable; they can do what they enjoy doing, and incursions on their turf are not demands but collaborations. On the other hand, low-key persons often will not respond to this type of school atmosphere. They feel lost in the busy shuffle, and cannot tolerate the high energy levels, the noise, or the distractions. However, the principal, who should be a quiet consensus builder, takes time to nurture, listen, and build support for programs and policies, and is valued in many communities. For example, Mr. Rider made all persons entering School #6 feel welcomed and valued. He arrived early in the morning and spent the hour before classes complimenting custodians, welcoming faculty, and asking children how the day was starting. This value produced an emotional environment that supported self-esteem of all persons associated with the school.

There are other variations on these two administrative styles. Mamie Johnson has made a success story of P.S. 146 in East Harlem by her combination of structure, enthusiasm, and family involvement (Clinchy, 1993). Quite a few schools begin an administrative era with one style in place, and then evolve to a comfort level tolerable for most teachers and community representatives.

Children sense the administrative tenor in buildings and adapt to it. They know what they can expect of principals and how far they can go in approaching them. This is all part of the "informal curriculum" discussed later in this chapter.

In the final analysis, it is the public served that determines the patterns and style for a school. A community gradually asserts its wishes for an organizational plan and climate that fits it best. Administrators must accommodate the community served if programs are to go forward.

Teachers

In keeping with administrative styles, teachers also bring a presence to schools. Much of the teacher's style is a function of philosophical orientation or belief about how children learn and how schools should work. Just as there are parenting styles (see Chapter 4), we find comparable teaching styles, which are merged with personal outlooks and ways of presenting. In general, these form a four-part grid on two axes (Table 7.2): warmth (responsive vs. nonresponsive) and control (demanding vs. undemanding). Note that Table 7.2's categories are similar to Baumrind's (1968) categories for parenting.

The demanding but responsive teacher, similar to the authoritative parent, is most popular because this person pursues plans aggressively but in a humane and friendly fashion. The style coordinates well with all curriculum orientations except personal relevance, where an undemanding but responsive teacher is more likely valued. The demanding and nonresponsive, or authoritarian, style can exist in traditional programs, but seems out of place in constructivist programs where human dynamics play such an important part. The undemanding and nonresponsive profile produces an indifferent demeanor, which has little chance of succeeding in any program.

Teaching styles relate to all levels of teaching, since volunteers, aides, and specialists all project a teaching style. Various styles can be successful in different venues and teachers are aware of this; however, all must be able to match children's learning modalities with different circumstances and different material (Dunn & Frazier, 1990; Hunt, 1961; Dunn & Dunn, 1978). Good and Brophy (1994) state that "different situations and goals call for different methods [and] a given method may have different effects on different students" (p. 375).

Service Personnel

While teaching and administrative staff dominate the adult interaction time with schoolchildren, other members of the school community project social and emotional qualities, too. Custodians, nurses, lunchroom workers, and secretaries all play a part in a school atmosphere. While teaching style is not an issue, the responsiveness that these adults show toward children and the manner in which they cooperate with teachers add to or detract from the overall school environment. Schools that are happy places have personnel who are responsive and genuinely interested in helping children grow and develop.

Physical Organization

The physical aspects and space associated with schools differ with age and location, but these elements always suggest what can happen in particular educational environments. A large majority of U.S. children of primary school age attend schools in classrooms containing 20 to 30 students and one teacher per group. The physical plant for most school programs is still the "egg box" type construction with a central hallway and branching individual classrooms. Variations exist for the basic plan, and also may exist within the egg box, including learning stations and highly flexible constructions and equipment.

One can see that physical organization of schools and classrooms relates to program (Figure 7.1). A traditionally organized room is likely to have a traditional orientation. This message communicates itself quickly to children and others who enter a school. Some older schools built for

TABLE 7.2
Different Teaching Styles

	Responsive	Nonresponsive
DEMANDING	Demanding but Responsive	Demanding and Nonresponsive
UNDEMANDING	Undemanding but Responsive	Undemanding and Nonresponsive

The "demanding but responsive" teaching style fits a variety of classroom venues.

traditional programs have been reorganized into settings containing open spaces, work stations, and resource areas. Space, including hallways and out-of-doors areas, can be used in an entirely different way to support a program where teachers want experiments and freedom in movement. Teachers who have reorganized their space have given new life to the adage "form follows function."

Open space schools were developed in the 1970s in many U.S. communities. In general, these were large buildings planned around "pods" or divisions that housed various grade levels or "families." The large spaces or pods were generally allotted to specific grade levels, and the teachers for each space developed the area as they saw fit. This often meant that one group of 25 second graders was within sight and hearing of two or more other groups.

With this plan, many activities in open space schools are total group events, and subgroups move between the designated sections in the pod. Noise levels tend to be higher in open space schools, but with carefully scheduled activities, study, and transition time the interruptions are minimized. The open space permits the flexibility to move to other groups, within or outside the pod, for specific activities or for partnerships, and then to move back when the home group is called to session. The plan fits well with the cognitive process (constructivist) orientation and other, more individualized, orientations. It does not jibe with academic or traditionalist patterns, and has for this reason lost popularity in many school districts.

FIGURE 7.1
Different classroom organization patterns.

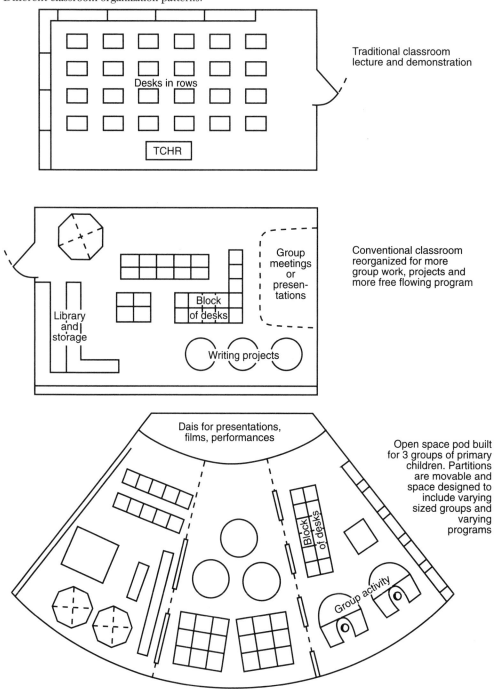

Traditional classroom lecture and demonstration

Conventional classroom reorganized for more group work, projects and more free flowing program

Open space pod built for 3 groups of primary children. Partitions are movable and space designed to include varying sized groups and varying programs

Physical arrangements and organization of learning areas have much to say about the curriculum that unfolds there. Consider the following three arrangements, related to the curriculum orientations discussed.

1. Regimented classes are in cordoned-off classrooms with little visiting, interaction, or exchanges with other classes or the community. This arragement bespeaks of traditionalism supreme. Seating is in rows. The teacher is most likely academically oriented, and carefully emphasizes a prescribed set of objectives. The room can be pleasant and focused, but students are directing their attention to individual learning and accomplishments.

2. Another room has been converted from a traditional arrangement so that large tables provide work space for conducting numerous projects simultaneously. Children are in self-selected teams for the week and are pursuing their projects by consulting with each other, by visiting others in the room, and by visiting the media center for resources. A few parents are volunteering, as one team wished to have counsel regarding some fabric designs they are developing. Space and equipment are used very differently in this classroom than in a traditional one.

3. In another classroom, children are visiting a community center to get information for their self-selected bridge building projects. Their teacher has suggested this as a place to seek ideas and information on construction. The students do not require any particular space or even much organization. They move to places where they feel comfortable and pursue projects in ways that interest them. It is a child-centered class.

CURRICULUM

Schools were established originally to teach areas of skill and knowledge more efficiently and with better results than could be achieved at home. Even though the nature of this task has changed and expanded over the years, the need for skills and knowledge is still the basis for school curriculum.

In the nineteenth century, the overarching objectives were to ensure reasonable competence in the ability to read, to compose written work, and to master computation skills and general problem solving. Schools were arranged exclusively on the traditional or teacher dominated plan. Schools assumed an extensive role in providing more and new content for children as time went by. At present, U.S. schools have curricula that include not only language arts and mathematics, but social studies, science, health and recreation, and fine arts as well. As we noted at the beginning of this chapter, the school curriculum has three distinct forms—formal, informal, and hidden. All are evident each day that children attend school.

The formal, or explicit, curriculum includes the established content, concepts, and skills found in curriculum guides and teacher plan books. It is the material included in textbooks or in the projects that teachers and students decide to pursue.

The informal curriculum includes the social learnings, the work and study habits, and the protocols that learners must master to fit into school life. Students learn these through modeling by school adults, by persuasion and advisement, and sometimes simply by having a buddy to associate with and thereby "learn the rules" from. This process compares to the etiquette practices of homes and with the social organization rules found in any subculture.

The hidden curriculum consists of unintentional learnings accruing to children from their school experiences. Informants in this case are frequently peers; children also absorb messages from adults by observation. Through the hidden curriculum, children learn such things as whether it is a good time to make a request, which teachers get the things they want from the school office, or that third-grade boys "do not play" with girls. They also learn how school personnel and peers view their habits, dress, and home life experiences.

Formal Curriculum

The formal, explicit, or intended curriculum of a school is the plan of action or experiences delivered to attending children. Curricula are promoted in different ways and, as noted, can differ considerably from one school to another depending on staff, district philosophy, materials and equipment involved, type of community, and acceptance level of teachers.

Often the curriculum is a detailed, written document, produced through the work of teacher study groups and disseminated from a central office. The content fits neatly into a scope and sequence chart, and material often correlates closely with published textbooks. Many state offices of education publish curriculum guides for particular grade levels, or subject matter guides for all grade levels, developing them in a manner similar to that of local school districts.

In each of the curriculum orientations discussed in this chapter, educators have different ways to organize and schedule curriculum content. In the following sections, we give examples of how formal curriculum is developed for each orientation in contemporary schools.

Formal Curriculum in Traditional Schools

Predetermined curricula fit academic or traditionally oriented schools, because the philosophy of such schools holds that there exists a common core of knowledge and that the facts, concepts, and skills of that core can be written down, turned into objectives, and then developed with children.

Schedule and structure. Grade levels for elementary schools established in the early nineteenth century have remained much the same to the present day. While somewhat arbitrary, and contributing to many lockstep curriculum designs, the practice arranges a considerable amount of content into grade-specific levels. Teachers in traditionally oriented classrooms organize a day primarily through various routines, then schedule lessons and practice followed by evaluation of some type. A typical day in a traditional school is shown in Table 7.3. This is a minimal plan, showing only the highlights, but suggests the extent of schoolwork for 6- to 8-year-olds in a traditional program.

Organization. An exception to the "self-contained" classroom with children of specific ages is the departmentalized program, where children move from room to room for instruction in particular subjects. Departmentalized plans, normally associated with upper elementary grades, also have been developed in primary areas. Teachers specialize in one or more areas; for example, one teacher develops reading, writing, and spelling (language arts) and handles those areas for two or more classrooms. Team teaching is another model that combines departmentalized features with group planning, support, and evaluation.

Cooperative learning models replace many individual assignments with a small-group focus and responsibility. Teachers may combine this strategy with most staffing arrangements and classroom organizations patterns; however, it blends most successfully with constructivist classrooms.

TABLE 7.3
Traditional Classroom Day—Grade 2

9:00	Opening activities
9:15	Reading and other language arts
10:15	Recess
10:30	Mathematics
11:30	Physical education
12:00	Lunch
12:45	Social and physical sciences
1:30	Art and music
2:00	Recess
2:30	Language arts review

Formal Curriculum in Constructivist Classrooms

A constructivist curriculum is carefully thought out. The teacher's plans are developed in conjunction with school and community expectations; children's developmental stages and individual patterns of growth are accounted for. A constructivist teacher may use a curriculum guide, but will freely interpret it as needed. Content covers all disciplines—reading, writing, math, social studies, science, fine arts, and physical education. Rather than a sequenced listing of content and concepts, we find classes pursuing investigations of topics, projects, or themes. The curriculum is integrated, and involves children in active learning. Through involvement with different issues in the units studied, children develop the same set of basic skills encountered in a traditional school plan. Teachers are responsible for content and for providing continuity of experience and opportunities for learners. Classroom social interactions, which are important to curriculum development, are provided through shared experiences, flexible groupings, interactions with the teacher, and opportunities for children to reflect on their learning.

A "constructivist at work" is presented in the following vignette, as one teacher tells visitors about her grade 3 unit on trees (adapted from Barbour & Seefeldt, 1993).

....

I operate my third grade by establishing a flexible schedule so I can reorganize, if interests and projects require more time. I have a framework of the subject area skills that children should acquire that I have pulled, along with themes and unit suggestions, from the curriculum guides. Beyond that, I try to be flexible enough to respond to children's interests and needs.

Planning for our tree unit went something like this: Children were just finishing explorations on different birds, when one child brought in an apple tree branch about to blossom. Children had all

sorts of questions, so I suggested that our next unit could be on trees. I encouraged children to bring some books about trees and I gathered several as well. The next day I read Parnall's Apple Tree, *and we discussed some of the things in the book that interested them. Some of the concepts were: trees provide food for us and for other animals, trees change during the seasons, trees provide joy and delight, and trees provide shelter for some creatures.*

Then I thought of some activities we could do that connected to our reading, social studies and science curricula. In reading we are looking at settings for stories, in social studies we are doing mapping skills, and in science we are studying the environment. So, I began to devise some projects that would engage the class in learning more about trees and their importance to the environment but that would still be linked to subject area skills.

In reading children are studying story settings, and from reading Apple Tree *and other books, they will examine settings, and thus learn about the environments that trees need.*

In social studies children are studying mapping skills. On global maps children will locate places where our "tree" stories take place. Children will then make topographical maps and place models of their trees appropriately. In art children will portray different houses that animals develop in trees.

In writing children will reflect in journals what they are learning about trees and what is of particular interest to them. Children are always encouraged to list new and interesting words, so as they attempt creative writing they will have a list of new words to use.

In science we will examine the different foods that trees provide. We will collect some of these foods for snacks on different days.

Some of the presentations or projects will be total class, and others will require children to work in groups or individually. As a total group we will discuss the findings and plan out the different projects: topography; reading discussion groups; snack preparations; creative stories or reports; house building projects. Four basic work areas will be prepared: maps area, house building area, food preparation area, and arts and creative writing area. But depending on children's discoveries and their interests, they can elect to be part of two, three or all four activities. There will be a formal independent reading time when children read from their selected books, and then meet in a discussion group to share information from their books. Discussions during snack time and after reading time, children's journals, their creative stories, and their art creations will provide me information on what students have learned. At the end of all our units, I ask children to reflect on what new information or skills they have acquired. You see, I'm trying to get them to become aware of their own learning.

The typical day in a constructivist class is organized through various routines, projects, meetings, and skill sessions. Activities are usually followed by evaluations, sharing, and exhibiting. A typical schedule for a constructivist school day is shown in Table 7.4.

The advantage of doing projects in the cognitive process and constructivist programs is that such work is more informal and lends itself to ex-

TABLE 7.4
Constructivist Classroom Day—Grade 2

9:00	Meeting time. Greet friends. Check and discuss schedule for day.
9:30	Reading & writing workshop
10:30	Class meeting
10:45	Recess
11:00	Skill session on subtraction
12:00	Lunch
12:45	Class meeting
1:00	Independent work time for projects
2:00	Art & music sessions
2:30	Presentations, publishing, & wrapup

perimentation and collaboration. Assignments tend to hold children's interest longer, especially when they get to help choose the topics and how to extend their study. Some sessions will seem disorganized, with children searching for material or collaborating with others, but the advantage is that the approach to mastering material is self-selected. In these programs, children feel empowered for much of their own learning and grasp concepts and skills far beyond traditional grade expectations.

A major disadvantage to constructivist plans is that projects can become trivial or repetitive. In addition, some teachers have difficulty incorporating or inserting reasonable skill development sessions in the investigations that classes propose.

Formal Curriculum in Personal Relevance Programs

A truly child-centered program is difficult to describe, since all content emerges from the interests of children involved. As an illustration, however, imagine that a small group of children has elected to consider frogs for a week while other groups or individuals are focused on different topics. The classroom teacher and aides would provide as much help, guidance, and support as possible for their study, and a scenario such as the following might develop:

- Teachers accompany children on a visit to a swamp, after they decide to observe frog habitats.
- Discussions about materials collected follow the visit and children ponder ways they wish to continue.
- Teachers assemble resources—books, magazines, films, and the like—while students explore what they wish to concentrate on.
- The group shares with the entire class, and children brainstorm, or at least discuss, how they could learn more. They consider books, museum exhibits, presentations by persons in ecology departments, and interactions with local specialists and with other classrooms or schools nearby. New members join the group.

- Students incorporate writing and mathematics into their study by keeping journals on experiences and planning experiments, such as hatching frog eggs in different media. Teachers help and provide information or instruction when needed.
- The project evolves into a larger study of swamp ecology, as it serves the interests of students and continues to be a stimulating topic.

Certain home schooling programs are conducted along this line, and evidence shows that children's interest blooms when they are given chances to investigate their surroundings. One fascinating example is the plan the Colfax (1992) family used with their four sons.

The content examples presented here are all explicit or intended curriculum activities of a school program. This means teachers feel a responsibility to plan for and to steer children toward some substance or experience. As we have stated, other forms of curriculum also are associated with all schools. The "informal curriculum" is acknowledged by most educators and parents as part of "what we come to school for." The "hidden curriculum" is rarely apparent to teachers and parents, but its effects often outlast those of the explicit curriculum. We discuss these curricula in the following sections.

Informal Curriculum

Much of the informal curriculum is implied and unplanned; it consists of those learnings teachers and parents expect to come about but rarely bother to state, plan for, or present to children. Much of the informal curriculum has to do with socialization into school life, and it is similar to the etiquette of other institutions in children's lives.

The implied curriculum includes events such as teachers expecting their new students to discover procedures for lining up, for passing in papers, for getting recognition in class, or for responding. No one plans the activities, but all are expected to follow the rules. Recall the vignette in

Chapter 4, where Greg helped Philip understand the teacher's request. Informal curriculum was at work when Greg instructed the younger child. The teacher expected Philip to know the practices but he did not, so the older child interpreted.

Teachers expect children to internalize a number of general school procedures and protocols. We find the following items of informal curriculum in typical U.S. schools:

- School activities are organized and differ from spontaneous situations at home. Children are expected to differentiate, to adapt, and fit in.
- Competition is a fact of life in U.S. schools. Teachers employ notions of being first, being best, and achieving more in all areas of classwork and sports. Children are expected to absorb this value.
- Time and schedules are paramount in school life. Children are expected to work on command, change quickly to new ventures, and meet deadlines many times per day.
- Group activities are common in all schools. Children are expected to learn group roles and to participate in groups cooperatively and smoothly.

The home curriculum is basically an informal curriculum (see Chapter 6), and learning accrues in a haphazard but reasonable way. Few formal or organized experiences are associated with the home—exceptions are music lessons, homework, and the like—unless parents have developed a "home schooling" program. Language skill is a good example of the informal home curriculum. There are no planned times for language instruction. However, by the time children enter kindergarten they have almost complete control of their native language, and it has all come through interaction with family, caregivers, and peers.

Hidden Curriculum

We have defined *curriculum* as those experiences that make up children's waking hours, and when you consider carefully, you can see that the thousands of impressions, interactions, and experiences children have each day do amount to a curriculum. Children constantly receive stimuli that contribute to learning. Some stimuli are intentional; adults plan things that children are "supposed" to learn through school, home, or cummunity instruction. But some learning is unintended; it comes about in informal and accidental ways as children observe phenomena, experience situations, and associate with others. This is often called "hidden curriculum," and makes a considerable impression, although its extent and effects are frequently ignored. Recall from the vignette in Chapter 4 Jana's drawings about her family configurations at different periods in her life. These drawings indicate Jana's evolving hidden curriculum.

Children continue to encounter the hidden curriculum after entering school. Examined closely, we find it occupies a large part of the school day. For example, first-grade teachers plan about five hours of in-class time per day, but when we calculate the time actually spent on planned activities, we often find that less than one-half is on-task work. In fact, some time-on-task studies

reveal that primary classrooms in some cases were on task less than one hour of the total day (Stallings, 1980). This leaves a large amount of in-class and out-of-class time, and time spent going to and from school, given over to the hidden curriculum. Whether beneficial or negative, it is a potent force in any child's learning.

....

Ryan only shrugged when, during dinner, his father asked him about his school day, but later when they were reading the comics page of their newspaper, some things came up about a new child in Ryan's class.

"I think Charlie takes money," Ryan said.

"Oh, really," said his dad.

"Yeah, he had three quarters that he spent on candy at Ed's Variety today . . . said he found 'em."

"Maybe he did," his dad replied.

"Yeah, but he didn't know where. . . . I think he stole 'em."

"Has Charlie been here visiting?" Ryan's father asked.

Some learning is unintended or accidental, coming about informally as children observe phenomena.

"Nope. I asked him over last week, but his Dad don't let him go places. It's funny, 'cause he knows a lot."

"Oh, that so?"

Ryan nodded and volunteered, "He told me all those dirty words on the fence back of the variety store."

"Hmmm, well . . . when . . .," his dad began.

But Ryan continued as he picked up the comic again, "There's those funny red marks on Charlie's arms. I'm gonna ask him tomorrow, if we walk home from school."

....

Ryan is a 7-year-old doing well in his traditional second-grade class, but you will note a host of items he is learning that are unrelated to school objectives. In his walk home with the new boy, Ryan is encountering a hidden curriculum. Its features are unrelated to his formal school curriculum, but the stimuli—scatological language, questions about theft, and hints of abuse—all have an impact on Ryan.

The unintended or hidden curriculum for at-risk children can, of course, have a negative impact, and may have heartrending consequences. Aspects of these experiences surface in media reports describing particularly poignant family situations. The distressing accounts of children's lives given in Chapter 4 present all too graphically a savage curriculum for some children, which cries out for redress.

RESULTS OF SCHOOL EDUCATIVE PROCESSES

Millions of children attend schools in the United States each year. Also each year, between three and four million young Americans (many of whom are dropouts) move beyond school to the work force, to college, to homemaking, or to unemployment (U.S. Bureau of the Census, 1993). It is common knowledge that a vast difference exists in

outcomes for differing educational environments, ranging from the sublime to the pathetic.

Schools differ in structure, in view of curriculum, in equipment, and in space. School leadership varies, as does the skill of staff members in charge of day-to-day activities. The background, support, and preparation that enrolled children possess will differ. All these factors contribute to differences in educational outcomes.

Changes are possible in all educational situations; the poor can be made better, the good can become outstanding, and highly rated programs can falter if factors change.

Differing curriculum orientations, coupled with various teaching strategies and techniques, may fit into the equation. All can be successful. The traditional teacher who demonstrates, explains, and then pursues application may be rewarded with inquisitive, enthusiastic students. The indirect teacher, with educational goals firmly in mind, also can stimulate and guide student interests to fruition, using the same basic equipment.

In the final analysis, teachers must know who they are, where they are going, and the best ways to get there. This means they must have a clear grasp of their own skills and preferred work style, and be able to see how their style matches children's interests and work habits. Teachers who are not self-aware in this way must depend on fortune to place them in comfortable situations with eager students. If circumstances change, positive interactions easily become reversed.

Some schools have an easy time. Schools accepting highly motivated, advantaged students with few deficits in background and experience can frequently produce quality results. With skilled administrators and energetic and focused staff members, students from these schools measure up against all expectations that communities could have. Selective private schools and well-endowed suburban schools in affluent areas show these results.

Other schools are far different, and need extraordinary energy from all sources to produce modest gains. Schools in disadvantaged areas frequently admit children with problems in nutrition, health, socialization, and even in emotional stability. The background of deprivation has taken a toll on interest and outlook and all things of an educational nature, for day-to-day survival is the paramount consideration in the United States's underclass (Schorr, 1988; Garbarino et al., 1992; Kotlowitz, 1991). The comprehensive nurturing from community families, needed to engender children's self-esteem and a high self-concept or readiness, is often lacking. These schools need outstanding teachers and skilled administrators, but often get neither, as staff assignments are often determined by length of tenure. How can schools like this compete? The answer is that they cannot. Most will continue to struggle unless and until receiving massive investments of support and supplements from outside, and well-organized cooperative action with the community served. In Chapter 10, we identify productive models for school–community partnerships.

SUMMARY

In this chapter, we have discussed the dimensions of school curriculum, the philosophical orientations associated with curriculum, and the variation in practices and structure found in U.S. schools. Philosophical orientations differ from school to school and from teacher to teacher, and orientation makes a great difference about what content teachers consider for classrooms as well as how they approach skills instruction. The physical organization of a school also reflects its philosophical orientation.

Formal, informal, and hidden curricula exist in all types of schools. The results of school educative processes can be positive or negative, and all results have implications for the school and the school program, the surrounding community, and the families involved.

Schools are taken for granted in U.S. society, and parents send their children to schools expecting them to partake in productive activities. The public expects schools to provide reasonable care and safety for children, stimulation of minds and bodies, and skills and knowledge for participation in adult life. Most parents

feel that home cannot provide the requisite skills even young children require today, and they do not trust themselves to guide children's interests or monitor their progress.

In productive schools, irrespective of curriculum orientation, children will master basic literacy skills, interactive and social skills, general study habits, computational skills, social and natural science concepts, and the ability to experiment and to learn through investigations. All schools have a duty to meet these basic features of curriculum, although each may approach this duty differently. Schools showing minimal or incomplete results for these basic expectations cannot survive in the twenty-first century.

SUGGESTED ACTIVITIES AND QUESTIONS

1. Observe the classroom behaviors of the teacher in your field assignment and determine from things said, assignments given, and general demeanor which of the philosophical orientations that teacher holds.
2. Think back to your own school years and identify three things you learned that were never part of the school curriculum. Compare with one of your colleagues. Are your memories academic, work-related, or social in nature?
3. Take the grid presented in Table 7.2 and use it to assess teaching styles of your college instructors and high school teachers, other teachers you recall, and classroom teachers you are in contact with now. What percentage of the total falls in each quadrant?
4. Develop a profile of interests, habits, and skills on one child you are working with now or one you know well. Determine which curriculum orientation would suit her or him best. Defend your choice.
5. Interview several children to identify the informal curriculum they experience at school. You will have to start them off with suggestions about lining up or taking breaks, and so on. Try to determine yourself, or get them to tell you, where the expectations originated. Were these rules stated, picked up through others, inferred, or carried over from other years?

RECOMMENDED READINGS

Bennett, K. P., & LeCompte, M. D. (1990). *How schools work: A sociological analysis of education.* New York: Longman.

Dunn, K., & Frazier, E. R. (1990). *Teaching styles.* Reston, VA: National Association of Secondary School Principals.

Good, T. L., & Brophy, J. E. (1994). *Looking in classrooms* (6th ed.). New York: HarperCollins.

Neill, A. S. (1960). *Summerhill.* New York: Hart.

Pratt, D. (1994). *Curriculum planning: A handbook for professionals.* New York: Harcourt Brace Jovanovich.

Ross, D. D., Bondy, E., & Kyle, D. W. (1993). *Reflective teaching for student empowerment: Elementary curriculum and methods.* Englewood Cliffs, NJ: Merrill/Prentice Hall.

Silber, J. (1989). *Straight shooting: What's wrong with America and how to fix it.* New York: Harper & Row.

Stiggins, R. J. (in press). *Student-Centered Classroom Assessment* (2nd ed.). Englewood Cliffs, NJ: Merrill/Prentice Hall.

U.S. Department of Education. (1993). *Goals 2000: Educate America.* Washington, DC: Author.

Wells, S. E. (1990). *At risk youth: Identification, programs and recommendations.* Englewood, CO: Libraries Unlimited.

Curriculum of the Community

Special attention must be given to building schools that transcend traditional distinctions between learning in and out of school, between schooling as a traditional process limited in time and place to the institution of school, and education as a continual life process that occurs in a variety of community contexts.

(Haberman, 1992, p. 35)

T he purpose of this chapter is to examine the rich, but often overlooked, features of the community for children's learning. Just as we have a curriculum of the school and of the home, so too we have a curriculum of the community. In reading this chapter you will learn that:

1. Organizations and agencies within a community provide many and varied learning opportunities for children.

2. Some community education is purposeful and planned by members of community organizations and agencies.

3. Much of children's learning within the community results from their observations of how things work and how people function and from their interaction with materials and people.

4. The physical and emotional attributes of a community will either support and extend or will hinder children's opportunities.

5. Social networks, involving both adults and peers, will affect the amount and quality of learning children derive from their community.

Whether or not educators recognize other curricula, children's knowledge and understanding come from various sources. The community, an amorphous mass surrounding us all, is one of these sources. As in the school and family curricula examined in chapters 6 and 7, community curriculum is affected by the type, location, and physical makeup of the region and its inhabitants.

In Chapter 1, we discussed the many influences on children's learning. All curricula are affected by these influences. The community curriculum determines many learning opportunities affecting children. Some are deliberately planned, and some exist by the very nature of the community's organization. Although we find great differences in communities, we also find many commonalities that suggest similar educational experiences.

Various organizations within the community offer different aspects of curriculum, and children have opportunities for learning by being exposed to these organizations. In addition, the physical and emotional environments children encounter in their immediate neighborhoods enhance or hinder intellectual development. No curriculum exists in a vacuum. Each community is composed of interconnected social systems, and how the people of these systems relate to one another greatly affects children's learning and development (Bronfenbrenner, 1979; Lightfoot, 1978).

In this chapter, we examine the context of the wider community and its potential for helping children grow. We examine community organizational structure and suggest how some of the diverse agencies "educate" children. The physical and social-emotional environments in a community together constitute a basic support system for all families, one that enables parents and child care workers to stimulate children in different ways. However, the level of children's participation in community and the social networks children establish depend on the interaction of community agencies with families, and with schools.

COMMUNITY STRUCTURE AFFECTS CURRICULUM

Although every community varies in structure and in the kinds of services available to its citizens, we find many common natural, human, and material resources. Table 8.1 presents a partial listing of these resources. A child's neighborhood may be in a city, a small town, a suburb, or a rural area. The resources available in each setting will vary, but all form the bases for a community curriculum. Whether in a rural area or in a city, children observe different aspects of nature. Trees, birds, animals, and stars at night are more available to rural children, but city children witness the warmth of the sun, wetness of rain, scrubby grass and small plants pushing up between concrete slabs, and ants or other creatures carrying away crumbs from garbage. Southern children know palm trees, northern children deciduous or fir trees, and southwestern children juniper and cacti.

Children constantly learn from persons in their neighborhoods. How much learning children gain from others, besides kin in the home, depends on how much association they have, how safe the neighborhood is, and how many community services and agencies parents use. Children, as they move beyond their homes, observe and normally interact with people involved in, as well as going to and from, the various activities. How different people dress, what distinguishes young people from old, what they do to cross the street, how they treat each other and children in passing, and many other qualities and interactions teach children about life.

Children learn from various materials generated by people in society. Some materials, such as a brochure about good eating habits for primary children, are prepared with educational intentions. Toy companies attempt to attract adults to buy various items for their children, and often advertisements will tell of a device's educational value. Children also learn from many other materials, including those adults consider "junk." From observing, touching, smelling, and manipulating wood scraps, earth and sand, styrofoam, bottles, shells, cans, and the like, children learn variations in texture, size, shape, and smell. Without adult support the learning may be minimal, but even children left on their own gain information and ideas about materials around them.

Every community has service agencies, political establishments, social-cultural agencies, and business enterprises. Just as schools and homes provide their curricula, so do community establishments and agencies. The efforts, products, and resources of each agency all provide formal, informal, and hidden curricula, similar to the school environment.

Children acquire knowledge, values, and social skills (positive as well as negative) from their experiences within their communities. We will find, of course, no single established curriculum for a community, any more than we find a common curriculum for all families. Resources vary, and how and to whom these resources are made available, plus the family's and children's ability to make use of them, determine learning potential.

Service Agencies

Service agencies provide families with health, transportation, protection, communication, and

TABLE 8.1
Community Resources That Educate Children

---

1. Natural Resources

Plants, animals, insects, fish, seashells, minerals, woods, ponds, streams, beaches, parks, nature preserves, farmland

2. Services

Educational: Zoos, museums, libraries, schools, parks

Communication: Telephones, radio, television stations, post offices, newspaper offices, computer networks

Entertainment: Theaters, music halls, movies, fairs, festivals, circuses, restaurants, television and radio stations

Recreational: Playgrounds, church or community clubs with athletic facilities, ballparks, public tennis courts, golf courses, parks

Transportation: Airports, train stations, bus terminals, taxis, gas stations, rental agencies

Commercial: Department stores, grocery stores, pharmacies, different types of farms (orchards, fish farms, dairy farms), specialty shops (toy stores, ice cream parlors, beauticians, pet stores, craft shops, and so on), factories, business enterprises

Professional: Offices of doctors, dentists, lawyers, and other professionals, fire and police departments, funeral parlors, courts, clinics, hospitals, political offices, state or local departments of education, universities

Service Agencies: Employment offices, social services and public assistance offices, counseling services, food co-ops

Living environments: Children's and teachers' homes, houses, apartment complexes, mobile homes, new home sites, real estate offices, retirement communities, nursing homes

3. Materials (available from most listed services)

Printed: Books, pamphlets, brochures, magazines, newspapers, advertisements

Audiovisual: Films, television, radio, audio- and videotapes, slide-tape shows, computer programs, exhibits, models

Collections of Recyclables: Scraps of fabric, carpet samples, wood scraps, buttons, ribbon, wallpaper samples, bottles, cans, boxes, wire, spools, paper scraps, large cartons

4. Social Networks

Adult: Friends, neighbors, colleagues and coworkers, social clubs, religious groups, sports groups, community theater

Peer: Young relatives, school and neighborhood friends, club and team partners

---

professional services. These agencies provide experiences from which children gain knowledge, both through the formal presentation of materials and in informal ways. Formal educational experiences from some agencies have been carefully thought through. Some prepared materials are directed towards parents or teachers to assist children in their instruction. Other materials or experiences are directed toward children. Children's first experience with the family dentist is one example of a community professional "educating" young clients.

Since Rodriquo was 3 years old, he accompanied his mother to the dentist for her semiannual checkup. While his mother was in the chair, he would sit in a nearby chair with a book and a toy. One day Dr. Garcelon asked him if he wouldn't like to sit up in the big chair where his mother had sat. As Rodriquo climbed up, the dentist allowed him to touch the instruments and told him what they were for. He encouraged him to press the water tap and to rinse out his mouth from the paper cup nearby. Gradually, over two or three visits, he introduced all the "cleaning" instruments and even turned on the polishing brush so Rodriquo could see how it vibrated. At first, Rodriquo refused to have the brush in his mouth, but gradually he became so intrigued with the instruments that he wanted to see what would happen. One day a small squirrel came to the dentist's window and chattered away. Dr. Garcelon and the young child took a moment to feed the squirrel, before the dentist gave Rodriquo a toothbrush and tube of toothpaste with verbal and written "picture" instructions on how to use the brush at home.

This dentist had a planned program for introducing dental hygiene to young patients. At first children observed parents' experiences—a rather informal learning experience. Parental comfort and the dentist's reassuring ways provided a safe and secure environment for the next phase. The formal instruction of what happens in a dentist's chair was designed to build children's trust, as well as to start them on the road to good dental hygiene. The pamphlet Rodriquo received had simple instructions with pictures so that even at age 4 he could see "how to brush his teeth." The squirrel was an accidental event, and Rodriquo observed an animal close up, discovered something about feeding animals, and experienced an adult's gentle treatment of the creature.

Just as teachers and homes vary in how they instruct children, so also do people in various agen-

cies and professions. Some dentists are not as thorough as Dr. Garcelon, giving information to parents whom they expect to instruct children. Many dentists work with schools and day care centers, and it is through schools that material and curriculum for dental hygiene are provided. Many physicians and dentists have instructional materials and toys in their waiting rooms, although their main purpose often is to ease the waiting period.

Most community agencies provide materials schools and parents can use to help children understand the purposes and functions of the agencies. Police and fire departments, for example, normally provide speakers for schools or encourage field trips to their stations. Some police officers and firefighters get special training in how to work with young children and children who visit are allowed to climb, under supervision, on fire trucks or into police cars. Representatives wear their uniforms, and explain the equipment they carry and use. They also explain what children are to do when a police officer or firefighter is trying to assist them.

Service personnel are trained in how to work with children, and children are permitted to explore vehicles and equipment.

Transportation Services

Transportation agencies provide learning experiences for children, and it is not uncommon to witness a group of children trooping through a bus terminal, airport, or train station, the bus, airline, and railroad companies collaborating with schools to provide a formal learning experience. Usually a company employee accompanies the class and informs children about the various services within the terminals. In some instances children get to board a train or plane and visit the engineer's or pilot's station. Not all children on regular plane flights get an opportunity to visit the cockpit, but on some flights with a long wait before departure, children are invited into the cockpit for a lesson on "what a pilot does." In addition to "formal" lessons, many unexpected events happen in transportation terminals that convey important messages to children. Teachers and agency personnel may capitalize on these events because of children's interest, as did Dr. Garcelon with the squirrel. The hidden or unknown curriculum emerges as children witness events around them and absorb different messages depending on their own prior experience. A guard running a metal detector over a passenger at the airport security checkpoint affects children differently. An astute guide might stop and explain what is happening, perhaps reassuring a child who has witnessed a neighbor being frisked by police. Without an explanation, the same child may reaffirm a fear of uniformed authorities.

Political Agencies

All communities have government agencies, school boards, and task forces or committees empaneled by the community government to provide different types of community curricula. The management decisions these agencies make will affect—directly and indirectly—the social, intellectual, and physical development of children in that community. As with social agencies, political agencies often provide written materials, films, or audiotapes designed to educate the public about their functions or about the community. Such agencies make use of newspapers, magazine articles, radio, and television to carry their messages to the public, and the assumption is that families and schools will then "educate" children.

In some communities the formal curriculum is more apparent, especially during election years, and is usually handled through the schools. Mock elections are held in some schools, using locally collected political campaign materials. Students sometimes visit local and state political offices, where teachers and political workers attempt to explain the functions and responsibilities of the resident officials. Children whose parents are active politically may begin to comprehend "how the system works." However, the political implications of messages are usually beyond the comprehension of primary-age children. Children whose parents use social services managed by political officials can acquire confusing notions of how the system works, especially when their parents have difficulty obtaining services. The political knowledge that children gain from such experiences tends to be serendipitous.

In the United States, we have no national policy that supports children and families, thus families benefit from such community resources only in relationship to the personal networks they establish within the community (Pardeck, 1990). Social policies, established by community leaders, affect the options that any family has in establishing networks and making use of available resources (Cochran & Riley, 1990). For instance, people living in wealthier communities often are able to negotiate with political figures for funding for well-equipped and -maintained parks or recreational areas. They see that libraries and museums have appropriate materials and outreach programs. Citizens in affluent areas have better access to child care support services, community-based activities, and protective and health services. Children reared in poor communities are often discriminated against and have fewer opportunities for learning. Parents in these neighborhoods appear to have less clout with governmental and management agencies, and they have to work harder to access fully the benefits of community learning. The following vignette illustrates different potentials for social, intellectual, and physical learning due to two different policies for park maintenance.

....

In Wexton, the recreation department has provided a park with grassy areas and paths. There are a few swings, one piece of climbing equipment, and a basketball court. Maintenance of the park is poor. Swings are always in disrepair; garbage and debris litter the ground. Parents, bringing children to the area, will briefly exchange a smile or a word with the everpresent "bag man," and occasionally with adults rushing through on their way to work or with those bringing dogs for an outing. Parents appear to use the park for children to have an outing, but display little sense of coming here to meet other people. Parents are likely to discourage their children from interacting with others in the park.

In Overton, situated near a small shopping area, the community has provided a small park, with lots of climbing equipment, paths for tricycles, a basketball court, bicycle paths leading off into an open grove area, and benches where parents sit and supervise their children's play. The park is well maintained, with little debris. Paths are well cared for, as is all equipment. Park maintenance people are seen frequently cleaning up the area and have been known to remind the older, often unsupervised, children to "watch out" for others as they play. In this park, parents chat with each other, watch their children interact with one another, and often begin to develop friendships. There is a sense of bringing children for outings, but one that expands parental contacts with others in the neighborhood.

....

Children in these situations will learn many things in both parks, but the park in Overton has greater potential for positive learning opportunities, where more people, material, and natural resources exist. In both parks, one observes children gaining physical skills, as they climb on equipment or play ball. Children use various strategies to engage other children in their play, and some appear to be skilled in interacting with other adults as they crouch to pet a visitor's dog. However, there are differences.

Safe and well-maintained parks provide opportunities for physical and other skills development.

In Wexton, there are fewer chances for personal interactions, since most parents discourage such interchanges, especially with "disreputable looking characters." Maintenance is poor, so children receive different messages about the value of a clean environment. Some adults, passing through the park, are seen picking up paper trash and throwing it in available receptacles, but children witness other adults carelessly dropping litter. More potentially dangerous spots exist in Wexton, and children learn to be chary of their environment and aware of the danger signals.

In Overton, a different learning potential exists. Safe paths for children riding bicycles and tricycles from their homes to the park provide more opportunities for expanded physical development. Adults feel more comfortable with each other. The ambiance is welcoming and the sense of trust among adults provides a stronger sense of trust in children. The park is kept free of debris, and maintenance personnel do not hesitate to remind children about respect for their environment and for each other. On the other hand, opportunities for learning danger signals may be more limited.

The community policy of providing and maintaining a park varies in these two communities. These policies are management choices, and affect children's learning opportunities. Certainly adults' abilities to use the resources available in the parks either enhance or limit what is learned in both situations.

It is not just with parks that communities provide options for adults to develop the social networks that enable them to use their community more advantageously. Governmental policy is inextricably interwoven with a community's social fabric. In some communities, policies regarding social service agencies make it much easier for adults to get the services they need.

Darlene, a shy person, had moved to a new community with her new baby and 4-year-old son. She needed help, but dreaded to apply for food stamps at the Women, Infants, and Children (WIC) program because of unpleasant experiences she had had when seeking welfare in her previous community. However, when in desperation she finally went, she was pleasantly surprised at the quality of support. A community health organization had pressured the mayor's office into allowing food stamps to be distributed at their well baby clinic. Also, a group of volunteers had begun a program of reading and talking to and playing with the babies and older children at the clinic while the parents waited for their appointments or discussed with the nurses the health and nutritional needs of their children. Darlene and the nurse discussed ways to entice children into good eating habits, and during her first visit, one of the volunteers invited her to attend a parent support group for mothers with new babies. At these meetings she gained new confidence in herself and new skills in raising her children.

Political decisions can affect the community curriculum presented to children. Not only is Darlene gaining help in feeding her children, but also she is learning to educate them about good eating habits. As a more subtle message, parents here are exposed to models of adults reading to and interacting with children, and thus may in turn provide expanded language experiences and positive social interactions for their own offspring.

Social and Cultural Agencies

The more skilled parents become at securing community services, the more opportunities they have to use other community resources, as illustrated in the following vignette.

Louisa's husband abandoned her and their two small children after they moved to a new state. There was little money and no extended family support. Louisa swallowed her pride and went to a church soup kitchen so she and her children could have one nutritious meal a day. A series of contacts with people at the center led her to the social agencies in her community, where she learned how to use resources for the welfare of herself and her children. It wasn't always easy, for some of the policies seemed to hinder Louisa's progress. The support systems she began to establish for herself, however, enabled her to continue. Louisa eventually was able to finish high school and find a part-time job. She presently has a federally funded scholarship to college. In the process, she expanded her network of friends in the service areas so she could use community programs to enrich her children's experiences, of which library and museum programs and a two-week summer recreational program were recent highlights.

Churches, libraries, theaters, and sport and recreational facilities are community agencies that supplement children's education. As with all situations, some children experience a richer curriculum than others. How well families are able to use available resources and how well agencies are able to reach all families in the community account for some of the disparity. These social and cultural agencies do not exist apart from one another, as the vignette illustrates. A church agency, providing physical and social nurturance, helped Louisa work through the governmental policies, which in turn helped her find other community resources for her children.

Governmental policies, concerned with separation of church and state, can limit the resources that a church provides a community. Church leaders, concerned with developing memberships, often wish to provide religious activities for young people within schools, but community policies normally exclude such events.

Librarians, theater personnel, and museum directors often try to develop programs with schools whereby children are invited to cultural offerings in their centers. But too often communities will not financially support such programs, or will believe that children are missing "schoolwork" so must not be permitted to go. Those children whose parents have financial and social capital are able to profit by such community curriculum offerings, while other children are left out. Some cultural agencies locate financial resources other than political agencies to help community programs expand their curriculum to include more children and families. In one community, when schools eliminated art programs due to cutbacks in funding, the local artists' association extended art lessons to all children in the community with help from a local community foundation.

Many social and cultural agencies provide a rich formal curriculum to children. Such settings have a strong impact on children's information-processing skills, as well as on physical, emotional, and moral development (Koran, Longino, & Shafer, 1983; Grumbine, 1988; Miles, 1986–1987).

Art museums offer both art instruction and art appreciation. Science museums and zoos often have formal presentations for young children. National and state parks have various educational programs that emphasize education both relating to the park theme and to conservation and environmental protection (Jacobson & Padua, 1992). Often theaters have acting lessons, summer camp experiences, children's performances, and lectures about plays and playwrights. Most libraries have educational lectures, storytelling events, and book talks. Hurst (1993) describes a library program in which she uses poetry to enhance knowledge and feelings about the weather. She extends the language of poems by having children use computer graphics to create the effects of storms. The theme expands as children use reference books to find facts about storms and storybooks for descriptions of storms. Children who participate in these literacy events expand their language, reading, writing, and computer skills, as well as personal interaction skills and knowledge about where to find information.

Churches offer religious education classes, and many of these classes integrate art, drama, and music as a part of the instruction. Recreational facilities offer instruction in different sports such as gymnastics, basketball, golf, or archery as well as health-related classes such as aerobics, nutrition, and physical fitness.

As with curriculum in any context, children acquire a great deal of knowledge through the informal and hidden curricula of these social and cultural agencies. For example, several church leaders provided a curriculum that went well beyond teaching the beliefs of that religious group to involve parts of the informal curriculum.

The instructors of a Sunday school class decided to make the Biblical story of Joshua and Jericho come alive for their 8-year-olds. As in a school curriculum, their activity focused on writing, creating, memorizing parts, and cooperating as children wrote a play, designed costumes and props, learned their parts, and supported each other in a final production. At the end of the performance, children passed a collection plate, imitating the adults in church. This included keeping an eye on their partners and nodding to each other before moving to the next row. It was apparent that children were learning the rituals of that congregation in following the collection procedures.

As in any curriculum, some learning is unintended and may be considered undesirable by the teachers. For example, at the reception after the performance, special bonbons were placed on a dish and one portly gentleman took five pieces. Travis, following suit, took five as well, but his mother reprimanded him, saying, "Think of others and take only one." Travis got mixed messages, perhaps one he resents: both he and the portly gentleman were rude, but only children are expected to be thoughtful.

Other social-cultural agencies also present formal and informal curricula through classes they offer and by the materials and facilities available to children. For example, posters announcing coming events and programs inform adults, but in indirect ways inform children as well.

In a local theater, while awaiting a performance, a 5-year-old observed an adult commenting and pointing to an announcement of the next play. "Oh, look, Bill Braunhof will be playing in Cats! I wonder what the dates are?" Running her finger under the date she exclaimed, "Oh, too bad, it's Wednesday the 22nd and we won't be here."

With no intent of teaching young children, theater personnel have provided materials which can and do instruct. The adult, in seeking information for herself, unwittingly demonstrated to the child that such a poster offers information and that pieces of that information are found in different places on the poster. The child may even have discovered that "C-a-t-s" spells *cats*, and recognized it when seeing it again, or that "22" means twenty-second.

Sometimes such informal teaching is intentional. In Overton, the community librarian discovered that children would pick up, look at, and often take home those books that were displayed attractively. He began to more carefully select for display outstanding books that had heretofore sat unused on the shelves. The quality of books selected by young readers took a quantum leap. He then began to coordinate his efforts with units of study done by local teachers. The teachers were pleased to find children bringing into class these extra resources from the local library for current topics.

Community clubs are another means of educating children. Scout organizations, trail clubs, outing clubs, ski and skimobile clubs, and so on often have projects in which students participate. Some take trips into the community and surrounding areas, where children cook outdoors, practice trail maintenance, observe different natural phenomena, and learn lessons in "getting along with others." Some lessons are intentional and some are unexpected. On one such trip, three 8-year-old boys came upon a family of skunks in a meadow. Wondering what the skunks would do if startled, the children gently tossed some pebbles toward the nest. To the boys' and the other campers' dismay, they learned how startled skunks respond.

Business and Commercial Enterprises

All communities have business and commercial enterprises. These establishments have identifying marks to advertise what they sell or what service they perform. Intentionally and unintentionally, adults and older children help younger ones sort out information regarding such businesses. You need only to walk down a street in any community and observe carefully what the buildings look like, the signs in and about the community, types of vehicles along the street, and displays in the windows to get a feeling for what children learning about their world must sort out.

Children hear comments from adults, note certain identifying characteristics of the buildings, and learn without specific instruction where to buy ice cream, get stamps, find interesting books, or buy a desired toy. Children begin to recognize similar and different shapes. The stop sign is always red and octagonal. Children may question why their parents are stopping, or may even figure out from adult conversations what *stop* means.

Business enterprises distribute advertising circulars as well as put signs in shop windows. Such materials provide information about prices and kinds of items a store sells. Window signs may also give information about events in the community. Children who become adept in using such resources acquire many skills about how to get information. They may also become skilled in using adults as resources for achieving certain purposes. Like other curricula, how and what children learn depend on many factors, including the kind of community in which they live, their developmen-

tal stage, and how significant adults share such information with them.

Parents, of course, are major influences and how much parents talk and interact with their children as they are involved in the community influences children's learning. However, sometimes an important community person compensates for parental neglect or disinterest. Comer (1988) tells about a shopkeeper in his community who taught a child, whom everyone believed couldn't speak, to talk. The shop was a candy store and the child would only point to candy when he entered the shop. By refusing to acknowledge the child pointing out candy, the owner gradually got the child to tell her what he wanted, and then eventually to talk to her.

Media

Extensive learning opportunities for children are offered through various forms of media. Some children's learning takes place serendipitously, but adults extend and enhance it. We have a number of educational television and radio programs for young children. The Public Broadcasting System (PBS) has for years provided educational programs, such as *Sesame Street, The Electric Company,* and *Mr. Rogers' Neighborhood,* which in spirited ways introduce children to the alphabet, to new words and concepts, and to interesting stories and facts about everyday events. Early research on *Sesame Street* and *The Electric Company* indicated that children watching such programs were learning the alphabet, numbers, and vocabulary faster than children not exposed (Ball & Bogatz, 1970; Bogatz & Ball, 1971; Rice, Huston, Truglio, & Wright, 1990). Subsequent analysis of *Sesame Street* indicated, however, that rather than being a boon to disadvantaged children, middle-class children were more likely to watch the show, and the gains children maintained were dependent on adult reinforcement of concepts (Cook et al., 1975). Some learning from these programs may have an unintentional and perhaps undesirable effect. Children become accustomed to fast-paced materials and do not develop longer attention spans or ability to sustain interest in events that aren't moving rapidly. On both educational and commercial radio and television stations, science and social studies programs, story reading, and reenactments of children's literature offer rich educational opportunities. In addition, network educational offices often provide teacher or parent guides for assisting children in gaining more from these programs.

Printed materials in the form of books, pamphlets, magazines, and newspapers also educate children through pictures and printed words. Printed language is different from oral language. Oral language and life experiences assist children in learning to read, but printed materials to which they are exposed also facilitate intellectual growth. For example, when reading Parnall's *Apple Tree*, children's knowledge and concepts expand as they view an artist's interpretation and hear language describing the different ways the

familiar features of apple trees are used. Children have experienced apples, if not apple trees, but may never have realized that ants and bugs feed from the trees, as do birds, who feed on the bugs.

Children grow emotionally and intellectually when they can find, through books, security in loving and being loved, even while learning academic content. In Bang's *Ten, Nine, Eight*, a loving father hugs and tucks in his child as the two count objects in the room. Such a book conveys many, and different, messages to children, besides the knowledge of rational counting. One child may be reaffirmed in his understanding of a caring parent, while another child may realize males as well as females can be nurturing. An Anglo child sees that African American children do things just like she does. Feelings of security come as children see that book characters like themselves can be angry, frightened, frustrated, hateful, sad, or lonely. Models for resolving conflict, as well as lessons, can be learned. In Zolo-

Some television programs offer rich educational opportunities for children.

tow's *The Hating Book*, children learn how misunderstandings come about when one listens to gossip and doesn't trust a friend.

Most newspapers have a special children's section, and some offer guidance on how to use the newspaper with children. Comics have always been a source for nudging children towards reading. Comer (1988) tells how his mother always read the comics from three different newspapers to her children each Sunday. This undereducated mother instinctively realized the importance of rereading the parts that especially interested each child and how this would assist them in learning to read.

Not all influence from printed materials is necessarily positive from an adult point of view. The excitement of Max chasing his dog with a fork in Sendak's *Where the Wild Things Are* may be so attractive that a mother of a 4-year-old finds her child imitating the action with another child. Stories and other printed materials, as with television programs, also can reinforce prejudice and bias when characters of different ethnic origin are interpreted as having "the characteristics" of a certain cultural group. Fairytales have been cited as reinforcing male and female stereotypes. It is possible to interpret such female characters as Cinderella, Snow White, and Rapunzel as passive women in need of rescue by active and handsome Prince Charmings. Many comic strips portray stereotyped characters and advocate violence for solving problems. Television and computer games have also been criticized for their violence.

When stories, other printed materials, television, and computer programs are not comprehensible or not within children's range of experience, then, without support from an adult, the influence may be harmful to children's self-concept, and to emotional, social, or intellectual development. Cornell (1993) maintains that this may be especially true for children coming from particular cultural heritages. For example, many European tales present witches as old, ugly, mean, and to be feared, but in Asian cultures the old are wise, kind, and to be revered. The clash of cultures may be confusing, especially to new immigrants, and can deter their understanding of and adaptation to their new country.

Not all books and printed materials are well written, and the language in some is stilted and uninteresting. Well-written materials are appropriate and have integrity, whereas poorly written books have "flagrant repetitiveness, stiff dialogue, a gross exaggeration of humor or fantasy, conflict between realism and fantasy, didacticism, superciliousness, or a use of language that is poorly chosen for the genre of the book or for the characters in it" (Sutherland & Arbuthnot, 1991, pp. 49–50). Children acquire language and richness of expression from books. Hackneyed, mundane expressions do nothing to enrich children's vocabulary or imagination.

A rich curriculum provided through printed materials requires adults (1) to be sensitive to children's acceptance or confusion about these materials and (2) to help them interpret printed matter in light of their own experiences.

The media also has an intentional curriculum that seeks to educate children through advertisements. Some altruistic advertisements are aimed at drug or sex education, but most are directed at enticing children to be consumers. The media also has its informal and hidden curricula. Much of television and radio programming is for adult consumption, but many children are exposed to programs that confuse, frighten, or misinform them when there is little or no adult guidance. Chapter 1 contains a more detailed discussion of media influence on children and illustrates the importance of adult intervention.

PHYSICAL, SOCIAL, AND EMOTIONAL ENVIRONMENTS IN A COMMUNITY

The physical and social-emotional environments in a community where children live provide a curriculum that both positively and negatively affects children's development. Children's chances of becoming confident and competent adults are greater when they have both a safe home environment and a safe neighborhood where they are able to play, explore, and form relationships (Garbarino et al., 1992). Unfortunately, today many children are exposed to dangers both within family situations and in their communities. When too many risk factors exist, children's emergent intellectual capacity and ability to benefit from environmental curriculum are hampered (Sameroff et al., 1987).

Social Networks

Children's ability to benefit from their neighborhood is influenced extensively by the social networks their parents have established. As children mature, they develop additional social networks within their peer groups. In earlier generations, families tended to be stable, and community members formed bonds that enabled them to look after each other's children and to some degree control children's peer groups. Today, communities tend to step in only when parents truly fail to support their children, and most parents have less control over their children's friendships. Yet, nowadays children and their families need community support more than ever, due to dual-income families, single parents, and greater mobility (Kagan, 1994).

Adults

In today's society, adults are likely to move often during children's growing years, and chil-

Children's chances of becoming confident and competent adults are greater when they have a safe neighborhood where they are able to play.

dren's development is affected by adults' ability to adapt to change. Some parents establish new relationships easily, thus helping their children profit by participating in neighborhood activities.

The ambiance of a particular neighborhood may be welcoming or may be threatening, making it easier or more risky to initiate social contact. For example, in one part of Eastern City homes, streets, and sidewalks are well maintained. One residential street is a dead-end street with little traffic, so residents sit outside on doorsteps and watch their children play close to the street. Families moving into this community feel secure in reaching out to others. Children come to know the adults in the neighborhood easily and are able to interact with them.

In another part of Eastern City, broken bottles litter sidewalks, poorly maintained buildings restrict families from venturing out, and illegal activities are common. Adults and neighborhood gangs are in such conflict with each other that children are unsafe, even in their own homes. The street violence causes such trauma for families

that children have difficulty learning anything positive from any community source.

Rural and suburban neighborhoods also vary in providing physical and mental safety for inhabitants, thus influencing learning. Poverty is perhaps the greatest deficit, as it limits families in making the diverse social ties that enable children to participate in a neighborhood's growth opportunities (Cochran, 1990). When children are able to move comfortably throughout their neighborhoods, socialization becomes more available and children benefit.

....

Janice and Peter lived on the same street in look-alike houses in a large suburban neighborhood. Although the yards were all fenced, children felt free to visit from one house to the other, stopping to watch and ask endless questions of kindly neighbors. One day Janice and Peter roamed and stopped to watch while one neighbor trimmed roses in the front yard and another washed his car. They even got to spray some water on the soapy

Parents who participate in neighborhood activities help children develop important social networks.

car, getting a bit wet themselves. After a while they wandered onto a nice muddy area in another neighbor's backyard. Making a few mud balls, they proceeded to toss the balls at the neighbor's garage. When Janice's mother caught up with them, she obtained buckets and water from the neighbors and insisted that the children clean up the mess they had made. With help from some of the older neighbor children, Janice and Peter managed to get the garage quite clean.

....

That day, among other lessons, Janice and Peter learned a bit about the why and how of gardening, how cars are cleaned, and what makes water spray. They may also have increased their throwing skills, while discovering that they would be held responsible for any mess they created. They learned about helping others when they received help from the older children. Of course, children's everyday lessons from the neighborhood are not always the ones adults might wish. Still, Cochran and Riley (1990) point out when children have more adults and older children with whom they do a variety of activities, they tend to do better in school. Children who have caring adults beyond family members to assist them in mastering skills and attitudes in a gradual way have greater metacognitive and problem-solving strategies.

Children learn how to cope with their environment differently depending on their circumstances, as the following vignette demonstrates.

....

By November, 4-year-old Tobias was able to go without his parents to the Head Start center down the street from his apartment. He had been to that building many times and knew just how to maneuver through the street. One day he noticed a folded dollar bill lying in the gutter. He picked it up and then proceeded down the street to the Mom and Pop store on the corner. He went directly to the aisle for cookies and found some of his favorite, which he took to the counter. Handing Mrs. Jameson the dollar, he asked, "Is this enough money?"

"Yes, and you'll get some change," she replied, then added, "Is this what your mom wanted you to buy?"

"She don't care. I found this dollar in the street." And with his cookies and change, Tobias hurried off to Head Start.

In Vermont, 4-year-old Clara also went to Head Start, but her mother took her every day, for they lived in the country and her mother didn't want her to walk the road to the church alone, although they had been there many times. One day Clara's mother was ill and Clara decided to go to Head Start by herself. She started down the road, but soon got lost. A neighbor, driving by, noticed Clara alone and stopped to pick her up. When she explained what she was doing, the neighbor said, "But, Clara, you are going in the wrong direction. I'll take you home and then to Head Start, if your mother would like."

....

Both children have been exposed to their community environment and both children have other supportive community adults who assist them. But Tobias is much more streetwise and able to maneuver than is Clara. Clara has always had the support of an adult and has never ventured down the road alone. Not all children have such extended support, and many could have unfortunate experiences in either of the above situations. Tobias might be able to negotiate problems more successfully than Clara, depending on the circumstances, and he is probably more alert than she to danger signs. In some ways, Tobias has had more opportunities to learn from his community and has become more independent. Kumove (1966) found that when children under age 7 were able to move more freely in their immediate environment, they became more independent than children whose parents found it necessary to keep them homebound.

Peer Groups

Tobias, in the preceding vignette, moves somewhat freely about his neighborhood. Even at his young age, he demonstrates knowledge of the social mores of his society. He knows where to find cookies and that he must pay for them, and feels comfortable interacting with the adults in the shop. Some of this learning is through observation and some through the impact of adult teaching. Tobias already shows considerable independence, and friends in the neighborhood will affect his learning more and more. Peers become strong socializing agents, and it is from them that children learn more about who they are and how they fit into society. Parents teach children moral and ethical values, but the peer group is powerful in setting the social tone and imposing behavioral patterns.

Even as young as 18 months children learn how their actions affect others, and thus begin the process of learning behavioral codes (Hartup, 1983). A toddler who tries to take a desired toy away from another child soon learns the consequences of the behavior. It may be an indignant yell; it may be a slap; it may be acquiescence and subsequent loss of a playmate. As children begin to form peer groups and play with each other, they begin to form rules of conduct so that they can continue to operate as a group. It is in peer groups that children learn to negotiate, problem solve, and compromise in order to continue to play and work together. Some children will be more dominant than others, and will learn the rules for domination and acquiescence. Children are rewarded by significant others in the group for conforming or they are ostracized (Elkin & Handel, 1989).

Children experiment with various roles (leader, compromiser, follower, negotiator, etc.) and discover from their peers how to act to fulfill roles, as well as how their peers respond to them. Children learn about their own abilities from their peers. They learn if they can run faster, jump higher, or read better as they compare their skills with others. But the group also dictates what skills are prized.

Although parents teach children about gender roles, by preschool, peers begin to segregate into boy and girl groups that dictate what roles each group is permitted to play. A physician's daughter, after beginning preschool, insisted that her doctor mother was really a nurse. At school she learned in her play group that doctors are boys and nurses are girls, even though her teacher and parents insisted differently. In addition, children learn cultural and social differences as they interact with their peers. They compare notes about their own family's customs, values, and ways of doing things. Peer group acceptance or rejection can influence how individual children change their own behaviors.

Sexual understandings and misunderstandings are learned from peers. Many young children learn the physical difference of boys and girls by examining each other. They often learn about birth when some "wiser" child informs them of their knowledge or misunderstanding. It is through such discussions, along with other teachings, that children figure out for themselves the confusing information they receive.

Cognitive information and development of numerous skills come from children's interactions with peers. Children have rituals and routines, just as adults do. Older peers teach to younger ones the chants and rhymes of childhood. Memory skills and counting as well as physical endurance are enhanced as children jump rope to such rhymes as "One Potato, Two Potato," or "First Comes Love, Then Comes Marriage." As they play together, children learn from more skilled peers how to climb higher, catch a ball, read a story, or add up their money for ice cream. Learning may result because of a desire to compete with a peer, or because the peer has more information and passes it on. Learning may also come because a new idea has been introduced and children need to test out the new concept.

....

Billy was watching Ahmed copy words from a book he was reading. "Whatcha doing?" asked Billy.

Children learn numerous skills
from interaction with peers.

"I'm making an 'r' for 'red'," replied Ahmed.

*"Nunh, nunh, that's not an 'R'. I'll show you
how to make an 'R'." Billy wrote a capital R.*

*Ahmed retorted, "Oh! That's a big 'R', and I'm
making a little 'r'!" After much discussion, Ahmed
in disgust turned to his book. "Look," he pointed,
"that says 'Red' and that says 'red.' See, that's a big
'R' and that's a little 'r'."*

Ahmed has challenged Billy's thinking about
r's. He now will have to examine writing in a new
way. New learning has been opened up to him by
a friend. Ahmed's scorn for his not knowing
seemed to spur Billy on, for later he got a book
and paper and came to sit beside Ahmed and
tried to make the "little 'r'," asking his friend for
help.

Not all learning from peer groups is positive.
Gangs can be a destructive force in any society, as
children seek approval and find that they must develop antisocial codes of behaviors to be accepted.
When a community provides opportunities for
children to develop social networks among different adult and peer groups, then children have
more options. When this happens, the lure of de-

structive peer groups is lessened and children are
helped to find more positive peer associations.

Natural Environments

As children move about their neighborhood, the
outdoor environment offers a rich curriculum
from which they gain understanding about their
world. This curriculum is, of course, all of nature.
Learning differs depending on the combination of
children's ability, social interactions regarding the
environment, and children's freedom of movement to explore. Louv (1990) discovered that
many U.S. children spend very little time outdoors. Although they do learn about nature in various ways, their understanding and appreciation
of nature are limited.

Studies on children's play activity indicate that
the quality of children's outdoor and indoor play
differs, and thus different learning opportunities
emerge. Children engage in more dramatic and
constructive play outdoors (Moore, 1985) and in
more exploratory play (Anderson, 1972; Wagner,
1995) where they feel, touch, examine, crunch,
and test materials, such as when learning the
sounds different rocks make when dropped into
the water. Children may climb indoors, but view-

ing the world from a tree branch gives them broader perspectives. "Twigs, soil, mud, stones, leaves, and grass are materials of sensory pleasure, play, and learning" (Dighe, 1993, p. 58).

Good children's books capture the many wonders of nature and can extend children's appreciation of what they experience, but without experiencing the reality of the world, their knowledge is limited.

Davon lived all his 5 years in Florida. He had read lots about snow and was especially fond of Ezra Jack Keat's The Snowy Day, *but had never seen real snow. While visiting his cousin in Boston one winter, he awoke to white flakes outside his window. He had never imagined snow to look like that. As the week wore on and more snow fell, Davon learned much more about the feel of* *snow on his face, and the taste of snow as he and his cousin held out their tongues to catch it. He learned how snow could limit and enhance activity and how it felt to walk through drifts.*

INTERACTIONS AMONG COMMUNITY AGENCIES, FAMILIES, AND SCHOOLS

The learning that took place in the vignettes in this chapter did not happen in isolation within these communities, for the community curriculum was affected by how the families and schools linked children to community resources and agencies (Figure 8.1). Stronger links heighten the potential for children's learning.

FIGURE 8.1
Community impact on children through the environment and from interactions among agencies.

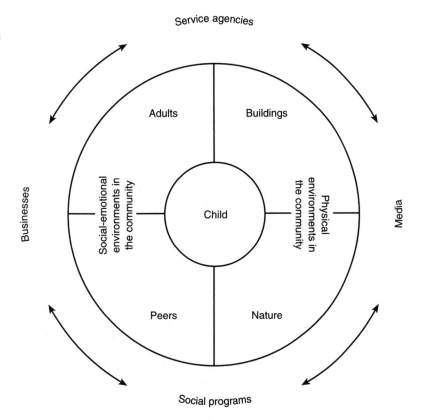

Many community agencies welcome children's visits, either with their families or with schools. Some agencies actively attempt to reach families of differing cultural and economic backgrounds. Other agencies limit their support to those families who can afford their services, or to those families who reach out. Louisa, in the vignette, was able to use more community resources because church members aggressively presented programs to assist her in her dilemma. As she became more confident of her ability to help her children, she more actively sought those recreational programs that provided richer learning experiences.

All families at some time use the business enterprises of a community. In today's society many families patronize large impersonal organizations for purchases, banking, and communicating, and the education that children receive is more limited than what happens in a small neighborhood. The Mom and Pop store in Tobias's neighborhood was used by his parents, so that Tobias felt comfortable in entering the store and asking for information. "Mom" knew the child well enough to check on him and offer advice. Clara, on the other hand, had more limited neighborhood resources, but her parents had developed connections with some neighbors. Clara was lucky that someone found her and helped her.

Many community agencies that offer programs to children depend on family or Big Brother/Sister–type support. A Scout-sponsored camping trip, for example, may include one or both parents or another adult accompanying children. Trail blazing and fire building lessons may be a planned part of the trip, but how the learning is extended depends on parental involvement with the organization. Some churches have family nights where leaders invite entire families to be involved in extended learning situations.

Communities and schools can collaborate to provide concrete experiences to extend children's learning, but this is not done as much as is possible. Trips into the community are enriched when the agencies have materials, people, and specific

events appropriate for the learning level of children visiting. When teachers make visits and discuss the trip with community agencies beforehand, learning is more likely to be enhanced. Unfortunately, some school trips within a community are not done collaboratively, and children's learning is limited, and may even be negative.

One child care center decided to make a trip to McDonald's without checking with the establishment. It was noon, and McDonald's was crowded. Children, when let off the bus, ran to the play area and began to play noisily. Teachers' attempts to find a place for children to eat together and to give them experience in selecting and ordering food were disastrous. The bus driver had gone, and the harassed teachers had to corral the children in the play area until he returned. The children finally received their food, but the bus arrived and the teachers had to hurry everyone on the bus, carrying uneaten food with them. The children, the teachers, and McDonald's personnel were all unhappy with the experience.

Many restaurants welcome children's visits and provide opportunities for them to visit the kitchen and to experience ordering and eating food in a relaxed manner. Lack of planning with the establishment in the above episode resulted in an unpleasant experience for both adults and children. It would be wrong to assume that no learning took place from this trip; however, with more care, the trip could have been more valuable and pleasant for everyone.

In community programs, where children interact with materials, observe events, or see animals acting in a natural situation, children usually learn more than in programs where adults lecture, expecting children to be enraptured with what they say. The community, through natural phenomena and by the nature of its organization, offers a rich curriculum for all children. Children learn from this curriculum in direct relationship to the social networks available to them.

....

Eve was on her way to Africa to visit her son and his family. In the local airport, Mrs. Thomas, a third-grade teacher, and an airline representative approached her and introduced themselves and Wrinkle. Mrs. Thomas, in collaboration with the airline, had devised a plan to enrich her children's knowledge of the world through Wrinkle. Wrinkle is a stuffed dog, and he has a notebook, in which his experiences can be noted. Mrs. Thomas wondered if Eve would be willing to take Wrinkle with her to Africa and keep Wrinkle's diary. When she was to return from her travels, the airline had agreed to assist her in finding someone traveling to another continent and request that Wrinkle accompany them. Wrinkle was to have an "Around the World in Eighty Days" experience.

Eve was delighted and in the process of educating Wrinkle, she, in collaboration with the airline personnel, Mrs. Thomas, and other friendly adults along the way, provided a rich curriculum for children in the third-grade class, for children traveling in the same planes and trains as Eve, and for the children in Eve's own community.

Eve dutifully wrote down Wrinkle's experiences, but she also had Wrinkle send postcards to the children in Mrs. Thomas's class, telling them what he was seeing. On one or two occasions Wrinkle met people who added something to the notebook or sent a postcard to the class, saying they had met Wrinkle. The airline hostesses knew about Wrinkle and during the trip to Africa used him to help other traveling children gain some insights. For example, one young child was traveling alone to Africa and was quite apprehensive. The airline hostess asked Eve to introduce Wrinkle to the child, and together they visited the cockpit where the pilot explained to them the many instruments. On returning to the cabin, the lad drew a picture of the cockpit and the pilot in Wrinkle's notebook, so "Wrinkle's children would see better

what a cockpit was like." Periodically, he, Wrinkle, and Eve would look out the window to see "where they were," how the sun looked coming up over the horizon and the size of the ships in a harbor. He even dictated a few sentences about his discoveries for Eve to put in the notebook. Eve returned to her home community before taking another trip to Hong Kong. In the school in that community Eve took Wrinkle to class and, using a map, described Wrinkle's trips. Some of these children communicated with Mrs. Thomas's class also, explaining how they had met Wrinkle.

Eve then took Wrinkle for new adventures to Hong Kong. Before boarding the plane for her return trip to America and with the assistance of the airline personnel, Eve found a family with young children returning to England, and so Wrinkle took off on another leg of his journey (Hamblett, 1994, personal communication).

....

A teacher collaborated with an agency in an imaginative way to provide an extended school curriculum involving community agents and an interested citizen. The community in this situation transcends the local one; people and natural and material resources from around the world provided an extended curriculum for children of Mrs. Thomas's class, and, incidentally, for other children along the way. The amount of learning for children in Mrs. Thomas's class will depend on their interest and developmental level, and on their families' ability to network and to make connections.

SUMMARY

....

Most community curriculum is not expanded to such a worldwide view as Mrs. Thomas was able to create. It can, however, be made equally rich and varied, depending on how adults in society structure the environment and how they develop supportive educational policies in various service agencies. Political, social, cultural, and business agencies offer, both intentionally and unintentionally, a learning environment for children in a community. Political agencies, for the most part, focus formal education about political endeavors toward adults or older children, expecting the teaching to be done by significant adults. However, political decisions in different communities—regarding management of a community and its social agencies—can result in children learning from totally different curricula.

Service agencies, transportation services, social and cultural agencies, and business and commercial enterprises produce a range of materials aimed at educating the public about their services. What children learn from these formal materials depends largely on the use parents and teachers make of them. Some agencies make deliberate attempts to offer educational opportunities for children, especially if schools have complementary programs. However, not all children are able to take advantage of the opportunities.

Like schools, all agencies provide informal and hidden curricula whereby children learn about their world. The natural and manufactured resources found within communities provide learning experiences even when there is little adult intervention. Children see signs, notice buildings, observe nature, note adult actions, and learn something from all their encounters. The ways important adults use the resources, explain things to children, and interact with each other all enhance children's learning.

Children who live in communities providing safe physical and emotional environments have more educational opportunities, for in these communities families are better able to establish social networks that enable them to tap community resources. For children outside such safe environments, schools and other agencies must work especially hard to compensate and must strive to build a solid curriculum so these children, too, will thrive in tomorrow's world.

SUGGESTED ACTIVITIES AND QUESTIONS

1. Take a two- to three-mile hike around your neighborhood. List all the natural resources, human resources, and materials that you observe. What is the learning potential for children living here?

2. Visit a business establishment in your community. Interview the owner or manager to learn if they have materials aimed at educating children, and how they distribute such materials. While there, ask yourself what children might learn just from being in the building.

3. Interview two peers, asking what they remember learning from friends, either now or when they were younger. Try to determine how they learned—by watching the friend, by having the friend tell, by having the friend demonstrate, or by the friend practicing the skill. Compare your peers' responses. How were they alike? How were they different?

4. From the list of community resources in this chapter, identify those your family was connected with as you grew up. List two or three things you think you learned from involvement with these resources.

5. Observe two or more children playing together. What learning do you think is taking place in this interaction? What community resources could support or hinder what these children are learning?

RECOMMENDED READINGS

Bronfenbrenner, U. (1979). *The ecology of human development: Experiment by nature and design.* Cambridge: Harvard University Press.

Cochran, M., Larner, M., Riley, D., Gunnarsson, L., & Henderson, C. R., Jr. (Eds.). (1990). *Extending families: The social networks of parents and their children.* New York: Cambridge University Press.

Comer, J. P. (1988). *Maggie's American dream: The life and times of a black family.* New York: New American Library.

Frost, J. L., & Sunderlin, S. (Eds.). (1985). *When children play.* Wheaton, MD: Association for Childhood Education International.

Garbarino, J., Dubrow, N., Kostelny, K., & Pardo, C. (1992). *Children in danger: Coping with the consequences of community violence.* San Francisco: Jossey-Bass.

Kagan, S. L., Powell, D. R., Weisbourd, B., & Zigler, E. F. (1987). *America's family support programs: Perspectives and prospects.* New Haven, CT: Yale University Press.

Louv, C. (1990). *Childhood's future.* Boston: Houghton Mifflin.

Traditional and Innovative Strategies for Working Together

Programs designed with strong parent involvement produce students who perform dramatically better than students in otherwise identical programs that do not involve parents at all, or as well.

(Henderson, 1987, p. 1)

Teachers have numerous ways for involving parents and community agencies in children's learning. In this chapter we examine traditional and innovative practices for collaborative action, and we also discuss items to consider when using these strategies. In reading this chapter you will learn that:

1. Teachers have long used traditional practices that involve parents in children's learning.

2. Creative teachers develop a variety of strategies to involve parents in their children's schooling.

3. Teachers have different effective strategies for communicating with parents.

4. Teachers establish parameters for the different roles parents have in classroom operations.

5. Successful home visits and parent-teacher conferences require careful consideration and well-planned strategies.

6. Many strategies for working with parents of children with special needs are similar to those for working with all parents, but you must consider different important factors as you work with different parent groups.

Our changing society, even with the advantages of mass communication systems, has evolved to a point in the late twentieth century where school programs alone are not sufficient for the task of formally educating children. The collaboration of parents and community agencies is essential if schools are to succeed in educating young children for a different society in the twenty-first century. A quarter of a century ago, Evans (1975) pointed out that the ultimate goal of active parent involvement is "enhancing the family's ability to respond to its children" (p. 11). This goal is as vital today as it was then.

Parental and community involvement has always been a part of U.S. education. As we have discussed, most parents historically have been totally responsible for their children's education, but beginning in the 1800s, schools accepted more responsibility for academic learning. Later, professional educators began to assume the responsibility for communicating with parents, instructing them on ways of helping their children for school, and even educating parents about children's growth and development.

By and large, parental cooperation in educational matters during the twentieth century has meant parental acquiescence to school suggestions, but in some ways this has begun to change. Parental and community involvement in some districts has moved gradually from teacher-dominated procedures to collaborations with parents and community agencies. In this chapter we discuss traditional, but still useful, strategies that teachers continue to use for involving parents, and note helpful variations and innovative practices.

Most teachers' established ways of communicating with parents and community members have proven to work well. But many parents are not reached by these methods. Teachers must find new, or develop variations on old, means to establish better communication between home, schools, and community. As teachers recognize that children have different learning styles, so they are beginning to understand that parents also have different communication styles. If children are to benefit, then teachers must learn to adapt to these differences and to respond to parents' interests, concerns, and needs.

We find in recent years that parents and community members feel more free to visit classrooms, becoming aides or volunteers in schools and contributing special expertise to children's learning. These individuals learn about the schools and about school culture, which enables them to help their children and to communicate to the larger community their sense of the importance of school programs.

The community is also an important educating force. Schools and families have always made excursions into their community for educational purposes, or have invited community members into the classroom. This involvement becomes more important as schools include community and environmental issues as part of the curriculum, and as community agencies become partners.

COMMUNICATION WITH PARENTS

Almost all parents are keenly interested in their children and what happens to them at school. And teachers, knowing of this concern, have developed various ways to communicate to parents about their children's school experiences. Parent-teacher conferences, newsletters, telephone contacts, and written communiques inform parents about children's progress, about school programs and curricula, and about ways parents can help their children. Most techniques have proved very successful, and many "new" or innovative ideas are variations on these basic strategies.

Parent-Teacher Conferences

Teachers have traditionally used conferences for telling parents about children's progress, informing them of the school's way of doing things, and soliciting their support and involvement. As schools begin to develop a sense of partnership, conferences, although not different on the surface, will become forums for mutual exchange. *Partnership conferences* mean both partners share examples of children's development, show respect for each other's responsibility, and propose ideas for continuing a program or changing direction. In successful conferences, both parents and teachers feel that they (1) gain new insights about children's learning, (2) have an opportunity to pose questions about school and home behavior, and (3) exchange ideas relating to children's needs (Rotter, 1987).

Establishing Collaboration Through Conferences
Teachers work from a sound traditional base when creating an environment for successful collaboration. Current strategies reflect changes in attitudes of teachers and parents. Figure 9.1 presents a general scheme that you as a teacher may use to ensure that your parent-teacher conferences result in effective collaboration (adapted from Coleman, 1991; Bjorklund & Burger, 1987; Seefeldt & Barbour, 1994).

Innovative Practices for Conferences
Although initiating conferences has traditionally been the teacher's responsibility, innovative schools encourage parents to suggest meetings and to come prepared to conferences. Student in-

In partnership conferences, both teachers and parents feel they gain new insights about children's learning.

volvement in conferences also has proven to be successful for all concerned.

Parental involvement. O'Brien (1989) offers suggestions for parents who are preparing for conferences. Innovative schools will make sure parents know about the following strategies:

1. Both parents should plan to attend, if possible. A single parent may bring a grandparent or a significant other person.
2. Parents should make the appointment a priority and get it on the calendar early.
3. Parents should talk with children about the conference and ask for their input about school and how they view their progress.
4. Organize any materials that parents and children want to share with the teacher.
5. Think through questions or concerns that parents wish to share with the teacher.

As with teachers, courtesy requires parents to thank the teacher for taking time for a conference, especially if it required special arrangements to accommodate busy schedules. Parents who talk positively about a conference afterward help their children see the relationship of the home environment to school life. A letter of thanks to the teacher stating what parents got from a conference clarifies for the teacher the parents' views of the situation. Parents and teachers all develop a sense of partnership in children's learning when they recognize the significant impact these meetings have on that learning.

Student involvement. Traditionally, students have had little say or involvement in parent-teacher conferences. But as parents assume responsibilities for conferences, both teachers and parents seek input from children regarding questions they would like the adults to discuss. Another facet of innovative conferences is including students themselves. For example, at Elbow Park Elementary School in Calgary, Alberta, students from K–6 were included in conferences, and parents also could have private interviews with teachers later. Students and parents were both prepared ahead of time for the new conference format, and many students wrote out questions to ask. Teachers prepared comments and questions addressed to students and parents, so that both could be actively involved in the discussion. At the end of the conference, teachers asked for an evaluation of the conference and suggestions for improving the process (Hubert, 1989).

FIGURE 9.1

Making parent-teacher conferences work.

PREPARATION FOR THE CONFERENCE

1. Develop mutual respect by scheduling conferences at convenient times for both teachers and parents.
2. Establish a sense of equality with seating arrangements. Avoid physical barriers by sitting beside parents at a table where everyone can view all materials.
3. Prepare an agenda and send it to the parents. Include a statement of purpose and allow time for parent input, your input, and questions from both you and parents.
4. Assemble materials from areas of the curriculum that demonstrate children's classroom work over time.
5. Invite parents to bring products their children have produced at home, demonstrating the value you place on parental teaching, such as charts of children's home responsibilities, craft projects or food children have made, letters they have written, any collections, or sets of favorite books.

THE CONFERENCE

1. Begin the conference on a positive note by sharing with parents children's accomplishments at school.
2. Invite parents to share their children's meaningful achievements at home.
3. Share your mutual academic and personal concerns.
4. Discuss ideas for resolving these concerns.
5. Allow time for parental questions. If parents appear reluctant to ask questions, assist them by suggesting what other parents often ask: codes of behavior for the classroom, academic questions not attended to in this particular conference, parent involvement in schools or in children's learning.
6. Keep conference to allotted time. If you need more time, schedule a new conference.

ENDING THE CONFERENCE

1. End the conference on a positive note, complimentary to the children involved.
2. Review conference highlights.
3. Restate your understanding of any decisions mutually made.
4. Indicate how information or material parents have shared has helped you understand their children better.
5. Thank the parents for coming and inform them of the next conference period, next school event for parents, or next PTA meeting.
6. Indicate your anticipation at seeing the parents again.

CONFERENCE FOLLOWUP

1. Write a brief summary for your records. Include any and all parental suggestions or questions.
2. Follow through on your promises and inform the parents of your efforts.

Home Visits

Visiting the homes of preschool-age children has been common practice for many years. Such programs have been and continue to be sponsored by school systems, and many earlier ones were sponsored by health departments and mental health agencies (Miller, 1987). Whereas early programs focused on health needs of young children, in recent years, home visiting has become a means of enhancing cognitive and social development (Powell, 1990).

Head Start is a federally funded program that requires home visitation. In the 1970s, the United States government funded Home Start, a component of Head Start, to create early intervention models that required home visits from specially trained persons. Three exemplars from this period were the Mother-Child Home Program (Levenstein, 1977), the Florida Parent Education Infant and Toddler Program (Gordon, Guinagh, & Jester, 1977), and the Early Training Project (Larner & Halpern, 1987). Today, Head Start continues to have a home visiting component, and many public preschool programs, day care programs, and private nursery schools also require teachers to visit children in their homes. Some programs are well defined, modeled after the early Home Start program and requiring specially trained home visitors. Most are aimed at assisting parents in providing better health care and obtaining needed social services as well as in becoming better teachers of their children.

Other home visiting programs are designed to establish home–school relationships early by helping children become acquainted with the teacher, and helping the teacher to understand the home situation. The responsibility for such visits always rests with the classroom teacher.

Traditional Practices

Traditional practices for making the home visit comfortable for both teachers and parents abound in early childhood literature. Recommendations include the following:

1. Clarify the purpose of the visit through an initial telephone call.
2. Arrange a convenient time so children will be part of the process.
3. Set a specific time for the visit. Arrive and depart on time, and leave earlier if events warrant it.
4. As a guest in the home, respect the cultural and ethnic values the family exhibits.
5. If other family members are present, include them in your conversation.
6. Be an attentive listener, but don't oversocialize or get drawn into family controversies.
7. Be prepared to suggest agencies and types of services that parents might pursue in getting help if the family asks.
8. Invite the parents to become active participants in the school program, suggesting several levels of involvement.
9. Follow up the visit with a thank you note and indicate action on what was agreed on during the visit.

Innovative Practices

In the traditional home visiting arrangement, the teacher was the resource person assisting parents in some way, especially by helping parents understand how they could support their children's education. Innovative programs change this relationship, making home visits collaborative efforts. This means parents can and should initiate visits, plan an agenda, and share educational aspirations for their children. Parents and teachers may then become equal partners in developing good educational programs for children (Powell, 1990).

The Family Matters Program at Cornell University is a home visiting program designed on the notion of parent empowerment. As the first step, program personnel recognize parents as experts in raising their own children. The home visitor acts as facilitator in the visit sessions, encouraging parents to share their understanding of their children's growth (Cochran, 1990).

No matter how home visiting is seen, it is apparent that successful programs depend on a teacher's ability to develop a trusting relationship with parents. These visits can provide teachers with new insights into the social and cognitive functioning of children. By working cooperatively, parents and teachers may more easily find solutions to children's problems. The following vignette portrays a home visit's positive outcome.

....

Jose Diaz, a third grader who had recently moved into the school district, was having difficulty in responding to and interacting positively with his peers. His written work seemed above average, but work with other children or in class presentations did not go well. Mrs. Cardenza, Jose's teacher, spoke with Mrs. Diaz, but the conversation shed little light on the situation. Mrs. Diaz said Jose was very interested in school and was always sharing ideas at home. Mrs. Cardenza then suggested a home visit, with Jose and his parents both present. Mrs. Diaz was delighted. Mrs. Cardenza found Mr. and Mrs. Diaz to be personable hosts. Jose was a model of charm, quite able to be part of the conversation. In the course of the visit, Mr. Diaz noted how Jose seemed to be adjusting quite well to his new school. But when Mrs. Cardenza asked Jose about his new friends, he described several adults in his neighborhood. Mrs. Cardenza learned that Mr. and Mrs. Diaz had traveled a great deal with their only child. Jose had not often interacted with his peers, but had spent most of his time among adults, being included in many of their activities.

For Mrs. Cardenza it was a revelation to see Jose so skilled socially. Mrs. Cardenza invited Mr. and Mrs. Diaz to visit the class. They were astonished to discover Jose had trouble interacting with his peers. During the visit they noted that his group work suffered, and he felt less secure in pre-

senting material to the class. When Mrs. Cardenza and the Diazes discussed the visit later, they devised plans to have Jose involved in more activities with peers.

Had Mrs. Cardenza not visited Jose in his home, she would never have seen how skilled he was socially, at least with adults. His difficulty was really with other 8-year-olds. When he presented work, his peers thought him a showoff. Mrs. Cardenza was able to work with him, pointing out in a nonthreatening way how his behavior seemed to turn off his classmates. At home the Diazes begin to encourage more involvement with neighborhood children, and gradually Jose learned to cooperate with peers and to share more freely.

....

Telephone Contacts

In the past, parents or teachers telephoned one another when concerned about children's progress. Today, the telephone is a tool for collaborating on children's education. As in all contacts, the communication should be a positive experience for both teacher and parent, even if the call is to discuss a concern.

Establishing good relationships early in the year is important. You can do this with a brief telephone conversation, if parent-teacher conferences or home visits aren't possible. In this first call, introduce yourself to the family and express pleasure in having their children in class (Gelfer, 1991). This also establishes the idea that you will use the telephone to contact parents about other things, such as children's progress, school events, or help in the school. Establishing communication early in the year enables parents and teachers to be comfortable about contacting each other when confusion or misunderstanding arises.

....

Melissa Jacobs was entering a new school during the third grade. She knew no one and was terrified, especially since she "didn't read so good."

Mrs. Jacobs was relieved when Ms. Thomas called to welcome Melissa to school and to invite the mother to come any time to visit. As the year wore on Mrs. Jacobs was delighted in Melissa's successful adaptation to school. She called Ms. Thomas one morning to check and see how Melissa's reading "was going."

The next day Melissa came home very angry, not wanting to go to school. "I don't see why I have to go to that dumb teacher and do phonics. I hate phonics!"

Distressed, Mrs. Jacobs immediately called Ms. Thomas to ask what was happening. Before Mrs. Jacobs could say much more than hello, Ms. Thomas said, "Oh, I am so glad you called. I was about to call you. I really don't think it is a good idea for Melissa to go to the special teacher. I know you are concerned about her reading, but she was just miserable today. Her reading is coming along well and she doesn't need this extra pressure."

In the course of the conversation it was clear there was a misunderstanding during the last telephone conversation. Mrs. Jacobs had intended to just maintain contact, and Ms. Thomas had interpreted it as concern. Since good communication had been established early, both teacher and parent could resolve the misunderstanding in good faith and do "what was best for Melissa."

Innovative Practices

Technology expands possibilities for communicating with parents. Electronic mail and telephone answering machines are two ways that teachers provide more information to parents. Bauch (1989) designed a program called the "TransParent School Model" that allows teachers to communicate daily with parents. Teachers have individual answering machines or electric mailboxes. At the end of the day they prepare a one- to three-minute message, noting homework assignments, events of the day, things children have been asked to bring to school, and upcoming meetings. Parents can call in at their leisure and have easy access to information (Bauch, 1989). Parents may also leave messages for the teacher.

Informal Contacts

Parents with children in preschool normally accompany their children to school, and this gives both parents and teachers a chance to talk informally. Allow time at the beginning and end of the day for brief conversations with parents. Parents like to hear what their children have been doing, and a brief statement such as, "Phil climbed to the top of the jungle gym for the first time today. He'll be excited to tell you about it," communicates to the parents that you are aware of what is happening with each child. Parents also must share in the communication process. Parents who comment about how their children are at home, or who note children's enjoyment of a school activity, communicate their involvement in their children's learning. By asking questions and by being attentive, you can help parents who are unsure of how to establish communication.

Lengthy conversations are a problem at the end of the day. Busy parents are anxious to get home, and busy teachers need to welcome other parents, get children organized, or clean up after a long day. Brief statements at this time are important, and if a parent needs more time, you may suggest either a scheduled conference or telephone call. When parents linger in the classroom, skilled teachers suggest they observe something special, or help their children in some constructive way.

Parents do not accompany their older children to school, but are often present in open schools where partnerships have been formed with parents and communities. These parents still anticipate brief words of welcome or an exchange about what is going on with their children. These contacts with parents are helpful if conversations are positive and demonstrate an interest in how children are learning in different settings. Such exchanges communicate to all parties, including children, that responsibility for educating the young is shared by the entire community.

Written Communications

Schools have traditionally made assignments with the hope that parents would oversee the homework and help their children as needed. Such homework provides children with practice on skills and concepts taught at school, and parents who review the work with their children get information about what they are expected to learn. In addition to homework, some schools have devised other interesting ways for communicating with parents about their children's school involvement, including bulletin boards, newsletters, and informal notes.

Bulletin Boards

All classrooms have bulletin boards, and most schools have boards in the halls. Traditionally, teachers place on these boards children's work, special events, and material for a particular unit. Parents coming to the classroom or school building gain information about the school through reading the boards. They see their children's artwork, their written or retold stories, books they are reading, and information on units they have studied. Many teachers also use photos with captions to show children's involvement in the activities.

Innovative schools have special bulletin boards just for parents. The interests of parents dictate what is posted on these boards. If teachers regularly change postings, parents will learn to look to the board for information. Teachers may post special articles regarding children's growth and development, information regarding meetings and availability of social services, and health and nutritional information. Parent volunteers often arrange the board or assist teachers in highlighting information, such as bibliographies of children's books, educational toy suggestions for birthdays or holidays, and recipes for nutritional snacks. Sometimes teachers photocopy materials and put them in a wall pocket for parents to take home.

Newsletters

Classroom and school newsletters, while varying in purpose, are traditional methods for schools to communicate with parents. Most newsletters communicate "school news," notices of school events, parent-teacher conferences, and other important meetings. Traditionally, most newsletters have also included tips on helping children at home and for parents seeking resources.

Innovative teachers find extended purposes for newsletters. Revised newsletters often contain children's work, whether poems, stories, artwork, or news of class events. One teacher includes in her newsletters artwork by children, photos of classroom activities, thank yous for parental and community support, examples of how children used the materials parents contributed, and extracts of discussions children had because of parental support. Such a complete newsletter provides parents with many examples of what and how children learn from various resources.

Informal Notes

Teachers' previous use of informal notes tended to inform parents of concerns teachers had regarding their children's work. However, now, more frequently teachers recognize the value of notes that reflect children's special accomplishments in developing social, cognitive, or physical skills, thus giving both parents and children a sense of well-being. Usually notes don't require a response, but you may occasionally wish to query how parents see children's skill development at home. You may also use notes to express concerns about children's changed behavior. When notes are positive in tone, even if you have some concern, parents come to understand the importance of working cooperatively to provide the best for their children. Most teachers believe it is wise to let children know about communications with their parents, and, in general, what the note contains. In classrooms where children's parents speak a language other than English at home, teachers have elicited the aid of bilingual parents in translating notes sent home. Students who are fluent in both languages can translate messages themselves. Children's involvement is important, for they need to know that parents and teachers are working together to help them learn.

Thoughtful, ongoing communication with parents is an important component of parent-teacher cooperation. It involves parents at a basic level in their children's education. Table 9.1 summarizes the traditional and innovative communication strategies discussed in this section of the chapter.

PARENTS IN THE SCHOOLS

When parents are in classrooms, they see first-hand how their children respond to the school learning environment. Though we find some exceptions, involved parents usually become strong supporters of their children's schools. They come to appreciate what schools are doing and what is involved in educating their children.

Parents can be observers, paid aides, or volunteers, or may serve as classroom resources. Whatever their role, it is important that parents have orientation or training for participation. Teachers are legally responsible for the children in their classroom, and if parents don't understand class-

room rules or procedures, conflicts can arise. Misunderstandings can result, and neither children, parents, nor teachers are well served.

School Visitations

Traditionally, parents are invited into children's classrooms on special occasions, such as National Education Week, or as audiences for special events. Innovative schools are establishing an open-door policy, welcoming parents whenever they wish to visit. This is a distraction for some teachers. Unless both parents and teachers understand the purpose for such visits and establish guidelines, people coming unannounced into the classroom can be disruptive. However, visits and observations may be productive and informative for parents and not distracting for teachers. The following paragraphs describe methods that creative teachers have discovered work for their classrooms.

Teachers who are more comfortable with announced visits make clear their feelings, and explain their reasons to parents during conferences and parent-teacher meetings. They establish

When parents volunteer in classrooms, they come to appreciate what is involved in educating their children.

TABLE 9.1
Parent and Teacher Communication Strategies: Traditional and Innovative

Conferences	
Traditional	*Innovative*
Teacher schedules and directs conference.	Parents prepare for conferences as well as teachers.
Teacher prepares materials, provides input, and strives for cordial and productive exchanges.	Parents schedule appointment.
	Child contributes ideas to conference and/or attends.

Home Visits	
Traditional	*Innovative*
Teacher attempts to understand home and establish positive relations.	Collaboration is sought.
	Parents become partners in planning visits and sharing ideas.
	Parent empowerment is sought.

Telephone Calls	
Traditional	*Innovative*
Teacher initiates calls when concerned.	E-mail allows either parent or teacher to initiate calls or leave messages.
Teacher uses phone as substitute for conference.	Answering machines with messages on schedules, homework, etc. permit exchange of information.

Informal Contact	
Traditional	*Innovative*
Beginning and ending of school day are times for brief exchanges between parent and teacher.	Parents can accept more responsibility for communication.
Demonstrating interest is goal.	

Written Communication	
Traditional	*Innovative*
Teachers develop bulletin boards.	Parents can help arrange bulletin boards or collaborate with school personnel in developing one.
Newsletters include school news, dates to remember and tips for helping children at home.	New items are included: photos of schoolwork, artwork, notes on parents' contributions, and how kids learn.
Informal notes are ways to keep in contact and inform homes.	Notes reflect children's special accomplishments.
	Notes designed to give both parents and children a sense of well-being.

guidelines for all visits held during regular class time, such as where to sit when visiting, things the parent might want to observe, and when it is appropriate for parents to approach the teacher.

Early childhood classrooms are active places, and children are not always sitting at desks involved in paperwork or listening to the teacher. In such classrooms, teachers find it helpful to explain to parents what the routines of the day are and how children are involved. In order not to disrupt the flow of activity, the teacher suggests where the parent may sit to "get the most out of their observation." If there is activity, which parents can observe better if they moved about the room, then the teacher suggests the best time to do so. If the class and teacher prefer that parents not interact with children, then the teacher explains why this is important.

Children are accustomed to adults in some classrooms, and are comfortable asking them for help. In cases like this, parents are advised that children will approach them. If parents are visiting to observe general classroom activities and how children interact with each other, then the teacher provides a list of things parents can watch for. If a parent is visiting for a particular reason, then parent and teacher confer regarding what to look for and how. Parents are encouraged to visit their children on the playground and during special activities. Teachers who use these visiting strategies believe that parents who understand about the total school program will be more supportive of it.

In some families, grandparents, uncles, and aunts are closely involved in children's lives. Teachers should make it clear that these other important people are welcome in the school. At the David A. Ellis School in Roxbury, Massachusetts, one grandfather explained how he was the one who brought his granddaughter to school and picked her up every day. By spending time with her, he was learning a great deal himself. He expressed his pleasure in the openness of the school by saying, "Boy, I'm telling you, what an education we are getting together" (Johnson, 1990).

Some day care programs encourage parents to drop in to observe or even to be with their children whenever they can. If a day care center is near a parent's workplace, parents come during breaks or lunch hour to have a snack, eat with their children, or even play with them for a few moments. Some parents are able to come before naptime to read to their children and tuck them in.

Most classrooms have special events to which teachers invite parents. Such occasions give children experiences in writing invitations, planning for the event, demonstrating some skill or talent, and even preparing special snacks. The list of events for such visits is almost endless. Some interesting examples are noted in Figure 9.2.

Children's Role in Visitation

Children need to be prepared for adults visiting their classroom. Teachers usually have explained to their classes that parents and other adults enjoy coming in to see what things they are doing. Traditionally, teachers introduce visitors to the classroom, explaining to children the purpose of the visits. Innovative teachers make such explanations a part of children's responsibility.

One teacher who had many visitors to her class established a "greeter" as one of the weekly classroom duties. She had children practice the role so they would feel comfortable with adults. When new adults came into the room, the greeter would quietly welcome them, take their coat, and suggest where to sit. The child would point out the daily schedule, which was always posted, and tell the visitors what was currently happening.

Parents as Aides or Volunteers

Recently, teachers have come to realize that having a paid aide or having parents volunteer to regularly assist children in the classroom pays off in a richer curriculum for students. Since most parents now work, these volunteers often fill the role of "other important adults" in children's lives.

Skillful teachers make good, creative use of volunteers. Although methods vary for training

FIGURE 9.2
Special events for classrooms.

1. *Stone Soup Day.* As part of their folktale study, a third-grade class invited their parents to celebrate the end of the unit. Children performed their version of Stone Soup and then had parents join them in eating a nutritious meal of "stone" soup and corn muffins, which they had prepared the day before.
2. *Celebrating Mrs. Jones.* Once a month, the second-grade class celebrated a special person in the school and invited her in for snack time. Besides preparing the snack, children always made a special gift, reflecting some aspect of their current study unit. Different parents joined to help with preparations and to express their appreciation for the person's services.
3. *Circus Day.* A kindergarten class invited parents to the culminating session of their circus unit. Their circus had only one ring, but all contributed special skills as acrobats, lions and dogs or trainers, clowns, and a ringmaster. One parent, a skilled pianist, accompanied the acts with appropriate music.
4. *Father's Day Breakfast.* A first-grade class invited their fathers, grandfathers, or special adult males to join them monthly for a special breakfast they helped prepare. As a variation, the class had unrelated adults from the school and community join parents and students for breakfast. The price for breakfast was $1.00; however, if a student found an unrelated adult to join her, then the student saved the $1.00 charge. At first teachers helped engage students and adults in conversations regarding school events. As the idea caught on, students began to seek out other volunteers, besides their parents, to join them. Not only did community volunteers get a better understanding of what happens in schools, but students began to appreciate the diversity of interests within their community.
5. *Coffee Hour.* At one school the principal, staff members, and teachers, on a rotating basis, were freed from responsibilities each Friday morning. Parents were invited in to have coffee and chat with them about school in general, and to get to know one another. As the year progressed, sharing "things that were working well" and "things that could work better" became part of the agenda. Gradually, the evolving good fellowship and trust led to both parents and school personnel taking responsibility for seeking solutions for expressed concerns.

volunteers, the following procedures have proven successful for many teachers.

Teachers solicit reliable, regular volunteers at the beginning of the year, and have a brief meeting to explain the classroom regulations and how parents can assist. Sometimes volunteers help individual children with projects or in practicing certain skills. They also may read to individual children, and when comfortable may read to small groups or to the class. Volunteers also may help the teacher prepare materials, or set up activities.

Volunteer schedules work more smoothly if teachers make a monthly calendar for parents and send home reminders of their volunteer days.

Each morning before children arrive, the teacher and volunteer(s) try to spend a few minutes discussing the events of the day. At the end of the day, they meet again briefly to discuss "how the day went." For the experience to be successful, both teachers and volunteers need to recognize that the teacher is the major decision maker and authority figure in the classroom. Teachers must respect the skills volunteers bring, but the rules of the classroom must be established by the teacher and communicated to volunteers, so children do not receive mixed messages.

One creative teacher has an open policy on volunteers, inviting working parents to observe and help whenever they have time off. He keeps a list of special activities that need extra classroom help. When parent volunteers arrive, the teacher is then ready to use them productively to assist children. This policy has been especially helpful in securing more male volunteers.

Parents as Classroom Resources

Teachers and schools are also finding other ways that parents and community members can assist them. Some programs use volunteers as tutors or mentors. Some tutors work with students having particular difficulties, while others work with gifted children who need enrichment programs for which schools lack resources. Other mentors work with children who have a special interest in their area of expertise.

Mentors with particular expertise are helpful to children with special interests.

Traditional Practices

Many programs use parents to read literature to children. Volunteers come regularly, take children to a quiet area, and read with and to them. Some programs even have special work sessions for volunteers, helping them develop skills for involving children in the reading (Lancy & Nattiv, 1992).

Volunteers with computer or clerical skills help office staff typing newsletters, preparing reports for a parent meeting, addressing letters, and even designing an attendance program. The custodial staff tends to the housecleaning and maintenance of the school, but volunteers have assisted this staff also when special projects required setting up different areas of the school, or when special carpentry work was required. In more than one preschool classroom, parents have joined the custodian in building a loft for a classroom, building

extra cubbies for children, preparing outdoor tables for a playground, or setting up playground equipment. When the staff and volunteers work together for children, all have a better sense of ownership in the school program.

When parents do not have time for regular classroom volunteer work, they help on special occasions, in many ways that parents have been traditionally involved. When children go on field trips, parents often accompany children or help the teacher in organizing the trip. All schools have nonclass functions where parents render support services, such as helping organize events for National Education Week, helping with fundraising activities within the school, or supporting the "Read a Book Club."

Innovative Programs

Some educators have devised plans whereby volunteers offer an enriched program for children in their school. In one Maryland program, on Wednesday afternoons, community members offer to children a variety of programs that reflect particular volunteers' skills and interests. For example, an expert quilter offered quilting lessons for six weeks. A bird carver introduced the beginning steps of carving. A computer programmer taught children how to create simple programs. A chef offered lessons in Italian cooking. A ballet dancer gave ten weeks of ballet lessons. There were flower growing and arranging classes, bird and rock identification classes, and discussions on topics from Caldecott and Newbery Award-winning children's books. At the beginning, volunteers wrote a brief description of their "course" indicating the number of lessons and appropriate age range. Children then signed up, but as the program developed, some adults began to join their children in taking the classes. Both children and adults found they enjoyed learning new skills in such multiage groupings.

Hunter (1989) describes a more formal approach, called "Par-aide." In this program, the parents receive a presentation format, and then are given suggestions for appropriate ways to present the materials to the age group they are teaching. Parents less secure in working with young children have found this approach more reassuring.

Volunteers in our schools today come in all ages. As more and more retirees seek ways to have a meaningful retirement, many are willing to volunteer their talents in schools. In addition to doing all types of volunteer work, they find themselves becoming friends and supporters of some of the young families in the schools. All volunteers support children's cognitive, social, and emotional development, but older adults give children a special insight into developing relationships across ages (Smith & Newman, 1993).

Expressions of Appreciation

Volunteers receive rewards for their efforts in different ways. Seeing children's progress is very satisfying and children have their unique ways of showing delight in having someone read to them or help them with a problem. Reaching to take the adult's hand, a hug, a sharing of, "I read this entire book to my mom after you helped me yesterday," or a special drawing of "us reading together" express better than anything how much children benefit. Letters of appreciation can come from children, teachers, and from the parent coordinator or the school principal. Many schools have special dinners or events to formally thank volunteers.

Parents and community members involved in classrooms or school events find themselves at a participatory level of involvement, from which they gain knowledge about their schools. Children's education is further enhanced when the entire community arrives at this level of cooperation and participation.

Parents as Advocates

In general, teachers and staff feel comfortable when parents are involved with children's education at the basic or the participatory level. Many teachers are willing to take responsibility for try-

Community members acquire a participatory level of involvement in schools by volunteering in the classroom.

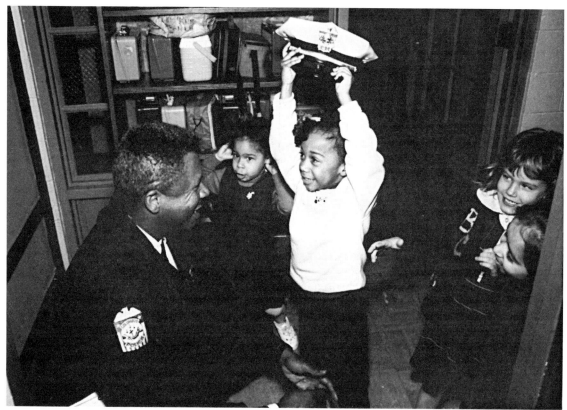

ing to get more parents involved, and they find it produces better results for their students (Bloom, 1992). However, there is a third level of involvement that teachers and school administrators are not always comfortable with, that of advocacy.

When parents or community members become advocates for children they become decision makers, serving as equal partners on school policy boards, curriculum committees, steering committees, and school councils. Some parents, in this role, work within the framework of committees and the administrative structure. However, parents who feel that the school policy is adversely affecting their children may initiate action. In such cases they meet with teachers, principals, school board members, and even local and state legislators to advocate a change in policy. Recall, it was a single parent, and then a group of parents on a grassroots level, that eventually succeeded in securing appropriate education for children with disabilities through PL 94–142, the Individuals with Disabilities Education Act (IDEA).

Other parents become strong advocates for change within an entire school system. Parents may seek election to school board positions because they wish to see change and feel that this is a way for their voices to be heard. Federal legislation also has resulted in some parents having a policymaking role. Head Start programs, Chapter I programs, and programs under IDEA are required to have parents on their policy level councils. These parents then have a voice in program development, in hiring teachers, in the kinds of training offered to teachers, and in other policies that affect the programs.

Not all school systems or teachers embrace parent advocacy enthusiastically, nor can all parents operate at an oversight level of involvement. Such advocacy and involvement work well only when both parties—parents and teachers—have a voice in the decisions and work cooperatively together. Some parents have served on curriculum committees, steering committees, or school councils and have advocated or demanded change only to find nothing changes. This means frustration. Only when parents, teachers, and school administrators are able to recognize each other's expertise and are willing to assume responsibility for pulling together can changes occur. Building coalitions of parents and teachers working for the best interests of their children is the most powerful advocacy role any person undertakes (Bloom, 1992).

PARENT EDUCATION

Since the early years of the twentieth century, parent education has been viewed as an important component for parental involvement in schools. In Chapter 2, we discussed the trends of parent education during this century. As we noted, in the early history of the United States, parents learned about educating their children from their own parents or relatives. Then, as psychology became a more honored profession, professionals became the experts and parent education regarding child development and wise parenting practices became a part of the school's responsibility.

Presently, we again find recognition of parents' skills and expertise. In some innovative programs, *parent education* means that teachers are learning new skills for interacting with parents. They value parents' ideas, help parents understand their own skills, and more effectively integrate home and community knowledge with classroom learning. Parent education and parent involvement thus go hand in hand.

Education Through Meetings and Classes

Programs of parent education range from meetings conducted by parents themselves to formal classes on parenting skills conducted by professionals. Traditional Parent-Teacher Association groups still provide support for schools and sponsor special parent programs or workshops. Professionals today are especially anxious to include those parents who have traditionally been excluded from such groups.

Innovative practices in parent education tend to reflect efforts to include parents from all economic and ethnic groups within a community. Some schools attempt to involve their parent group in those education programs that parents themselves see as particularly needed. Seefeldt and Barbour (1994) describe a program of outreach where a principal succeeded in getting parents involved by allowing parents to choose and plan their own topics. Many "hard to reach" parents became intrigued and began coming to these informal but educational sessions.

Some schools find that developing a parent center within the school gives parents a sense of belonging, and they feel more comfortable attending classes geared towards their needs. Classes in parent centers run the gamut from good child-rearing practices, to dealing with behavioral problems and drugs in the community, to language instruction for non-English speakers. The meetings are often unstructured, led by lay persons, and involve a great deal of discussion and idea exchange among the participants.

Several specially designed programs exist for training parents to develop skills in working with their children. When implementing, leaders typically follow the format described by the programs' creators. Parent Effectiveness Training (PET) (Gordon, 1975), Systemic Training for Effective Parenting (STEP) (Dinkmeyer & McKay, 1983), and Active Parenting Discussion Group (Popin, 1990) are three popular program models used during the last twenty years.

The Parenting Center at Marquette University developed a series of introductory parenting classes aimed especially at parents of young children (Fox, Anderson, Fox, & Rodrigues, 1991). The objectives of that program are to teach parents the STAR (*Stop, Think, Ask, Respond*) approach to parenting, specific strategies for dealing with behavioral problems, and reasonable behavioral and developmental expectations for their children. Strategies used in parental instruction include lecture/discussion, practice sessions using parenting techniques, responses to particular problems parents are currently having, and homework assignments.

The Center for Young Children at the University of Maryland developed a program especially for fathers of young children (Lamb, 1986). This program engages fathers in twelve two-hour Saturday sessions, divided between playing with their children and group discussion with other fathers. During the first hour, fathers and children engage in such activities as exploring a new toy, building with blocks, tasting new foods, or reading a special book together. While aides look after children, the fathers spend the second hour in a discussion group on such topics as child development, what it means to be accessible and responsible for children, and parenting in general (McBride, 1989).

Education Through Materials

With research indicating the importance of parents' involvement in their children's education, schools are increasingly looking for ways to reach parents at home. Homework has traditionally been the device teachers have used to increase children's skills, and they assumed parents would supervise the work and thus come to know what school expectations were. All too often that homework consisted of ditto sheets to complete or drill work on specific skills. Recently, different types of materials are being sent home that serve to involve parents with their children's education, and at the same time educate parents for helping their

children learn. Learning Packets (Spewock, 1991) and Family Theme Bags (Helm, 1994) are two innovative practices that teachers have devised for helping parents of at-risk children.

In both programs parents receive a packet of information and ideas for how to interact with their children in a way that increases children's early literacy development. Learning Packets are sent to parents of newborns, and each succeeding year until age 5 the child receives a birthday card plus a new packet. The packet contains information about child development, ideas for fostering growth, and tips on good parenting strategies. Ideas include such things as ways to share books, simple games to play at each age level, and arts or crafts to create with inexpensive materials (Spewock, 1991).

Family Theme Bags are cloth bags sent home with preschoolers that contain a stuffed animal, a journal, a file-folder game, "What if . . . ?" cards, songs/fingerplays, a storybook, and art supplies. An introductory letter outlines the purpose of the bag and the value of the activities suggested. The stuffed animal or puppet provides a theme, and games, songs, and activities relate to that theme. For example, the Zoo Bag contains ideas for making zoo sandwiches, a song about an elephant, and a simple board game with a zoo pattern. The journal is provided so parents can write how children responded to the materials and games. When children return the bags, the teacher reads the journals to the class (Helm, 1994).

Parent education programs differ in how they are structured and delivered, but all are designed to help parents become more involved in their children's education. When parents are active participants and decision makers in the developing programs, then new understandings are likely to be long lasting.

COMMUNITY INVOLVEMENT

Although much can be accomplished when parents and teachers form a strong partnership, children receive even richer educational experience when the larger community is included. As discussed in Chapter 8, the community is a strong educational force in children's lives. Places exist in all communities that children should know about and visit, and all communities have material resources teachers and parents can use in the educative process. Businesses and social service agencies can often provide support systems enabling children to develop the traits that make them productive citizens. Teachers have traditionally tapped many of these resources, but we are finding new ways for teachers and parents to engage community services for children's education.

Trips into the Community

All children have experience with their community, and have learned many different concepts from these encounters. Traditionally, preschool and primary schools take field trips focusing on specific aspects of community life, which provide children with new and extended insights.

Carefully planned field trips enhance and make more meaningful the objectives of a unit of study. Students studying economics, for example, can set up a bank and a store in their classroom and practice using the bank and store in ways they learned from their parents or from books they have read. However, a trip to an actual bank and store, where they can ask specific questions, allows them to view how adults behave in such places. It gives them "behind the scenes" experience. When children have particular questions to ask, or things to see or do, they gain skills in observing, collecting information, making inferences, comparing information with others, and drawing conclusions. Also, trips produce new ideas, which children transfer to their dramatic play, their reading, their writing, and other classroom instruction. A trip provides motivation for further interests and learning, as for the first graders in the following vignette.

Field trips produce new ideas, which children transfer to other classroom instruction.

Nigel's class, accompanied by several parents, took a walking trip to the pet store to get food for the cicada they had found in the play yard and were now studying in class. While at the store, they were fascinated by a hermit crab and convinced their teacher to buy one for further study. Nigel became so interested that with his parents' help he visited the local aquarium. A naturalist at the aquarium told him more about hermit crabs and where they lived. With this information, the family took a trip to the seashore, and all were able to observe hermit crabs in their natural habitat. Nigel's stepfather videotaped the family's excursion, and Nigel shared the tape and his experience with his classmates.

Community members, family, and teachers can all become involved in children's learning when schools plan and carry out field trips. Nigel's teacher needed parents to go on the trip. She also needed the support of the pet store owners to have the trip become meaningful enough to be worth the effort. Then Nigel's family extended the learning for the whole class by arranging a family trip, using as a resource aquarium personnel, and bringing back results. Teachers organize and plan children's formal education, but when a community and parents are interested and involved, enhanced exposure and greater learning emerges.

Innovative Trips

Trips into the community are not restricted to gaining understanding of the neighborhood. Children can make trips intended to contribute in some way to the community, such as by enhancing the local environment. Trips around the school can focus on cleaning up the area or on planting flowers, trees, or shrubs. Some organizations "adopt a highway," assuming the responsibility to clean up litter. Classrooms can adopt a neighborhood park, a playground, or a street and keep it attractive. Besides picking up trash, children often find ways to make the area more pleasant, such as by planting and caring for flowers. Extending the idea, children could notify a sanitation department to ensure proper trash pickup, and present posters to local newspapers and shopkeepers urging people to keep the area clean.

A visit to a nursing home or hospital presents opportunities for children to share with elderly or ill people their artwork, some special songs, or a dramatic presentation.

One kindergarten teacher hit on an idea that not only had her 5-year-olds doing something for the community but involved their parents, as well. The class made class jokebooks called *Laugh with the Kindergarten* and distributed them to medical facilities and doctors' offices in the area. The teacher, Ms. Patchin, sent home a jokebook with each child and asked parents to read the jokes to the children and help them pick out the

ones they liked. The parents helped write the joke on a five-by-seven-inch card, and children illustrated it. Parents were encouraged to research other joke sources, so children could find additional items to include. Volunteers helped in the classroom to laminate and assemble the collection (Patchin, 1994). This idea would also work well for second and third graders, who are beginning to develop both a sense of humor and a social conscience for helping others.

A related idea became a project for older children, who followed the Foxfire concept of visiting and interviewing older residents to hear their stories of yesteryear. The class collected and published the stories and sold them at school functions. In this case the intent was not to help other people, but to help children interact, appreciate, and be involved with an older generation. Also, when children became responsible for the sale of the books, they learned something about economics.

Community as a Resource for Materials

Children can travel in their community for educational purposes, but it is also possible to provide community resources within the classroom. Community members play roles in the school similar to parental roles. Community members with special expertise may be willing to present their craft, knowledge, or skills for children's enlightenment. Traditionally, teachers have invited doctors, dentists, firefighters, or police to share their services with children, but imaginative teachers have found others to extend or enhance a unit. One university biology professor enjoyed taking part of his collection of rare butterflies to a second-grade classroom each year during their "butterfly unit." In the spring, he walked in nearby fields with children hunting out cocoons or newly hatched butterflies. In one kindergarten classroom, an ornithologist shared her knowledge of birds, using stuffed exhibits and special bird books to point out their characteristics. She left the books and birds on display, and for days children could be seen examining the materials and painting their favorite birds in sometimes remarkable detail.

As in planning for field trips, teachers need to plan for special guests. They tell children about the guest, encourage them to think of things they want to know, and help them understand how they are expected to act during the visit. It is important that teachers remind visitors of children's interest level, attention span, and need for hands-on experience. Followup activities are similar to those for field trips. Relating the visit to classroom events through discussions, reading, writing, and projects enables children to integrate their learning.

Some resources from the natural environment can be brought into the classroom for closer examination. Teachers must carefully choose these resources. Endangered plants must not be disturbed, and certain animals are unsafe to bring into classrooms. But colorful leaves, nuts, and fruit, or twigs fallen from trees, rocks and seashells, minerals embedded in bits of rock, insects in aerated jars, and pond creatures for classroom aquariums are specimens that children can examine and study in the classroom. Some teachers have been successful hatching baby chicks or watching a cocoon develop into a moth or butterfly. Often, classroom volunteers have an interest or particular knowledge about these materials, and will be able to supervise children's involvement.

Community service agencies and businesses often have materials that classrooms can recycle, such as scraps of materials, boxes, bottles, juice and coffee cans, buttons, wire, and different types of spools. Some offices have old uniforms and business supplies representative of their occupation. These materials can be put in prop boxes for dramatic play or for presentations.

Often agencies also have printed materials, models, or audiovisual materials that are appropriate for classroom use. Some local television studios have tapes of educational programs that teachers may borrow and show. Community volunteers are often willing to assume responsibility for obtaining such materials.

Involving the Business Community

Businesses have provided support for schools in various ways for many years, most often in the form of funds for some particular project or materials. Band uniforms or costumes for a school production are items that local businesspeople take pride in providing for community junior high and high schools.

Lately, primary schools have also profited from business support. One kindergarten teacher doing a panda project convinced a local toy store manager to subsidize part of the unit. In addition to finding and donating toy pandas in different sizes, the manager agreed to donate money for children's books and other appropriate classroom materials. Although she didn't pay for the zoo trip the class took, the manager did subsidize the venture so all children were able to go. Other businesses have contributed classroom equipment including typewriters, calculators, and computers. A school supply store agreed to provide one enterprising kindergarten teacher with a year's supply of fingerpaints when her classroom budget was reduced. In return, children's work, demonstrating the creative potential of fingerpaint, was exhibited in the store.

Businesses have also provided programs for helping children understand what different jobs in their businesses entail. Hyatt Hotels collaborate with schools nationwide in a career day designed to teach children about opportunities in the hotel industry. A class spends a day at the Hyatt doing a two-hour shift with different Hyatt employees, from chef to sales manager. When children arrive at the hotel, they have breakfast and an orientation, then an introduction to their working partners and uniforms that fit their type of work. They then work with their partners, take a lunch break with them, and conclude the day in a recap session with hotel executives. Both hotel personnel and students receive preparation for the event, and those working with children are informed what to expect and how to proceed (F. R. Cook, personal communication, 1994).

Businesses also cooperate with schools by providing release time for employees to volunteer in the schools. In some instances, it is parent employees who wish to be a part of their children's classroom, but in other instances it is to allow unrelated employees to share special expertise with children. Project TEACH, in West Virginia, was organized by the chamber of commerce so classroom teachers could receive computer training. Area businesses were asked to release employees willing to substitute in classrooms while the regular teachers attended computer instruction. The volunteers received brief inservice training, which included modeling of good teaching practices and introduction to a teaching kit. The kit included information on child development, sample lesson plans, and suggested appropriate materials (Cowan, 1989).

Collaborating with business for better schools requires a spirit of mutual respect and reciprocity of benefit. For partnerships to be effective, teachers must visit the business establishment to determine what its educational possibilities are, and business personnel should visit schools to become acquainted with their function, goals, and daily operation. Each partner needs to know the other's resources, ideas, and commitments. Committees for each organization need to make decisions affecting the support and purpose of the collaboration. Teachers must be represented on the appropriate business committee, and involved business personnel should be a part of the school planning committee. Through such collaborations, teachers, parents, and community members gain new understandings of the importance of good schools to a community and of how the community can contribute to their excellence.

WORKING WITH SELECTED FAMILIES

The strategies used for collaborating with parents of all children in your classroom can be effective, no matter what the circumstances are. However, some groups need special consideration, especially when traditional methods are not working.

Parents of children with disabilities, members of ethnic minorities, homeless families, and gay and lesbian parents often find that schools do not reach out to them as easily as they do to other parents. It is imperative that schools reach all parents, and some teachers and administrators have found ways to be sensitive to special needs children. The first step is for teachers to examine their own feelings toward parents who are outside the mainstream and who may be more difficult to reach. It is natural to feel angry, guilty, frustrated, exhausted, even disapproving when no communication seems to work, or when others exhibit different priorities or a different lifestyle. Being honest about your feelings and discussing them with others will help to avoid using terms or making statements that hurt or anger parents who may have been rejected in other situations (White & Phair, 1986).

Children with Disabilities

All professionals must know the legal rights and the responsibilities parents have with regard to their children's education. Public Law 94–142 requires that parents of children with disabilities participate in planning and implementing educational programs for their children. Parents also have the right to challenge an educational plan if they deem it necessary. Regulations regarding educational planning include the following requirements, intended to establish positive communication between home and school (Gearheart, Weishahn, & Gearheart, 1996):

1. In discussions, the parents' native language must be used, with an interpreter if needed, so that good communication can be established.
2. Parents must give permission for assessments to be done on their children and must be informed about conferences whenever results are being considered.

3. Parent(s) should attend the meeting when children's Individualized Educational Plan (IEP) is confirmed. The law requires the time and place to be convenient for the parents.
4. Parents have a right to review their children's school records and ask for amendments if they feel records are inaccurate. If they disagree with the records or the evaluation, they have the right to an independent evaluation.

Parents of children with disabilities often feel alone and as if they were walking on a tightrope (Griffel, 1991). Many need to be treated more sensitively than do typical parents. Educators must make a special effort to be knowledgeable about disabilities and the implications these have for families. It is all too easy to use specialized language and educational jargon when discussing learning principles and teaching techniques, and most parents do not understand the terms. With the increased amounts of communication between teachers and parents of children with disabilities, we must be especially clear and precise about procedures and objectives.

Special workshops may be held to help teachers learn how to communicate without offending. Also, workshops in which parents of children with disabilities and teachers participate together are particularly valuable in facilitating cooperation. Parents and teachers need these workshops to share information, deal with everyday situations, help all parties cope with stress, and cement bonds with others.

Ethnic Diversity

When working with ethnically diverse families, teachers must understand what differences exist between the language of the school and that of the home. Remember that over 13 million residents of the United States do not speak English well, so if parents speak limited English, it is important to find someone who can translate. When teachers work with different linguistic groups, learning some words and expressions in the other language(s) communicates to parents that the teacher values their language and accepts the two-way responsibility for communicating.

Educational activities designed to respect all cultures in the classroom enhance communication between home and school. But teachers must make special efforts to involve minority parents in classrooms. Most parents have special knowledge of their heritage and culture that they will share with a class when approached in a positive way.

In one California school, parents of different ethnic backgrounds contributed in several ways. A Mexican American parent helped children prepare tacos for snacktime, and a Japanese American mother showed children how to make origami birds. A Native American father invited a second-grade class to his workshop and demonstrated basic skills in silver work. A recent German immigrant brought her collection of dolls to the school and explained the regional costumes the dolls wore.

Parents become much more involved in their children's learning when they help gather materials that children share in the classroom. This is especially beneficial for ethnically diverse families. One teacher developed a "Me-Museum," where each child displayed objects and pictures that reflected favorite objects from family life. The class's parents had helped their children collect and label the items, at times using native expressions as well as English translations. Parents and grandparents were encouraged to come with children also, to explain in more detail about the objects (Anderson & Suntken, 1989).

Prop boxes have been used in many early childhood classrooms as a means of providing enrichment for children's dramatic play, and this idea can be extended to include the home. The teacher can send theme prop boxes home with children to be used as stimuli for reading, writing, and play. For example, a grocery prop box would contain empty food boxes, play money in a box, signs for the items, and a pad for writing a grocery list. Inviting parents to add special items to the prop boxes from their family's cultural experience gives a multicultural aspect to the play, and also connects children's home experiences to the school (Neuman & Roskos, 1994).

Homeless Parents

Working with homeless families is one of the most challenging tasks a teacher faces. In spite of the McKinney Homeless Assistance Act of 1987 (PL 100–77), which requires states to guarantee access to education for homeless children, many homeless children are not in school. The requirements for registration, such as proof of residency, age, immunizations, and health records, are too much for many homeless families to cope with, and they find it easier to keep their children out of school (Eddowes & Hranitz, 1989). When children do have access to schooling, they often are not there long, as parents are forced to move again. Often these parents also are struggling with other problems, such as spouse abuse, depression, and poverty. Most need assistance in securing social services and if asked to help a school educate their children, the request will be beyond the skill of most homeless parents.

When homeless children are in a school, personnel need to unite their efforts to find support services that will enable parents to support their children's education. The following list contains several suggestions for teachers to assist parents in homeless situations (McCormick & Holden, 1992; Quint, 1994):

1. Provide information about availability of various services and funding options, and how to qualify for mental health services, day care, afterschool care, and transportation arrangements.
2. Suggest options for parent involvement in the school. Although regular commitment to volunteering in classrooms is beyond most homeless parents, it is wrong to assume they are unable or unwilling to help. They may spend a day tutoring or supervising. When they give comfort to another child, they receive the joys of assisting someone else.
3. Be sensitive to parents' ability to provide baked goods, pay for special class events, or have children bring materials for classroom projects. Children whose families cannot provide such materials are often discriminated against by other children and even by teachers. Consider asking homeless parents to assist in a cooking experience in the classroom.
4. Homeless parents, too, need parent workshops and opportunities to share their concerns and "stories." Often, it takes special handling to get these parents to trust enough to be a part of these sessions.
5. Coordinate efforts with local shelters. Some school programs or workshops can be started at shelters, but we must not segregate the homeless, denying children and parents opportunities for interaction with diverse groups.

Gay and Lesbian Parents

Most teachers today are sensitive to different family structures and are trained to support children when families are in the process of change due to death, divorce, remarriage, or adoption. Less attention has been given to working with gay and lesbian parents. Although a relatively small group, supporting these parents as partners in their children's education requires special efforts by school staff. Teachers may need workshops to enable them to come to grips with their feelings about homosexuality and to find ways to support children whose parents live this lifestyle.

In a diverse society, parents need to understand that all family structures presented in the classroom will be treated with dignity and respect. Beyond this, it is important for educators to be sensitive to the needs of children from gay and lesbian households. Teachers must help these parents support their children's learning as they do all others. Terminology used for diverse groups should always be that which is currently acceptable—in this case, *gay* and *lesbian* are appropriate (Clay, 1990).

When children of gay and lesbian parents experience difficulty in school, teachers must approach the parents to discuss their problems. By noting harassment, as well as by noting special friendships, teachers and parents can work together to help children deal with negative experiences. Janosik and Green (1992) have substantial recommendations for working with families that include gay members. Selected books also may help (see listing in Appendix).

SUMMARY

Forming special relationships with parents and communities to enhance the education of children is not a new concept in the United States. As educators have gained more responsibility and authority over children's education, they have realized that parental education and parent involvement also become part of the equation. And although educators have normally considered themselves experts in teaching children, they acknowledge that without parental and community support their job is more difficult.

Teachers over the years have developed many effective strategies for involving parents in children's education. Many traditional strategies still work very well. But when these strategies are not sufficient or have been outmoded, creative teachers and administrators must test innovative means for reaching parents.

Frequent communication between home and school is important. Parent-teacher conferences, newsletters, phone calls, home visits, and having parents participate in classroom and school activities are more effective when teachers experiment with different strategies so each family is reached at some level.

Teachers have developed many effective traditional and innovative strategies for parent education, for involving the community, and for working with parents of children with special needs. Most traditional strategies can be extended in innovative ways.

Educators do not see all parental involvement as positive and beneficial, but many educators now recognize that, when teachers, parents, and community members form a relationship of equality and shared responsibility, schools become strong and children acquire greater cognitive and social skills.

SUGGESTED ACTIVITIES AND QUESTIONS

1. Ask your parents (or someone you know well) about parent-teacher conferences or home visits in which they were involved. Determine how useful they felt such activity was. If you know a parent of a primary school-age child, ask the same questions and compare to see if there are differences in strategies and parental reactions.
2. Interview parents who volunteer in their children's classroom. Solicit their opinion of this involvement, asking how often they volunteer, how they became involved, why they think it is important, and what they are learning from the experience.
3. Locate a commercial establishment that displays children's work and ask how the school became involved. Compare notes with classmates who have interviewed other establishments to determine what kinds of involvement your community appears to have with schools.
4. Visit a school and check the bulletin boards in the hallways and in different classrooms. Identify the kinds of information these boards communicate to parents. Look for other signs that indicate whether parents are involved in the schools.
5. Obtain from a school administrator (or parents of a schoolage child) copies of newsletters sent home to parents. In your class, organize the collected newsletters by type and compare the kinds of information they contain. Discuss whether some are more "parent friendly" than others, and why.
6. Observe the neighborhood of an elementary school and identify a location you think would provide a good field trip for a primary-grade classroom. Plan an imaginary trip for a grade of your choice, noting what in the community you are valuing as good educational resources. Present your planned trip to your class for review.

RECOMMENDED READINGS

Cochran, M., Larner, M., Riley, R., Gunnarsson, L., & Henderson, C. R., Jr. (Eds.). (1990). *Extending families: The social networks of parents and their children.* New York: Cambridge University Press.

Coleman, J. (1991). *Policy perspectives: Parental involvement in education.* Washington, DC: U.S. Department of Education, Office of Educational Research and Improvement.

Henderson, A. T., Marburger, C. L., & Ooms, T. (1986). *Beyond the bake sale: An educator's guide to working with parents.* Columbia, MD: National Committee for Citizens in Education.

Hymes, J. (1974). *Effective home school relations* (Rev. ed.). Sierra Madre, CA: Southern Association for the Education of Young Children.

Rotter, J. C. (1987). *Parent-teacher conferencing: What research says to the teacher.* Washington, DC: National Education Association.

Swap, S. M. (1984). *Enhancing parent involvement in schools: A manual for parents and teachers.* Boston: Wheelock College.

Topping, K. J. (1986). *Parents as educators: Training parents to teach their children.* Cambridge, MA: Brookline.

Models for Parent-School-Community Partnerships

I n this chapter, we detail particular program models, examining the various components leading to successful changes for school-based collaborations. We also discuss other promising initiatives occurring in different parts of the United States. In reading this chapter you will learn that:

1. Home–school–community partnerships work because of thoughtful planning, careful implementation, straightforward accountability, and honest communication.

2. Four major partnership projects have provided a framework for operation and have designed activities that now serve as models for other programs.

3. Parents and community members become involved in partnerships at different levels—from occasional volunteer work to advocating for children.

4. In addition to developed and well-defined partnerships, small projects also involve parents, schools, and communities in collaborative efforts.

5. Partnership models vary considerably, but quality programs have many common features.

Parent–school–community collaboration is not a recent phenomenon in the United States. The Cooperative Nursery School Movement, at the beginning of the twentieth century, required parents and teachers to cooperatively plan education and work with children. Community schools in the 1960s integrated many community services into school programs. A hallmark of collaborative efforts for U.S. schools began in 1965 with Head Start.

The Head Start and later Follow Through programs were established to provide comprehensive services for poor families. Parental and community involvement was mandated for these federally funded plans, and the programs were required to support parents as they learned new roles for educating their children. These early programs provided patterns for later ventures in home–school–community partnerships.

In 1988, when federal legislation established the Educational Partnerships Program, the concept of partnerships was extended to include alliances between different community organizations and public schools. As a result, a small number of programs began in the early 1990s. Some were initiated to unite social services, public schools, and business organizations, while others focused on educational improvements through gradual changes within school systems (Danzberger & Gruskin, 1993).

In this chapter, we describe several current program models and note research studies that confirm the importance of such programs for children. Though these programs differ in content from one another, all validate the notion of drawing efforts and resources from all major social settings in children's experience. We also find in these models certain planning procedures and strategies that seem to ensure successful programs that result in meaningful change.

COMPONENTS OF SUCCESSFUL CHANGE

Research studies show that children improve academically when schools work for better school and community involvement (Thompson, 1993; U. S. Department of Education, 1994; Epstein, 1987). Because of this promise, and through administrative campaigns, a number of school districts are now caught up in the rhetoric of "collaboration." Some have taken serious steps to establish links with social service agencies and arrange for more parental involvement. Some have struggled and had little success, and others have gotten only to goal statements and committee assignments (Tushnet, 1993).

As more businesses become involved with schools, one detects a danger that some business executives see this relationship as an opportunity to garner customers for their products or ideas. In any collaboration, parents and teachers must assume the ethical responsibility for ensuring that commercial enterprises understand children's developmental levels and their vulnerability. If businesspeople usurp teachers' and parents' rights and responsibilities, then children can become victims. Successful partnerships mean shared responsibilities. The rewards for involvement must be more fully educated children, not more consumers of given products. Most school personnel want parents and community members to share in the responsibility of educating children, and they seek outside support for school events and for resolving nonacademic problems. However, in academic matters, educators are more hesitant to in-

volve parents and community members. Yet successful schools mean that parents, school personnel, and community groups share responsibilities for decision making regarding all educational matters.

The work does go on, and we find glimmers of hope regarding collaboration from time to time. In some communities, schools and social services have coordinated services so that families receive more comprehensive assistance and less hassle. And, indeed, some schools, after struggling to expand home–school–community relationships, have found that both student achievement and faculty expertise in curriculum development improved, and that the business community valued their efforts more highly.

The programs that have been successful have different strategies for achieving collaboration, but all have certain elements in common, which Gardner (1993) calls "the hooks, glue, and joint ventures" (p. 15). All good programs have a planning process, an implementation process, and an accountability process (Carter, 1993). Equally important is that, in each process, all involved pay constant attention to establishing good communication and developing trust, familiarity, and understanding (Smrekar, 1993).

Planning

Collaboration requires a community-wide team. Members of social agencies, businesses, and government agencies, and teachers, administrators, and parents come together in some fashion, and all make a commitment to work for the benefit of the community's children. The community team needs a strong leader, and all participants must be willing to work out differences when necessary. Key people in the community are crucial for the project. Trust and respect for other viewpoints are even more vital.

During planning, the team determines the needs of children in the community, develops goals, and designs procedures for accomplishing these goals. The team identifies children's particular needs within the various community contexts, then assesses the community to identify resources to meet these needs. Communication, collaboration, and cooperation among the various team members mean that all agencies will surrender some power, autonomy, and turf in seeking solutions, but in so doing all recognize the mutual benefits from the project. The team first develops long-term goals, then specific immediate objectives so implementation can proceed.

Implementation

As the collaboration team develops procedures for implementing strategies, members ascertain which agencies can provide personnel and financial resources. Implementation is guaranteed greater success when a team has provided orienting and training sessions, ensuring that parents, teachers, and community people have collaborative skills.

A major step in beginning collaboration is providing workshops that help reduce the social distance among participants and that also improve relationships among parents, school staff, and students. Another involves understanding the interests and expertise of teachers, parents, and other volunteers, so that all can contribute their best. All contributions must be respected and, ideally, all gain an understanding of how their service contributes to the goals and objectives.

After the team prioritizes the community's needs, it begins to plan and collaborate on such activities as providing families with needed services, improving school and home discipline, adapting curriculum to particular community needs, establishing appropriate social activities, and developing program evaluation strategies.

Assessment

People working with collaborative programs have ways to determine how well their goals are being met. Most projects will review students' classroom work, and many programs develop questionnaires to get feedback from the community about the success of their activities. Data are collected and interpreted regularly, and strategies are altered or continued accordingly. Parents, school staff, and community members are kept informed about progress, assessments, and changes being made to improve conditions. Project members annually summarize progress for the community at large.

Communication

The success of all collaborative programs depends on good communication and careful monitoring of activities. Parents must feel welcome to visit schools and to participate, and teachers must feel they are able to visit homes as needs arise. Community persons must also be part of the communication loop. All must feel welcome in schools, and feel free to offer suggestions.

Many avenues provide parents and community members with information about school activities and what is happening with the collaboration. Routine notices, telephone messages, personal notes, newsletters, articles in local papers, and the direct approach, which volunteers employ in contacting "hard to reach parents," are all used. Parents are encouraged to write notes or call teachers when concerns arise, and are encouraged to express appreciation as well.

Features of Successful Collaboration

New partnerships are beginning slowly but surely across the United States, and though the stimulus varies, often projects start in response to educational problems at the local and state level. Irrespective of the motivation, we find that collaborative efforts do result in greater opportunities for students when the "whole child, whole community" concept is adopted (Davies, 1993). Each successful partnership will be unique, but all seem to include the following features (Davies, Burch, & Palanki, 1993; Decker & Decker, 1988; Tushnet, 1993):

- Programs comprehensively and intensively integrate educational and social services for all children, but especially for needy families.

Collaboration requires a broadly based community team working for the benefit of the community's children.

- Parents, school personnel, and community members are empowered to make decisions about, plan for, and implement changes for their community's children.
- School bureaucracy reduces and involvement of community and home in school management increases.
- Schools become family centers to promote better interactions among teachers, parents, and community members.
- Programs include strong volunteer programs, with parents, grandparents, and community members contributing expertise to support children's learning, and to assist in school operations.
- Community and home are viewed as important children's learning environments and are integrated into school learning.
- University programs provide training for the establishment of successful partnerships.
- Faculty and staff have time for training, and develop skills needed to build and maintain relationships of trust and respect with children and families.
- Researchers, teachers, and parents work together in assessing the successes of school programs.

PROGRAM MODELS

Head Start

When Project Head Start was conceived in 1965, authorities acknowledged that children were not only family members but also community members. Thus, if Head Start was to succeed in changing the lives of children, then parental involvement and community commitment to the program's goals were paramount. Through this involvement and commitment, Head Start began to provide in holistic rather than fragmented ways comprehensive services in health, economics, nutrition, as well as school readiness for children and their families.

Purpose

The purpose for involving communities in Head Start was to make the community aware of the importance of providing adequate health, educational, and nutritional services for children's development. If skills developed in the Head Start programs were to be sustained, then parents and community had to reinforce the learning. Parent involvement reached even further, for the programs created avenues for parents to gain skills for participating in different social contexts and to gain greater self-confidence and self-esteem.

Types of Parental Involvement

Parents may assist in a variety of ways at Head Start centers or in classrooms. The *Head Start Manual of Policies and Instruction,* still in force today, outlines the types of parental involvement available.

Parents as partners. Parents are partners with professionals in the decision-making process, and we find two levels open to parents of Head Start children. At the informal level, parents work with center staff on determining program content and how their children will participate. At a more formal level, parents serve on a parent policy committee or council. Fifty percent of council membership must be parents of current Head Start children, and must be elected to the council by parents of participating children. Council parents are involved in program improvements, parent activities, recruiting volunteers, and planning and developing a budget for the parent activity fund. They are also involved in decisions about program goals, criteria for selection of children, hiring Head Start staff, and major changes in budget and work programs.

Parents as observers. Parents participate in Head Start classrooms as observers, volunteers, and as paid aides, to observe different ways of working with their children. They gain a better understanding of what their children are learning, and what they can do to assist them at home. Children seeing their parents in the classroom know their parents are interested in their learning and see the cooperation and support that parents and teachers give one another. When parents become more involved as volunteers or as paid aides, they gain skills and confidence, which in turn help them qualify for employment elsewhere.

Parents as learners. Head Start parents become involved in their own learning by planning and identifying opportunities that correspond to their own interests and aspirations. Workshops and other learning experiences for a center are often requested by and designed by parents, who in this fashion increase their own education. Career ladders have been developed where parents are able to progress through workshops to obtain their GED. Some parents in Head Start programs have continued their education at technical schools, community colleges, and four-year colleges, increasing their opportunities for employment.

Supporting children's learning. Parents work at home with their children to support and reinforce children's Head Start experiences. Center personnel create and distribute ideas and suggestions for home activities, and often visit homes to observe and suggest ways family members can support children's education. As parents become aware of their impact on children's learning, they become confident about helping them grow and develop (Head Start Bureau, 1980; Greenberg, 1990).

Research

Since Project Head Start's inception, the effects of early intervention on children's development have been a subject of much research and public concern. Initial research by Westinghouse Learning Corporation–Ohio University (1969) indicated cognitive gains for Head Start children after the first year, but by the third year these gains had nearly disappeared.

The study had many critics who pointed to several limitations of the study, including viewing all Head Start programs as if they were of equal quality, examining only one aspect of potential benefits, not recognizing the importance of medical and nutritional benefits, and ignoring the unproven validity of some evaluation instruments

(Evans, 1975). The study did alert the public that a basic assumption of the War on Poverty was unrealistic—a single summer or one-year program could not produce rapid academic results for economically disadvantaged children.

Long-term studies of the initial programs, however, reveal that Head Start has been both cost effective and beneficial to society. Both the Consortium for Longitudinal Studies and The Perry School Project indicated that children of poverty had indeed profited from Head Start experiences. Though initial achievement gains tended to disappear, and Head Start children never "caught up" cognitively with their middle-class peers, by high school these children demonstrated significant differences from those disadvantaged children who had not attended Head Start. Head Start children did better in school, repeated fewer grades, and were less often placed in remedial classes. As adults, they were less likely to end up in jail than their peers who had not attended Head Start (Lazar & Darlington, 1982; Schweinhart & Weikart, 1980).

Studies revealed also that Head Start children's social development improved, to equal their middle-class peers. They became more task oriented, sustained attention to task longer, and developed curiosity about learning. Children with disabilities appeared to benefit the most after involvement in Head Start programs. Collins's (1984) synthesis of over 1,500 Head Start studies confirmed the positive impacts on children's cognitive, social, and health development, as well as improvements in parenting.

Many Head Start programs successfully coordinated health and social services for their children. As a result a large percentage of participants maintained their immunizations, as well as medical and dental exam schedules. Due to this medical attention and to the sound nutritional school programs, Head Start participants are found healthier today than other disadvantaged children.

As noted, parental involvement is a requirement of Head Start programs, and was really the first large-scale involvement of parents in children's formal education. Parents have served as policy makers, teachers, aides, and volunteers, and two of every three students in Head Start have parents involved in one of these above capacities. There is an additional payoff for that connection: studies indicate that children of involved Head Start parents had higher academic achievement, were more likely to graduate from high school or college, and were more apt to have full-time employment. A further benefit, for a small percentage of Head Start parents, was assistance in finding jobs and in continuing their education (Collins 1984).

Communities that established and maintained Head Start programs have benefited, as well. A number of poor and minority parents in these communities have moved into the work force, and area public schools changed because of the models that Head Start provided, including strategies for parental participation, implementing developmentally appropriate curriculum, mainstreaming children with special needs, modifying health services, and implementing practices accommodating the needs of poor children and minorities.

Certainly, Head Start has not succeeded in fulfilling the dream of eliminating poverty in the United States or in filling in all learning gaps, but its impact has been positive and its benefits, for helping poor and minority families become partners in their children's education, outweigh the costs. All collaborative efforts can profit from the procedures and experiences of this model.

Home-Based Programs

With the lessons of Head Start came the realization that children—even before the age of 4—needed help if we were to overcome the debilitating effects of poverty. The realization of the importance of parents as children's first teachers led to ideas for developing home-based programs. Several such programs were funded by the U.S. Office of Education in the late 1960s and 1970s. Ira Gordon,

Two of every three students in Head Start have a parent involved as a volunteer, aide, teacher, or board representative.

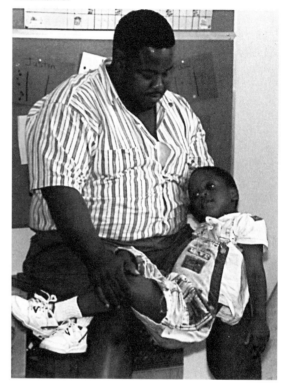

David Weikart, Phyllis Levenstein, and Susan Gray were among the first educator/researchers who developed model programs. Many communities adapted one or another of these models as extensions of their Head Start programs. Other home-based programs have been developed and funded by private foundation monies and/or because of local and state initiatives.

Purpose

The intent of all home-based programs is to use the home as a beginning point in children's education. The concept recognizes that parents are children's first teachers, and that it is important to help and train parents to become more effective teachers. The emphasis in the 1990s for many home-based programs has been family literacy.

Recognizing that "the family is the primary system for the transmission of values from adults to children" (Smith, 1994, p. 2), these home visiting programs attempt to make parents aware of the power of their influence on the development of their children's prereading skills.

Types of Involvement

The focus of individual programs depends on the needs of families in particular communities. Gordon's (1969) Parent Education/Involvement Model was replicated throughout the United States, and still serves as a model for communities reaching out to families. The program had direct links to Head Start Programs, because the Head Start teacher and parent educator worked together and planned appropriate activities to be carried out in homes. In many programs today, the parent educator is associated with a center-based program, and collaborates with a teacher or supervisor in that program.

In Gordon's original model, the parent educator, a person from the community served, was the key component of home visiting. These parent educators spent half of their time in homes demonstrating prepared lessons and the other half in classrooms working with teachers and children. In homes they engaged parents in role-playing lesson activities as well as in discussions of the intent and purpose of the teaching. In the classroom they became better acquainted with the children and learned techniques for the school curriculum. Changing school curriculum to meet the needs of parents served was not a goal; instead, the activities for home-based programs were intended to extend and build on the cognitive and affective development of children to get them ready for a school environment (Gordon, 1969).

Many activities were language related, and the home teaching encouraged parents to follow the demonstrated strategies closely in order to understand effective teaching. Considerable emphasis was on extending parents' ability to use an elaborated language code, which would in turn extend children's language development. The model emphasized both positive reinforcement strategies and techniques for explaining and eliciting explanations and questions from children.

Today, many programs still seek a trained person from the community, although some programs have professional social workers, early childhood specialists, or nurses. Ideally, this person has specialized training in the development of infants and toddlers and in the specific needs of parents with very young children. Many programs are adapted from the early models, but currently educators establish trust and encourage more collaboration as they build on the skills parents already possess. Programs differ, but for many the home curriculum emphasizes the role of play in children's development, the importance of reading to young children from infancy, and the value of quality interaction between parent and child. Nutritional and health and safety information is still a feature of many programs (An Ounce of Prevention Fund, 1994).

Many home-based programs have special features, which are developed outside the home. Well-equipped parent resource centers provide materials for families and for children. Planned neighborhood gatherings enable infants and toddlers to have opportunities to play together, and give parents the chance to socialize and discuss their children's learning. Opportunities to hear experts in early development are available, as is participation in more formal discussion groups (Florida State Department of Education, 1992; Hedrich & Jackson, 1977).

Research

Although research on home-based programs encounters many of the same difficulties associated with the Head Start and Follow Through projects, evaluation results indicate that participants showed increased self-confidence in parenting ability, in the quality of mother–child interactions, and in skill development of the children involved (Florida State Department of Education, 1992; Gordon, 1969).

Comer's School Development Program

In 1968, James Comer and his colleagues at the Yale Child Study Center began the School Development Program, a collaboration with two New Haven elementary schools to increase parental involvement in the education of their children. Both schools were located in low-income areas, all children were African American, and parent participation in school activities was very low. When examining parent interest and involvement, the team discovered three levels or patterns that revealed home–school connections. One, most parents expressed interest in the activities their children participated in at school. Second, some parents were also interested in volunteering for particular activities in the school. Third, a few parents were interested in curriculum and how teachers instructed their children (Comer & Haynes, 1991). With this knowledge, Comer and his team began a series of experiments and adjustments that used parents' interests to bring about collaboration. Now, over two decades after the conclusion of the project, the experiment has become a highly touted model for involving parents.

Major Goals

The initial School Development Program evolved over a five-year period. Participants gradually adjusted the structure as programs evolved and needs changed. A steering committee, formed of administrators, teachers, parents, aides, professional and nonprofessional support staff, and the Yale Child Center mental health team, established major goals for the project (Comer, 1980):

- Modify the social and psychological climate of the school to facilitate greater student learning.
- Improve students' basic skills.
- Raise students' motivation for learning and their academic and occupational aspiration level.
- Create a sense of shared responsibility and decision making among parents and staff.
- Connect child development and clinical services to the educational program of the schools.

Structure of the Program

The program now consists of three teams: the school planning and management team (originally called the steering committee), a Yale Child Study Center mental health team, and the pupil personnel team, plus four major features: a parent program, a focus program, workshops, and an extended day program.

School planning and management team. The original steering committee was made up of "stakeholders" in the school, and its purpose was overall guidance of project planning, implementation, and evaluation. This committee has now become the school planning and management team (SPMT), which develops and implements academic and social programs, designs staff development, evaluates the program, and makes necessary adjustments. From experience with difficulties and various experiments, three important guidelines evolved for the SPMT: (1) solving problems with a no-fault approach, (2) using principles of child development for decision making, and (3) ensuring that collaborative management does not paralyze the school principal when important administrative decisions must be made (Comer & Haynes, 1991).

Mental health team. The mental health team consists of a child psychiatrist, two social workers, an educator with early childhood education training, an educator involved in teacher training, and a psychologist/program evaluator. Its main purpose is assisting school staff in understanding and applying principles of social and behavioral science to school problems and opportunities. The mental health team at first helped parents and school staff develop skills of cooperation, and assisted teachers in managing behavior problems and in changing or creating school rules. Since behavior problems decreased at the school, the team now provides help for curriculum planning and facilitates communication between school personnel and families, between teachers and students, and among teachers, administrators, and nonprofessional staff.

Pupil personnel team. A pupil personnel team initially cooperated with the principal, community social service personnel, and special teachers by giving services directly to students who needed such support. As conditions in the school have changed and behavioral problems lessened, this service is now more educational in nature and less behavioral.

Parent program. A parent program started with a small group of parents receiving a stipend for assisting teachers. This core group formed the nucleus of the parent group and served on governance bodies and subcommittees that helped plan social and educational programs. Their function was to "bring attitudes, values, ways, and needs of the community to these committees and activities" (Comer, 1980, p. 65). As the program changed to meet school and community needs, the parent program has evolved to include parent involvement at three different levels.

Presently, at the first level, five or six parents are elected to serve on the school planning and management team where decisions about programs and operations are made. These parents become a source for enlisting parents for other levels of participation, and help overcome barri-

ers that inhibit "hard-to-reach" parents. They also bring a community perspective to the planning process, assisting teachers in planning culturally appropriate programs.

At the second level, 5 to 10 percent of the total parent group are involved in helping in classrooms or in sponsoring and supporting school programs. The strength of this involvement is that parents and teachers work together to motivate students to achieve academically and socially.

At the more modest third level, parents become involved in activities in which their children are engaged. They attend student performances and other teacher–parent activities where "good news" is shared, and generally support the program from a distance.

Focus program. At the start of the project, a focus program was established to help children one or more years behind in reading and math skills. Three times a week, these children were taught in groups of two to six to supplement classroom teaching of reading and mathematics. Currently, the focus groups change as children's learning needs are identified.

In the community model, the "focus program" helps individual children develop reading and math skills.

Workshops. At the beginning, two-week summer workshops allowed parents and teachers to get to know each other and share their perspective on the academic and social experiences they felt children needed. Workshops are ongoing now and are offered when teachers or parents indicate a need.

Extended day programs. Initially, teachers were required to attend afterschool programs, for which they received a small stipend. This program included workshops for teachers to learn more about child development and behavior, teaching and curriculum development, and the use of arts in promoting academic skills. In addition, teachers developed skills in meeting with parents and planning parent participation projects. These extended day programs have ceased, and any needs are now addressed in the workshops.

Social skills curriculum. In establishing community involvement, Comer's team found that many distinctions between low-income and middle-income children involved differences in social skills that middle-income children acquired in their homes. As a result, the team devised a social skills curriculum for inner-city children, consisting of four units: politics and government, business and economics, health and nutrition, and spiritual and leisure time. Field trips, visits by community members, and lots of hands-on activities enabled low-income children to enhance their interpersonal skills, writing skills, and interactive skills with adults. A banking unit provided experiences in receiving a "bank check" for work done and then spending the check or learning to save it for a purpose. A gospel choir helped students learn responsibility to a group and to plan, organize, and select programs, as well as rehearsal procedures and performance demeanor. In the government unit, students learned to write and give speeches, then hold a miniconvention and election. Other innovative programs, such as a Discovery Room, continuing with same teacher plan, and a support system for new students, were developed as the team reached out to solve student and parent problems. Many aspects of the social skills curriculum continue today.

Research

After five years of working through problems and modifying procedures, rules, teaching strategies, and programs, the School Development Program showed remarkable success. The two participating schools progressed from having the worst attendance records in the city to having the best. Overall academic achievement went from third from the bottom to among the top schools in the city. Behavior problems were greatly reduced, and parent–teacher misunderstandings lessened as parental participation in school activities increased. When the program started, only 30 parents participated at a major Christmas program; four years later 400 parents attended. Major activities attracted an average attendance of 250 for a school population of 300 (Comer & Haynes, 1991). The consensus is that home, school, and community links growing from the School Development Program in New Haven have provided essential ingredients for children's healthy development.

The Comer model has been replicated in over 500 schools across the nation. In Washington, DC, several neighborhoods have successfully changed their schools from places where violence, drugs, and crime were paramount to schools where students, parents, and community are reenergized with meaningful and engaging activities, where "high expectations and everyone working together . . . has become an attitude, a way of learning and an education for life" (Ramirez-Smith, 1995, p. 19).

Schools Reaching Out Project

In collaboration with the Institute for Responsive Education, the Schools Reaching Out project began in Boston and New York City during 1988, with two laboratory schools trying new strategies to build closer relationships among families, communities, and schools (Heleen, 1990). The schools enrolled primarily African American and Hispanic students with basic skills scores in the lowest quartile. The intent was for researchers and teachers working together to find out which collaborative strategies worked and why.

Basic Assumptions

The project started with the premise that attitudes toward family involvement in learning could be altered by changing the structure and manner in which teachers and parents interacted. All workers were convinced that if the project schools were to succeed, then family involvement was a necessity and that all parents, even those "hard to reach," could be involved (Heleen, 1990). A guiding principle was that children achieved better in school when home and school maintain a continuity of values, expectations, and attitudes. A second principle was that it is imperative for school personnel to help parents understand what and how schools teach their children, so that parents can reinforce these efforts at home (Swap, 1993).

Structure of the Program

Each school formed a school–community council that made decisions regarding objectives, policies, and strategies for involving parents. Both schools were required by the Institute to have a parent center, a key teacher, a home visitor program, and a teacher action research team.

The parent center was a room especially for parents, where they could meet with other parents, relax, and hold special meetings. The room was to make parents feel comfortable and welcome in the school and give them a place within the school they could "own."

The key teacher, released from classroom teaching, became the coordinator of most project activities. In both schools, surveys dictated some of the activities that the key teacher supervised, such as English as a second language classes (Heleen, 1990).

The home visitor program stressed the importance of family empowerment, building on family strengths, and building family involvement in neighborhood networks. Four paid parent support workers, trained in counseling and work in community settings, provided three types of service in the home. They distributed information about school programs, homework requirements, and special events. They assisted children in the home and demonstrated to parents various ways to help children develop academic and social skills. They met with teachers to exchange information about children in their classes and to make suggestions on how teachers could help parents.

Teacher researcher teams studied home–school relationships and devised strategies to include more parents in work with schools. After conducting surveys and interviews, one small teacher action research team designed several programs that helped parents enrich their children's learning activities, including a toy lending library (Davies, 1990).

Selected Activities

Activities in these programs included GED courses for parents and English as a second language classes to assist parents in increasing language proficiency. To develop more idea exchanges, grade-level breakfasts were held. When one school launched a "whole language" initiative, a parent and community volunteer group assisted teachers in teaching reading and writing. Special projects were established, such as the toy lending library, a clothing exchange, and a school store. Trips, social events, and workshops where parents, teachers, and community members could work and play together were carried out (Davies, 1990; Heleen, 1990).

Extension of the Project

In 1990, the Schools Reaching Out project became the League of Schools Reaching Out, and as of 1993 had become a network of over 80 schools nationwide, involving homes, schools, and communities in collaborative efforts. The major goal for all programs now is to provide academic and social success for all children, but different schools provide various activities for children and their families. Two key elements we see in all programs are that collaboration is a requirement for

The home visitor program demonstrates to parents ways to help their children.

delivering comprehensive services to a community, and that multiple ways exist for families, communities, and schools to share responsibility for making good partnerships work (Davies, Burch, & Palanki, 1993).

Epstein's Levels of Partnership

The league has adopted Epstein's (1992) typology of six family and community involvement activities to keep track of and to ensure progress for programs for the League of Schools Reaching Out. We describe this typology in the following subsections, and give examples of how league schools adapted activities (examples adapted from Davies, Burch, & Johnson, 1992; Davies, Burch, & Palanki, 1993; Epstein, 1992).

Basic obligations of families. Families are responsible for providing children with the basic health, emotional, social, and educational support to enable them to develop in increasingly complex ways. Schools help families develop childrearing practices with strategies such as the following:

- Parent education workshops
- Family resource centers
- Home visitor program involving trained parent outreach workers
- Grade-level meetings with parents to discuss curriculum, learning goals, and how parents and teachers can work together to help children achieve goals
- Trips for parents and teachers to cultural events
- Before- and afterschool care in cooperation with other agencies

Basic obligations of schools. Schools are responsible for communicating with parents regarding their children's progress and the school programs. Partnerships are strengthened when there is effective two-way communication, including the following:

- Teachers visiting homes
- Parent–teacher conferences and report cards
- School handbook, fliers, newsletters, and activities calendar
- Dial-a-Teacher program and student homework club
- Phone conferences

Involvement at school. Parents are involved in league schools in two ways: (1) they attend school events to show support for their children and for schools; and (2) they are volunteers, helping in classrooms, offices, the library, or in special areas. Schools vary schedules so more parents can become involved, and recruitment and training events help volunteers understand the routines and objectives of the teachers. Parents assume some of the following activities:

- Recruiting other volunteers
- Organizing and assisting in field trips
- Organizing summer enrichment programs
- Volunteering as classroom aides, librarians, and clerical assistants, or as lunchroom and playground aides
- Organizing special programs and fairs
- Becoming tutors for other children

Involvement in learning activities at home. Teachers collaborate with parents in supporting children's learning at home. They coordinate home and classroom learning and provide enrichment activities. Teachers help parents understand the academic skills children need at each grade level. Activities include the following:

- Toy and book lending libraries
- Specially designed materials for parents to use with children at home
- Workshops on how to use materials
- Home visitors who work with parents on use of materials
- Special reading and math projects for parents to do with their children

Involvement in decision making, governance, and advocacy. Parents become part of the policy-making team for the school. Parents are trained in decision-making skills, how to communicate with all parents they represent, and how to use community advocacy groups to address issues of school improvement, through the following methods:

- Workshops to train parents for advocacy
- Participation in selected school councils and committees (school management teams, Chapter I and Head Start councils, curriculum committees, budget committees, social committees)
- Participation in community decision-making councils

Collaboration with community organizations. Schools collaborate with social service agencies, business organizations, and cultural and social organizations to extend children's learning experiences in communities. They share responsibility with these other organizations to assist families in obtaining support services and information about community resources that strengthen their children's learning. League schools and communities have collaborated in the following ways:

- Partnerships with specific businesses in a community
- Fulltime community service personnel on school staff
- Civic leaders meeting regularly with parent and teacher groups regarding neighborhood and school issues
- Partnerships with local police, fire, drug abuse, and child abuse officers to provide families with information, prevention, and tutoring services
- Partnerships with radio and TV educational networks to develop programs and activities that involve families in educational and community endeavors

Research

The Institute for Responsive Education studied 42 urban schools in the national network of League of Schools Reaching Out (Davies et al., 1992). The intent of the investigation was to examine the practices of urban schools for involving parents in collaborative efforts, and to determine how the policies affected these practices. The study drew the following conclusions.

Many of the schools are becoming "community institutions" by serving families and by exchanging resources with other community agencies. The level of activity proved high in all the schools, and partnership activities had increased.

Although researchers found that traditional strategies for communicating with families were predominant, all schools showed they used multiple means for linking up with families. Parent volunteering was high, and the range of volunteer activities had expanded to accommodate needs of working parents. Multiple advisory and policy councils existed in all schools studied.

Support from the school principal was essential for League of Schools Reaching Out member schools to achieve their goals.

Other Promising Initiatives

In the past decade, a number of collaborative ventures have emerged in different U.S. communities to improve education of children in their areas. Many communities have adopted comprehensive models, like the Comer model, and these adaptations have proven successful. Other communities are trying small projects, expanding their focus as they meet important goals. In some projects, schools work with a single organization; others involve alliances with several organizations. Most projects have had some success. Commitment and dedication to the idea that collaboration can make a difference in children's education are underlying features for all projects.

Adopt-a-School

The first Adopt-a-School program was established in Boston in 1978 as an outgrowth of the Boston Compact with area colleges, and its goal was to assist public schools in desegregation efforts. As more businesses became involved, the focus changed from racial balance to concerns about early childhood education, decreasing drop-out rates, and decentralizing school governance (Grobe, Curnan, & Melchoir, 1993).

Texas and Tennessee both have exemplary Adopt-a-School programs. The programs involve the business community in the educational process, and businesspersons try to help communities understand the schooling process and what each community school needs to provide better education. In all plans for these two states, coordinators identify needs of the schools and resources of the business community, and then try to match schools to appropriate businesses.

Activities in Adopt-a-School plans vary, but providing tutors and mentors for children with specific talents or needs is common. Other typical

Partnership programs have expanded to meet more needs of working parents.

activities include speakers for classrooms, pen pals, tours of business enterprises, scholarships for both teachers and students to attend specific meetings, classroom presentations, perfect attendance incentives, career workshops, educational films, and judges for school events. Other developments include workshops or services for teachers. One business enterprise even formed a volleyball team that played on a regular basis to raise funds for a schoolwide project (Brooks & Powell, 1986; Decker & Decker, 1988).

Lighthouse Project

Seeking a pilot program to guide change, the Bennington (Vermont) School District launched the Lighthouse project in 1994 (Webster, n.d.). The project is based on the concepts of collaboration, choice, and consensus. The initiative was preceded by discussions and meetings among concerned parents, teachers, and administrators to discuss changes in their schools. The meetings resulted in a governance board of faculty, parents, and administrators who began to examine curriculum and to develop strategies for increasing community involvement in schools.

The board selected one school site that served families from all economic levels; however, the "choice" concept allowed area parents to participate or choose to send their children to more traditional classes in the district. Parents applied for openings in the pilot project and administrators selected participants so as to reflect a cross section of the Bennington community.

As the program progresses, developmental learning is stressed in this pilot program as children attend multi-age classrooms for the following age ranges: 5–8, 7–10, and 9–13 years. A thematic curriculum is designed by the team of teachers, parents, and administrators, using an interdisciplinary approach for acquiring skills and subject matter. One hundred percent parent involvement is the project goal, but the plan permits several levels of involvement for different families.

The governance team has worked to build trust and secure commitment of all parents and community volunteers related to the school. Program decisions are made as a result of consensus building. Professional development is ongoing for all participants, and staff and parents attend workshops after the groups identify areas they need help with.

Authentic assessment is a major focus of the Lighthouse project. Participants search for different strategies to assess what has been taught, and experiment with means to give appropriate feedback to students, and to parents and teachers. In this way, they believe that all concerned can best adjust to curriculum and lesson development requirements.

Initial success of the program is evidenced in the enthusiasm children have for the many projects undertaken so far. Strong community support for the program is evident also, and community members have stepped in to help when family members are unable to meet commitments. Parents are enthused and recognize the hard work necessary for building schools. Even more importantly, they see that children's education must involve the entire community.

Model Programs in Oregon

Most large school districts in Oregon have business–education partnerships (Oregon Department of Education, 1990). The Governor's Outstanding Partnership Awards and the State Superintendent's Business–Education Partnerships' Awards reflect a range of business enterprises engaged with schools in improving educational opportunities for Oregon students. The following are common characteristics of these partnerships, and key findings from partnership experiences:

- Mutual benefits accrue to partnership members.
- Face-to-face contact for teachers, students, and businesspeople spontaneously brings out interests and needs.
- Partnerships mutually establish specific goals pertaining to learning outcomes.
- Flexible involvement allows for different levels of participation depending on time and commitments.

- Communication between schools and businesses is consistent and effective.
- Clear monitoring of projects and personnel makes adjustments easier.
- Key people, committed to the project, are identified.
- Volunteer efforts are recognized.
- Partnership members provide annual reports to all parties involved and establish a sense of working together.

Activities for different partnerships in Oregon vary. The most common show business community involvement through contributions of material or equipment, business employees teaching in classrooms, job fair events, and school staff use of business facilities. The following examples illustrate.

Gove's Market's involvement with Eastwood Elementary School was a partnership where mutual benefits accrued. Every student in grades K–6 displayed a piece of art in the store. Along with the artwork, the market displayed information about school events, with student photos. As an incentive for good behavior, the market provided "Eastwood Bucks," which students could exchange at the market for special treats. In addition, personnel from the market assisted teachers in many out-of-class activities, and besides a feeling of good will, the store has benefited from increased business.

The Gresham Area Business and Education Partnership involved several industries working with Centennial School District in Oregon. In addition to such regular, ongoing events as workshops for teachers and employment fairs for students, many partnerships were formed by informal contacts that teachers and children had with business leaders during field trips. For example, a business executive and a principal met at a visit to Viking Industries, and discovered a mutual concern regarding drug abuse. As a result, a program was developed whereby elementary students assisted in a drug awareness program for employees of Viking Industries. Such a program is an example of both parties benefiting, with students doing some of the giving.

Charter School Movement

As of 1994, 11 states had passed laws permitting the formation of "charter schools." This recent reform plan, which draws on features of voucher plans, alternative schools, magnet schools, and private education, has grown out of attempts to cope with big-city bureaucracy and from campaigns for alternative schooling. The projects, highly diverse in nature, have serious implications for the organization and funding of public schools in the United States. They conceivably could "light the way" for significant school reform measures in many areas, but also hold the potential to institute a new form of segregation in public schools. Several projects have already been challenged in court.

As with regulations on home schooling, laws vary from state to state on the definition of a charter school, who grants the charter, how many charters can be granted, who can apply for a school charter, and how long the charter extends. In some states the local school authority grants the charter, in other states it is the state education department, and a few allow the boards of community colleges and universities to grant charters. Missouri initially permitted only 3, Massachusetts granted 17 charters for the 1995–1996 school year, and in Michigan there is no limit. All charter schools must conform to either a district's or a state's learning outcomes. Promoting accountability, states do not renew the charters of those schools that fail to meet their required standards (Raywid, 1995).

Charter schools already operating, and those in development, vary greatly in conceptual base and in organization because of state legislation enfranchising them. For example, the 1993 Massachusetts Education Reform Act allows parent groups, businesses, educators, social agencies, or groups of interested citizens to form alternative schools. The Massachusetts schools, which opened in September 1995, receive per-pupil funds from the local school districts in which they are located, but are freed from most of the constraints that apparently hamper change in traditional school districts. Though all new charter schools in Massachusetts must abide by rules governing children's safety, civil rights issues, and financial disclosure, they will receive waivers exempting them from local school policies, state education codes, and teacher union contracts (Harrington-Lueker, 1994b). In other states the conditions are very different, and some schools are subservient to local school boards.

Charter schools vary widely in their concept of "good schooling." One chartered school in the southwest United States adheres to an academic curriculum, using Hirsch's cultural literacy outline, and has a principal making all decisions. Another school in the same district has a very permissive program. Instead of a designated administrator, a group of parents, teachers, and community members work together to provide for the learning needs of the students (Raywid, 1995).

A common belief in granting charters is that without the encumbrances of regulations these schools will be able to work more closely with parents, respond better to children's needs, and reflect the aspirations of families served (Harrington-Lueker, 1994a). We believe that some of these programs are likely to fulfill the notions of this text—harnessing more and greater family and community resources than has been the case historically. The experiments bear watching, for some will become exemplars, showing what happens when we ask more of the adults involved in a school endeavor.

Educational Partnerships Program

In 1993 the federal government funded 30 projects under the Educational Partnerships Act of 1988. The programs encompass a range of activities and have been funded for small and large communities, and also for businesses. Each project includes different partners, but school districts, private businesses, museums, libraries, parent organizations, nonprofit organizations,

and social service agencies are all involved. The projects' goals are for the public and private sectors to join forces in encouraging excellence in education, in improving education for disadvantaged as well as talented students, and in appropriating community resources for the improvement of education (Danzberger & Gruskin, 1993).

The Educational Partnership Program of Meade County, South Dakota, serves all students K–12, but targets those at greatest risk. Partners in the project include the school district, a university, several nonprofit organizations, and local cultural organizations. Major goals are to increase academic achievement, higher-order thinking skills, sense of community responsibility, competency in more than one language, and acceptance of cultural diversity, and to develop quality parent–community–school partnerships. The project has training components for key personnel who in turn work with parents, school personnel, and community members in forging alliances. Models are being developed for K–12 curricula that integrate local history, Native American culture, and citizenship responsibility into academic subjects such as math and science.

With such promising projects, we have hope that other communities will look for more responsibility in participating in education. Educators can help out by presenting the evidence and the suggestion. Certainly, improvement in education for all children will result.

Critical Features of Partnerships

All partnership models and collaborative arrangements are different, but we find most of the following features appearing in quality programs:

1. Change in educational structures is slow, and workers recognize that alterations cannot be rushed.
2. Each participant must surrender some decision-making power in order to find common ground for collaborating.
3. All program steps require careful planning, and modification of plans is done when necessary.

4. It is imperative to establish goals before implementation begins.

5. Continuous assessment is needed to determine progress.

6. Redirect focus of objectives when necessary to overcome barriers.

7. All participants must work at sharing feelings and reactions to keep communication channels open.

8. The entire community must stay informed of progress.

9. All participants must respect the skills, knowledge, ideas, culture, and values of all partnership members.

10. Programs integrate learning experiences from all social settings.

11. Parents and community groups participate in educational decision making.

12. Collaboration requires strong leadership to begin and to survive.

13. For programs to survive, partners must identify the power brokers in social settings and gain their support.

14. Collaborative ventures require capable and committed coordinators.

15. The program must recognize and reward participants' efforts.

SUMMARY

The factorylike and bureaucratic school developed in the early 1900s is not viable for the twenty-first century, but the task of changing schools so that families and communities work in partnership is not easy, either. Model inter-institution collaborations have succeeded in changing and improving schools to enhance the social, intellectual, moral, and physical potentials of children. All professionals must work vigorously to extend these models.

Educators, parents, and businesspeople have found the road to workable collaborations difficult and tenuous, but in reaching out, have discovered processes others can emulate for successful change.

Although its main goal was to "make war on poverty," Project Head Start initiated an era of collaborative work for schools, homes, and communities that continues as an exemplar of uniting social settings. Home Start and Follow Through programs extended Head Start's beginnings, and increased the amount of experimentation with partnerships. Another boost to partnerships from the federal government came with the Educational Partnerships Act of 1988.

Comer's School Development Program and the League of Schools Reaching Out demonstrate clearly that families, schools, and communities can work together in strengthening educational progress. Many communities experimenting with these collaborations have not achieved total involvement, but even the small steps taken have meant additional opportunities for children. In Adopt-a-School programs, businesses and community organizations find ways to support schools and teachers. Some states, such as Oregon, foster collaboration by recognizing outstanding programs. Many school systems lack the finances to launch a major change, but are able, as in Bennington, Vermont, to start with a small step. Educational Partnerships programs, such as that in Meade county (South Dakota), are allowing both small and large communities to explore changes within their districts to enhance curriculum.

Schools and communities have different models to guide them as they work toward partnerships. Many strategies work, and several elements are common to most projects. The strongest components for success appear to be the motivation in a community for solving some of its problems and the commitment of key people involved.

SUGGESTED ACTIVITIES AND QUESTIONS

1. Contact the superintendent of schools in your area to identify any local partnership programs. Interview the project coordinator. Ask how the program got started. What is the structure of the program? What activities are parents, teachers, and community members involved in? How does the coordinator view the results of the collaboration? What difficulties have arisen in implementing the plans?

2. Compare this program to one of the model programs discussed in this chapter. How is the

structure similar? How is it different? What activities, if any, do they have in common? How do the program's successes compare to the research on the model program?

3. Read James Comer's *Maggie's American Dream* and discuss with classmates the impact the book has on you. From your reading, what home and community influences do you think might have affected the way Comer engineered his School Development Program?

4. With a group of classmates, design a hypothetical collaborative project that would benefit an imaginary class. Members should select one social setting (home, school, or community) that they will represent. Plan the steps of the process, assigning roles and responsibilities for implementation. What problems did you encounter in coming to agreement on collaboration?

RECOMMENDED READINGS

Comer, J. P. (1980). *School power: Implications of an intervention project.* New York: Free Press.

Davies, D., Burch, P., & Johnson, V. R. (1992). *A portrait of schools reaching out: Report of a survey of practices and policies of family–community–school collaboration.* Boston: Center on Families, Communities, Schools, & Children's Learning.

Decker, L. E., & Decker, V. A. (1988). *Home/school/community involvement.* Arlington, VA: American Association of School Administrators.

Hechinger, F. M. (1992). *Fateful choices: Healthy youth for the 21st century.* New York: Carnegie Corporation.

Kindred, L. W., Bagin, D., & Gallagher, D. R. (1990). *The school and community relations.* Englewood Cliffs, NJ: Prentice Hall.

Swap, S. M. (1993). *Developing home-school partnerships: From concepts to practice.* New York: Teachers College Press.

Tushnet, N. C. (1993). *Educational Partnerships Program as a force for educational change: Findings for a national study.* Paper presented at the meeting of the American Educational Research Association, Atlanta, GA. (ERIC Document Reproduction Service No. ED 360 731)

U.S. Department of Education. (1994). *Strong families, strong schools.* Washington, DC: Author.

Effective Social Settings for Learning

> *. . . recognition is spreading that schools as narrow, bureaucratic providers of academics for children are incapable of preparing our communities for a future that includes anything like prosperity or stability.*
>
> *(Thompson, 1993a, p. 1)*

After looking at the various curricula found in homes, schools, and communities, it is well for us to identify those settings that will provide the best possible educational experiences. In this chapter, we examine the features that normally produce effective homes, schools, and communities. In reading this chapter you will learn that:

1. Particular characteristics identify effective homes, schools, and communities.

2. Educators have tools we may use to evaluate the different social settings.

3. Connections are needed between and among the three social settings, in which all children live, to produce the best educational environments.

4. The school is the logical choice and most capable force both to begin and to nurture partnerships that unite the three social settings.

Well-functioning homes, effective schools, and dynamic and prosperous neighborhoods and communities are goals to which all cultural groups and political units aspire. This situation does exist in some areas across the United States, heralded in media reports under banners such as, "most desirable location in America." But investigators inform us that many towns and cities in the United States are suffering, have damaged parts, and show stress (Kotlowitz, 1991; Garbarino, Kostelny, & Dubrow, 1991; Quint, 1994). Consider the following descriptions of two very different U.S. communities:

1. The southwestern city has the most sought-after climate in the United States. Days are sunny, atmosphere is clear, and the demeanor on city streets is uplifting. Careful development from the area's small town origins produced wide streets, pleasant parks, and pleasantly designed neighborhoods. The multiethnic population flows in a harmonious way and appears to be truly integrated. Electronics production provides a strong economic base, and poverty seems completely absent. Crime statistics are the lowest in the United States for small cities, and a pleasant ambience is felt by even short-time visitors. All schools are new, spacious, and well equipped. The curriculum for students is conservative but apparently in keeping with community wishes. It seems an almost utopian setting (adapted from A. B. Prescott, 1994, personal communication).

2. The public housing project is an impoverished community with rat-infested apartments, where plumbing often does not work and there is almost no maintenance. Buildings and grounds are in constant disrepair—windows are boarded up and the effects of vandalism are seen everywhere. The project is also dangerous. Crime has increased 400 percent in recent years, and death is so frequent that young children play "funeral" in the afterschool program. Gangs and drug lords dominate the community, instilling fear in all residents. Conditions have made families into "internal refugees," and rules that parents give their children reflect the sobering conditions: "Don't go out in the hallway. Stay away from windows. Stay together all the time. When you hear shots, hit the floor" (adapted from Garbarino et al., 1991, pp. 130–142).

The two settings described result from the overarching social, political, and economic forces at work in their respective communities. Certain fortuitous circumstances produced one venue; a series of misfortunes and miscalculations produced the other. It is beyond the scope of our text to define or explain even part of the dynamics producing quality and distressed areas in any city. However, we can identify characteristics of effective social settings and recommend ways to make our own workplaces effective examples.

All three social settings in children's lives naturally affect their learning and experience. Also, for good or ill, one setting will affect the other two. Viewed negatively, problems in one setting can make functioning in the others more difficult. However, the positive effects of two settings often counterbalance an inferior third. For instance, effective homes can and do offset negative community influences (Comer, 1988; Clark, 1983), and effective school programs can make a difference for struggling families and peer groups (Thompson, 1993a; Friedman, 1990; Quint, 1994). From the model programs discussed in Chapter 10 we take assurance that better things are possible for chil-

dren's experiences in the United States if more cohesion develops among the major social settings. So, how do we get there?

We must first assess what exists in children's lives. Then, we may establish goals for improvement, and create a plan of action for meeting the goals. One underlying thesis of this text is that schools are best situated to assess the social settings of an area, make plans for remediation, and begin the process of drawing institutions together for the betterment of children.

Collaborative efforts are easily instituted in vigorous and healthy social settings; when deficits and problems exist in the settings, the challenge is of course far greater. In problem settings, agents of change must be more engaged, must work harder, and must experiment aggressively to bring about improvements.

In this chapter, we examine the features of competent families, effective schools, and effective communities. We include the converse of some features when they illuminate explanations. We conclude by examining the role of the school as broker for linking social settings.

COMPETENT FAMILIES

As we noted in Chapter 4, U.S. families have different organizations, values, and socioeconomic bases, and different approaches to health care, nutrition, and the like. Few families are perfect, and most have their particular strengths. Families evidence a difference of degree rather than a complete absence or possession of skills and abilities. All families function in the context of a community and in association with a school, and the quality of this interaction determines to a large extent the success or failure of children attending a school.

Areas of home and family competence that we explore in this section are organization and management, beliefs and value structures, intellectual stimuli, parental knowledge of child development, health and nutrition practices, social and emotional environments, and social networking. All these areas have a serious impact on children's growth and learning, so, what if problems exist in one or more? As stated, many families have deficits, but the issue is the extent of deficit. Recall the Sameroff et al. (1987) research and the Werner and Smith studies (1992), which inform us that at-risk children with one or two problem areas can manage well when compensating help is available from other social settings (see Chapter 4). So, one or two problems do not doom children to failure.

Organization and Management

As we discussed in Chapter 3, the United States contains numerous cultures, and each represents a somewhat different pattern of childrearing. But, also across cultures, we find strands undergirding the competent home and differentiating it from less effective ones.

We discussed family management styles in Chapter 4. These styles bear repeating here. Since the Bernstein and Baumrind studies in the 1960s, social scientists recognize several discernible management styles in U.S. homes. The styles overlap and combinations exist, but most families tend toward one style or another. Baumrind (1966, 1968) labeled three basic parenting styles: authoritarian, authoritative, and permissive. Others refined Baumrind's terms somewhat and added different labels, but in essence all authorities focus on similar major categories. The authoritative, or sponsored independence, style is the one we associate with the effective family. Family members managing according to the authoritative style are democratic and controlling, but warm and receptive. These contrast with the authoritarian's detached control, and the noncontrolling and nondemanding approach of the permissive style.

Maccoby and Martin (1983) and Dornbusch, Ritter, Leiderman, Roberts, and Fraleigh (1987) failed to find the same relationships that Baumrind's Anglo population revealed between style and schoolwork in selected ethnic families. However, Clark's (1983) teams looked at Caucasian, Mexican, and African American homes to identify the effective families in difficult living conditions. He found that particular attitudes and behaviors—generally the authoritative style—that parents displayed toward their children made the difference between success and failure in school and life for children in his studies.

A significant finding in Clark's (1983) work is that "these [effective] families believe they can make a difference in a child's life, and they are not overwhelmed by circumstances" (p. 198). He identified 10 characteristics of effective families, irrespective of socioeconomic condition (Clark, 1983):

1. A feeling of control over their lives
2. Frequent communication of high expectations to children
3. A family dream of success for the future
4. Hard work as a key to success
5. An active, rather than sedentary lifestyle
6. Twenty-five to thirty home-centered learning hours per week
7. Family viewed as a mutual support system and problem-solving unit
8. Clearly understood household rules, consistently enforced
9. Frequent contact with teachers
10. Emphasis on spiritual growth

It is easy to view these as characteristics of the "Protestant ethic"—a hallmark of prospering U.S. families; however, Clark found these characteristics in poor homes having many economic and social disadvantages.

So what can we do about the families that lack many of these features? It is useless to wring our hands and write off 20 percent or more of U.S. homes as unsalvageable. Changed circumstances for families with children are key. Government policies must aim to improve health conditions, stimulate economic opportunities, and attempt to redirect living conditions of those in poverty. Even without government intervention, school and community groups working together can bring about changes in the perceptions families have of themselves. Good schools and humane communities do make a difference in the pressures affecting families, and can provide incentives for families to grow in effectiveness. Model programs show this!

In some instances parents are so remote and out of touch that the best teachers can do is to give constant support, believe in children, and hope some success unfolds in the classroom. However, some hard-to-reach parents can be included, through new ways of communicating and by emphasizing their strengths and their successes with their children. Parent education can no longer mean simply telling parents what they must do. It means seeking ways to support parents to gradually accept responsibility for their children's education—and at parents' level of ability. It means trying out different things, such as listening to parent responses, building on what works, and trying new strategies. As in teaching children, teachers must be ready to listen, to observe, and to support parents' efforts before offering new challenges.

Beliefs and Value Structures

Most studies show that children's attitudes, beliefs, and values resemble those of their parents (Berns, 1993; Scarf, 1995). Parenting practices thus become critical in children's lives.

Educating about stealing, lying, and disorderly conduct is normal in most families, although the education can take different forms. Some parents teach morals and values through intimidation and punishment, while others approach the challenge by explaining children's problems and the impact of one's actions on others. This last approach, called *induction,* results in stronger development of conscience and internal control (Sadker & Sadker, 1991). The effective family will focus on values, morals, and attitudes by modeling behaviors and discussing them with their children, reasoning through solutions, and labeling the behavior when seen in public (Figure 11.1).

Encouraging children's special interests promotes the development of their internal locus of control.

Literary and Intellectual Stimuli

Competent families provide children with life-long learning interests as they go about their daily lives. Families that provide intellectual stimuli stimulate children's interest in natural phenomena and sharpen their skills used in acquiring knowledge from different media. Parents encourage these practices by conversing, questioning, demonstrating, and modeling use of literary, problem-solving, and investigative skills.

Language Patterns

Language is absorbed through family interactions. Children's vocabulary and grammatical ability are patterned almost totally after caregiver modeling (Heath, 1983; Sigel et al., 1984). Competent homes provide a rich language environment where conversations, active listening, and interactions with all members are valued and demon-

FIGURE 11.1
Helping children develop an internal locus of control.

1. Be responsive to children from the moment they are born. Be affectionate, comforting, attentive. They need to know someone will respond to their actions or else they will feel they have no control over their own actions.
2. Let children accept consequences for their actions. If they spill milk, give them something with which to clean it up.
3. Avoid performing tasks children can do for themselves. Encourage effort, allow children to make mistakes, don't expect adult performance.
4. Give children developmentally appropriate responsibilities. For example: age three, put toys away; age five, make bed; age seven, set or clear table.
5. Give feedback. Let children know if they have performed well and, if need be, how they can improve.
6. Be an example of a person who makes things happen, rather than waiting for things to happen.
7. Encourage children's special interests—those things they initiate themselves.
8. Set standards and limits for behavior. Explain the reasons for the rules. [You need to be home by six, so we can all have dinner together.]
9. Show respect for children and for their accomplishments. [What an interesting painting; can you tell me about it? rather than, What is that? It doesn't look like a kitty.]
10. Allow children to make appropriate decisions that affect them. [You can have six children at your party; whom would you like to invite? Do you want to play soccer this year?]

Source: From *Child, family, community: Socialization and support* (3rd ed.) (p. 455) by R. M. Berns, 1993, New York: Harcourt Brace Jovanovich. Reprinted by permission.

strated. Bernstein (1972) noted the elaborate codes that middle-class families use that prepare children for interaction and communication within schools and the greater community. In homes where multiple languages or dialects are used, competent parents through their demonstrations ensure that children learn "code-switching" to deal with different social venues.

Published Materials

Competent families read, have books, and use other publications in the home. Numerous studies confirm that the amount of reading in homes is directly related to children's success in reading as well as in other subjects at school (U.S. Department of Education, 1986). Quality day care arrangements and Head Start programs contribute to literacy, and their efforts can compensate somewhat for deprived circumstances, but the major influence still comes from the family.

Some school–community collaborations are intended to increase the amount of reading in homes, as in the following vignette.

....

The Growing Up Reading program in a small New England community is a community–school–home collaboration directed at improving literacy. Books are delivered to homes of new babies born in the community, and then each preschool birthday is celebrated with another good, age-appropriate book. "Grandparent" volunteers deliver the books to homes and share with parents and children through home teaching. Parents are invited several times a year to attend birthday celebrations for children involved. At these celebrations, parents and teachers exchange stories, demonstrate techniques of book sharing, and discuss ideas of how to use other materials.

....

Illiteracy is a lingering problem afflicting many marginal homes. The United States has a surprising number of functionally illiterate young parents, who have few printed materials in their homes, and therefore meager ways of stimulating the prereading skills and interests of their children. Collaborations and networks, as in the vignette, to involve these parents are critical. School early intervention plans are backup strategies when collaborations are not available.

Use of Television

As is *not* the case with published materials, almost every home in the United States has a television set. How each family uses television is, of course, the salient factor. Sitcoms, game shows, and soap operas, while providing some stimulation, give children few readiness skills for reading. Children's shows are aired in all areas of the country, but unless parents and children both watch them they are of no benefit.

Positive links to achievement have been found when children viewed television programs such as *Sesame Street* and *Mr. Rogers' Neighborhood.* In addition, some researchers have found benefits when parents watched television with their children and then discussed the program (Singer & Singer, 1980). Here again it is the effective family that pursues the objective of tapping the educational dimensions of television. To ensure that disadvantaged children can maximize learning from television, community and school programs must be instituted where advocates can influence home behaviors (parent education).

Parental Knowledge of Child Development

In effective family situations caregivers are aware that children move through developmental stages and that instruction and expectations depend on where children are in their growth.

Some young parents have the advantage of extended families and other social networks of neighbors to inform them about normal and reasonable stages of children's growth. Others have

books, such as the guides published by Dr. Spock, Dr. Berry Brazelton, and others, from which to view their children's progress. Others will depend on services gained through clinics, such as WIC programs, well baby clinics, and family health centers. Still others remain quite ignorant of the basics of child development and depend on intuition and even on folklore.

When communities address child development needs, results are haphazard at best. Adult education programs on child care and community outreach programs are available in some areas, but historically these attract few parents. Some high schools provide a basic course on home management and child development for students. These opportunities, such as the Dunbar High School (Baltimore) program for pregnant teens and young mothers, provide some knowledge and experience about developmental concepts and nurturing. However, information is constantly challenged by the ever-present television, which promises much and implies that young mothers must shower their children with material things.

Health and Nutrition

Health implies attention to complete personal well-being, not just the absence of disease or infirmities. Competent parents provide safe and healthy environments in which children develop and prosper. Most health and safety concepts derive from parents and caregivers, and grow out of situations associated with everyday living. Due to poverty and depressed living conditions, marginalized families frequently suffer from chronic health problems, accidents, and inadequate nutrition. A surprising 33 percent of Americans have little or no health care plans, and children are often in that group (Children's Defense Fund, 1992). Illness and health problems become all too often a function of income.

Health problems affect all poor families. Inadequate housing, high population densities, poor sanitation, poor diets, smoke, and poor habits in managing resources engender unhealthy homes.

Some problems stem from ignorance about basic home maintenance, some come from poor habits and substance abuse, and much from the inability of persons to secure and follow through on available care and help from social agencies. Clearly, one way to address problems is through parent education.

Competent families, on the other hand, know about health practices, the basics of nutrition, and how to secure medical attention. When health and nutrition standards are preserved, we observe the following in competent homes:

Nutrition
- Meals with food from major food groups
- Reduced use of prepackaged, treated foods containing fat, salt, and additives
- Reduced use of sweets, soft drinks, and fatty products
- Regular eating habits and sensible snacks

Hygiene and physical health
- Immunizations
- Annual checkups and evaluations
- Adequate lighting, ventilation, and heat in homes

Sanitation
- Avoiding toxic substances
- Washing before meals and food preparation
- Regular bathing
- Keeping rubbish cleared away
- Sensibly maintained home space

Most of these practices can be extended to all homes when strong collaborations emerge.

Consistent Social and Emotional Environments

Effective homes develop environments that nurture children's social and emotional well-being. The overriding dimension is one of care and interest. Too often children state that they are not watched over, that no one cares. And this situation worsens when we encounter families in stress—7 percent of our poor children state that no one cares about them (Noddings, 1992). Children's range of perceptions about self, from confidence to spiritual growth, will be affected by this feeling.

Parents' workplaces affect their perceptions of life and the way they interact with children and other family members (Bronfenbrenner & Crouter, 1982). In turn, these perceptions foster parenting styles that conform to parents' experiences and how they see themselves in the world. On the positive side, we have the effective families investigations (Clark, 1983; Rich, 1987) showing that the functioning family views itself as a problem-solving unit with a mutual support system, and that valuing spiritual life is important.

How can we encourage parents in guiding and nurturing their children and in establishing contacts outside of home? Workshops, modeling, and discussions are only part of the answer. Supporting families through family–school–community collaborations and involving parents in extended networks will enhance social and emotional health in homes.

Childrearing patterns certainly affect children's level of moral development. Children's attitudes are formed early, and parents and peers have a significant impact through instruction, modeling, rewards, and punishments. Children's values tend to reflect those of their family. Other experiences also affect this development; individuals exposed to many socializing agents are more likely to achieve a higher level of moral reasoning than those exposed to only a few (Bronfenbrenner et al., 1984; Kohlberg, 1976).

Locus of control is directly related to parenting (see Figure 11.1). Whether children see themselves or others in control determines the way they look toward the future.

Developing Interactive Skills
Competent families engender interactive skills that permit children to interact with the world with their values and moral notions in place. Modeling, discussions in the home, and being a part of the larger community, i.e., extending children's social contacts so they use more than one interactive style (Salzstein, 1976), all help children develop these skills. Children's growth will reflect their participation and experience.

Developing Problem-Solving Skills

Homes foster problem-solving skills through participation and experimentation. By modeling problem-solving skills and exploring problems and solutions with children, parents steer them toward competence. Homes where highly directive and punitive behaviors are the norm actually discourage interest and skill for analyzing tasks, and some even produce a sense of helplessness (Bronfenbrenner et al., 1984).

Teaching Coping Skills

Children able to confront adversity and seek ways to approach difficulties usually have had guided experiences in approaching tasks. Competent families entertain questions about solving problems. This means caregivers verbally or kinesthetically lead children through a series of tasks, and also frame questions leading to a reasonable conclusion. Children with experiences in considering alternatives and choices have a background for confronting challenges and even adversity. Of course, parental orientation is crucial. Domineering, prejudiced, or autocratic adults engender thinking for one "correct" set of rules or format. This does little to help children develop coping skills.

Recreational Pursuits

Competent homes value recreation, gaming sessions, and play. Children normally select their own levels of participation in play, sports, and creative work, but parents and other family members may encourage and support their interest. Children require time, space, and equipment to pursue recreation, and effective parents will plan for this, support it, and even participate. Few things solidify families better than recreational pursuits. Benefits children derive include the following (Seefeldt & Barbour, 1994):

1. Working with others
2. Small and large muscle exercise
3. Establishing fitness
4. Lifelong interests and attitudes
5. Guided exploration of challenges and new ventures

Competent homes value recreation, gaming sessions, and play.

FIGURE 11.2
Evaluating family effectiveness.

In evaluating effective families, assessors will answer "yes" for most of the following questions.

1. Is an authoritative parenting style evident?
2. Is there consistency in home management, family routines (bedtime, meals, and relaxation), and regulations?
3. Are rules and codes of conduct understood and consistently enforced?
4. Are discussions, conversations, and interactions noticeable and frequent?
5. Do children have responsibilities in the home?
6. Are expectations of children in keeping with their stages of development?
7. Do parents have high hopes for children's success?
8. Do family members evince a sense of success and pride?
9. Are good nutrition practices observed?
10. Are sanitary practices in evidence?
11. Do family members know where others work, play, and socialize?
12. Is there warmth in the home—do members accept others?
13. Do family members encourage and praise each other?
14. Does the family have a social network of friends?
15. Are values and moral codes apparent in the family?
16. Are literary and other intellectual stimuli present in the home?
17. Do members read to each other?
18. Does family show skill in using the social and welfare services available to them?
19. Are health checkups done regularly and immunizations scheduled?
20. Can parents verbally and kinesthetically lead children through tasks and problems with appropriate questions, comments, and demonstrations?

Source: Adapted from Berger, 1995; Berns, 1993; Curran, 1983; Galinsky, 1987; Gordon, 1975; Rich, 1992.

---

6. Sensible and accurate use of equipment
7. Release from tension

Figure 11.2 provides questions that professionals may wish to use when evaluating whether a family is effective. An effective family will display a high percentage of the features, though not necessarily all.

EFFECTIVE SCHOOLS

Often we think that standardized achievement test results are proof of what happens in schools. When related to aptitude scores, program resources or support, and considerations of community SES, these tests may statistically indicate whether particular school programs have realized expected gains. But the results of norm-referenced tests should not necessarily be accepted at face value.

If overall success rates are high when comparing achievements among schools, then educators and citizens alike often assume all is right at their school and that programs must be appropriate. Few are motivated to investigate crucial details. However, group tests often hide areas of deficiency, and often fail to assess specific children's skills. For example, a test may be inappropriate for a particular subgroup in the school, or some gifted children, while performing adequately in school, on tests receive lower than anticipated results.

Teachers must incorporate the results of several assessment forms when considering additional attention, remediation, or program changes.

When problems appear, for example, if scores are well below an area norm, then educators, parents, and other community citizens wonder what the school is doing or not doing that results in such lower scores, and usually demand explanations. Are community problems or area demographics confounding parts of the program and school curriculum? Are scores lower because schools are reserving time for nonacademic areas, such as developing esteem and readiness or expanding cultural background, before returning to achievement-tested basic skills? Again, standardized tests measure particular academic skill levels and do not assess achievements in all the curriculum areas schools work with today (see Chapter 7). Schools can determine children's achievement quite well using tools other than repeated batteries of norm-referenced tests. (For a thorough discussion of the relative strengths and weaknesses of the different types of assessment available to teachers, see Stiggins, in press.)

Positive School Features

Some program attributes are necessary for all productive schools, and the presence of other features can hamper efforts in any school.

School effectiveness researchers have identified several characteristics that are observed consistently in schools demonstrating good achievement gains (Good & Brophy, 1986; Good & Brophy, 1994; Cruickshank, 1990). The following items appear consistently on most lists:

1. Strong academic leadership that produces consensus
2. A safe, orderly school climate
3. Positive teacher attitudes toward students
4. High expectations regarding children's abilities
5. Efficient use of instructional time
6. Careful monitoring of progress
7. Strong parental involvement programs
8. Emphasis on importance of skills and achievement
9. Frequent use of praise and encouragement
10. Support for different learning modalities

The preceding are general school practices and will fit with almost any program, goal, or strategy. The curriculum content, the teaching strategies, the equipment used, and level of instruction to develop a program vary greatly among classrooms and schools. Two effective teachers can develop a topic in very different ways, and both can still have successful outcomes. One may use direct instruction (showing and telling) to establish ideas of growing plants or writing poems, while the other uses inductive thinking (discovery) with several experiments so that children arrive at the same understandings. Successful classrooms use a variety of models, and successful teachers understand how to apply different models, techniques, and strategies when appropriate.

Impediments to Effective Schools

Some schools do less well than others in supporting educational opportunity. Problems may exist only in certain areas, or may range through the curriculum, administration, and school life. Impediments to learning come from such things as inappropriate curriculum, negative teacher attributes, bias, problems in physical plant, and community forces such as special interest groups, defensive attitudes, and dangerous streets.

Inappropriate Curriculum

Schools occasionally miscalculate when selecting and implementing curriculum, such as when choosing content that doesn't relate to the developmental stages of children served, concepts too advanced for children, or material that is redundant and too simplistic. Some material may also be inappropriate because of social or cultural mores in a community.

Some teachers lack motivation and a sense of urgency about education. They excessively repeat material or resurrect old material and keep stu-

Successful classrooms are ones where teachers understand how to involve children and adults working and playing together.

dents "busy" with worksheets unrelated to the day's activities. Large segments of time can be absorbed in mindless tasks that go nowhere. Children quickly tire of repetition and use their time to make excuses for avoiding work. The myth of "boring school" thus becomes reality.

Negative Teacher Attributes

While it is difficult to accept the notion that teachers can be less than helpful, from time to time it is true. Some individuals come to teaching for the wrong reasons, perhaps because they wish to dominate situations, or enjoy pontificating and expounding. Others want children to look up to them, and use instruction as a device to hold attention as on a stage. These individuals rarely fulfill the requirements of guide, director, or supporter of learning, and may overlook children's needs or misunderstand children's perceptions of skills and concepts being addressed.

At times a teacher's personality does not support learning situations. Brittle, cold, and demanding personalities logically do not serve children; neither do indifferent, sarcastic, or introverted temperaments. It is paradoxical that persons with these characteristics wish to be in a "helping profession," but we meet them once in awhile.

Bias

Our society still works to shed the problems associated with racism, ethnocentrism, elitism, and sexism, but these qualities unfortunately still affect some schools. Perpetuating stereotypes in monocultural schools is a problem. Stereotyping restricts everyone's social competence. The situation may become worse in ethnically integrated schools if hints of bias and careless use of sexist and ethnocentric language appear. When demeaning language surfaces, minority persons are affronted, their aspirations suffer, and children's growth in social competence is diminished (Comer, 1988; Sadker & Sadker, 1991). For all persons involved, bias is costly.

Physical Plant Problems

Limited physical facilities, while sometimes adaptable by creative people, become burdensome for inexperienced teachers. Poorly functioning buildings, ill-lit or poorly ventilated areas, and a badly maintained plant become difficult to work in, and are dangerous and depressing. Normal school space can also be misused. Rooms too large or too small for instructional activity are a problem; poorly arranged materials contribute to confusion.

Poor and inappropriate equipment does not serve a facility well, since maintenance is always high and use is unpredictable. In addition, sometimes machines and supplies are stored at a distance from classrooms, requiring unneeded traffic and additional time spent in securing equipment and moving materials about a building. For example, one Chicago principal secured a grant to buy 12 computers for an early literacy program at her inner-city school. The machines were fitted with programs for young children to use in creating stories. The objective was excellent and first and second graders enjoyed using the new equipment, but the logistics of scheduling became a burden.

The computers were housed in one secured room to prevent theft, which was understandable. However, this meant that eight groups of children had to be scheduled to travel en masse to and from the room once each day. Time with each group was spent leaving the classroom, traveling to the writing room, waiting for the previous group to finish, and moving in for the 22-minute period. The problem of trooping about the building on schedule, and everyone's feeling that they had insufficient time actually working on the computers, depressed enthusiasm for the literacy program. A better plan would have maintained the computers on mobile carts and assigned one or more to each primary room for individual use during the regular school day, returning them to the secure room at the end of the day.

Special Interest Groups

Special interest groups can be advocates and sources of support for schools. Groups formed to lobby for school funding or to increase interest in a new building are positive in impact. However, some special interest groups are formed, as in the following vignette, to counteract school projects or to prevent curriculum from being implemented.

A group of parents and other interested persons organized themselves into a "review committee" in one Texas community. When they reviewed the "reproduction of creatures" unit in the second-grade classrooms, the books and charts used became a highly charged topic. Complaints about the material became intense; parent visits to the school caused confrontations and wild charges. One teacher resigned because of accusations, and emotion dragged on for weeks before the administration abandoned the unit. Even though the unit had been developed in previous years and had been accepted by the health education committee, a militant anti-sex education group spread dissension. Community and school working relations were set back considerably for more than a year.

Too often schools acquiesce to pressure from special interest groups, and programs can suffer in scope and purpose. Censorship of books in public school is a common occurrence in some large school districts (Sutherland & Arbuthnot, 1991).

Other Challenges

Community violence can spill over into schools. Weapons are carried to school by too many children who seek to protect themselves, to prey on others, or to maintain status in a peer group. Of course, weapons have an unsettling effect on any school climate. Whereas some schools have been considered safe havens from distressful conditions in a neighborhood, too often this haven is savaged by intrusions, bullets, and intimidations during gang activities. In the hands of secure teachers, the trauma resulting from witnessing violence can become a part of the school curriculum. One teacher, trying to resolve fears in a Baltimore neighborhood experiencing periodic violence, used story writing and sharing to deal with children's anxieties, and to help them understand about precautions and safety measures (Notar, 1992).

Changes in Schools

Schools in the United States are always evolving. New building plans, new procedures, new equipment, curriculum innovations, and new strategies appear on a regular basis. But one cannot say that basic schooling changes in a dramatic way from year to year. Adjustments appear that seem serious or far-reaching at times, but in fact schools change very slowly (Webb et al., 1996; Bennett & LeCompte, 1990).

It takes time for a school staff to adopt a new method of teaching; before new materials are in hand, inservice has been arranged, and teachers are convinced of the method's efficacy. Turn-around time is not fast, and even though some teachers implement a new plan, the school as a whole often lags behind. Consider the phased-in "writing to read" program in the following vignette.

In fall 1989, a school system set up a "writing to read" workshop. Two second-grade teachers from Elwood Elementary, in the district, were interested in trying the new plan immediately, and this experiment encouraged them. The two gave glowing reports at faculty meetings the following spring, but only one third-grade and one first-grade teacher agreed to try the next year. Halfway through the year, the first-grade teacher supplemented her program with basal readers, and her evaluation of the experiment was iffy. With heavy urging, two more teachers agreed to experiment later that year. At the end of three years, only half of the primary teachers in the building were involved. Although most evaluations were positive, the principal still wondered how she could in-crease participation. It took five years, and repeated reports of success, before most of Elwood's primary teachers adopted the program.

Schools change faster socially than they do academically. Neighborhoods can change quickly in urban and suburban areas, and the cultural and socioeconomic mix can alter demographics in a school within a few years. Many U.S. schools have experienced this phenomenon in recent years (see the demographic changes discussed in Chapter 3). For many reasons, a large number of schools are less successful in the 1990s than in the previous two decades or so. Achievement results, SAT scores, school attendance, the rising amount of school-identified disabilities, crime, and other social problems have alarmed many. The result has been a host of studies and evaluations to assess what is happening in U.S. education.

National Reports and Activities

A number of task forces representing various interests have conducted national studies to identify problems in U.S. education. Some offer recommendations to correct the problems they find. Some results have to do with school practices and curriculum, but many have implications for huge changes in society at large, regarding health care, prevention of substance abuse, correcting violence, changing U.S. attitudes, and so on. Some studies also include new plans for teacher preparation.

A Nation at Risk

In 1983, the National Commission on Excellence in Education produced the warning *A Nation At Risk* (NCEE, 1983). The study identified the following indicators of risk: (1) higher illiteracy in the United States; (2) decreasing achievement in school; and (3) lack of preparation for military and business careers. The commission found four aspects warranting concern: content, expectations, time, and teaching. These findings, while considered a "thunderclap across the landscape"

(Bell, 1993, p. 593), were hardly revolutionary—educational leaders had known of them for years. The report did succeed, however, in energizing discussion of the issues. Unfortunately, attracting public attention to education concerns has been the only significant outcome (Lund & Wild, 1993). No improvement in achievement, teacher preparation, or time in school has been documented (Lund & Wild, 1993; Bell, 1993).

A Nation Prepared

The influential Carnegie Forum on Education and the Economy (CFEE) (1986) followed the Commission on Excellence with a report focused on changing the preparation of teachers. The report, *A Nation Prepared: Teachers for the 21st Century*, quickly affected programs in the United States and inspired the American Association of Colleges for Teacher Education (AACTE) and individual state certification offices to recast accreditation standards. Using a purely economic rationale, the Carnegie forum concluded that a constructivist curriculum directed by more intellectually skilled and empowered teachers was the only way the United States could retain its competitive edge in a global economy.

The objective was to ensure that schools produce students "who have the tools they need to think for themselves, people who can act independently and with others, who can render critical judgment and contribute constructively to many enterprises, whose knowledge is wide ranging and whose understanding runs deep" (CFEE, 1986, p. 20). The forum recommended the following to accomplish this objective (CFEE, 1986):

- Create a National Board for Teaching Standards.
- Restructure schools to provide a professional environment for teaching—allowing teachers to decide programs and holding them accountable.
- Set up a new plan for Lead Teachers to provide leadership in schools.
- Require a bachelor's degree in arts and sciences before study for teaching.
- Develop an education curriculum for a Master of Arts in Teaching.
- Bring more minorities into teaching careers.
- Relate incentives for teachers to student performance and provide technology, services, and staff needed for teacher productivity.
- Make salaries competitive with other professions.

Government Action

The accumulation of education reports prompted both the Bush and Clinton administrations to address the problems perceived in U.S. schools. Their initiatives started with the annual Conference of Governors in 1989, which normally reviews social problems and often devises goals to address them.

The Bush administration in 1990 advanced *America 2000: An Education Strategy* (U.S. Department of Education, 1991a), a formula for addressing the large problems in the country's education. The objectives are very sound and desirable (see the listing in Chapter 2), but the means for implementation were not clear. Authorities generally applauded the plan and asked for the time, money, and training to bring about the goals. At the end of the Bush administration, the plan remained as it started—a desirable goal statement.

The Clinton administration followed in the footsteps of the previous plan, and the Goals 2000: Educate America Act (1993) extended the *America 2000* plan to add family involvement (U.S. Department of Education, 1993). Even though the administration has steadily emphasized social reconstruction and help for social problems, implementation of the principles to achieve Goals 2000 remains at the starting point.

The awareness of difficulties and needs in the United States has reached high levels. Problems with schools and student achievement appear to worry many, but movement is slow. Colleges and universities have only begun to redefine programs, and federal action is still at the report level. In fact, federal financing for educational programs has decreased steadily over the last decade (Lund & Wild, 1993). Fortunately, some communities have started experimental programs, and these do provide models for use (U.S. Department of Education, 1994). All professionals must rethink the evaluations that have appeared, and set new objectives for addressing them.

Evaluating Schools

Nationwide, the present state of U.S. schools appears fairly stable (Lund & Wild, 1993; Elam et al., 1994). Phi Delta Kappa's annual survey even shows some gains in public attitudes about America's schools. In regard to particular areas and projects, we find amazing success stories (Thompson, 1993b). In others, such as in most inner cities,

polls show conditions, services, and outlooks deteriorating badly (Garbarino et al., 1992; Kotlowitz, 1991).

Figure 11.3 presents questions that professionals may wish to use when evaluating the effectiveness of a particular school. An effective school will display a high percentage of the features indicated. The questions reveal much about a school's effectiveness, adequacy, chances for success, and readiness for change.

The quality future school will arise from the connections among homes, schools, and communities as these become complementary and supplement all school objectives. But educational change and enhancement affect more than academic achievement. Also linked to school success

FIGURE 11.3
Assessing schools for effectiveness.

For effective schools, assessors will answer "yes" for most of the following questions.

1. Is consonance of philosophy found among board of education members, administrators, and teaching staff members, as well as aides and volunteers?
2. Are school plant and facilities adequate?
3. Is the school plant maintained and serviced well?
4. Is space used appropriately and efficiently?
5. Does continuity of content and concepts exist between grade levels and from home experiences?
6. Are collaborations between home and school evident?
7. Do children evidence achievement in social and academic skills through their practices and activities?
8. Do teachers show a command of various teaching strategies and techniques?
9. Are teaching techniques varied for different children?
10. Are children constructively engaged in projects, in followup activities, or in application of ideas? Or, are they nonfocused, disruptive, glancing about, wandering from place to place?
11. Is time off task kept to a minimum?
12. Do children evince various levels of thinking as they work and investigate?
13. Is a pleasant climate for learning and enthusiasm noticeable?
14. Are children allowed opportunities to interact with others and grow in social relationships?
15. Do teachers display command of several teaching models (direct instruction, discovery learning, roundtable discussion)?
16. Are teaching approaches sensible and realistic for the particular classrooms?
17. Do teachers praise and encourage learners as well as value different contributions to classwork?
18. Do all children succeed from time to time?

Source: Adapted from Doll, 1989; Good & Brophy, 1986; Joyce, Weil, & Showers, 1992; Rich, 1992.

are changes in health care, improved living conditions, improved interethnic relations, and diminished crime in neighborhoods.

EFFECTIVE COMMUNITIES

Because communities are made up of sets of subsystems, research on competent communities is problematic. It is difficult to determine cause and effect relationships within a community, especially those that affect children. Also, such terms as *community* and *neighborhood* are not yet perceived as important referents by authorities in the field of child development. They therefore give less attention to the influences of this third social setting (Bronfenbrenner et al., 1984).

However, substantial research is available on the effects of community on family health and prosperity and school attainment (Quint, 1994; Bronfenbrenner et al., 1984). Evidence shows that some communities enjoy more positive results than others. For instance, communities with consolidated health services support prenatal and perinatal situations better than those without such consolidation. Researchers identify a number of features of more promising communities, irrespective of economic base, that can be linked with children's educational achievements.

Community Organization

Formal community organizations that we find almost everywhere are health services, welfare and social services, religious institutions, civic services, businesses, and media. Informal organizations that develop, but which are far less obvious, are (1) special interest groups, and (2) the social networks that individuals and families form.

Health Services
Children must remain healthy to develop properly, yet access to a health care system depends on the community children live in and on the economic status of the family. It is well documented that poor families have greater health

problems, including chronic health problems, more infectious diseases, higher incidence of low birth weight babies, and higher infant mortality rates.

The effective community will have comprehensive care systems striving to serve citizens impartially. Many communities have both neighborhood health centers (such as those funded through the Office of Economic Opportunity) and a private health care system. By uniting family care offices in one setting, officials diminish the expense, frustration, and transportation problems that poor families experience when seeking services.

In addition to health care, all medical facilities have an educating function. Important features of health services include distributing materials about disease prevention and counseling by personnel who are positively oriented to their clients.

Welfare and Social Services
While directed primarily at those in poverty, welfare and social services are relevant to the larger community. Employment offices, legal aid offices, and counseling centers cut across socioeconomic levels and are needed in addressing concerns for most U.S. communities. Unfortunately, welfare services in the United States have always carried a stigma, and only in recent years have programs such as Head Start led to changed attitudes and the welcome involvement of middle-class citizens (Bronfenbrenner et al., 1984).

As with health care, accessibility of social services is a key to their use. Media, local directories, and interagency referrals are the normal channels for distributing information on services, and word of mouth is of considerable importance. One community established a family services office in its new elementary school. An active director and proximity of services led to teachers reevaluating the types of services available for families and children. Increased accessibility brought more parent visitors to school, and all persons involved showed a greater acceptance of the need and benefits of the programs.

Religious Institutions

Religious institutions have always been a feature in human communities. Churches, synagogues, and mosques were and are central facets of most communities. Religious associations have dominated large portions of community life in the United States, representing a large part of the out-of-home activity for pre-twentiethth century Americans.

National surveys reveal a drop in religious participation for recent decades, but still more individuals belong to church-related groups than to any other voluntary grouping. Religious institutions continue to influence many segments of U.S. communities, promoting ethnic as well as theological identity. With outreach programs and social action objectives, many houses of religion now provide social, cultural, and other support for their communities as well as spiritual nurturance for their membership groups. Food pantries, soup kitchens, and drug abuse and family counseling services are all operated by or through religious organizations in thousands of communities. With the new norm of dual-income homes and employed single parents, day care for preschoolers and afterschool care for older children become necessary in even the smallest community. Many care programs are not-for-profit arrangements developed and maintained by local religious organizations. All these features boost the social welfare of communities. Most citizens find religion-related programs to be desirable community features.

Civic Services

All communities require fire departments, sanitation programs, and public safety offices. Supported by tax revenues, these services provide for the general stability and safety of the community.

In addition, community services provide an educative function for children. What goes on in those departments, how the jobs are done, and the problems they encounter are of interest to all children. Most offices publish materials and have personnel who head information programs for schools and other local groups. Children learn to understand the meaning of organized communities and the interdependence of community residents. They learn how these services affect their lives and perform for them as individuals.

Businesses

Most communities contain private commercial enterprises linked to daily life in those venues, such as the filling stations, newsstands, and "mom and pop" groceries we find in nonindustrialized suburbs. (The so-called "hypermarts" are both replacing these businesses in many communities and retaining their function as informal links in the lives of community residents.) Other communities contain factories, wharves, large merchandise outlets, and financial and information processing establishments that employ residents and give a flavor to the community. As children become acquainted with local businesses, they become knowledgeable about economics of their town—where people work, what they produce, and where products go. They also learn of the need for many specialties, becoming attuned to the world of work and the effects each institution has on community life and interaction.

In effective communities, commercial establishments cooperate with schools and families. Such cooperation demonstrates commitment to the interdependence of community settings and to the need for mutual support. (See chapters 8 and 10 for discussion of and models for such collaboration.)

Media

With the explosion and transmission of knowledge in the Information Age, communities are engulfed with media of all kinds. From standard newspapers through television programs to the Internet, visual and aural messages descend in increasing amounts across the United States. Whether in an isolated prairie town or an urban neighborhood, the impact of media is all encompassing.

Media affect all other institutions of a community. The type, quality, and amount of information an area receives produces responses from individuals, families, and schools. Effects can be positive

Community services provide an educative function for children.

or negative, but are rarely neutral. Since most media are protected under provisions of the First Amendment to the U.S. Constitution, media outlets are largely self-policing, and public acceptance of the products determines the boundaries for individual distributors.

Appropriateness of media products is a significant issue when we consider children's education. Many publications and recordings are adult oriented in topic, format, and relevance, but children are nonetheless exposed to large amounts of them. It is the responsibility of homes, schools, and other community agencies to make available and encourage use of appropriate materials for children in their care. Media products that fall outside a community's standard invite thoughts of censorship. Problems always surface when community persons confront such issues. It is desirable for communities, through public forums, to

reach consensus on acceptable quality, and then to work for that standard through educational programs and lobbying efforts when required.

Strictly speaking, adults can withhold from children only those materials prohibited by law. All adults working with children must educate them about appropriate and inappropriate materials. Reasonable objectives for media can evolve through the work of churches, civic associations, schools, and neighborhood groups. The effective community is knowledgeable about its media, the effect it has, and the sentiments of its citizens.

Special Interest Groups

In the late twentieth century, the United States has witnessed the formation of numerous special interest groups, from the small group of citizens seeking to exert pressure on schools to include or exclude something, to the highly organized lobbying groups seeking changes in legislation. In general, a *special interest group* has a particular cause and stance (e.g., anti-nuclear energy, save the whales, anti-pornography, pro-choice or pro-life regarding abortion). Many groups disappear after accomplishing their mission; others become entrenched because their cause is ongoing.

Special interest groups are grassroots associations and are very American in concept. Taking as their basis the Constitutional amendment protecting association and assembly, citizens come together to work for or against something. In this way, altruistic groups have formed to gain privileges for disenfranchised persons, such as the education for disabled persons legislation started in the 1970s, or for highlighting a public problem, such as cleaning up the Nashua River (Cherry, 1992). Other groups form to oppose regulations or practices. A nonsmoking lobby is one example; a group censoring local library materials is another.

When special interest groups are headquartered in a particular community or the issue that concerns the group is present in a community, then their presence is clearly felt. The resulting campaigns will affect many community establishments, in particular media, political offices, and schools.

How do communities respond to special interest groups? If partnerships are in good working order, we normally find that special interest group pressure can be accommodated and processed in a healthy fashion. All too often this is not the case, and a part of the community bows to the pressure of the campaigning group. For example, a local library contained several volumes on cults and pagan rituals. When a member of a PTA subgroup saw these volumes, the group started a search through the library to identify and condemn all volumes containing information about the occult. Having no agency and little organization to counter the arguments of the group, library staff quickly acquiesced to the demands and removed all offending materials. This established a dangerous precedent for library materials in this community. The campaign ultimately removed even chil-

dren's innocent fantasy books featuring ghosts and goblins.

Social Networks

The informal everyday contacts of relatives, neighbors, friends, and colleagues produce social networks for adults and children in almost all neighborhoods. These groupings, which can cross gender, age, and socioeconomic status lines, provide useful support for individuals.

Adult Groups

Social science research shows the importance of friends and relatives in providing exchanges of goods and services, as well as psychological support (Coleman, 1991). Werner and Smith (1992) and Bronfenbrenner et al. (1984) indicate that support groups are especially important for at-risk families—to provide emotional support to adults for child raising, confronting adversity, and integration into the community. Healthier adult groups mean healthier environments for children. Information about social services, work opportunities, or new resources in a community is often delivered through social networks of adults, and this benefits children.

Children's Peer Groups

Children's social networks, often called *peer groups*, are natural and can have desirable results, although at times certain combinations may become destructive. The effect on a community may be extensive when children associate in groups. Loosely affiliated groups of children often tour malls and parks, visit businesses, and play games with pleasant and positive results. Other groups may harass citizens and damage property.

Children's contacts beyond the home are necessary as they mature, and the emotional support and exchange of information within networks are powerful influences for all children. When conducted in supervised and constructive ways, peer groups are essential for adequate socialization and maturation, and offer opportunity for many educational insights. Through networks, children

FIGURE 11.4
Assessing the competent community.

Assessors will find most of the following characteristics in effective communities.

1. A workable health care system available to all income levels
2. Social programs, health facilities, and health offices clustered to maximize usage and cut logistics
3. Community programs designed to educate as well as serve
4. Religious institutions participating in community life and demonstrating concern through social action programs
5. Religious associations that nurture children's ethnic and spiritual identities
6. Municipal service departments that are stable, well maintained, and available for educational visits
7. Commercial enterprises that welcome visits and conduct information sessions
8. Commercial establishments that see adopt-a-school plans as an enhancement to the business
9. Media producers who realize the effects of mass communication and who responsibly produce material appropriate for young children
10. Communication between media outlets, schools, and community agencies regarding available media
11. Special interest groups responsive to community questions about their objectives and policies
12. Positive social networks in evidence (social gatherings, block parties, community clubs)
13. Social clubs for children (sports programs, scout programs, 4-H clubs, seasonal recreational facilities)
14. A populace interested in community schools, in neighborhoods, and in individual children

learn physical skills for games, such as baseball, hopscotch, or jump rope, and develop negotiating skills when settling disputes.

Healthy communities recognize the presence of social networks and endorse the formation and continuation of groups of individuals. Effective communities have ways to monitor children's social networks and to steer them in constructive ways (Figure 11.4).

EFFECTIVE PARTNERSHIPS

Schools as Brokers for Social Settings

When viewing the three major social settings in children's lives, we can see the overlap and interlocking nature of the curricula for any one child. One sees areas of effectiveness in each setting, and their relation to outcomes for children's lives. However, these connections do not necessarily form the three settings into a partnership or any type of collaborative venture. No requirement exists in any community for collaboration, and institutions do not collaborate unless an agent appears and serves as catalyst.

We do not need to wait for the fortuitous appearance of persons who will engineer collaborations. We have one institution now that can provide the incentive and stimulus, that has the position and requisite skills to best solicit effective social settings in which children prosper. That institution is the school.

This position means schools must prepare themselves with information and background, establish a plan for making connections among the social settings, and implement that plan. It is hard and extensive work, involving the commitment of instructional staff and administrators who must redefine their own roles and work piecemeal to get consensus among all forces in the community.

One required change is in thinking about what schools are for. The traditional view of teaching has been remediative, that is, filling in the knowledge gaps and developing skills. But schools can no longer consider themselves as compensating for inherited faults and inabilities. For too long, schools have thought of the communities and the families with which they work as possessing "deficits" that must be overcome or accommodated. Schools must now articulate the roles that communities and families can and should bear, and devise ways to steer, guide, and collaborate with them to best accomplish these roles.

What would it take to effect such a plan? School personnel must be educated in the ways of collaboration, and teachers must work hard at "figuring" out the community served, to discern steps and approaches necessary to accomplish the job. Schools may then use their broker position to farm out responsibilities, then to coordinate activities and findings that concern the in-school lives of children served. To start a true collaborative plan is a major effort for most communities. Leadership is essential, and the steps will most likely be taken slowly. But involving families and community must begin somewhere (see the following section).

Programs for Teacher Preparation

Empowered school staffs are needed for any plan based on partnerships and collaborations. Many present staff members will require educating for the role. New teacher programs must include work in sociology of education, work with volunteers, work with adult learners, and collaboration as a skill, and internships with social agencies or community organizations. This implies a very different teacher preparation program and emphasis than currently implemented in most districts, and universities must attract the most talented candidates for these roles. Schools will require fewer teachers, but the core staff must be skilled assessment people who can program and unite efforts.

Few courses exist for this particular focus. One effort was begun a few years ago at Wayne State University (Kaplan,1992).

Filling a new niche in the home–school–community matrix, teachers will require more skill and training to establish their role, which is primarily that of convener, diagnostician, and guide, as illustrated here:

....

When approaching the classroom, the newly empowered teacher will think of herself as an "at-home" Peace Corps worker who takes stock of situations and then figures out how best to serve the population with which she finds herself. Starting with the literacy skills, she will ask herself, Where are students in their reading and writing development? When the diagnosis is accomplished, she will meet with parents or others, conducting demonstration lessons, and conferring on objectives and ways to attain them. She will use suggestions and ideas that people present about resources in the community that can be used beneficially to teach or illuminate any subject matter, project, or skill area. For instance, her class may accept an invitation to the area water treatment plant to learn about its operation and effect on the community. They would plan the trip, use investigative skills to study and analyze the site, use cooperative learning and coaching skills to reason out the benefits, and then use literacy skills to describe it for parents, other school students, and community members.

....

Such partnership activity would be followed by others, as the school becomes a different entity in its community. The partnership replaces the school where teachers welcome groups of 25 or more children and teach from a traditional curriculum: distributing books, conducting a reading lesson, assigning a writing lesson, then proceeding to the next subject. Traditional schools consume a large amount of time learning rules and classroom protocols, lining up, moving to and fro, collecting papers, distributing and collecting books, and so on. These ritual-filled classrooms exist all over the United States, and teach little beyond what each child is motivated to seek. The time has arrived to move beyond these tightly structured schools.

SUMMARY

We have defined effective families, schools, and communities as those in which children have maximum opportunities to grow, develop, and prosper. We have discussed effective social settings, and provided models of effective settings working together.

General guidelines exist by which you may examine families, schools, and communities, assess the social settings you encounter, and ascertain how each measures up to standards of effectiveness. Imperfect settings exist for different reasons, many beyond the reach of educators acting alone. Providing individual support in areas where deficits exist is an option, and persons associated with a given social setting have sometimes been able to give that support. The best resolution for most deficits lies in linking the strengths of all social settings.

The road to stronger relationships is simplified when each social setting is effective in itself. When this is not the case, then persons in the different settings look for ways to pull together to help children obtain more benefits. Each setting affects the others, and the strength of one bolsters another. The school must be the place where interactions are coordinated. Schools need to become the brokers for new learning communities, which may then thrive in the support and contributions of all three institutions.

SUGGESTED ACTIVITIES AND QUESTIONS

1. Take the assessment questions given in the chapter and relate them to (1) a home you are acquainted with, (2) a school you know well, and (3) the community in which you are located. What

profiles do you find? Did anything surprise you? Which social setting seems strongest?
2. Take the profiles from question one and compare them with those obtained by a classmate. What differences do you find?
3. Assume now that you are to be the director of a new collaboration involving the three settings. As the school administrator, what will be your three greatest challenges in establishing a collaborative effort? Are all three from one setting? What are your chances of accommodating the three challenges?
4. Describe a hypothetical competent family of a 6-year-old child. Describe a less competent family for another 6-year-old. Speculate how you could use your knowledge of the competent family to assist the less competent one.
5. Imagine that you are working on a new home–school–community collaboration. An official from your state Board of Education is visiting to view your district's new plan. Develop an outline of your working partnership to show the visitor how the three social settings support each other.

RECOMMENDED READINGS

Bennett, K., & LeCompte, M. D. (1990). *How schools work: A sociological analysis of education.* New York: Longman.

Clark, R. M. (1983). *Family life and school achievement: Why poor black children succeed or fail.* Chicago: University of Chicago Press.

Curran, D. (1983). *Traits of a healthy family.* Minneapolis, MN: Winston.

Lund, L., & Wild, C. (1993). *Ten years after a nation at risk.* New York: The Conference Board.

Quint, S. (1994). *Schooling homeless children: A working model for America's public schools.* New York: Teachers College Press.

Rich, D. (1992). *Megaskills: In school and life—the best gift you can give your child.* Boston: Houghton Mifflin.

Thompson, S. (Ed.). (1993). *Whole child, whole community.* Boston: Institute for Responsive Education.

Werner, E. E., & Smith, R. S. (1992). *Overcoming the odds: High risk children from birth to adulthood.* Ithaca, NY: Cornell University Press.

Working Together

Much is right with U.S. educational experiences in spite of some glaring and well-publicized problems. Education planners and other workers in most communities have both a suitable base to build on and numerous models to draw from to bring about improvements. The future will be positive for children's education if citizens can build on the processes and worthwhile creations already in action.

We address in this final chapter the issues for working together. In reading this chapter you will learn that:

1. Collaborations among families, schools, and communities entail several levels, or stages, of involvement.

2. Certain conditions enhance the growth of partnerships, and other factors present barriers to forming good working relationships and collaborations.

3. Six particular criteria demonstrate the status of partnerships, and we can also use them to design new collaborative ventures.

4. Both "bottom-up" and "top-down" approaches can succeed at bringing families, schools, and communities together.

While seldom using the term *collaboration*, residents in rural and urban communities have always had ways of influencing the upbringing of their youngest citizens. In the following vignette, a teacher recalls her childhood years in a poor rural community of the 1930s, and indicates directions that would serve us well as we begin a new century.

The minister, the school principal, and the town's mayor all discussed educational problems, recommended solutions, and showed great concern for their community's children. Their efforts were supported by local parents. A "party line" telephone system, where most families could listen in, aided their communication. For example, one child, late coming home from school on a spring day, was easily found, reprimanded by a passerby, and sent on his way with knowledge that the parents at home would follow through on the reprimand. Children who needed clothes and extra food were identified at school, and with the support of "town fathers," teachers and others visited the homes. Food, clothing, and other resources were found and delivered, and, at times, negligent par-

ents were counseled. Teachers taught formal lessons in their schoolrooms, but often walked home with their students, continuing their education as they observed and discussed nature about them. The community was the children's playground, and adults who were present supervised the children. Older children educated younger ones in many skills and safety rules. One could feel this was a cohesive community and one marked by caring. It was, of course, not an ideal system; a few children didn't reach their potential and one didn't even survive. But an overarching support system enhanced opportunities and of 13 children in my first-grade class, all completed high school and 7 went on to college.

....

The narrator of the preceding vignette demonstrates how parents, schools, and community members all assumed responsibility for children's development. Times were simpler then, and many communities were more closely knit than now, but the lesson of communal caring and the need for shared expectations are quite valid today. Author James Comer also lived in a close-knit city community during his childhood, and he tells of a similar collaboration of the social institutions which cared for him. In *Maggie's American Dream: The Life and Times of a Black Family*, Comer (1988) recalls his parents, neighbors, and teachers reinforcing each other's goals for children's engagement in learning. The process in Comer's case wasn't formal either. Individuals in each social setting seemed to understand each other's roles. In both stories, neighborhood children whose parents were sympathetic to the school's goals were more successful than were children whose parents were out of touch.

Society in the late twentieth century is different from that at the century's beginning. It is harder to establish common objectives, where social institutions can work effectively together. Families have new worries and heavier burdens,

and children have fewer advocates. In many situations schools have assumed more of the educative, counseling, and social oversight for children, but from many accounts it is apparent schools cannot effectively do the job alone (U.S. Department of Education, 1994; O'Callaghan, 1993). And the most disturbing fact in the United States is that our society is annually writing off as dispensable a large fraction of its youth, condemning them to lives of dysfunction and nonproductiveness (Zinsmeister, 1990; Kotlowitz, 1991).

However, some accounts show that different outlooks have appeared in our nation's communities in recent years. A significant number of professionals and lay persons have taken a position that education is much more than school buildings, books, and daily schedules. We find a growing recognition that lifestyle diversity and multiculturalism are here to stay, and that it makes sense for all residents to pull together in making communities more liveable and schools more productive.

Amid the high hopes and *vision* for redoing the educational landscape, practical considerations sober us; we know change comes slowly. Some workers will have to settle for small victories. But, small steps can be beneficial; they represent building blocks. For example, getting cooperation and involving parents and community associations in building playground equipment for a North Carolina school helped hundreds of citizens in that community become familiar with and interested in school functions. Getting local businesses involved in science and math projects for third graders in a rural Michigan town pulled education very close to the lives of many citizens. Small steps do provide a base.

In this chapter, we offer our recommendations for working together. We first discuss the levels of involvement in partnerships; we then identify conditions for healthy working relations, as well as barriers to them; and finally, by examining experiments in two different idealized communities, we present accounts of growing partnerships.

LEVELS OF INVOLVEMENT
IN COLLABORATIONS

Partnership relations are built on basic premises about leadership, participation, and involvement. Good collaborative efforts mean that individuals in any group must recognize different levels of involvement. Though educators are in the best position for encouraging and establishing partnerships, some teachers, parents, and community members will assume stronger leadership roles. Others will contribute at minimum levels. For persons involved in a collaboration, there is always a hierarchy of involvement (Henderson et al., 1986; Wissburn & Eckart, 1992). Some will participate at a minimum level, others at an associative level, and still others at a decision-making level.

Understanding Involvement

Laypeople interpret parental and community involvement in different ways. Some citizens are proactive and feel connected to schools, but a larger group continues to view teachers as having total control of children's education, and either do not seek involvement or feel shut out of the process. They tend to view schools from afar, but often are critical or resentful when their children don't progress well or they feel tax dollars are being misspent. This view, of course, contributes very little of substance, and we have a duty to continue to attract this part of the constituency and work for more participation.

So, how much involvement is productive? Different programs will call for differing amounts of involvement and, generally, participatory intensity varies with level. Most parents and community members can be involved in some school activities; only a few will be present for others. The key to successful collaboration is for all community citizens to be involved in one level or another, with a few individuals contributing at all levels.

Minimum Level

Teachers and school administrators reach out to parents and community members in various ways, seeking support for school programs. This has been the case for several generations. For example, children have homework that teachers request parents to supervise. The homework might involve interviewing neighbors or finding information about different community businesses. Teachers expect that parents and other community members will respond to these requests and help them with the projects.

The community at large is normally invited to school-sponsored events, and teachers often seek assistance other than for simply taking attendance. For example, parents and community members often help make costumes or props for school plays. Schools have various fundraising events, including bake sales, fairs, and selling of particular products. Again, school personnel seek cooperation from parents and others in the community to contribute items, and to support and help with events. Teachers also seek cooperation from parents and various agencies as they collect materials for children to manipulate and use in school projects. Calls go out for empty egg cartons, juice cans, carpet samples, and the like.

The above are all examples of minimal involvement, and most readers will recognize and recall similar events from their own childhood. It is commonplace, it serves a definite purpose, and it is a good foundation from which to start working for more complete participation.

Children benefit from this type of involvement from homes and community. They are drawn into the practical stages of education and often see the application of schoolwork to the real world. The more persons involved, the greater the benefits to children. Successful collaborations mean that a large percentage of parents and community members are involved with their schools at this beginning level.

Associative Level

Some parents and schools seek more than minimal participation and association. Many teachers request parents and community members to become classroom volunteers on a regular basis. Volunteers assist teachers in various ways—from making and copying materials for classrooms to reading for children and assisting them in activities. Some volunteers tutor children who have difficulty with assignments, and others assist in the library or school office. Still others become "room mothers (or fathers)," organizing other community members, helping supervise children on school trips, or making calls to solicit different kinds of classroom support. Some volunteers become involved in enrichment programs where they share their special expertise with children in a classroom. In one primary school, a choral director organized the primary-age children into a singing group to develop a program of Christmas music, which children performed at several community functions during the holiday season.

At the associative level, community members also participate in local organizations that support schools. Parent-Teacher Association (PTA) chapters have traditionally supported schools, as parents and teachers cooperated in school improvement ventures. At times PTAs center on fundraising events; at other times they may become a political force in the community to improve conditions for children. In one Virginia community, when the school board decided to eliminate some kindergarten positions, make kindergarten classes larger in all schools, and transport extra children to nearby schools, the PTAs at these schools banded together to protest the decision. Board members, recognizing the opposition, found other ways to cut their budget. PTAs and similar organizations have served as advocates for school plans and have interpreted curriculum for community members. Still other groups have been responsible for arranging parent education classes and parent support groups.

These actions draw schools closer to their parent and community groups, creating significant communication links.

Children benefit from involvement at the associative level; expectations are clearer and communication is facilitated. Stronger ties mean stronger programs, and divisiveness is far less likely when schools and communities enjoy this level of interaction. At any point in time, fewer parents will be involved at the associative level than at the minimal level. Comer (1980) notes that if 5 to 10 percent of parents became actively involved at this level, then an adequate group of parents assisting and acting as advocates is present, as long as they represent a cross-section of the community.

Decision-making Level

The third level of parent and community involvement in schools is the decision-making level. At this level individual parents, business persons, professionals, and community leaders assume the right to make decisions for the education of their children.

Parent participation works with little controversy at the minimum and associative levels of involvement. Teachers and school administrators are still in charge of all educational decision making, and parents and community members assist and support these decisions. However, when parents and others become involved in decision making, friction can emerge. Controversy that paralyzes is, of course, not in the best interests of children. Successful collaboration of parents, teachers, administrators, and community members at this level requires mutual respect and a new definition of shared responsibility and accountability (Bloom, 1992; Wissbrun & Eckart, 1992). Acting at this level requires hard work.

Parents at the decision-making level move beyond being committed advocates for their children into sharing responsibility for providing quality (school) education for their own and other

FIGURE 12.1
Three levels of involvement.

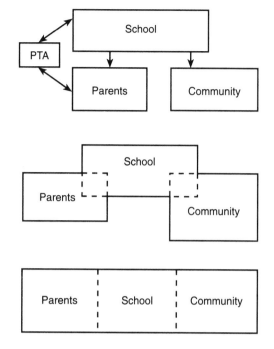

Minimal
School tells, informs
and requests from
homes and community.

Associative
School involves
parents in many ways.
School communicates
with community.

Decision-making
Schools, homes and
communities all work
together as equals
to devise good
educational opportunities
for all children.

children. They serve on curriculum and other educational committees, identifying goals and objectives and deciding how to achieve them. At this level, parents are expected to serve on committees that hire school staff. They also might assist in forming advocacy groups to secure necessary local, state, or federal funding, so that local schools may provide programs important for the community.

Usually, parent and community involvement at this level requires only a small percentage of parents, but these representatives *must* represent the different constituencies within the community. Such involvement dictates changes within the school hierarchy, and such a change can be detrimental unless teachers, administrators, parents, and community members work carefully and with genuine mutual respect to bring gradual change. Gradual change, steadily enhancing school programs, is by far the most productive.

Figure 12.1 illustrates the collaborative relations of each level of involvement.

HANDLING RELATIONSHIPS

Conditions for Positive Relationships

As noted in earlier chapters, we have a long history of parental involvement in U.S. schools. Some relationships have been very positive for particular parents, teachers, and community members. But good relationships do not just happen. Both internal and external conditions and factors help establish better relationships.

One important human factor for developing positive collaborations is mutual respect. Each party in a collaborative effort needs the concern of the others, as well as the expertise, viewpoints, and experiences others possess.

Recognizing and supporting the expertise of others is not always easy. Comer (1980), in developing his collaboration model, maintains that the project nearly failed several times. It took three years to develop the trust and respect necessary for the school to begin a change process that would offer equal access and opportunity for all students. Commenting on this, he states, "In order to provide good learning experiences for students, trust and respect must exist so that behavior, teaching, and learning issues can be addressed. Such a climate cannot be imposed: it must grow out of governance and management arrangements and ways of working based on knowledge of social conditions and human and system behaviors" (p. 230).

Developing such respect requires compassion, a willingness to listen to others' points of view, and a willingness to compromise. Often it is school personnel who must take the initiative in establishing a sense of respect. No one right way exists to accomplish this, but concerned teachers and administrators devise ways that improve communication with their students' parents through face-to-face communication, and use of electronic and written communications (D'Angelo & Adler, 1991).

An important component in establishing good partnerships is people's ability to really listen to each other. Unfortunately, although professional adults are involved in communication activities about 70 percent of the time, less than half of that is spent listening, and even at that, the listening is not done well (Studer, 1993–1994). Individuals can improve their ability to listen. When both teachers and parents are willing to learn about and practice communication skills, student success increases (Miller, 1991).

Beyond the willingness to establish respect and develop good communication, external factors help collaborative efforts to function. It is important to establish support systems, such as workshops to assist people to develop better communication skills. Time must be provided for meetings to discuss needs and objectives. To meet parent, teacher, and community members' time constraints, schedules must remain as flexible as possible. Teachers may need to be released from classes or compensated for evening meetings. Businesses need to examine the possibility of flexible hours of operation or flexible working hours for their parent employees. Having options for

parent and community member involvement establishes a good basis for collaborative efforts, allowing all who are or wish to be involved to select a comfortable participation level.

A welcoming physical environment always helps to establish good relationships. Schools must place a priority on image, for sometimes a simple change in what parents see when entering a building makes a great difference. A welcome sign directing visitors to the principal's office helps. Student artwork and other projects brighten up an entrance. Space where parents can comfortably wait, perhaps with a coffee pot and some interesting literature about schools, gives visitors a sense of being welcome.

The process of collaboration is one of identifying, establishing, and cultivating positive factors to support interactions. Many ideas make sense for cooperative arrangements—the strategies of most any helping profession may be adapted appropriately. If schools are to become engaged in true partnerships, all concerned must expand and refine these skills of communication, negotiation, and cooperation.

Barriers to Good Relations

No matter how well intentioned people are, some barriers surface that will result in breakdowns of communication and good relationships. One basic hurdle revolves around the different philosophical positions and perspectives persons have regarding how children learn and what they should be taught.

For example, if a school attempts a constructivist approach to learning and parents do not understand how their children are learning to read, write, and learn number facts, a barrier can develop. Parents could well become angry and accuse the school of ignoring discipline and not teaching the basics.

Different beliefs about how and who should teach sex education can create misunderstandings among schools, parents, and community. Parents may consider discipline measures as either too

A welcoming physical environment always helps to establish good relationships.

harsh or too lenient, and these different perceptions will cause friction between homes and schools. Issues such as these can spark problems, and they will fester and add to existing subsurface distrust if no mechanism is present to address them. Parents and teachers must openly examine their philosophical viewpoints so they may establish better relationships.

Attitudes can also present barriers to good relationships. Parents and community members have feelings and attitudes about school that date back to their own childhoods. Parents who had unpleasant school experiences are often reluctant to become involved with their children's schools. A diminished self-concept is often present in such cases, and the isolation breeds more fear. Such parents resist contact with schools from fear of criticism of themselves and their children. This circumstance helps no one, least of all the children. Schools need to work gently but with determination to overcome negativism and encourage positive contact.

Nonverbal interactions often cause barriers to good relationships. Teachers or parents may state one thing while their nonverbal stance communicates another (Seay & Alterkruse, 1979). For example, during a conference, one parent crossed her arms, saying, in what seemed an annoyed tone, "I thought Janey did well on that project." The teacher interpreted this to mean, "I don't agree with what you said." The teacher then paused, moved slightly away, and murmured, "Well, it was an interesting project." When both moved on to another topic, the real significance of Janey's effort was lost. Both left the situation feeling defensive, because the non-verbal behavior of both parties cut off further communication.

Fear affects teachers as well as parents, and they may do little to encourage parental or community involvement. When teachers are uncertain or insecure about their own teaching skills, they fear criticism of how they do their job and discourage parent participation in their classrooms. When we have local criticism of schools, teachers become tired of being "scapegoats" for all the wrongs of society, and they often express a desire "to be left alone" to teach. When such attitudes permeate the school, parents are made to feel unwelcome in many different ways.

Admonishments and other external features can become barriers to positive home–school relationships.

When wide socioeconomic and cultural differences exist between school personnel and local families, misunderstandings can cause friction and often anger. Barriers are created when value systems differ and neither party is willing or able to examine differences and find common ground.

External features may also become barriers. Entering a school for the first time can be daunting even for the experienced. In some instances, doors are locked for safety reasons and one must ring to enter. Sometimes the first thing one sees on entering a school is the notice, "All Visitors Must Report to the Principal's Office." Parents who were sent often to the principal's office during their school years will not feel very welcome. When the office is difficult to find, and no one is around to assist, schools again communicate that visitors are unwelcome. Office personnel are sometimes too busy to assist, or may appear annoyed at the interruption, or may ask in an intimidating way, "Do you have an appointment?" Unwelcoming signals are easily discerned, and too often found.

Teachers and administrators are busy people struggling to maintain productive environments for student learning. That is their most important task, and many think the time and energy needed to add parental and community involvement to their workloads just isn't available. Such school personnel communicate the unimportance of parental involvement.

Parents also find external barriers as they try to maintain a commitment to schools (Swap, 1993). Many have busy schedules, and families who live a distance from the school may have a problem with transportation. When involvement means going to school in the evenings, child care may be difficult to arrange. Few businesses have flexible hours that allow parents to meet teachers during daytime hours. Hotlines and help lines can resolve some time and schedule conflicts when schools have a priority for maintaining communication.

ACHIEVING PARTNERSHIPS

In Chapter 10, we noted program models showing that true collaboration can emerge when properly nurtured. These model collaborations took time to build, and take even more time to monitor and fine tune to keep healthy. As such models show, however, the effort is worthwhile. Anyone interested in achieving partnerships for their schools should carefully examine established programs. Information about the sustainability of these programs is helpful for beginners developing their plans, and the reported educational benefits to children and communities are inspirational.

In the rest of this chapter, we consider two idealized communities that are struggling with collaborative efforts. We have adapted Davies's (1993) six criteria for assessing collaborations as a template for viewing the stages of development. These descriptions provide a reasonable guide for the processes that communities move through when forming partnerships with schools and parents. Stated as imperatives, the criteria are as follows:

1. Neutralize bureaucratic resistance to change.
2. Reinvent community.
3. Provide support for families.
4. Integrate educational and social services.
5. Involve those affected by change.
6. Base policy and practice on research.

Woodland

This New England community of 3,000 people has long traditions and a stable population. Ethnically, the town is almost totally Anglo-American, but pronounced economic differences appear for the residents. You could say that the community consists of "haves," "have nots," and a few "have-somethings" in the middle. All citizens use the town's services. Individuals greet each other daily, and hire and consult each other, but live in separate worlds.

Differences have become more intense in recent decades as affluent families continue to send sons and daughters to college, to develop land, and generally live pleasant lives. The "have nots" have suf-fered more from a deteriorating local industry and the distress, reduced wages, and anxieties that accompany it. More than those of the "haves," their lives are beset with divorce, substance abuse, single parenting, and diminished living conditions. Lacks in education nudge almost all young people from the lower economic level into the limited service and manual labor jobs in the area. The result is frequent unemployment, welfare dependence, and substandard housing.

Disparities between the two groups appear in community schools. Little segregation by "class" is evident, but the existence of cliques is apparent. Participation in social functions, sports, and cultural activities is similarly lopsided. Teachers adjust to these conditions and observe protocols for both subgroups, but are candid about the growing school failure rate for the "have nots."

But Woodland is beginning to change through grassroots efforts. Two years ago, reports of lower achievement scores, students failing college entrance exams, and parents sending children to private schools became the impetus for several community groups to take action. Individual groups have designed various programs for helping improve conditions for children. The school board authorized a community planning committee to proceed with developing long-range goals for schools. As need for a new elementary school building became apparent, a communitywide committee began to devise plans. In response to literacy needs, a large volunteer community group started to serve children and parents in new ways: delivering books to infants and toddlers; reading to children at school; providing storytelling hours at libraries and in homes; offering literacy programs for adults; and assisting children with homework during after-school programs. Groups of volunteers now offer summer camp experiences for children. A group of parents who thought their school was "gloomy" organized to repaint the foyer and provide bulletin boards on which to display children's work. When materials for artwork and dramatic presentations ran out, a group of churchgoers collected and organized art materials for teachers. Organizations with volunteer help now support the school with several projects including art appreciation, integrating arts into the curriculum, and special art classes for gifted and talented students.

For the most part, social service and health agencies still work separately from the schools. But several projects now unite social and medical services with school projects. Volunteers read to children while mothers wait at the local clinic for medical and social services. Social service personnel have begun to work with teachers and community volunteers both during school and in after-school programs. Local businesses have organized an educational foundation, which collects and invests money to fund creative activities. Ironically, Woodland has high community involvement without any systematic approach for developing partnerships. No leadership really unites the efforts.

Although this groundswell of concern and interest exists, lethargy and resistance are found in many quarters, too. Attitudes of parents and teachers with respect to one another change slowly. Many parents still feel alienated, but most officials feel comfortable with the status quo and resist different ways of operating. With so many programs, some teachers have begun to feel the school doesn't belong to them.

Yet change will come, and Woodland is poised to take some important steps to assure more benefits for children of their community. With leadership from community officials and school administrators, the community could flourish in the "bottom-up" flow of interest that has begun. Many individuals are now engaged at the associative level of involvement. Using Davies's (1993) criteria, we can speculate about outcomes that may evolve for Woodland. In the following subsections, we discuss methods by which Woodland may enhance and encourage its budding partnerships.

Neutralize Bureaucratic Resistance to Change

Though only a slender community government exists, resistance to change in Woodland is diffi-

cult to overcome. Strong leadership is needed to do this, and a school board member, a principal, or a superintendent of schools could be the pivotal person. In any new project, the first task always is convincing school personnel, families, and community that change is needed. For example, the community is grappling with building a new elementary school. This is under study by community groups, but the school board and town government have not as yet authorized any development. The following are ways of neutralizing resistance to this change:

- Publish figures on current school statistics.
- Publish alternatives for present school programs.
- Identify leaders within the community to get their ideas.
- Notify citizens about ways to get involved.
- Schedule information-sharing sessions.
- Sponsor research to show the weaknesses and strengths of different alternatives.

Reinvent Community

The patterns of past generations are still at work in any community, even though needs change. In Woodland, an influx of new residents with different ideas about education has caused wide differences in expectations. A productive route is needed to redefine inclusiveness in this community so miscommunication does not reinforce the resistance.

Rediscovering community may be more appropriate in this case. The different family groups work together, but their work must move beyond the superficial links if a new community feeling is to emerge. New residents need a voice in the community's future, and may certainly contribute significantly to long-term goals by stating their objective opinions on community development, school curriculum, and participation in this process. But families who have lived in the community for generations must be given a voice for maintaining their cultural expectations, too.

Establishing cross-group committees is one way to bring a diverse agenda of desires and hope

In Woodland, volunteers provide summer camp experiences for children.

into the open. The community will need to develop workshops so the different groups learn strategies for communicating. Establishing common goals will help clarify community beliefs concerning what and how to educate all children. The community must consider seriously the future of all its young citizens, since a large number of them remain in the town to be future leaders and contributors.

Provide Support for Families

Some families in Woodland need support desperately. While crime and abject poverty are still rare, some families live a "hand-to-mouth" existence that has become a lifestyle. The results are low aspirations and high dependency. Immediate gratification, in the form of fast cars, snowmobiles, and unhealthy substances, dominates the interests of many.

Woodland can take several steps to assist families. Community members must study family needs, then build on their strengths, coordinating activities to improve confidence and aspirations. Information for determining family needs may be obtained in the following ways:

- Anonymous questionnaires
- Telephone or home interviews with sample families
- Statistical analysis of local government records
- Small focus groups within the community sharing their particular interests

Those involved must not make their information gathering offensive to residents. Making clear the intention for gathering information, being respectful of parents, and demonstrating that their ideas will be heeded will all improve the process. Evidence of cultural values and strengths will emerge in most families. Planners must incorporate these values and strengths into any developing support systems.

Several projects already started in Woodland build on family strengths. A nutritional program demonstrates the value of different foods and how

variety of preparation provides interest in healthy eating. Another project, a family reading program, brings quality books to all new parents. The community's preschoolers receive gift books as a strategy to inject books into family life, and one criterion for selections is that books must reflect the cultural patterns of the community. Offshoots of the plan call for young mothers and their children to gather socially to discuss interests in the books and how they use them. A related objective is to develop a writing program in which young mothers share stories of their own lives with their children.

Several projects are underway as a result of information gathered through a local Women, Infants, and Children (WIC) program, which provides basics for low-income families with small children. A new regional mental health project is poised to render support for needy families. Workshops and adult education offerings also have started recently as a result of citizen requests.

Additional support for families, particularly young and struggling families, is needed to bring all to participate in the life of their town. The Woodland school district, which up to this point has stood apart from family connections, must pull all families closer to school operations. Woodland needs a parent program to introduce skills to enable young people to lift aspirations and discover their abilities to be worthy parents. A parent center would also make families feel more welcome in the school program. Small steps have begun.

Integrate Educational and Social Services

In spite of many community activities to enhance children's education, true partnerships do not yet exist in Woodland. The minimal social services presently available have only a small connection with the school and other educational endeavors. The feeling in the community has been that these services must be separate, that there is no logic to combining them. However, researchers now realize that social services linked to schools have much greater chances for success. Any community can take steps to strengthen its disparate activities, and Woodland is beginning.

A new building presents a marvelous opportunity for the community to integrate a social services center within the school itself. Social services such as counseling, abuse prevention, GED programs, nutrition, and job training are logically housed in the local educational facilities. Much of the work overlaps and can be coordinated for recipients. Not every community can build a new building, but when services are coordinated, logistics for offering the services can be worked out.

In Woodland, some projects are beginning to be linked through a single coordinator. A social service coordinator who works with community people and teachers administers nutrition programs in the schools, the WIC program at the community health center, volunteer reading programs, and a community program for involving children in gardening. Local business people have begun to contribute by providing resources and welcoming students for field trips. When services are linked, open decision making follows readily.

Involve Those Affected by Change

Seemingly, in a small town most citizens would and could be involved in change—after all, the New England town meeting is the true example of grassroots democracy. Sadly, in Woodland, only about 10 percent of the residents attend and participate in town government. Many feel that town affairs are already out of their hands and their voices will not be heard. Community principals must persuade residents to learn about participation.

In Woodland, the immediate goal is to consolidate the work of many people. The first step is to secure strong leadership committed to establishing school, family, and community group links for all the various programs. School personnel must be the arbiters and promoters for developing and supporting this leadership, and may wish to hold workshops to enhance leadership and communication skills for all persons involved.

A partnership team must be formed whose members represent the different interest groups in the community. All members must recognize its authority and be committed to assuming their responsibility, including assisting in communicating to the public the many activities already supporting community involvement and the benefits accruing to children. When grassroots programs proliferate as they have in Woodland, one great risk is burnout of teachers, parents, and volunteers. Team members also must serve as a filter to prevent overlap, as different parent, community, and school organizations sponsor new initiatives, and as a support group for fledgling programs, overseeing their assessment and evaluation. The team's final responsibility will be to communicate school successes resulting from collaborations.

Base Policy and Practice on Research

Often political and educational organizations are estranged from researchers. The irony is that both camps are often looking at the same phenomena, and each has part of the answer to questions that arise. Politicians reason through situations and act on hunches, while educational researchers study circumstances and then experiment. Situations improve when both agencies cooperate and value the viewpoints and findings of the other.

School and community leaders have much to gain by using information gathered by quantitative and qualitative researchers. But in Woodland, outside researchers are viewed with suspicion. Local residents operating on hunches, knowledge of community, and common sense are viewed as more credible than people with charts, calculators, and questionnaires. One can see that educators must move carefully to raise the perceived value of research efforts.

If a partnership becomes established and the assessment process begins, then the Woodland partnership team can easily secure information regarding changes within the schools. Then, as schools in the community seek new methods of assessing their work, it will be necessary to conduct other research. We believe that if the first five criteria are met, in all likelihood this last area of a new partnership will also fall into place.

Big City

....

This major U.S. city has a varied population, a tradition of strong leadership, and a history of economic ups and downs. As in all large cities, great affluence exists in some areas, and abject poverty in others. The ethnic mix varies considerably from one part of the city to another, but overall the population is typical of most large urban centers today. We center our discussion on School District 5, which typifies many large cities in the 1990s.

Big City has a large welfare budget, which is kept completely separated from all school affairs. Different city agencies working with the same family groups in District 5 almost never collaborate. But Big City has a reputation for moving rapidly on projects, in securing funding for experiments, and managing events well. The "can do" attitude permeates the city government to a point where schools and other city agencies are brought along as silent partners. While the management shows efficiency, it is a paternalistic style allowing for little involvement of citizens and subgroups.

District 5 includes 100,000 people, mostly of African American and Anglo-American descent, plus smaller numbers of recent Hispanic and Asian immigrants. The district is almost totally residential and family incomes range from below the poverty level to middle income. The district is made up of older homes in long-established neighborhoods, and most civic associations throughout the area are traditional in nature. One school was recently constructed, but all others are older establishments. Elementary school curricula throughout the district are traditional, although there is some experimentation, and two schools have attempted closer connections with students' families.

The new regional superintendent in District 5 has expressed concern about traditional curricula

in the area. She has championed the cooperative learning ventures at Expo School and the school–family partnerships at Demo School and seems anxious to reestablish program innovations that arrived more than a decade before. Most middle-level administrators and directors demonstrate less concern.

District 5 is in an interesting stage. From prior administrations, most personnel have more than fleeting knowledge of cooperative efforts between homes and schools. In fact, several major studies on school partnerships conducted in the city schools have received national recognition. But many administrators have short terms to serve until retirement and give only lip service to new endeavors. Coupled with a constant battle to maintain adequate school budgets, this has produced slow reform on home–school–community work.

The district population is about 60 percent African American, and over 70 percent of school students are members of ethnic minorities. The district has a good record in race relations; however, schools are segregated by income. Two elementary schools contain half of all the Anglo-American children in the district, and these schools reflect middle-class values. Parts of District 5 have high crime levels; nightly violence and constant police surveillance seem a fact of life in these neighborhoods.

Considerable change has come to Demo School since the new principal has forged ahead in altering its operating policies. She has installed a parent council that meets to consider school problems and develop community outreach programs. Parent and community representatives are noticeable in the school and local support for any program or project is bestowed lavishly. These innovations are applauded by the new regional superintendent. While middle-level support seems minimal, the effect does not dampen efforts at Demo School. For this one school in District 5, change is noticeable and the effects are promising. For most other parts of the district old procedures and a stifling bureaucracy remain in place.

....

We consider Davies's (1993) criteria for establishing school and home connections with regard to District 5.

Neutralize Bureaucratic Resistance to Change

Two superintendents in recent decades tried to decentralize management of schools in Big City, and they fostered new thinking about communication with communities and parents. Modest success appeared in several schools, but interim superintendents depended on previous policies; thus headway on site-based management has not been extensive in the last decade. Fortunately, research studies carried out in several schools have kept district personnel cognizant of efforts in partnership. Teachers and administrators are familiar with the language of cooperation, and most are acquainted with positive results in schools that have experimented. However, even with the new regional superintendent's objectives for innovations, bureaucratic resistance exists in most central offices of the district.

Demo School has established itself as a partnership model, showing that change in school–community relationships is quite possible. District 5 has always maintained itself adequately, and there is no groundswell for change. Its problems are not as intense as elsewhere in Big City, and many educators feel comfortable with preserving the status quo. The two small projects (Demo School and Expo School) that foster cooperative work are heralded as pacesetters. It appears the district is pleased to have them as representatives, but opts out of the work needed to emulate them. District 5 must be judged as modest in neutralizing resistance to change at present, but the district could flourish with cooperative ventures if the new leadership prevails over entrenched bureaucracy.

Reinvent Community

District 5 has made reasonable progress in race relations. Demo School is situated in the poorest section of the district, and has succeeded in "reinventing" a community that now supports it and collaborates with its programs. While still at the stage of minimal to moderate involvement, school personnel have demonstrated clearly how productive work with a community can be, in setting up parent groups and gaining confidence of community members.

Mothers, fathers, and extended family members regularly visit the school and participate in supportive ways. Demo School has developed a parent volunteer group to support teaching projects and uses parents as short-term substitutes in classrooms. Area residents, working with the principal, have successfully brought immunization clinics to the school for neighborhood children. Strides have been made in valuing and promoting education, especially among residents of low-income homes. Parent skills are acknowledged in newsletters, on bulletin boards throughout the school, and in school presentations. A feeling of joint purpose pervades this low-income school community.

Reinventing community has been a success in Demo School, but a sister school only several blocks away has almost an opposite quality. No parents visit unless summoned, and no joint school–home activities are developed. Most of District 5, in spite of the progress at Demo and Expo schools, seems locked in a period of partnership stagnation. Community in District 5 has been only partially reinvented.

Provide Support for Families

Supporting families means sustaining them emotionally as well as financially, and these separate objectives rarely come together in Big City. With the exception of Demo School, family members in the district keep their social welfare and school affairs far apart. Big City school administration and welfare offices have not established any arrangement to bring two or more city services together.

To focus on children's total "curriculum," their experiences at home, in the community, and at school, requires treating all conditions as a single global issue, with the parents at the heart. Supporting parents means uniting services and helping them make decisions for their children. Most

Reinventing community means family members regularly visit school and participate in supportive ways.

District 5 school personnel know little about their neighborhoods and about the children who live there, where they go and what they do after school. Such lack of knowledge is neither helpful nor supportive, and changes must begin within the educational bureaucracy.

In Demo School, the principal is a strong leader. From the beginning of her tenure she has trained, organized, and supported teachers in the school's new plan for reaching out to families. She initiated a family center in the school and invited parents to join her and other teachers in discussing their children's needs. Early discussions took place over coffee with one or two parents and a teacher. These parents were instrumental in getting other parents involved. At present, we find

high parental involvement in the school, and the neighborhood takes great pride in the changes in enthusiasm and skill development of its children.

Integrate Educational and Social Services

Big City is replete with bureaucracy, extending to all offices and agencies within the urban boundaries. To bring about even modest change requires reinvention of agency processes. As noted, District 5, except for the few integrated services at Demo School, has little connection to community resources. The gaps among city agencies, even while serving the same populations, keep operations, records, and budgets entirely separate. Each time a service is rendered, both the agency personnel trying to meet family needs and the recipients of benefits must travel to where those services can be found. Misunderstandings abound in these circumstances, and children are left with few advocates.

In Demo School, the parent council succeeded in convincing two city agencies to provide services within the school for community families. The principal found office space and provided a family service coordinator who serves as an advocate for children and families. A computer program, which lists family needs and services provided, helps the coordinator keep up to date. This major step has brought considerable publicity to Demo School and has caused at least two exploratory plans to begin in other schools.

Involve Those Affected by Change

As noted, the new regional superintendent is committed to change and reinforces collaboration with families and community agencies. However, preserving the status quo is an underlying priority for many in the schools. At Demo School, parents have been involved in deciding about integration of city services, and have served as representatives in meetings with other city agencies. All agree that involving the persons affected by change is healthy for this school, but similar concern does not appear elsewhere in the district.

Curriculum matters and assessment procedures are a different matter. Nowhere in District 5 are parents or community members involved in reviewing curriculum, evaluating teachers, or employing staff members. Even at Demo School, where parents are welcomed into school life and involved as volunteers, educators reserve curriculum decisions for themselves. The final step of giving decision-making power to those affected is still missing.

Most of District 5 has a long way to go in bringing parent and community groups into educational planning and participation. Currently there are few demands for a community voice in school matters, and this gives educators more time to consider the wisdom of moves to increase outside involvement. But the picture is not a bleak one in

the district, and the modest experiments at Demo School and Expo School do provide a positive background. As Davies (1993) notes, "It is much easier to plan, execute, and evaluate programs for [others] than it is to involve the clients or the end-users from the beginning in all aspects of change" (p. 71).

Base Policy and Practice on Research

District 5 has had numerous funded projects, associated with nearby universities, which were directed at curriculum and school organization. Research endeavors are common in most of the area schools, and school personnel are quite sophisticated in accommodating experiments and discussing projects. The district has significant experiences in research and a wealth of information to draw on. Administrative and community attitudes toward research appear positive.

However, as in other school districts, positive attitudes and involvement in research do not necessarily translate to implementing the findings of successful projects. This is the case in most of District 5. Findings from some studies carried on within the district have been published nationally, but, with the exception of Demo School, few changes have been made. The energy and leadership, particularly at middle levels of school administration, to push for implementation appears to be a prime missing ingredient. A large part of Demo School's success in basing policy and practice on research comes from the interest and strong leadership of the new principal. This is a testament to the fact that leadership undergirds almost all program and success in schools today.

Assessing the Partnership Experiments

The two examples described in this chapter show the particular school districts in a state of "becoming." We note some progress in each area for bringing schools closer to their natural allies, the homes and communities. But complete linkage is yet to be for both Woodland and District 5.

What will it take to bring real change? Both school districts portrayed are typical across the

United States. Woodland is an interesting example of "bottom-up" influences—the agitation for change resides in the community and in homes. Nearly all improvements have come from the population served. Here is a community that has discovered the value of partnership, in a naive fashion, and started to agitate for more involvement before the school department has discovered its potential. In District 5 of Big City, the opposite situation, one of "top-down" influence, is emerging. The leadership by the principal and one central office has initiated and spurred the growth toward collaboration. The community is placid and is not campaigning for involvement, but some school leaders see the benefits and have started to collaboratively involve the population served.

Partnerships could flourish in each district with reasonable effort. Careful, committed leadership in both cases could move teachers, parents, and community members to accept responsibility for changing and adapting their old patterns of behavior.

Individual Responsibility

Even strong leaders cannot accomplish any task alone. They require the participation and cooperation of many people. All parents, teachers, and community members have a responsibility to become involved at the different levels of participation. At a minimum level, just as some parents are active only in supporting schools and helping children with homework, there will be teachers who will limit their involvement to the ways described in Chapter 9. They will take advantage of the community programs that serve children's educational needs. Some teachers will seek more involvement as they plan their curriculum for parent and other volunteer support in the classroom. They will participate in workshops with parents and serve on committees with them as equal partners. A few teachers will be involved in decision making and will serve on partnership teams.

Committed people can make a difference, and partnerships can begin with a single teacher and parent collaborating in a classroom. Possibilities exist for enthusiastic colleagues and parents to expand a program. But there are important additional steps.

A team considering collaborations must define objectives and agree on what changes are necessary. They must find out how collaboration has worked for others. They need to try out their ideas, locate resources, involve others, and decide how to assess their progress. Communication is often a problem as more people become involved. Teachers and parents must be alert to how they are communicating and how different messages are being interpreted.

Total community involvement requires breaking down bureaucratic resistance. Administrators, district officials, leaders of parent groups, and directors of business and community organizations eventually must participate and must commit to involving themselves and their employees at all three levels—from minimum to decision making. For grassroots programs, researchers and planners may eventually assist in getting needed resources and in evaluating programs.

REALIZING THE DREAM

Realizing the dream of partnerships takes more than the effort exhibited across the United States today. A spirit for undertaking change has germinated in many areas, but seems slow to blossom fully. But change takes time! The recent surge of interest at state and federal levels must be viewed positively. Publications, funding, and legislation now provide a fertile base for more collaboration.

When reading about model programs, we can certify that those programs with a research and assessment dimension have made great strides in reaching a new level of participation. We find from the models that exciting things happen when new ideas are introduced, nurtured carefully, and built as change mechanisms. The models reinforce the desirability of bringing more collaborative work to our nation's schools.

The following requirements are prerequisite for planning and implementing home–school–community partnerships in education:

1. Community spirit is primary. Success comes naturally for dedicated and committed people working together.
2. Interested planners, leaders, and researchers must initiate, guide, and polish emerging plans.
3. Financial resources, such as grants, must be available to subsidize pilot programs.
4. Interested citizens and community officials must commit to enacting and supporting partnerships. (Such people are often present, for most homes and communities wish for better connections to their schools.)
5. Educators must want better communications with homes and community agencies.
6. Training and development programs must be available to nourish beginners and provide new leaders (too many programs erode when a strong leader leaves).

SUMMARY

When schools are brokers for new learning communities, and invest time and energy in forming links with homes and communities, exciting and productive results materialize. We have so much evidence that this is true. The work of James Comer in New Haven, the synthesis of Schorr's (1988) ideas in *Within Our Reach*, and the expansion of the League of Schools Reaching Out, to name but a few, show that we have both reason and compelling need for communities to reach further to obtain better functioning school operations.

New collaborations can mean reaching objectives by somewhat different routes. For example, we have found school programs to be faltering in some quarters (usually in economically disadvantaged areas), but setting an enviable pace in others. Implementing the principles of partnerships in part of a district enriched the experiences of other students. These different routes can take more energy, more careful planning, and more financial commitment, but the result is a far better and richer product.

Schools are still the catalysts in the new endeavor. No other social institution in the United States occupies the comprehensive position or has the trained personnel to serve in this capacity. Partnership programs may start with a few small projects, as in Woodland, or may grow from a well-conceived and well-directed program, such as that in District 5's Demo School. However it grows, a plan must call for teachers and administrators to be committed to the new practice. Commitment, gaining knowledge about other programs, devising a plan, establishing means of communicating the plan, and involving others are necessary to the success of any project.

If we are to achieve the type of social and educational change we advocate, we must find and nourish ways to make real the practices behind partnerships. This means setting aside some of the highly competitive stances that our society sponsors and working for the common good. Everyone will benefit, and the least fortunate will win a larger share.

SUGGESTED ACTIVITIES AND QUESTIONS

1. Talk with three teachers about parent involvement in their programs. Have them describe the things parents do when they come to school. Compare their statements to the three levels of involvement discussed in this chapter. What levels of involvement do you find?
2. Interview three parents to learn how they have participated in their children's school programs within the last year. What levels of involvement do you find?
3. Examine a school district with which you are acquainted to ascertain its stage of evolution in collaborative efforts. Does it resemble Woodland? District 5 in Big City? How does your district compare to the two examples in terms of economic status, administrative situation, and problems faced?

RECOMMENDED READINGS

Bloom, J. (1992). *Parenting our schools: A hands-on guide to education reform.* Boston: Little, Brown.

Davies, D. (1993). Looking backward. In S. Thompson (Ed), *Whole child, whole community* (pp. 67–72). Boston: Institute for Responsive Education.

O'Callaghan, J. B. (1993). *School-based collaborations with families.* San Francisco: Jossey-Bass.

Powell, D. R. (1989). *Families and early childhood programs.* Washington, DC: National Association for the Education of Young Children.

Rich, D. (1987). *Teachers and parents: An adult to adult approach.* Washington, DC: National Education Association.

Swap, S. M. (1993). *Developing home-school partnerships: From concepts to practice.* New York: Teacher's College Press.

U.S. Department of Education. (1994). *Strong families, strong schools.* Washington, DC: Author.

Annotated Bibliography of Children's Books

If we are fortunate, we . . . belong to a small, more particular community, defined by ethnicity or kinship, belief system or geography. It is in this intimate circle that we are most "ourselves," where our jokes are best appreciated, our special dishes most enjoyed. These are the people to whom we go first when we need comfort or empathy, for they speak our own brand of cultural shorthand, and always know the correct things to say, the proper things to do.

(Dorris, 1993, p. 1)

The following selected bibliography of children's books portrays a variety of American family structures where individuals are learning together in the home, the school, and the community.

- **H** indicates the book reveals children learning through the home environment
- **S** indicates children from different family structures learning together at school
- **C** indicates different family members sharing and learning from their community environment

DIFFERENT CULTURES

Ashley, Bernard. (1991). *Cleversticks.* Illustrated by Derek Brazell. New York: Crown. An Asian American boy can't seem to be clever at anything at school, until the day his talent with chopsticks is revealed. **S**

Barrett, Joyce Durham. (1989). *Willie's Not the Hugging Kind.* Illustrated by Pat Cummings. New York: Harper Trophy. Willie's best friend Jo-Jo thinks hugging is silly, so Willie stops letting his family hug him even though he misses the affection. African American family. **H**

Breckler, Rosemary K. (1992). *Hoang Breaks the Lucky Teapot.* Illustrated by Adrian Frankel. Boston: Houghton Mifflin. A Vietnamese immigrant boy breaks the *gia truyen*, or teapot, that houses May Man, a good spirit. He tries to keep evil away by fixing the pot. **H**

Bunting, Eve. (1990). *The Wall.* Illustrated by Ronald Himler. New York: Clarion. A Hispanic American boy and his father visit the Vietnam memorial to leave a photo for the boy's grandfather. The boy is glad to hear about his grandfather, but wishes he had known him. **C**

Bunting, Eve. (1993). *Someday a Tree.* Illustrated by Ronald Himler. New York: Clarion. A family enjoying a picnic under an old oak realizes something is wrong with the tree. Discovering the tree has been poisoned, neighbors and community members pitch in to save the tree. **H, C**

Cisneros, Sandra. (1984, 1994). *Hairs/Pelitos.* Illustrated by Terry Ybanez. Translated by Liliana Valenzuela. New York: Alfred A. Knopf (Apple Soup Books). A simple text describes in both English and Spanish the variety of hair possessed by each of a child's family members. Especially appropriate for early readers. **H**

Clifton, Lucille. (1974, 1992). *Three Wishes.* Illustrated by Michael Hays (1992). New York: Dell. Two African American children find a lucky penny and learn the value of friendship. **C**

Cohen, Barbara. (1972, 1987). *The Carp in the Bathtub.* Illustrated by Joan Halpern. Rockville, MD: Kar-Ben Copies. Jewish American siblings try to save a carp from becoming gefilte fish for the Seder. **H**

Cohen, Miriam. (1977). *When Will I Read?* Illustrated by Lillian Hoban. New York: Greenwillow. Ever since arriving in school, this first grader has been anxious to learn to read. He is surprised to find out he has been "learning" while engaged in so many activities. **S**

Cohen, Miriam. (1979). *Lost in the Museum.* Illustrated by Lillian Hoban. New York: Greenwillow. Danny, excited about finding the dinosaurs during his class's visit to the museum, manages to get half of the class lost, and then found again. **S**

Cohen, Miriam. (1989). *See You in Second Grade.* New York: Greenwillow. One boy in a multiethnic classroom makes a sacrifice to enable a girl to join others at the year-end beach party. **S**

Cross, Verda. (1992). *Great Grandma Tells of Threshing Day.* Illustrated by Gail Owens. Morton Grove, IL: Albert Whitman. It is threshing day in the early 1900s and a girl and her brother help as neighbors gather to assist in threshing. The day ends when men return to the feast neighbors have prepared. **H, C**

Cummings, Pat. (1991). *Clean Your Room, Harvey Moon!* New York: Macmillan. An African American mother and her son don't have the same concept of a clean room. **H**

DeVeaux, Alexis. (1987). *An Enchanted Hair Tale.* Illustrated by Cheryl Hanna. New York: HarperCollins. A boy suffers ridicule for his strange-looking hair, but he learns to like having dreadlocks. **S**

Dooley, Norah. (1991). *Everybody Cooks Rice.* Illustrated by Peter J. Thornton. Minneapolis, MN: Carolrhoda. As Carrie searches the neighborhood, she discovers everyone is making rice for dinner, even though each family is from a different country. Includes recipes from Barbados, Puerto Rico, Vietnam, India, China, Haiti, and Italy. **H, C**

Franklin, Kristine L. (1994). *The Shepherd Boy.* Illustrated by Jill Kastner. New York: Atheneum. When school is out, a Navajo boy cares for his family's sheep. One night he rescues a lost lamb. **C**

Friedman, Ina R. (1984). *How My Parents Learned to Eat.* Illustrated by Allen Say. Boston: Houghton Mifflin. A young girl tells how her American father and Japanese mother dated in Japan after World War II and learned to eat according to each other's custom. **H, C**

Gardella, Tricia. (1993). *Just Like My Dad.* Illustrated by Margot Apple. New York: HarperCollins. A young lad and his cowboy dad spend the day in routine activities of mending fences, roping, branding, and herding cattle. **H**

Garza, Carmen Lomas. (1990). *Cuadros de familia/Family Pictures.* San Francisco: Children's Book Press. A Mexican American artist illustrates growing up on the border of Texas and Mexico. English and Spanish text. **H, C**

Good, Merle. (1993). *Reuben and the Fire.* Illustrated by P. Buckley Moss. Intercourse, PA: Good Books. An Amish boy has five bossy sisters and trouble being allowed to drive the pony cart. When a neighbor's barn burns, Reuben and his friends help rescue the animals. A barn raising follows. Depicts Amish unity. **C**

Greenfield, Eloise. (1976, 1991). *First Pink Light.* Illustrated by Jan Spivey Gilchrist. New York: Black Butterfly. An African American boy and his mother wait for his father to return home from taking care of Grandma. **H**

Hamm, Diane Johnston. (1991). *Laney's Lost Mama.* Illustrated by Sally G. Ward. Morton Grove, IL: Albert Whitman. When a young African American girl and her mother lose each other in a department store, they rely on good thinking to find each other again. **C**

Hartman, Wendy. (1993). *All the Magic in the World.* Illustrated by Niki Daly. New York: Dutton. Lena feels very small and clumsy until Joseph the odd-job man shows her how to make beautiful things from his ordinary junk. **C**

Havill, Juanita. (1989). *Jamaica Tag-Along.* Illustrated by Anne Sibley O'Brien. Boston: Houghton Mifflin. African American siblings resolve the conflict that emerges when a younger sister always wants to tag along with her older brother. **H, C**

Hill, Elizabeth. (1967). *Evan's Corner.* New York: Holt. There isn't much room in this tiny apartment and Evan would like to have his own space. His mother helps him find a corner, but he learns about sharing when his little brother wants to visit his space. African American family. **H, C**

Hines, Anna Grossnickle. (1986). *Daddy Makes the Best Spaghetti.* New York: Clarion. The entire process from shopping to cooking to eating to cleaning up afterwards is enjoyed when Corey and his dad cook spaghetti for dinner. **H, C**

Hoffman, Mary. (1993). *Henry's Baby.* Illustrated by Susan Winter. New York: Dorling Kindersley. Henry wants to be a part of a special group at school, but feels the only special thing he has is a baby brother, and that is hardly cool. When Henry is forced to invite the gang to his house, he learns what cool really means. **H, S**

Hoyt-Goldsmith, Diane. (1990). *Totem Pole.* Photographs by Lawrence Migdale. New York: Holiday House. A Native American boy describes with pride his father's woodcarving and its importance in his Klallam tribe. Story includes tribal legends. **H**

Hu, Dakari. (1993). *Joshua's Masai Mask.* Illustrated by Anna Rich. New York: Lee & Low. Joshua fears his friends will ridicule him if he plays the kalimba in the talent show. He solves his problem by hiding behind a Masai mask only to learn his friends appreciate him for himself. **S**

Johnson, Angela. (1989). *Tell Me a Story, Mama.* Illustrated by David Soman. New York: Orchard. An African American mother and daughter share stories of the mother's childhood, which the child relates to her own experiences. **H**

Johnson, Angela. (1990). *Do Like Kyla.* Illustrated by James E. Ransome. New York: Orchard. A young African American girl imitates her older sister all day long. Shows sound sibling relationship. **H**

Johnson, Angela. (1991). *One of Three.* Illustrated by David Soman. New York: Orchard. An African American girl describes daily life as part of a threesome with her two older sisters. **H**

Keats, Ezra Jack. (1962). *The Snowy Day.* New York: Viking. Peter watches the snow fall and goes out to spend a lovely day in the snow. Trying to save a snowball, he discovers what happens when he brings it inside. **C**

Kendall, Russ. (1992). *Eskimo Boy: Life in an Inupiaq Eskimo Village.* New York: Scholastic. Norman is a 7-year-old Inupiaq Eskimo. A day of his life in this village is described in photographs and simple text. **C**

Ketterman, Helen. (1992). *Not Yet, Yvette*. Illustrated by Irene Trivas. Morton Grove, IL: Albert Whitman. An African American girl and father throw a surprise birthday party for her mother, a veterinarian. The story leads nicely from cake-baking to the climax. **H**

Kroll, Virginia. (1994). *Masai and I*. Illustrated by Nancy Carpenter. New York: Four Winds. Linda learns about East African life and imagines what her life would be like if she were a Masai. **C**

Mandelbaum, Pili. (1990). *You Be Me, I'll Be You*. Brooklyn, NY: Kane-Miller. A child of an interracial marriage playfully changes roles with her white father, evoking an amused reaction from her African American mother. **H**

Markhun, Patricia Maloney. (1993). *The Little Painter of Sabana Grande*. Illustrated by Robert Casilla. New York: Bradbury/Macmillan. School is out for Fernando and he can spend the summer painting in his small Panamanian village. But alas, he has no paper. Convincing his parents that he could use the walls of their adobe home for paper he changes not only his home but the community. **C**

McCloskey, Robert. (1952). *One Morning in Maine*. New York: Viking. "One morning in Maine Sal woke up . . ." and so begins the story of one small girl and her family as she helps her father dig clams, take the boat to Buck's Harbor for groceries, and finally goes home to dinner. **H, C**

McPhail, David. (1993). *Farm Boy's Year*. New York: Atheneum. A young lad of the late nineteenth century enjoys life on a New England farm. **H**

Ormerod, Jan. (1991). *When We Went to the Zoo*. New York: Lothrop. Two children relate their experiences as the family takes a trip to the zoo and finds a pair of sparrows and their nest. **C**

Pinkney, Andrea Davis. (1993). *Seven Candles for Kwanzaa*. Illustrated by Brian Pinkney. New York: Dial. Elaborates on the origins and practices of Kwanzaa, the seven-day harvest festival, as celebrated by one family of African descent. **H**

Pinkney, Brian. (1994). *Max Found Two Sticks*. New York: Simon & Schuster. Max, an African American, begins to beat out the rhythms of the things he sees and hears around him in the neighborhood. Family and friends keep asking what he is doing, but he continues his rhythms. **C**

Polacco, Patricia. (1990). *Just Plain Fancy*. New York: Simon & Schuster. Naomi wishes she could be more fancy than her Amish culture permits. When a special egg hatches she discovers a fancy "chicken" indeed. Worrying this chicken will be too fancy for the community, she tries to hide Fancy. When the community discovers Fancy, Naomi is surprised by the results. **C**

Polacco, Patricia. (1994). *My Rotten Redheaded Older Brother*. New York: Simon & Schuster. Patricia is forever annoyed with her older brother, who can always best her at everything. Her attempts at outdoing him are hilarious. **H**

Quinlan, Patricia. (1987). *My Dad Takes Care of Me*. Illustrated by Vlasta van Kampen. Toronto: Annick. Luke doesn't want to admit his father lost his job, but he really enjoys having his father fix meals, read, and play with him. When he finds another boy whose father stays home, he feels better about his dad's role. **H**

Rochelle, Belinda. (1994). *When Jo Louis Won the Title Fight*. Illustrated by Larry Johnson. Boston: Houghton Mifflin. Jo is reconciled with her unusual name when her grandfather tells why she got it. **H**

Samuels, Vyanne. (1989). *Carry, Go, Bring, Come*. Illustrated by Jennifer Northway. New York: Four Winds. A young African American boy gets overwhelmed by his role as a gofer during the preparations for his sister's wedding. **H**

Smalls, Irene. (1994). *Dawn and the Round To-it*. Illustrated by Tyrone Geter. New York: Simon & Schuster. A touching story of an African American child who solves the problem of family members who spend time with her when they "get around to it." **H**

Sonneborn, Ruth A. (1970, 1987). *Friday Night is Papa Night*. Illustrated by Emily Arnold McCully. New York: Puffin. A Puerto Rican American family prepares for their father's weekly return home. **H**

Soto, Gary. (1993). *Too Many Tamales*. Illustrated by Ed Martinez. New York: G.P. Putnam's Sons. Maria fears she lost her mother's ring while making tamales for her Mexican American family's Christmas gathering. **H**

Surat, Michelle Maria. (1993). *Angel Child, Dragon Child*. Illustrated by Vo-Dinh Mai. New York: Carnival. Ut, an immigrant child from Vietnam, has difficulty adjusting to school in America. She misses her mother in Vietnam. and classmates help her solve her dilemma. **S**

Taha, Karen T. (1986). *A Gift for Tia Rosa*. Illustrated by Dee deRosa. Minneapolis, MN: Dillon. A Hispanic American girl has a close relationship with her elderly neighbor and finds a meaningful way to celebrate her life when she dies. **C**

Villanueva, Marie. (1993). *Nene and the Horrible Math Monster.* Illustrated by Ria Unson. Chicago: Polychrome. Nene, a Filipino American, is worried her teachers will expect too much of her in math, because Asians are supposed to excel in math and she doesn't. As she confronts the myth she learns to overcome her fear. **S**

Walter, Mildred Pitts. (1990). *Two and Too Much.* Illustrated by Pat Cummings. New York: Bradbury. An African American boy volunteers to help his mother and ends up struggling to get through a day with his active 2-year-old sister. **H**

Watkins, Sherrin. (1994). *White Bead Ceremony.* Illustrated by Kim Doner. Tulsa, OK: Council Oak. The Greyfeather clan holds a Shawnee naming ceremony for Mary. Includes Shawnee vocabulary. **C**

Weiss, Nicki. (1992). *On a Hot, Hot Day.* New York: Putnam. Enjoying life throughout the year in a closely knit Latino neighborhood, Angel plays with the fire hydrant in the summertime, drinks chocolate with his mother in Pepe's Luncheonette, and admires his mother's herb garden. **C**

Wells, Rosemary. (1991). *Max's Dragon Shirt.* New York: Dial. Max's sister takes him shopping to buy some trousers, but all Max wants is a dragon shirt. **C**

Wells, Rosemary. (1993). *Waiting for the Evening Star.* Illustrated by Susan Jeffers. New York: Dial. In the time before World War I, Berty believes nothing is better than his family's Vermont farm. His brother Luke, however, wants to travel and yearns to leave the placid life. **H**

White Deer of Autumn. (1992). *The Great Change.* Illustrated by Carol Grigg. Hillsboro, OR: Beyond Words. While fishing, a Native American grandmother and granddaughter discuss the circle of life and the meaning of death. **C**

Williams, Vera. (1990). *More, More, More Said the Baby.* New York: Greenwillow. Using simple text, the author/illustrator shows three babies of different races in loving relationships with a father, grandmother, and mother. **H**

Wright, Courtni C. (1994). *Jumping the Broom.* Illustrated by Gershom Griffith. New York: Holiday. Life in the slave quarters holds some delight for Lottie as her family makes quilts and sister Tillie gets married by jumping the broom. **C**

Yamate, Sandra S. (1991). *Char Siu Bao Boy.* Chicago: Polychrome. Charlie, a Chinese American child, likes strange food, according to his classmates, but Charlie and his friends learn to appreciate cultural differences. **S**

Yashima, Taro. (1955). *Crow Boy.* New York: Viking. Chibi and his Japanese classmates learn that each child has something special to offer. Differences in home life are shown to be unimportant as children share their talents. **S**

Zolotow, Charlotte. (1969). *The Hating Book.* Illustrated by Ben Shecter. New York: Harper. Friendship is tested when two girls both listen to what someone else tells them they have said about each other. Friendship is restored when both ask what was really said. **C**

DIVORCED FAMILIES

Baum, L. (1986). *One More Time.* Illustrated by Paddy Bouma. New York: Morrow. A young boy is reluctant to leave the visit with his father and keeps asking to do things one more time before going home to his mother's house. **H**

Boegehold, B. (1985). *Daddy Doesn't Live Here Any More.* Illustrated by Deborah Borgo. New York: Western. Casey is very unhappy that daddy isn't going to live with them anymore. She pretends to be sick and tries to run away to make daddy stay, but finally becomes reconciled to the situation. **H**

Girard, Linda Walvoord. (1987). *At Daddy's on Saturdays.* Illustrated by Judith Friedman. Morton Grove, IL: Albert Whitman. When Katie's parents divorce, her dad moves away and she visits him on weekends. **H**

Helmering, Doris W. (1981). *I Have Two Families.* Illustrated by Heidi Palmer. Nashville, TN: Abington. Patty and her brother live in two different houses since their parents divorced. The children manage to establish regular lives in two homes, though they live mostly with their father since he has regular working hours. **H**

Hazen, Barbara Shook. (1983). *Two Homes to Live In: A Child's View of Divorce.* Illustrated by Peggy Luks. New York: Human Sciences. Niki's mom and dad are divorced. Though she wishes they would get married again, gradually she understands both parents love her and that she can be happy with each parent in separate homes. **H**

Mayle, Peter. (1988). *Why Are We Getting a Divorce?* Illustrated by Arthur Robins. New York: Harmony. A matter-of-fact book that goes into depth about divorce. **H**

Stinson, Kathy. (1982). *Mom and Dad Don't Live Together Any More.* Illustrated by Nancy Lou Reynolds. Toronto: Annick. The story follows a family through the stages of divorce. **H**

Vigna, Judith. (1984). *Grandma Without Me.* Morton Grove, IL: Albert Whitman. A young child will not be going to Thanksgiving at Grandma's for the first time, because his mom and dad are divorced. The child resolves his conflict by keeping a scrapbook he can share with his grandmother. **H**

Watson, Jane Werner, Switzer, Robert E., & Hirschberg, J. Cotter. (1988). *Sometimes a Family Has to Split Up.* Illustrated by Cat Bowman Smith. New York: Crown. The story follows one child as his parents move from fighting to divorce. **H**

BLENDED FAMILIES

Boyd, Lizi. (1987). *The Not-So-Wicked Stepmother.* New York: Viking Penguin. Over the course of a summer spent with her father and new stepmother, Hessie unlearns her prejudices about how horrible stepmothers are supposed to be. **H, C**

Boyd, Lizi. (1990). *Sam Is My Half-Brother.* New York: Viking Penguin. Hessie gets to know her new stepbrother while living with her dad and stepmom for the summer. **H**

Jukes, Mavis. (1984). *Like Jake and Me.* Illustrated by Lloyd Bloom. New York: Alfred A. Knopf (Dragonfly Books). Alex's stepfather Jake isn't sure Alex can help him on the farm. When Alex saves him from a wolf spider crawling down his back, affection begins to grow between the two. **H**

MacLachlan, Patricia. (1985). *Sarah, Plain and Tall.* New York: Harper & Row. Sarah is a mail-order bride who goes to the Midwest to marry a widower with two children. The children come to love Sarah and worry when they think she has gone home. **H**

Ransom, Candice F. (1993). *We're Growing Together.* Illustrated by Virginia Wright Frierson. New York: Bradbury. Portrays the emerging relationship between a young girl and her mom's new husband, as they experience things together over the course of a year. **H, C**

Vigna, Judith. (1980). *She's Not My Real Mother.* Chicago: Albert Whitman. Miles is not happy visiting his father and his new wife. It takes a visit to an ice show for him to realize that she can be nice and he can still love his real mom. **H, C**

Vigna, Judith. (1982). *Daddy's New Baby.* Morton Grove, IL: Albert Whitman. A little girl is unhappy about Dad's new baby, because things are different when she visits. But when she can't attend a puppet show, she discovers that helping her dad take care of the baby can be fun, too. **H**

Willner-Pardo, Gina. (1994). *What I'll Remember When I Am a Grownup.* Illustrated by Walter Lyon Krudop. New York: Clarion. Daniel's mother won't tell him the surprise that his father and stepmother have for him. When his stepmother tells him she's pregnant, his mind fills with memories and worries. **H**

SINGLE-PARENT HOUSEHOLD AND SPECIAL RELATIONSHIP WITH ONE PARENT

Ackerman, Karen. (1994). *By the Dawn's Early Light.* Illustrated by Catherine Stock. New York: Atheneum. Two African American children spend the early morning with their mother, who works the night shift. **H**

Bang, Molly. (1983). *Ten, Nine, Eight.* New York: Greenwillow. An African American father puts his young child to bed by counting backward from ten. A warm loving relationship is revealed through the pictures. **H**

Bunting, Eve. (1994). *Smoky Night.* Illustrated by David Diaz. San Diego, CA: Harcourt Brace Jovanovich. Daniel and his mother watch urban riots and their Korean neighbor suffers. After the families meet at a shelter, Daniel is relieved to find his cat and Mrs. Kim's are now friends, after suffering similar trials. **C**

Clifton, Lucille. (1977, 1992). *Everett Anderson's 1, 2, 3.* Illustrated by Ann Grifalconi. New York: Holt. Everett Anderson's African American mother is considering remarriage. He considers 1, 2, and 3, and sometimes the numbers seem lonely, sometimes crowded, and sometimes just right. **H**

Cooper, Susan. (1993). *Danny and the Kings.* Illustrated by Jos. A. Smith. New York: Margaret K. McElderry.

Danny so wants a Christmas tree for his brother, but his mother can't afford one. In a near accident, Danny meets three racially different truck drivers, Kings of the Road, and tells them his story. Later when he returns from school he finds his wish come true. **C**

Greenfield, Eloise. (1988). *Nathaniel Talking*. Illustrated by Jan Spivey Gilchrist. New York: Black Butterfly. Nathaniel, a spunky 9-year-old African American child, rhymes and raps about his family, friends, and school experiences. **H, S, C**

Haggerty, Mary Elizabeth. (1993). *A Crack in the Wall*. Illustrated by Ruben de Anda. New York: Lee & Low. While his mother looks for a job, a Hispanic American boy creatively transforms his fear of a crack in the wall of their apartment. **H**

Lindsay, Jeanne Warren. (1982, 1991). *Do I Have a Daddy? A Story About a Single-Parent Child* (2nd ed.). Illustrated by Cheryl Boeller. Buena Park, CA: Morning Glory. A boy wonders where his dad is, and his mom explains how she came to be a single parent. **H**

Maury, Inez. (1979). *My Mother and I Are Growing Strong*. Illustrated by Sandy Speidel. Translated by Anna Munoz. Berkely, CA: New Seed. Emilita works hard in Ms. Stubblebine's garden with her mother, Lupe, because her father is in prison. Emilita and her mother grow strong caring for themselves and preparing for father's release. Text is in both Spanish and English. **H, C**

McCully, Emily Arnold. (1992). *Mirette on the High Wire*. New York: Putnam. Mirette is eager to learn tightrope walking from a boarding house guest. The story, set in Paris, portrays warm loving relationships, as Mirette learns a new skill. **C**

Peterson, Jeanne W. (1994). *My Mama Sings*. Illustrated by Sandra Speidel. New York: HarperCollins. Mama sings special songs when they are together, but after a bad day at work she stops singing and playing with the little boy. He starts a new song asking his mama to play, she responds, and then they sing together again. African American family. **H**

Saller, Carol. (1991). *The Bridge Dancers*. Minneapolis, MN: Carolrhoda. Two African American sisters live in the mountains with their mother, the community healer. The younger sister helps when her elder sister injures her leg. **H, C**

Say, Allen. (1989). *The Lost Lake*. Boston: Houghton Mifflin. A boy spends the summer with his dad and they learn to communicate during a camping trip. Asian family. **C**

Sharp, N. L. (1993). *Today I'm Going Fishing With My Dad*. Illustrated by Chris L. Demarest. Honesdale, PA: Boyd's Mill. A young boy loves spending time fishing with his dad even though he doesn't particularly like fishing itself. **C**

Smalls, Irene. (1992). *Jonathan and His Mommy*. Illustrated by Michael Hays. Boston: Little, Brown. Jonathan, an African American child, and his mother move about their community walking and talking in different ways. They greet and talk with all the people they meet. **C**

Steptoe, John. (1980). *Daddy Is a Monster . . . Sometimes*. New York: Lippincott. In this African American family, the single-parent father at times seems like a monster as he struggles to provide the necessary nurturance for his two children. **H**

Tran, Kim-Lan. (1994). *Tet: The New Year*. Illustrated by Mai Vo-Dinh. New York: Simon & Schuster. Friends help a newly immigrated Vietnamese father and son celebrate the Vietnamese holiday. **C**

Vigna, Judith. (1987). *Mommy and Me by Ourselves Again*. Morton Grove, IL: Albert Whitman. A girl feels hurt and disappointed when her mom's former boyfriend forgets her birthday, but is comforted by her mother and other relatives. **H**

Waddell, Morton. (1994). *The Big, Big Sea*. Illustrated by Jennifer Eachus. Cambridge, MA: Candlewick. A young girl and her mother walk along the beach in the moonlight. The special walk builds a bond between mother and child as they explore the sea in the moonlight. **H**

ADOPTIVE FAMILIES

Banish, Roslyn, with Jennifer Jordan-Wong. (1992). *A Forever Family*. Photographs by Roslyn Banish. New York: Harper Trophy. Jennifer describes life as she moves from different foster families to her present adopted family. The multiethnic family provides stability for Jennifer, who adapted to many families before becoming a "forever family." **H**

Bloom, Suzanne. (1991). *A Family for Jamie: An Adoption Story*. New York: Clarkson N. Potter. Before Jamie was born, her mother and father were good at making lots of things, except babies. Finally they decided to adopt Jamie and the entire extended family rejoiced in the event. **H**

Bunin, Catherine, & Bunin, Sherry. (1976). *Is That Your Sister?* New York: Pantheon. An African American child tells what it is like to be adopted into a multi-ethnic family. She relates how she learns to accept a new adopted member into the family and how she comes to accept the abandonment by her natural mother. **H**

Caines, Jeannette Franklin. (1973). *Abby.* Illustrated by Steven Kellogg. New York: Harper. A small African American girl learns about her adoption and how special she is to all the family, even her older brother. **H**

Girard, Linda Walvoord. (1986). *Adoption Is for Always.* Illustrated by Judith Friedman. Morton Grove, IL: Albert Whitman. An adopted child works through her struggle with the notion of her adoption, wondering why her birth mother left her. **H**

Girard, Linda Walvoord. (1989). *We Adopted You, Benjamin Koo.* Illustrated by Linda Shute. Morton Grove, IL: Albert Whitman. Not until second grade does the Korean child realize he doesn't look like his Anglo-American family. But surrounded by caring adults he realizes love isn't related to ethnicity. **H, S**

Kasza, Keiko. (1992). *A Mother for Choco.* New York: Putnam. A lonely little bird searching for his mother looks different from others. Finally Mrs. Bear finds him and takes him home to share the household with her other adoptive animals—a hippopotamus, an alligator, and a pig. **H**

Keller, Holly. (1990). *Horace.* New York: Greenwillow. A spotted leopard feels sad when he realizes he is different from his tiger family. However, Horace comes to realize he can love his adoptive parents without betraying his own heritage. **H**

Lifton, Betty Jean. (1993). *Tell Me a Real Adoption Story.* Illustrated by Claire Nivola. New York: Alfred A. Knopf. A child requests the true story of her adoption before going to bed. **H**

McCully, Emily Arnold. (1994). *My Real Family.* San Diego, CA: Harcourt. Sarah, the youngest of the Bear family, is distressed with the attention given to Blanche, an orphaned lamb. When the family contemplates adopting Blanche, Sarah runs away, but in the end she understands the important place she has in the family. **H, C**

Pursell, Margaret S. (1978). *A Look at Adoption.* Photographs by Maria S. Forrai. Minneapolis, MN: Lerner. Explains the process of adoption and how each family must decide the type of children they wish to adopt. **H**

Rosenberg, Maxine. (1984). *Being Adopted.* Photographs by George Ancona. New York: Lothrop. The author points out the difficulties children of different heritages have in being adopted into Anglo-American homes. In the stories, the children learn the important lessons of love and permanence in an adoptive home. **H**

Turner, Ann. (1990). *Through Moon and Stars and Night Skies.* Illustrated by James Graham Hale. New York: Harper & Row. An Asian child retells how he had to fly a day and a night through moon and stars to a room of his own, a house of his own, and, very best of all, a loving mother and father of his own. **H, C**

FOSTER CARE AND ORPHANAGES

Bemelmans, Ludwig. (1939). *Madeline.* New York: Viking. Madeline and eleven other little girls live in an old house in Paris and are cared for by nuns. When Madeline has to go to the hospital, her friends visit her and she shows them her scar. **C**

Cannon, Janell. (1994). *Stellaluna.* San Diego: Harcourt. A baby bat, separated from her mother, is adopted by a family of birds. After her joyful reunion with her mother, Stellaluna remains in contact with her bird "siblings." **H, C**

Carlson, Natalie Savage. (1957). *The Happy Orpheline.* Illustrated by Garth Williams. New York: Harper. Brigitte is about to be adopted, but she wants to remain in the orphanage. She knows she must do a wicked deed to prove she isn't fit for adoption, and the hilarious stunt does keep the orphans together. **C**

Herbert, Stefon. (1991). *I Miss My Foster Parents.* Washington, DC: Child Welfare League of America. A real-life story of a boy and his sister adopted after three years in foster care. Though the transfer to adoption seems well thought through, the children make it clear they miss their warm relationship with their foster family. **H, C**

MacLachlan, Patricia. (1982). *Mama One, Mama Two.* Illustrated by Ruth Lercher Bornstein. New York: Harper. A foster child receives loving care from her foster mother while her own mother recovers from mental depression. **H**

Steptoe, John. (1969). *Stevie.* New York: Harper. Robert is bothered and a bit jealous when Stevie comes to live with them. However, a special bond begins to grow between the two and Robert misses Stevie when he leaves. **H**

MULTIGENERATIONAL HOUSEHOLDS AND EXTENDED FAMILIES

Akerman, Karen. (1988). *Song and Dance Man.* Illustrated by Stephen Gammell. New York: Alfred A. Knopf. When three children visit their grandpa, he shows them his old vaudeville costumes. Big hugs come after the children watch Grandpa perform for them. **H**

Bunting, Eve. (1991). *Sunshine Home.* Illustrated by Diane DeGroat. New York: Clarion. Tim's grandmother must leave for a nursing home when she breaks her hip. Tim helps his parents express their unhappiness. **H**

Burden-Patman, Denise, with Kathryn D. Jones. (1992). *Carnival.* Illustrated by Reynold Ruffins. New York: Simon & Schuster. Rosa lives with her aunt, uncle, and cousins in New York City but misses her father in Trinidad and misses the Caribbean, especially at Carnival time. **H, C**

Casely, Judith. (1986). *When Grandpa Came to Stay.* New York: Greenwillow. A Jewish boy explains the process of having his grandfather move in and how he tries to help his grandfather cope with the death of his grandmother. **H**

Chiemruom, Sothea. (1994). *Dara's Cambodian New Year.* Illustrated by Dam Nang Pin. New York: Simon & Schuster. Dara's grandfather misses Cambodia, so Dara uses her artwork to brighten his New Year celebration. **H**

Choi, Sook Nyul. (1993). *Halmoni and the Picnic.* Illustrated by Karen M. Dugan. Boston: Houghton Mifflin. Yunmi's grandmother has come to live with them and walks Yunmi to school each day. Yunmi is afraid her grandmother will want to go back to Korea. However, Yunmi's classmates help make Halmoni feel especially welcome on the class picnic. **S**

Crews, Donald. (1991). *Bigmama's.* New York: Greenwillow. An African American family comes to grandmother's Florida farm for the summer. They feel comforted in finding the security of an extended family and rituals of being together again. **H, C**

Dorros, Arthur. (1991). *Abuela.* Illustrated by Elisa Kleven. New York: Dutton. A young girl loves taking walks with her *abuela* (grandmother) and imagines flying over New York City with her. Spanish and English are used effectively. **C**

Flournoy, Valerie. (1985). *The Patchwork Quilt.* Illustrated by Jerry Pinkney. New York: Dial. Three generations of an African American family work on a memory quilt. **H**

Fox, Mem. (1989, 1994). *Sophie.* Illustrated by Aminah Robinson. New York: Harcourt. Sophie's grandfather comes to live with them, and a special relationship develops between child and grandparent. **H**

Greenfield, Eloise. (1988). *Grandpa's Face.* Illustrated by Floyd Cooper. New York: Philomel. In this three-generation household, an African American girl is frightened when she sees her grandfather's angry face as he rehearses for a play. **H**

Guback, Georgia. (1994). *Luka's Quilt.* New York: Greenwillow. A Hawaiian child and her *tutu* (grandmother) disagree over the design of a quilt, but eventually compromise. **H**

Hoffman, Mary. (1991). *Amazing Grace.* Illustrated by Caroline Binch. New York: Dial Books for Young Readers. Grace works hard to get the Peter Pan role in a school production. Presents mother, daughter, and grandmother relationships in an African American household. **H, S**

Howard, Elizabeth F. (1991). *Aunt Flossie's Hats (and) Crab Cakes Later.* New York: Clarion. Sunday afternoons are Sarah and Susan's favorite times to visit their great Aunt Flossie and try on her hats. She shares with them her stories, and the African American family enjoys crab cakes. **H, C**

Khalsa, Dayal Kaur. (1986). *Tales of a Gambling Grandma.* New York: Clarkson Potter. A young child tells the story of her grandma's colorful life, particularly as she shares in adventures with her. **H, C**

Lobel, Anita. (1981). *Uncle Elephant.* New York: Harper & Row. Uncle Elephant cares for his nephew whose parents are lost at sea, and a loving and fun relationship develops. When Uncle Elephant returns his nephew to the rescued parents, he knows a new relationship has developed between them. **H**

MacLachlan, Patricia. (1991). *Journey.* New York: Delacorte. Two siblings, living with grandparents after being abandoned by their mother, cope with accepting the loss and learn to live as part of a new family structure. **H**

Mathis, S. B. (1975). *The Hundred Penny Box.* Illustrated by Leo & Diane Dillon. New York: Viking. The story focuses on Michael's fascination with his 100-year-old great, great aunt when she moves into his family's home. **H**

McCully, Emily Arnold. (1993). *Grandmas at Bat.* New York: HarperCollins. Pip's two grandmothers join forces to rescue his baseball team so they don't forfeit a game. At first the grandmothers embarrass the Stings, but their cheering rallies the team to win. **C**

McFarlane, Sheryl. (1991, 1993). *Waiting for the Whales.* Illustrated by Ron Lightburn. New York: Philomel. When a daughter brings her baby home, the grandfather and granddaughter form a special bond, sharing a ritual of waiting for the whales. **H, C**

Miles, Miska. (1971). *Annie and the Old One.* Illustrated by Peter Parnall. Boston: Little, Brown. A Navajo girl tries to delay the approaching death of her grandmother, but learns to accept the last stages of life. **H**

Nomura, Takaaki. (1991). *Grandpa's Town.* Translated by Amanda Mayer Stinchecum. Brooklyn, NY: Kane/Miller. A Japanese boy visits his grandfather to persuade him to come live with them. Grandpa and Yuuta enjoy a wonderful visit meeting Grandpa's friends, and Yuuta comes to understand why he can't leave his town. **H, C**

Polacco, Patricia. (1988). *The Keeping Quilt.* New York: Simon & Schuster. The story of a quilt is traced over four generations of a Jewish American family. **H**

Polacco, Patricia. (1990). *Thunder Cake.* New York: Philomel. A *babushka* (grandmother) helps dispel her granddaughter's fear of thunderstorms. **H**

Polacco, Patricia. (1992). *Mrs. Katz and Tush.* New York: Bantam (Little Rooster). An African American boy befriends a widowed Jewish neighbor, and his "adopted" grandma, Mrs. Katz, continues to be part of his life through adulthood. **C**

Poydar, Nancy. (1994). *Busy Bea.* New York: Macmillan. Bea can never find her own possessions, but somehow manages to find things for her grandmother. **H**

Rylant, Cynthia. (1985). *The Relatives Came.* Illustrated by Stephen Gammell. New York: Bradbury. A rollicking story of a huge extended family coming for a visit. Life for a rural mountain family is lovingly portrayed. **H**

Say, Allen. (1993). *Grandfather's Journey.* Boston: Houghton Mifflin. Grandfather was born in Japan and moved to California as a boy, but later he returned to Japan to live. **H, C**

Scheffler, Ursel. (1986). *A Walk in the Rain.* Illustrated by Ulises Wensell. Translated by Andrea Mernan. New York: Putnam. Josh and his grandmother walk in the rain and discover tiny insects and animals in the city streets, and their day ends back at home with grandfather reading a story. **H, C**

Swartz, Leslie. (1992, 1994). *A First Passover.* Illustrated by Jacqueline Chwast. New York: Simon & Schuster. A Jewish immigrant family of grandfather, parents, and child from Russia celebrates Passover in their new country. **H**

Swentzell, Rita. (1992). *Children of Clay: A Family of Pueblo Potters.* Photographs by Bill Steen. Minneapolis, MN: Lerner. Describes the traditional process of pottery making as practiced by an extended family of Tewa Indians in New Mexico. Especially appropriate for older readers. **C**

Wild, Margaret. (1994). *Our Granny.* Illustrated by Julie Vivas. New York: Ticknor & Fields. The book describes many grandmothers, but focuses on one in particular who lives with her grandchildren. **H**

HOMELESS FAMILIES

Barbour, Karen. (1991). *Mr. Bowtie.* San Diego: Harcourt. A homeless man is reunited with his family after two children befriend him. A gentle story focusing on positive interactions between a homeless man and a loving family. **C**

Bunting, Eve. (1991). *Fly Away Home.* Illustrated by Ronald Himler. New York: Clarion. A homeless father and son live in a busy airport. The boy spends time with an extended community of airport dwellers while father works. **C**

Carlson, Natalie. (1958). *The Family Under the Bridge.* Illustrated by Garth Williams. New York: Harper. Armand's snug corner under an old bridge is usurped by three children. Their adventures lead them to find happiness as a family. **C**

DiSalvo-Ryan, DyAnne. (1991). *Uncle Willie and the Soup Kitchen.* New York: Morrow Junior Books. On the boy's day off from school, Uncle Willie takes him to the soup kitchen, where the lad gains insights into the homeless of the community and how volunteers provide support for these people. **C**

Hathorn, Libby. (1994). *Way Home.* Illustrated by Gregory Rogers. New York: Crown. A homeless boy adopts a stray cat and guides it safely through the often frightening streets to his place. **C**

Sendak, Maurice. (1994). *We're All in the Dumps With Jack and Guy.* New York: HarperCollins. Jack and Guy are two homeless children who look after other homeless children in their neighborhood. **C**

MIGRANT WORKERS AND IMMIGRANTS

Bunting, Eve. (1988). *How Many Days to America? A Thanksgiving Story.* Illustrated by Beth Peck. New York: Clarion. "It was nice in our village. Til the night in October when the soldiers came." So begins the story of a Cuban family's flight by sea to America, arriving in time to celebrate Thanksgiving. **C**

Bunting, Eve. (1994). *A Day's Work.* New York: Clarion. A Hispanic boy learns the value of truth-telling when he and his grandfather are hired to garden for a day. Grandfather is a new immigrant. **H, C**

Isadora, Rachel. (1991). *At the Crossroads.* New York: Greenwillow. South African children wait several days at the crossroads for their fathers to return from the mines. Finally the fathers arrive and the families are together again for a little while. **C**

Rosenberg, Maxine. (1986). *Making a New Home in America.* Photos by George Ancona. New York: Lothrop. The story introduces four children who have recently arrived in America where they are living as immigrants and resident aliens. **H**

Williams, Sherley Anne. (1992). *Working Cotton.* Illustrated by Carole Byard. San Diego, CA: Harcourt. Shelan, an African American child of migrant workers, tells of a day in the fields helping her family. She helps her mother pick cotton, plays with her baby sister Leanne, and befriends other children. **C**

GAY AND LESBIAN FAMILIES

Bosche, S. (1983). *Jenny Lives With Eric and Martin.* London: Gay Men's Press. Jenny lives with her two fathers, who take very good care of her and love her very much. **H**

Brown, Forman. (1991). *Generous Jefferson Bartleby.* Illustrated by Leslie Trawin. Boston: Alyson Wonderland. Jefferson's friends, who have no fathers, are jealous that he has two dads who do lots of fun things with him on weekends. He gets into trouble when he loans both dads to friends on the same weekend. **H, C**

Elwin, Rosamund, & Paulie, Michele. (1990). *Asha's Mums.* Illustrated by Dawn Lee. Toronto: Women's Press. Asha and her class are going to the Science Museum, but Asha can't go because two moms signed her permission slip. Asha's mom Alice comes to school to straighten things. **S**

Heron, Ann, & Maran, Meredith. (1991). *How Would You Feel if Your Dad Was Gay?* Illustrated by Kris Kovick. Boston: Alyson Wonderland. Two children deal differently with the fact that their father is gay. Discusses varied family lifestyles. **H**

Newman, Leslea. (1989). *Heather Has Two Mommies.* Illustrated by Diane Souza. Boston: Alyson Wonderland. Heather and her two mommies are portrayed in conventional daily lives. **H**

Newman, Leslea. (1991). *Belinda's Bouquet.* Illustrated by Michael Willhoite. Boston: Alyson Wonderland. In trying to help her son's best friend improve her self-image, a lesbian mother tells the story of the foolish gardener who tried to make all the flowers look alike only to discover the best gardens are those with lots of different blooms. **H, C**

Newman, Leslea. (1991). *Gloria Goes to Gay Pride.* Illustrated by Russell Crocker. Boston: Alyson Wonderland. Gloria is excited about attending the Gay Pride festivities with her two moms. Also describes other aspects of their family life, such as how they celebrate Chanukah. **H, C**

Quinlan, Patricia. (1994). *Tiger Flowers.* Illustrated by Janet Wilson. New York: Dial (Penguin). A boy's beloved uncle, his mom's gay brother, lives with the family while he is dying of AIDS. **H**

Willhoite, Michael. (1990). *Daddy's Roommate.* Boston: Alyson Wonderland. A boy describes life shared with his divorced father and his father's roommate. The story demonstrates a healthy relationship among the three as well as with the boy's mother. **H**

Willhoite, Michael. (1993). *Uncle What-Is-It Is Coming to Visit!* Boston: Alyson Wonderland. Brother and sister let their imaginations run wild as they anticipate meeting their gay uncle for the first time. **H**

FAMILY MEMBERS AND FRIENDS WITH SPECIAL NEEDS

Alexander, Sally Hobart. (1990). *Mom Can't See Me.* Photographs by George Ancona. New York: Macmillan. A 9-year-old details life with her mother, who is blind. The story fully illustrates that her mom is a capable individual while also explaining what makes her a unique mom. **H**

Alexander, Sally Hobart. (1992). *Mom's Best Friend.* Photographs by George Ancona. New York: Macmillan. The child explains the process of her blind mother getting a new guide dog when the beloved old one dies. **H**

Clifton, Lucille. (1980). *My Friend Jacob.* Illustrated by Thomas Di Grazia. New York: Dutton. Eight-year-old Sam's friend is the mentally retarded teenage boy who lives next door. Sam tries to teach Jacob many things, but he accepts what Jacob can do and enjoys the relationship. **C**

Cohen, Miriam. (1983). *See You Tomorrow, Charles.* Illustrated by Lillian Hoban. New York: Greenwillow. Children in this multiethnic classroom are worried about saying, "See you" to blind Charles. When Charles leads the children out of a dark room in a very confident way, the class gains new respect for his capabilities. **S**

Cowen-Fletcher, Jane. (1993). *Mama Zooms.* New York: Scholastic. Simply told story of what a boy does with his mother, who uses a wheelchair. **H**

Dugan, Barbara. (1992). *Loop the Loop.* Illustrated by James Stevenson. New York: Greenwillow. Anne notices Mrs. Simpson, a wheelchair patient, arching her wrist and spinning a yo-yo. Anne learns to spin the yo-yo as their friendship grows and Mrs. Simpson's health deteriorates. **C**

Fassler, Joan. (1973). *Howie Helps Himself.* Illustrated by Joe Lasker. Morton Grove: IL: Albert Whitman. Howie, a child with cerebral palsy, struggles to maneuver his wheelchair by himself. **S**

Hines, Anna Grossnickle. (1993). *Gramma's Walk.* New York: Greenwillow. A boy's gramma uses a wheelchair. The two of them repeat a special ritual of going on an imaginary walk together. **C**

Kroll, Virginia. (1993). *Naomi Knows It's Springtime.* Illustrated by Jill Kastner. Honesdale, PA: Boyd's Mill. A young blind girl explains how she knows the changing seasons. **C**

Lakin, Patricia. (1994). *Dad and Me in the Morning.* Illustrated by Robert O. Steele. Morton Grove, IL: Albert Whitman. A young boy and his father go to the beach to watch the sunrise. Although the boy is deaf, he and his father have many ways of communicating and sharing the joys of the sunrise. **C**

MacLachlan, Patricia. (1980). *Through Grandpa's Eyes.* Illustrated by Deborah Kogan Ray. New York: HarperCollins. A young boy learns a magical way of experiencing the world through his blind grandfather's eyes. Evocative portrayal of how time spent together creates bonds between grandparent and grandchild. **C**

Martin, Bill, Jr., & Archambault, John. (1966, 1987). *Knots on a Counting Rope.* Illustrated by Ted Rand. New York: Holt. A blind Native American boy and his grandfather use a counting rope to recount many amazing things the boy has accomplished during his life. **C**

Miller, Mary Beth, & Ancona, George. (1991). *Handtalk School.* Photographs by George Ancona. New York: Four Winds. Documents a typical day at a residential school for deaf children. Families visit for a special play before the Thanksgiving vacation. **S**

Muldoon, Kathleen M. (1989). *Princess Pooh.* Illustrated by Linda Shute. Morton Grove, IL: Albert Whitman. Patty Jean resents the special treatment her sister gets because she uses a wheelchair until one day when she decides to use the "throne" for herself. **H**

Osofsky, Audrey. (1992). *My Buddy.* Illustrated by Ted Rand. New York: Holt. A boy with muscular dystrophy describes the process of training his assistant, a dog named Buddy, who helps him be less dependent on other people. **H, C**

Rabe, Berniece. (1988). *Where's Chimpy?* Photographs by Diane Schmidt. Morton Grove, IL: Albert Whitman. A child with Down syndrome searches for her favorite toy at bedtime. Eventually she and her father find Chimpy. **H**

Rosenberg, Maxine B. (1988). *Finding a Way: Living With Exceptional Brothers and Sisters.* Photographs by George Ancona. New York: Lothrop. The story describes three sibling relationships in which one sibling in each story has a physical disability. **H**

Thompson, Mary. (1992). *My Brother Matthew.* Rockville, MD: Woodbine House. A boy has a special relationship with his younger special needs brother, and shares some of his experiences in living with Matthew. **H**

Waddell, Martin. (1990). *My Great Grandpa.* Illustrated by Dom Mansell. New York: Putnam. A girl takes her great grandpa for rides in his wheelchair. They travel down familiar streets, stop in special shops, and visit the park. When her great grandpa gets sick, she and gramma take good care of him. **C**

Walker, Lou Ann. (1985). *Amy: The Story of a Deaf Child.* Photographs by Michael Abramson. New York: Lodestar. Deaf Amy's life as a fifth grader is told through text and photos. **S**

DEFINING FAMILIES

Jenness, Aylette. (1990). *Families: A Celebration of Diversity, Commitment, and Love.* Boston: Houghton Mifflin. Nonfiction text and photos depict lives of seventeen American families. Step-relatives, divorces, gay parents, and other diverse family constellations are included in this text. **H**

Kroll, Virginia. (1994). *Beginnings: How Families Come to Be.* Morton Grove, IL: Albert Whitman. Contains several stories in which a child's parent tells how the child came to be part of a particular family. Includes adoptive, single-parent, and interethnic families. **H**

Morris, Ann. (1990). *Bread, Bread, Bread.* Photographs by Ken Heyman. New York: Lothrop, Lee & Shepard. Portrays families from all over the world eating, working, playing, and sharing their lives together. **H**

Simon, Norma. (1976). *All Kinds of Families.* Illustrated by Joe Lasker. Morton Grove, IL: Albert Whitman. Nonfiction text tells what makes a family a family. **H**

Strickland, Dorothy S., & Strickland, Michael S. (Eds.). (1994). *Families: Poems Celebrating the African American Experience.* Illustrated by John Ward. Honesdale, PA: Boyd's Mill Press (Wordsong). An anthology of poetry and songs relating to a variety of African American families. **H**

Thomas, Marlo. (1987). *Free to Be a Family: A Book About All Kinds of Belonging.* New York: Bantam. A collection of stories, poems, and songs about different types of families and family relationships. **H**

Valentine, Johnny. (1994). *One Dad, Two Dads, Brown Dad, Blue Dads.* Illustrated by Melody Sarecky. Boston: Alyson Wonderland. A lighthearted story of children comparing notes on their parents. Points out that differences may not be as dramatic as we imagine them. **H**

OTHER STORIES REFERRED TO IN TEXT

Brown, Marcia. (1972). *The Three Billy Goats Gruff.* New York: Harcourt. The classic fairy tale, told with verve. **C**

Cherry, Lynne. (1992). *A River Ran Wild.* San Diego, CA: Harcourt. A group of schoolchildren observe pollution in their river, and then with adult help take on the project of cleaning up the river. **C**

Macauley, David. (1988). *How Things Work.* Boston: Houghton Mifflin. With concise text and simple drawings, Macauley describes how our simple, and not so simple, machines work. **C**

Parnall, Peter. (1987). *Apple Tree.* New York: Greenwillow. The apple tree is host to all kinds of creatures that feed from it, as the tree changes from season to season. **C**

Sendak, Maurice. (1963). *Where the Wild Things Are.* New York: Harper & Row. When Max gets into mischief his mother sends him to his room. There, Max sails away to the land where the wild things are, only to return and find supper waiting. **H**

Glossary

academic curriculum The objectives, procedures, and materials schools use to ensure children's acquisition of the knowledge and skills affirmed by the community.

academic learning The acquisition of knowledge and skills relating to subject matter disciplines and organized fields of study.

academic rationalism Curriculum focused on education as the pursuit of knowledge in specified study fields and subject matter disciplines, to develop the rational mind.

acculturate Modification of an individual's cultural behavior patterns by another cultural group (usually the dominant group).

adoptive family A family unit with at least one legally adopted child.

advocacy The process of publicly supporting a group, person, or cause.

afterschool care Providing care for working parents' children (usually 5–10 years of age) during afterschool hours.

alternative schools Schools organized with curricula different from, and usually in reaction to, conventional public school curricula.

assessment Evaluation or determination of extent of learning or change in behavior.

at-risk children (families) Children or families in danger of experiencing developmental gaps and problems due to poverty, abuse, illness, or social disturbance.

authentic assessment Using assessment strategies based on group or individual needs and the kinds of activities undertaken.

authoritarian parenting style Baumrind's term for an autocratic, controlling, and somewhat detached method of raising children.

authoritative parenting style Baumrind's term for a receptive and somewhat democratic, though firm and in control, manner of raising children.

autonomy The ability of persons to regulate and determine their own behavior.

behavioral objectives Intentions of education stated in terms of observable actions.

behaviorism A belief that learning occurs because of a system of rewards, punishments, and reinforcements.

bilingual education Teaching practices designed to encourage fluency in two languages.

blended family Two basic family units with children that join together to form a single family unit; often a remarriage, but some partners choose to forego wedlock.

bonding Establishment of a long-lasting affectionate relationship between an infant and a significant adult.

bottom-up Practices and procedures designed to bring about changes or learning through local efforts or individuals' wishes.

charter school An authorized school designed to improve educational opportunities, which is supported but not regulated by local or state authority.

child-centered curriculum Teaching practices and materials focusing on children's interests, needs, and desires, with teachers responding to these interests by providing materials and guidance.

child care center A facility providing programs (frequently educational) for 2- to 5-year-old children.

code switching The ability to move easily from one language or dialect to another.

cognitive process A series of actions producing changes in learners' methods of thinking, organizing perceptions, and solving problems.

collaboration Two or more persons or groups working together on joint endeavors for mutually determined objectives.

concrete operational thinking The third stage of Piagetian developmental theory (ages 7–11), characterized by the child's use of logical thought processes applied to real objects or events. At this stage the child does not yet apply logic to abstract or hypothetical problems.

constructivist curriculum Curriculum based on the premise that the goal of education is for children to learn how to learn; when the individual is active in the learning process and is internally responding to outer stimuli.

criterion-referenced tests Tests designed to examine how well students have mastered a set of materials, based on specified instructional goals and predetermined criteria.

cultural literacy The corpus of knowledge of major historical and literary events all literate persons should know to be considered "educated" by their culture.

cultural background The traditions, customs, knowledge, beliefs, art, morals, and regulations adhered to by a given group of people.

cultural pluralism The concept that all cultures have value and contribute to society.

cultural deprivation Used formerly to describe the problems of certain families and groups. The notion that individuals lacked certain skills for productive school learning due to gaps in cultural background.

custodial parent The parent to whom a court assigns the primary responsibility of a child's care and upbringing.

day care Programs provided for children whose parents work outside the home.

day care providers The adults who care for a group of children in a day care setting.

departmentalized program School practices in which students are taught different academic subjects by specialists in these academic fields.

Distar A curriculum designed by C. Bereiter and S. Englemann based on behavioral principles of instruction and learning.

dual-income family A family where both parents or resident adults have income.

egg-box type construction A popular school design of the 1950s and 1960s. The building resembled an egg box, with a central corridor and classrooms on each side.

elaborated language code Syntactically complex speech that requires persons one communicates with to use judgment, imagination, and reason to interpret ambiguities and abstractions.

enculturation The process by which one learns the mores and habits of a particular cultural group.

ethnic orientation Relating to the complex set of characteristics and values, including national origin and linguistic, physical, and religious traits, by which a social group identifies itself.

extended community The area and population beyond the immediate neighborhood or local environment.

extended family The kin of the basic family unit who are economically dependent on and/or emotionally attached to the household.

family Two or more persons living together and linked for emotional and economic support.

fixed curriculum The curriculum, often perceived to be mandated by local, state, and national education boards, that has been determined for a particular classroom.

Follow Through U.S. government-sponsored program that supports students after Head Start programs through kindergarten and the primary grades. (*See* Head Start.)

formal curriculum The curriculum, authorized by state and local education boards, that is public, usually printed, and which indicates the objectives, procedures, and materials for student learning.

formal community structures The organizations and agencies within a community that support services for that community.

foster family A family unit where adults offer support to children who are not related by blood or adoption.

gay and lesbian Persons with a sexual preference for their same sex. *Gay* is a generic term; *lesbian* refers specifically to women.

general equivalency diploma (GED) A means of acquiring a high school diploma without having graduated from an accredited high school.

Head Start Comprehensive federally funded program for poor preschool children and their families. It is designed to provide health, nutritional, social, and educational experiences to compensate for the negative effects of poverty.

hidden curriculum Instructive events in a child's life that influence learning and attitude, often seen as hindering the stated goals of the school.

home schooling The education of children undertaken completely by parents and done in the home environment.

homelessness A chronic condition in which a person has no permanent place of residence and thus constantly moves from one place to another.

hyperactivity Behavior characterized by excessive or abnormal body movements and high expenditure of energy.

Individualized Educational Program (IEP) A program, mandated by law, developed by those responsible for the education of a particular child with special needs.

industrial model A model for educational practice based on the manner in which industry operates.

informal curriculum All the events, stimuli, and activities that children undertake outside classrooms from which learning occurs.

informal community structures The personal relationships that families establish with members outside the home or extended family.

interethnic family A family unit that has more than one ethnic group represented in the unit. Blood parents may be of different groups, but also children of different groups may be adopted by parents of a single group.

itinerant family A family unit that moves regularly, often following crop harvests or engaged in other limited-time work.

kinesthetic orientation A manner of human functioning that best produces learning through the sensations of touch or body movement.

latchkey children Children of school age who return after school to an empty house, because all resident adults are at work.

learning modality Consistent set of behaviors and performances by which an individual approaches tasks to be learned.

literacy development The process of acquiring meaning from signs and symbols and of transferring meaning to signs and symbols.

local educational authority (LEA) The agency with the obligation and rights to oversee the education of children in its jurisdiction.

locus of control The perception one has of where responsibility for one's actions lie. May be internal or external.

lower working class That part of the population, usually consisting of unskilled laborers, who are less secure financially, at risk of unemployment, and at times receiving government assistance with basic living needs.

magnet schools Schools organized around a particular focus, such as math or drama, and drawing students from a large area (metropolitan or state).

mainstream Integrating special needs children into the regular classroom.

marginalized families (children) Persons, responsible for the welfare of children, who are unable or unwilling to provide for basic needs and nurturance.

melting pot thesis Concept that a single culture will emerge if children are educated for one set of behavior patterns and beliefs.

mentors Persons serving as guides or teachers to others, on a one-to-one basis.

metacognition The processes one uses in understanding how one gains knowledge.

middle class That part of the population whose income falls within the median range for the whole. Professionals and businesspersons are often in this class.

monocultural Reflecting the beliefs, behavior patterns, and characteristics of a single cultural group.

mores Those rituals, traditions, customs, and behavior patterns seen as essential for a social group's survival and well-being.

multicultural Association with and appreciation for the practices of different cultures, religions, and ethnic groups.

National Council for the Accreditation of Teacher Education (NCATE) National organization that sets standards for and evaluates teacher education programs.

networking A system of making connections with individuals and groups that allows communication and involvement as a unit.

norm-referenced testing Assessment where evaluation is based on comparison to a predetermined control group, often peers of the individual tested.

nuclear family A family unit consisting of two parents and their biological children.

nursery school Program, usually private, designed for 2- to 5-year-olds. Often a half-day program, but may have a full-day schedule.

open space schools Schools with large open spaces or "pods" in which several teachers organize the space to fit the needs of their particular students.

parent cooperatives Private nursery schools where parents share both the teaching and the administrative decision making.

parent empowerment A process whereby parents become decision makers, often in collaboration with school personnel, for the education of their children.

parent center Specific location, usually within a school, where parents can work and socialize, and feel a part of the school.

partnerships Relationships among different groups in which each group has equal influence on decision making.

perceptual field Human range of recognition and organization of sensory input.

permissive parenting style Baumrind's term for a manner of raising children that is nondemanding and noncontrolling, allowing children to develop according to their natural instincts.

person-oriented family Manner of behaving in which the family unit focuses on the future development of individual children.

personal relevance curriculum Curriculum based on the belief that the goal of education is to provide personally satisfying experiences for each student.

phonics The letter–sound relationships of a language.

play school or group Program designed, usually for toddlers, to focus on the importance of children engaging in play as a means of enhancing development.

position-oriented family Manner of family functioning that is present oriented and object oriented and that assigns roles according to position in the family.

power brokers Members of a community or group with enough influence and power to become major decision makers for that community or group.

preoperational thinking The second stage of Piagetian developmental theory (ages 2–7) characterized by symbolic functions. The child moves from functioning as a result of sensorimotor stimuli to developing the ability to internally represent events and act on this memory.

proof of equivalency A requirement that home schoolers have proof that the education they provide for their children is equivalent to what children would receive in the formal school.

resilient Ability to cope and manage in spite of debilitating environmental circumstances.

restricted language code A manner of speaking that is syntactically simple and direct, and that has concrete meanings.

role expectations Behavioral expectations for an individual depending on status or function within the family, peer group, school, or community.

Scholastic Aptitude Test (SAT) Norm-referenced exams for high school students. Often used by colleges and scholarship boards to determine ability for advanced study.

scope and sequence charts Lists of important skills for children's achievement, arranged on two dimensions: (1) the broad extent of the skill; (2) the order in which a skill or set of related skills is learned.

secular humanism Belief that the goals of education are to develop children's sense of personal growth, integrity, and autonomy, but should not encompass the religious or spiritual part of the person.

secular education Education in which there is no religious or spiritual training.

self-fulfilling prophecy A concept that expectations of others shape and reinforce one's behavior such that the expectations are eventually met. Also known as the "Pygmalion Effect."

sensory mode The manner of receiving information through the five senses.

service agencies Organizations within a community that provide those health, educational, transportation, protection, and communication services necessary to that community's citizens.

significant adults The adults in children's lives who are particularly important to them. This relationship exists independently of any biological or formal social relation between child and adult.

single-parent family A family unit consisting of one parent, either mother or father, and children, and no other adults.

site-based management A procedure for managing schools in which organizational and educational decisions for children at a particular school should be made by persons at that school.

social capital The amount of human connections and relationships resulting in learning.

social climate The attitudes, feelings, and relationships people within a community maintain toward one another.

social networks Parallel relationships developed among individuals in a community that foster communication and a sense of belonging.

social reconstructionist curriculum Curriculum based on the thesis that the goals of education are to effect social change. Students learn social needs and values and how to use these concepts in critical thought processes.

social setting A place, such as home, school, or community, where interactive events between or among individuals happen naturally.

socialization skills The acquired ability to interact within the norms, values, and mores of a social group.

socioeconomic status (SES) The economic and social level to which one belongs because of wealth, occupation, and educational background.

special interest groups Groups with a narrow purpose or agenda organized to influence others to their point of view.

sponsored independence parenting style Clark's term, similar to Baumrind's *authoritative style*, describing a manner of raising children. Indicates a rational, receptive, warm, but demanding style.

stages of development Distinct steps in the growth process that individuals pass through from infancy through adulthood.

standardized tests Tests with scientifically chosen items, given under similar conditions, that enable persons to be compared to a group standard. Tests may be either criterion referenced or norm referenced.

sub-family A family cluster living with other adults or families, in which the parent(s) in the cluster is not the central family figure in the household.

technologist curriculum A curriculum based on the notion that the primary goal of education is for students to master the basic skills of reading and computing in order to function in present society.

theme-focused programs A phase of curriculum, based on a particular theme, where important objectives are identified and activities are prepared so students acquire knowledge and skills relating to that theme.

three-group rotation A technique for schooling that organizes a class of children into three groups and then rotates groups throughout the day into different learning centers or events.

time on task The actual amount of time a student is engaged in or attending to a particular assigned task.

top-down Practices and procedures designed to didactically bring about changes or learning. Typically, changes are initiated at the administrative or supervisory level and imposed on groups, classrooms, or schools.

traditional curriculum Curriculum based on the notion that the objective of education is for students to acquire knowledge in subject matter disciplines and specified fields of study. Similar to *academic curriculum.*

underclass That part of the population limited in opportunity and resources and locked into a cycle of poverty and despair.

units of study Part of a curriculum based on a particular theme, around which learning activities are organized. Similar to *theme-focused programs.*

unstructured learning Learning resulting from incidental and self-selected experiences in which children become interested and involved.

upper working class That population group represented by skilled laborers, who are financially able to cope but severely affected by economic conditions.

upper class The most economically advantaged group of a population; often wealth is inherited.

voucher plans Plans whereby parents receive certificates indicating the financial support for their children's education. Parents have the right to select a school and use the certificate to pay the cost of education.

well baby clinic   Health clinics or hospital programs where parents can, without cost, bring their children for regular checkups and discussions regarding ways to provide healthy environments.

whole language programs   Curriculum practice emphasizing the totality of language, presuming that chil-dren should learn to read the same way they learn to speak; i.e., holistically with respect to their environ-ment. Reading, writing, speaking, and listening are all aspects of language learned in conjunction.

writing-to-read   A strategy for teaching reading in combination with teaching writing.

References

Adams, H. B. (1907). *The education of Henry Adams.* Boston: Massachusetts Historical Society.

Adams, M. J. (1990). *Beginning to read: Thinking and learning about print.* Cambridge, MA: MIT Press.

Ahlburg, D. A., & DeVita, C. J. (1992). New realities of the American family. *Population Bulletin, 47*(2), 2–40.

American Academy of Pediatrics, Task Force on Children and Television. (1990). *Children, adolescents and television.* Elk Grove Village, IL: Author.

American Association of School Administrators. (1986). *Religion in the public schools.* Arlington, VA: Author.

American Civil Liberties Union. (1995). *Religion in the public schools: A joint statement of current laws.* New York: Author.

Anderson, J. W. (1972). Attachment behavior out of doors. In N. Blurton Jones (Ed.), *Ethological studies of child behavior* (pp. 199–215). New York: Cambridge University Press.

Anderson, J., & Suntken, J. (1989). The me-museum. In D. Strickland & L. M. Morrow (Eds.), *Emerging literacy: Young children learn to read and write* (pp. 42–55). Newark, DE. International Reading Association.

Anthony, K. H., Weidemann, S., & Chin, Y. (1990). Housing perceptions of low-income single parents. *Environment and behavior, 22*(2), 147–182.

Apple, M. W. (1979). *Ideology and curriculum.* London: Routledge & Kegan Paul.

Applebee, A. (1978). *Child's concept of story: Ages 2–17.* Chicago: University of Chicago Press.

Argulewicz, E. N. (1983). Effects of ethnic membership, socioeconomic status, and home language on LD, EMR, and EH placements. *Learning Disabilities Quarterly, 6*(2), 195–200.

Asher, S., & Coie, J. (Eds.). (1991). *Peer rejection in childhood.* New York: Cambridge University Press.

Bailyn, B., Dallek, R., Davis, D. B., Donald, D. H., Thomas, J. L., & Wood, G. S. (1992). *The Great republic: A history of the American people* (4th ed.). Lexington, MA: D. C. Heath.

Ball, S., & Bogatz, G. (1970). *The first year of Sesame Street: An evaluation.* Princeton, NJ: Educational Testing Service.

Banks, J. A. (1993). Multicultural education: Development, dimensions, and challenges. *Phi Delta Kappan, 75*(1), 22–28.

Barbour, N. H., & Seefeldt, C. (1993). *Developmental continuity across preschool and primary grades.* Wheaton, MD: Association for Childhood Education International.

Barker, P. (1990). The home schooled teenager grows up. In A. Pedersen & P. O'Mara (Eds.), *Schooling at home: Parents, kids, and learning* (pp. 203–208). Santa Fe, NM: John Muir Publications.

Barth, R. (1983). Social support network in services for adolescents and their families. In J. K. Whittaker & J. Garbarino (Eds.), *Social support networks* (pp. 289–331). New York: Aldine.

Bauch, J. F. (1989). The TransParent school model: New technology for parent involvement. *Educational Leadership, 47*(2), 32–34.

Baumrind, D. (1966). Effects of authoritative parental control on child behavior. *Child Development, 37,* 387–407.

Baumrind, D. (1968). Authoritarian vs. authoritative parental control. *Adolescence, 3,* 255–272.

Baumrind, D. (1971). Current patterns of parental authority. *Developmental Psychology Monograph, 75,* 43–88.

Bedell, K. B. (Ed.). (1993). *Yearbook of American and Canadian churches, 1993.* Nashville, TN: Abingdon.

Bell, T. H. (1993). Reflections one decade after a nation at risk. *Phi Delta Kappan, 75*(8), 593–597.

Belmont, L., & Marolla, F. A. (1973). Birth order, family size and intelligence. *Science, 182,* 1096–1101.

Belsky, J., Lerner, R. M., & Spanier, C. B. (1984). *The child in the family.* New York: Random House.

Bennett, K. P., & LeCompte, M. D. (1990). *How schools work: A sociological analysis of education.* New York: Longman.

Bereiter, C., & Englemann, S. (1966). *Teaching disadvantaged children in the preschool.* Upper Saddle River, NJ: Prentice Hall.

Berger, E. H. (1995). *Parents as partners in education: Families and schools working together* (4th ed.). Englewood Cliffs, NJ: Merrill/Prentice Hall.

Berns, R. M. (1993). *Child, family, community: Socialization and support* (3rd ed.). New York: Harcourt Brace Jovanovich.

Bernstein, B. (1972). A sociolinguistic approach to socialization with some reference to educability. In J. Gumperz & D. Hymes (Eds.), *Directions in sociolinguistics* (pp. 465–497). New York: Holt, Rinehart & Winston.

Bettelheim, B. (1976). *The uses of enchantment.* New York: Knopf.

Bianchi, S. M. (1990). America's children: Missed prospects. *Population Bulletin, 45*(1), 7–10.

Binford, V. M., & Newell, J. M. (1991). Richmond, Virginia's two decades of experience with Ira Gordon's approach to parent education. *The Elementary School Journal, 91*(3), 233–237.

Bjorklund, G., & Burger, C. (1987). Making conferences work for parents, teachers and children. *Young Children, 42*(2), 26–31.

Black, J. K., Puckett, M. B., & Bell, M. J. (1992). *The young child: Development from prebirth through age eight.* Englewood Cliffs, NJ: Merrill/Prentice Hall.

Blau, J. (1992). *The visible poor: Homelessness in the United States.* New York: Oxford University Press.

Bloom, B. S., Englehart, M. D., Furst, E. J., Hill, W. H., & Krathwohl, D. R. (1956). *Taxonomy of educational objectives, handbook I: Cognitive domain.* New York: McKay.

Bloom, J. (1992). *Parenting our schools: A hands-on guide to education reform.* Boston: Little, Brown.

Bogatz, G., & Ball, S. (1971). *The second year of Sesame Street: A continuing evaluation.* Princeton, NJ: Educational Testing Service.

Bossard, J., & Boll, E. (1949). Ritual in family living. *American Sociological Review, 14,* 526–530.

Bradley, R. H., Caldwell, B. M., & Elardo, R. (1979). Home environment and cognitive development in the first two years: A cross-lagged panel analysis. *Developmental Psychology, 15,* 246–250.

Brantlinger, E. (1991). Home-school partnerships that benefit children with special needs. *Elementary School Journal, 91*(3), 249–259.

Braverman, L. B. (1989). Beyond the myth of motherhood. In M. C. McGoldrick, C. M. Anderson, & F. Walsh (Eds.), *Women and families* (pp. 227–243). New York: Free Press.

Bronfenbrenner, U. (1979). *The ecology of human development: Experiment by nature and design.* Cambridge: Harvard University Press.

Bronfenbrenner, U. (1986). Ecology of the family as a context of human development: Research perspectives. *Developmental Psychology, 22,* 723–742.

Bronfenbrenner, U., & Crouter, A. (1982). Work and family through time and space. In S. B. Kammerman & C. D. Hayes (Eds.), *Families that work: Children in a changing world* (pp. 39–83). Washington, DC: National Academy Press.

Bronfenbrenner, U., Moen, P., & Garbarino, J. (1984). Child, family, and community. In R. D. Parke, *Review of child development research: Vol. 7. The family* (pp. 283–328). Chicago: University of Chicago Press.

Bronfenbrenner, U., & Weiss, H. (1983). *Beyond policies without people: An ecological perspective on child and family policy.* New York: Cambridge University Press.

Brooks, J. G., & Powell, D. (1986). *Adopt-a-school program 1985–1986.* Fort Worth, TX: Division of Curriculum Development. (ERIC Document Reproduction Service No. ED 287 191)

Buchwald, A. (1994). *Leaving home: A memoir.* New York: Putnam.

Bullivant, B. M. (1993). Culture: Its nature and meaning for educators. In J. A. Banks & C. A. M. Banks (Eds.), *Multicultural education: Issues and perspectives* (2nd ed., pp. 29–47). Boston: Allyn & Bacon.

Bullock, H. A. (1967). *A history of Negro education in the South from 1619 to the present.* Cambridge, MA: Harvard University Press.

Bumstead, R. A. (1979). Educating your child at home: The Perchemlides case. *Phi Delta Kappan, 61*(2), 97–100.

Butler, R. D. (1976). Black children's racial preference: A selected review of literature. *Journal of Afro-American Issues, 4*(2), 168–171.

Calderone, M. S., & Ramey, J. W. (1982). *Talking with your child about sex.* New York: Random House.

Calvery, R., Bell, D., & Vaupal, C. (1992). *The difference in achievement between home schooled and public schooled students for grades four, seven, and ten in Arkansas.* Paper presented at the Annual Meeting of the Mid-South Educational Research Association, Knoxville, TN. (ERIC Document Reproduction Service No. ED 354 248)

Carlsson-Paige, N., & Levin, D. E. (1987). *The war play dilemma: Balancing needs and values in the early childhood classroom.* New York: Teachers College Press.

Carnegie Forum on Education and the Economy. (1986). *A nation prepared: Teachers for the 21st century.* New York: Carnegie Corporation.

Carter, D. A. (1993). Community and parent involvement: A road to school improvement. *ERS Spectrum, 11*(1), 39–45.

Carter, T. P., & Sequra, R. D. (1979). *Mexican Americans in school: A decade of change.* New York: College Entrance Examination Board.

Center for the Study of Social Policy. (1989). *The challenge of change: What the 1988 census tells us about children.* Washington, DC: Author.

Center for the Study of Social Policy. (1992). *The challenge of change: What the 1990 census tells us about children.* Washington, DC: Author.

Cherry, L. (1982). *A river ran wild.* San Diego, CA: Harcourt Brace.

Children's Defense Fund. (1981). *How to help handicapped children to get an education: A success story.* Washington, DC: Author.

Children's Defense Fund. (1990). *S.O.S. America: A children's defense budget.* Washington, DC: Author.

Children's Defense Fund. (1991). *The state of America's children.* Washington, DC: Author.

Children's Defense Fund. (1993). *The nation's investment in children: An analysis of the president's FY 1993 budget proposals.* Washington, DC: Author.

Clark, R. M. (1983). *Family life and school achievement: Why poor black children succeed or fail.* Chicago: University of Chicago Press.

Clawson, B. (1992). Preparing for successful children. In L. Kaplan (Ed.), *Education and the family* (pp. xix–xxii). Boston: Allyn & Bacon.

Clay, J. W. (1990). Working with lesbian and gay parents and their children. *Young Children, 45*(3), 31–35.

Clay, P. (1981). *Single parents and the public school.* Washington, DC: National Committee for Citizens in Education.

Clinchy, E. (1993). Building an extended family in East Harlem. In S. Thompson (Ed.), *Whole child, whole community* (pp. 28–34). Boston: Institute for Responsive Education.

Cochran, M. (1990). The network as an environment for human development. In M. Cochran, M. Larner, R. Riley, L. Gunnarsson, & C. R. Henderson, Jr. (Eds.), *Extending families: The social networks of parents and their children* (pp. 265–277). New York: Cambridge University Press.

Cochran, M., & Riley, D. (1990). The social networks of six-year-olds: Context, content, and consequence. In M. Cochran, M. Larner, D. Riley, L. Gunnarsson, & C. R. Henderson, Jr. (Eds.), *Extending families: The social networks of parents and their children* (pp. 154–179). New York: Cambridge University Press.

Cohen, D. L. (1992). Children without "traditional family" support are posing complex challenges for schools. *Education Week, 12*(15), 5.

Cohen, D. L. (1994). Carnegie Corporation presses early-years policies. *Education Week, 13*(29), 1, 13.

Cohen, S. (1974). *A history of colonial education, 1607–1776.* New York: Wiley.

Coleman, J. S. (1966). *Equality of educational opportunity.* Washington, DC: U.S. Government Printing Office.

Coleman, J. S. (1987). Families and schools. *The Educational Researcher, 16*(6), 32–38.

Coleman, J. S. (1990). *Foundations of social theory.* Cambridge, MA: Harvard University Press.

Coleman, J. S. (1991). *Policy perspectives: Parental involvement in education.* Washington, DC: U.S. Department of Education, Office of Educational Research and Improvement.

Colfax, J. D., & Colfax, M. (1992). *Hard times in paradise.* New York: Warren.

Collins, R. C. (1984, April). *Head Start: A review of research with implications for practice in early childhood education.* Paper presented at the annual meeting of the American Educational Research Association, New Orleans, LA. (ERIC Document Reproduction Service No. ED 245 833)

Comer, J. P. (1980). *School power: Implications of an intervention project.* New York: Free Press.

Comer, J. P. (1988). *Maggie's American dream: The life and times of a black family.* New York: New American Library.

Comer, J. P. (1993). *The components of a successful education. Summer 1993 Chautauqua Lecture Series.* Chautauqua, NY: Chautauqua Institution.

Comer, J. P., & Haynes, N. M. (1991). Parent involvement in schools: An ecological approach. *The Elementary School Journal, 91*(3), 271–277.

Comstock, G., & Paik, H. (1991). *Television and the American child.* San Diego, CA: Academic Press.

Cook, T., Appleton, H., Conner, R., Shaffer, A., Tamkin, G., & Weber, S. (1975). *"Sesame Street" revisited.* New York: Russell Sage Foundation.

Cornell, C. E. (1993). Language and culture monsters that lurk in our traditional rhymes and folktales. *Young Children, 48*(6), 40–46.

Cowan, H. G. (1989). Project TEACH: How business helps our schools. *Educational Leadership, 47*(2), 6.

Cremin, L. A. (1961). *The transformation of the school: Progressivism in American education, 1876–1957.* New York: Alfred A. Knopf.

Cremin, L. A. (1982). *American education: The national experience, 1783–1876.* New York: Harper & Row.

Cruickshank, D. (1990). *Research that informs teachers and teacher educators.* Bloomington, IN: Phi Delta Kappa Educational Foundation.

Curran, D. (1983). *Traits of a healthy family.* Minneapolis, MN: Winston.

D'Angelo, D. A., & Adler, C. R. (1991). Chapter 1: A catalyst for improving parent involvement. *Phi Delta Kappan, 72*(5), 350–355.

Danzberger, J. P., & Gruskin, S. J. (1993). *Project abstracts: Educational Partnerships Program. Programs for the improvement of practice.* Washington, DC: Office of Educational Research and Improvement.

Dash, J. (1992). *Daughters of the dust.* New York: New Press.

Davies, D. (1990). Shall we wait for the revolution?: A few lessons from the Schools Reaching Out Project. *Equity and Choice, 6*(3), 68–73.

Davies, D. (1993). Looking backward. In S. Thompson (Ed.), *Whole child, whole community* (pp. 67–72). Boston: Institute for Responsive Education.

Davies, D., Burch, P., & Johnson, V. R. (1992). *A portrait of schools reaching out. Report of a survey of practices and policies of family–community–school collaboration.* Boston: Center on Families, Communities, Schools, & Children's Learning.

Davies, D., Burch, P., & Palanki, A. (1993). *Fitting policy to family needs: Delivering comprehensive services through collaboration and family empowerment.* Boston: Center on Families, Communities, Schools, & Children's Learning.

Davies, D., Palanki, A., & Burch, P. (1993). The whole school for the whole child. In S. Thompson (Ed.), *Whole child, whole community* (pp. 18–23). Boston, MA: Institute for Responsive Education.

Decker, L. E., & Decker, V. A. (1988). *Home/school/community involvement.* Arlington, VA: American Association of School Administrators.

Dewey, J. (1913, 1975). *Interest and effort in education.* Edwardsville, IL: Southern Illinois University Press.

Dighe, J. (1993). Children and the earth. *Young Children, 48*(3), 58–63.

Dinkmeyer, D., & McKay, G. D. (1983). *Systematic training for effective parenting.* Circle Pines, MN: American Guidance Service.

Doll, R. C. (1989). *Curriculum improvement: Decision making and process* (7th ed.). Boston: Allyn & Bacon.

Dornbusch, S., Ritter, P. L., Leiderman, P. H., Roberts, D. F., & Fraleigh, M. J. (1987). The relation of parenting style to adolescent school performance. *Child Development, 58*(5), 1244–1257.

Dorris, M. (1993). Foreword. In M. Roesell, *Kinaalda: A Navajo girl grows up* (pp. 1–2). Minneapolis, MN: Lerner.

Dreeben, R. (1970). Schooling and authority: Comments on the unstudied curriculum. In N. V. Overly (Ed.), *The unstudied curriculum: Its impact on children* (pp. 85–103). Washington, DC: ASCD.

Dunn, K., & Frazier, E. R. (1990). *Teaching styles.* Reston, VA: National Association of Secondary School Principals.

Dunn, R., & Dunn, K. (1978). *Teaching students through their individual learning styles: A practical approach.* Englewood Cliffs, NJ: Prentice Hall.

Durkin, D. D. (1966). *Children who read early.* New York: Teachers College Press.

Dworetzky, J. P. (1990). *Introduction to child development* (4th ed.). New York: West.

Ecksel, I. B. (1992). Schools as socializing agents in children's lives. In L. Kaplan (Ed.), *Education and the family* (pp. 86–99). Boston: Allyn & Bacon.

Eddowes, E. A., & Hranitz, J. R. (1989). Educating children of the homeless. *Childhood Education, 65*(4), 197–200.

Educational Research Service. (1992). Children with disabilities: Educational status and trends. *ERS Research Digest, 18,* 1–4.

Educational Research Service. (1993). Education of migrant children. *ERS Bulletin, 20*(4), 10.

Edwards, C., Gandini, L. & Forman, G. (Eds). (1992). *The hundred languages of children: Education for all of the children in Reggio Emilia, Italy.* Norwood, NJ: ABLEX.

Eisner, E. W. (1994). *The educational imagination: On the design and evaluation of school programs* (3rd ed.). Englewood Cliffs, NJ: Merrill/Prentice Hall.

Eitzen, D. S. (1992). Problem students: The sociocultural roots. *Phi Delta Kappan, 73*(8), 584–590.

Elam, S. M., Rose, L. C., & Gallup, A. M. (1993). The 25th annual Gallup/Phi Delta Kappa poll of the public's attitude toward schools. *Phi Delta Kappan, 75*(2), 138–149.

Elam, S. M., Rose, L. C., & Gallup, A. M. (1994). The 26th annual PDK/Gallup poll of the public's attitudes toward the public schools. *Phi Delta Kappan, 76*(1), 41–56.

Elgin, C. Z. (1990). Representation, comprehension and competence. In V. A. Howard (Ed.), *Varieties of thinking* (pp. 62–75). New York: Routledge, Chapman & Hall.

Elkin, F., & Handel, G. (1989). *The child and society* (5th ed.). New York: Random House.

Elkind, D. (1981). *The hurried child.* Reading, MA: Addison-Wesley.

Elmer-Dewitt, P. (1993). Too violent for kids? *Time, 142*(13), 67–72.

Emery, R. E. (1988). *Marriage, divorce, and children's adjustment.* Beverly Hills, CA: Sage.

Epstein, J. L. (1987). Parent involvement: What research says to administrators. *Education and Urban Society, 19*(2), 119–136.

Epstein, J. L. (1992). School and family partnerships. In A. Alkin (Ed.), *Encyclopedia of educational research* (pp. 1139–1151). Englewood Cliffs, NJ: Merrill/Prentice Hall.

Erikson, E. (1963). *Childhood and society.* New York: Norton.

Estrada, L. F. (1993). The dynamic demographic mosaic called America: Implications for education. *Education and Urban Society, 25*(3), 231–245.

Evans, E. (1975). *Contemporary influences in early childhood education* (2nd ed.). New York: Holt, Rinehart, & Winston.

Farenga, P. (1990). Methodologies and curricula. In A. Pedersen & P. O'Mara (Eds.), *Schooling at home: Parents, kids, and learning* (pp. 95–104). Santa Fe, NM: John Muir Publications.

Fine, M. J. (1993). Current approaches to understanding family diversity. *Family Relations, 43*(3), 235–237.

Fine, M. J., & Henry, S. A. (1989). Professional issues in parent education. In M. J. Fine (Ed.), *The second handbook on parent education: Contemporary perspectives* (pp. 3–20). New York: Academic Press.

Fitzgerald, J., Spiegel, D. L., & Cunningham, J. W. (1991). The relationship between parental literacy level and perceptions of emergent literacy. *Journal of Reading Behavior, 23,* 191–214.

Fitzpatrick, M. A., & Vangelisti, A. (1995). *Explaining family interactions.* Thousand Oaks, CA: Sage.

Florida State Department of Education. (1992). *Florida's First Start Program planning and implementation.* Tallahassee, FL: Author. (ERIC Document Reproduction Service No. ED 374 859)

Fox, R. A., Anderson, R. C., Fox, T. A., & Rodriguez, M. A. (1991). STAR parenting: A model for helping parents effectively deal with behavioral difficulties. *Young Children, 46*(4), 54–61.

Friedman, S. (1990). *Small victories.* New York: Basic Books.

Frost, E. A. (1988). Does home-schooling work? Some insights for academic success. *Contemporary Education, 59*(4), 223–227.

Frost, S. E., Jr. (1966). *Historical and philosophical foundations of Western education.* Englewood Cliffs, NJ: Merrill/Prentice Hall.

Fuller, M. L. (1986). Teacher's perceptions of children from intact and single parent families. *School Counselor, 33*(7), 365–374.

Galinsky, E. (1987). *The six stages of parenthood.* Reading, MA: Addison-Wesley.

Galle, O., Gove, W., & McPherson, J. (1972). Population density and pathology: What are the relationships for men? *Science, 176,* 23–30.

Gandini, L. (1993). Fundamentals of the Reggio Emilia approach to early childhood education. *Young Children, 49*(1), 4–8.

Garbarino, J., & Abramowitz, R. H. (1992). The family as a social system. In J. Garbarino (Ed.), *Children and families in the social environment* (2nd ed.) (pp. 71–98). New York: Aldine de Gruyer.

Garbarino, J., Dubrow, N., Kostelny, K., & Pardo, C. (1992). *Children in danger: Coping with the conse-*

quences of community violence. San Francisco: Jossey-Bass.

Garbarino, J., Kostelny, K., & Dubrow, N. (1991). *No place to be a child: Growing up in a war zone.* Lexington, MA: D. C. Heath.

Garcia, J. (1993). The changing image of ethnic groups in textbooks. *Phi Delta Kappan, 75*(1), 29–35.

Gardner, H. (1983). *Frames of mind. The theory of multiple intelligences.* New York: Basic Books.

Gardner, S. (1993). Failure by fragmentation. In S. Thompson (Ed.), *Whole child, whole community* (pp. 11–17). Boston: Institute for Responsive Education.

Gearheart, B. R., Weishahn, M., & Gearheart, C. J. (1996). *The exceptional student in the regular classroom* (6th ed.). Englewood Cliffs, NJ: Merrill/ Prentice Hall.

Gelfer, J. I. (1991). Teacher-parent partnerships: Enhancing communications. *Childhood Education, 67*(3), 164–167.

Gerbner, G., & Signorielli, N. (1990). *Violence profile 1967 through 1988–89: Enduring trends.* Philadelphia: PA: University of Pennsylvania, Annenburg School of Communication.

Gersten, J. C. (1992). Families in poverty. In M. E. Procidano & C. B. Fisher (Eds.), *Contemporary families: A handbook for school professionals* (pp. 137–158). New York: Teachers College Press.

Gestwicki, C. (1991). *Home, school, and community relations: A guide to working with parents* (2nd ed.). Albany, NY: Delmar.

Giroux, H. A. (1978). Developing educational programs: Overcoming the hidden curriculum. *The Clearing House, 52*(4), 148–152.

Goffman, E. (1967). *Interaction ritual: Essays on face-to-face behavior.* New York: Harper & Row.

Good, T. L., & Brophy, J. E. (1972). Behavioral expression of teacher attitudes. *Journal of Educational Psychology, 63,* 617–624.

Good, T. L., & Brophy, J. E. (1986). School effects. In M. C. Wittrock (Ed.), *Handbook of research on teaching* (3rd ed.) (pp. 570–604). Englewood Cliffs, NJ: Merrill/Prentice Hall.

Good, T. L., & Brophy, J. E. (1994). *Looking in classrooms* (6th ed.). New York: HarperCollins.

Gorder, C. (1990). *Home schools: An alternative. You do have a choice!* (3rd ed.). Tempe, AZ: Blue Bird.

Gordon, I. J. (1969). *Reaching the child through parent education: The Florida approach.* Gainsville, FL: Gainesville Institute for Development of Human Resources. (ERIC Document Reproduction Service No. ED 057 880)

Gordon, I. J., Guinagh, B. J., & Jester, R. F. (1977). The Florida Parent Education Infant and Toddler Program. In M. C. Day & R. K. Parker (Eds.), *The preschool in action* (2nd ed.) (pp. 95–127). Boston: Allyn & Bacon.

Gordon, T. (1975). *Parent effectiveness training.* New York: Peter H. Wyden.

Gorsuch, R. L. (1976). Religion as a major prediction of significant human behavior. In W. J. Donaldson, Jr. (Ed.), *Research in Mental health and religious behavior* (pp. 206–221). Atlanta: Psychological Studies Institute.

Graham, P. A. (1993). What America has expected of its schools over the past century. *American Journal of Education, 101*(2), 83–98.

Graue, M. E., Weinstein, T., & Walberg, H. J. (1983). School-based home instruction and learning: A quantitative analysis. *Journal of Educational Research, 76,* 351–360.

Gray, P., & Chanoff, D. (1984). When play is learning: A school for self-directed education. *Phi Delta Kappan, 65*(9), 608–611.

Greenberg, P. (1990). Head Start—Part of a multipronged anti-poverty effort for children and their families. Before the beginning: A participant's view. *Young Children, 45*(6), 40–73.

Griffel, G. (1991). Walking on a tightrope: Parents shouldn't have to walk it alone. *Young Children, 46*(3), 40–42.

Grobe, T., Curnan, S. P., & Melchoir, A. (1993). *Synthesis of existing knowledge and practice in the field of educational partnerships.* Washington, DC: Office of Educational Research and Improvement.

Groover, S. V., & Endsley, R. C. (1988). *Family environment and attitudes towards homeschoolers and non-homeschoolers.* Unpublished master's thesis, University of Georgia, Athens, GA. (ERIC Document Reproduction Service No. Ed 323 027)

Groves, B., Zuckerman, B., & Marans, S. (1993). Silent victims: Children who witness violence. *Journal of American Medical Association, 269*(2), 262–265.

Grumbine, E. (1988). The university of the wilderness. *Journal of Environmental Education, 19*(4), 3–7.

Gutek, G. L. (1986). *Education in the United States.* Englewood Cliffs, NJ: Prentice Hall.

Guterson, D. (1992). *Family matters: Why homeschooling makes sense.* New York: Harcourt.

Haberman, M. (1992). Creating community contexts that educate: An agenda for improving education in inner cities. In L. Kaplan (Ed.), *Education and the family* (pp. 27–40). Boston: Allyn & Bacon.

Haley, A. (1976). *Roots.* Garden City, NJ: Doubleday.

Hallpike, C. R. (1986). *The principles of social evolution.* New York: Oxford University Press.

Harrington-Lueker, D. (1994a). Charter "profit": Will Michigan heap money on an electronic charter school? *The American School Board, 181*(9), 27–29.

Harrington-Lueker, D. (1994b). Charter schools. *The American School Board, 181*(9), 22–26.

Hartup, W. W. (1983). Peer relations. In P. H. Mussen (Ed.), *Handbook of child psychology: Vol. 4. Socialization, personality, and social development* (pp. 103–196). New York: Wiley.

Head Start Bureau. (1980). *A Handbook for involving parents in Head Start* (DHHS Publication No. OHDS 88-331187). Washington, DC: U.S. Government Printing Office.

Heath, S. B. (1983). *Ways with words: Language, life, and work in communities and classrooms.* New York: Cambridge University Press.

Heath, S. B., & MacLaughlin, M. W. (1989). A child resource policy: Moving beyond dependence on school and family. *Phi Delta Kappan, 68*(8), 576–581.

Heaverside, S., & Farris, E. (1989). *Educational partnership in public elementary and secondary schools.* Washington, DC: Office of Educational Research and Improvement.

Hedrich, V., & Jackson, C. (1977). Winning play at home base. *American Education, 13*(6), 27–30.

Heleen, O. (1990). Schools reaching out: An introduction. *Equity and Choice, 6*(3), 5–9.

Helm, J. (1994). Family theme bags: An innovative approach to family involvement in the school. *Young Children, 49*(4), 48–52.

Henderson, A. T. (1987). *The evidence continues to grow: Parent involvement improves student achievement.* Columbia, MD: National Committee for Citizens in Education.

Henderson, A. T., Marburger, C. L., & Ooms, T. (1986). *Beyond the bake sale: An educator's guide to working with parents.* Columbia, MD: National Committee for Citizens in Education.

Hess, R. D., & Holloway, S. D. (1984). Family and school as educational institutions. In R. D. Parke (Ed.), *Review of child development research: Vol. 7. The family* (pp. 179–222). Chicago: University of Chicago Press.

Hetherington, E. M. (1988). Parents, children and siblings six years after divorce. In R. A. Hinde & J. Stevenson-Hinde (Eds.), *Relationships within families* (pp. 311–331). Oxford: Oxford University Press.

Hetherington, E. M., & Camara, K. A. (1984). Families in transition: The processes of dissolution and reconstitution. In R. D. Parke (Ed.), *Review of child development research: Vol. 7. The family* (pp. 398–439). Chicago: University of Chicago Press.

Hewison, J., & Tizard, J. (1980). Parent involvement and reading attainment. *British Journal of Educational Psychology, 50*(3), 209–215.

Hill, E. (1967). *Evan's Corner.* New York: Holt.

Hodgkinson, H. (1987). *All one system: Demographics of education—kindergarten through graduate school.* Washington, DC: Institute for Educational Statistics.

Hoffer, T. B., & Coleman, J. S. (1990). Changing families and communities: Implications for schools. In B. Mitchell & L. L. Cunningham (Eds.), *Educational leadership and changing contexts of families, communities and schools: Eighty-ninth Yearbook of the NSSE, Part II* (pp. 118–134). Chicago: National Society for the Study of Education.

Hoffman, L. W. (1984). Work, family, and the socialization of the child. In R. D. Parke, *Review of child development research: Vol. 7. The family* (pp. 179–222). Chicago: University of Chicago Press.

Holt, J. C. (1964). *How children fail.* New York: Pitman.

Hubert, B. D. (1989). Students belong in the "parent-teacher" conference, too. *Educational Leadership, 47*(2), 30.

Hunt, J. M. (1961). *Intelligence and experience.* New York: Ronald.

Hunter, M. (1989). Join the "Par-aide" in education. *Educational Leadership, 47*(2), 36–41.

Hurst, C. O. (1993). Teaching in the library: Dark and stormy reading. *Teaching Pre K–8, 23*(5), 92–94.

Huston, A. C. (1991). Children in poverty: Developmental and policy issues. In A. C. Huston (Ed.), *Children in poverty* (pp. 1–22). New York: Cambridge University Press.

Huston, A. C., Donerstein, E., Fairchild, H., Feshback, N. D., Katz, P. A., Murray, J. P., Rubenstein, E. A., Wilcox, B. L., & Zuckerman, D. (1992). *Big world, small screen: The role of television in American society.* Lincoln, NE: University of Nebraska Press.

Iverson, B. K., & Walberg, H. J. (1982). Home environment and school learning: A qualitative synthesis. *Journal of Experimental Education, 50*(3), 144–151.

Jacobson, S. K., & Padua, S. M. (1992). Pupils and parks: Environmental education in national parks of developing countries. *Childhood Education, 68*(5), 290–294.

Janosik, E., & Green, E. (1992). *Family life: Process and practice.* Boston: Jones & Bartlett.

Jencks, C., Smith, M. S., Acland, H., Bane, M. J., Cohen, I., Gintis, H., Heyns, B., & Michaelson, S. (1972). *Inequality: A reassessment of family and schooling in America.* New York: Harper & Row.

Jeub, C. (1994). Why parents choose home schooling. *Educational Leadership, 52*(1), 50–52.

Johnson, V. R. (1990). Schools reaching out: Changing the message to "good news." *Equity and Choice, 6*(3), 20–24.

Jones, K. (1988). *Interactive learning events: A guide for facilitators.* New York: Nichols.

Joyce, B., Weil, M., & Showers, B. (1992). *Models of teaching* (4th ed.). Boston: Allyn & Bacon.

Kagan, S. L. (1987). Home-school linkages. In S. L. Kagan, D. R. Powell, B. Weisbourd, & E. F. Zigler (Eds.) *America's family support programs: Perspectives and prospects* (pp. 160–181). New Haven, CT: Yale University Press.

Kagan, S. L. (1994, March). *Families and children: Who is responsible?* Paper presented at the annual meeting of the Association of Childhood International, New Orleans, LA.

Kantrowitz, B., & Wingert, P. (1990). Step by step. *Newsweek, 94*(27), 24–34.

Kaplan, L. (1992). Parent education in home school and society: A course description. In L. Kaplan (Ed.), *Education and the family* (pp. 273–278). Boston: Allyn & Bacon.

Katz, P. A. (1976). The acquisition of racial attitudes in children. In P. A. Katz (Ed.), *Towards the elimination of racism* (pp. 125–154). New York: Pergamon.

Kellogg, J. B. (1988). Faces of change. *Phi Delta Kappan, 70,* 199–204.

Kelly, K. (1993, November). Shock wave (anti) warrior. *Wired,* 4–6.

Kerman, K. (1990). Home schooling day by day. In A. Pedersen & P. O'Mara (Eds.), *Schooling at home: Parents, kids, and learning* (pp. 175–182). Santa Fe, NM: John Muir Publications.

Kidder, T. (1989). *Among school children.* Boston: Houghton Mifflin.

Kidwell, C. S., & Swift, D. W. (1976). Indian education. In D. W. Swift (Ed.), *American education: A sociological view* (pp. 329–390). Boston: Houghton, Mifflin.

Knowles, J. G. (1989). Cooperating with home school parents: A new agenda for public schools? *Urban Education, 23*(4), 392–411.

Kohlberg, L. (1976). Moral stages and moralization. In T. Lickona (Ed.), *Moral development and behavior.* New York: Holt, Rinehart & Winston.

Koran, J., Longino, S., & Shafer, L. (1983). A framework for conceptualizing research in natural history museums and science centers. *Journal of Research in Science Teaching, 20*(4), 325–339.

Kotlowitz, A. (1991). *There are no children here: The story of two boys growing up in the other America.* New York: Doubleday.

Kozol, J. (1967). *Death at an early age.* Boston: Houghton Mifflin.

Kozol, J. (1988). *Rachel and her children: Homeless families in America.* New York: Crown.

Kozol, J. (1991). *Savage inequalities: Children in America's schools.* New York: Crown.

Kumove, L. (1966). *A preliminary study of the social implications of high density living conditions.* Toronto: Social Planning Council of Metropolitan Toronto.

Lamb, M. E. (1986). The changing roles of fathers. In M. E. Lamb (Ed.), *The father's role: Applied perspectives* (pp. 3–27). New York: Wiley.

Lancy, D. F., & Nattiv, A. (1992). Parents as volunteers: Storybook readers/listeners. *Childhood Education, 68*(4), 208–212.

Larner, M., & Halpern, R. (1987). Lay home visiting: Strengths, tensions, and challenges. *Zero to Three, 8,* 1–7.

Lazar, I. (1977). *The persistence of preschool effects: A long-term follow up of fourteen infant and preschool experiments.* Washington, DC: Administration for Children, Youth, and Families.

Lazar, I., & Darlington, R. (1982). *Lasting effects of early education: A report from the Consortium for Longitudinal Studies.* Monographs of the Society for Research in Child Development, Serial No. 195, Vol. 47, Nos. 2–3.

Leacock, E. B. (1969). *Teaching and learning in city schools.* New York: Basic Books.

Leibert, R. M., & Sprafkin, J. (1988). *The early window: Effects of television on children and youth* (3rd ed.). New York: Pergamon.

Levenstein, P. (1977). The mother-child home program. In M. C. Day & R. K. Parker (Eds.), *The preschool in action* (2nd ed.) (pp. 27–49). Boston: Allyn & Bacon.

Levin, H. M. (1991). Cost benefit and cost effectiveness analyses of interactions for children in poverty. In A.

C. Huston (Ed.), *Children in poverty: Child development and public policy* (pp. 222–240). New York: Cambridge University Press.

Levy, D. E. (1992). Teaching family ritual: Sunday, sausage, and solidarity. *Teaching Sociology, 20*(4), 311–313.

Lightfoot, S. L. (1978). *Worlds apart: Relationships between schools and families.* New York: Basic Books.

Lines, P. M. (1991). *Estimating the home schooled population* (Report No. OR 91–537). Washington, DC: Office of Educational Research and Improvement. (GPO ED 1.310/2:337903)

Louv, C. (1990). *Childhood's future.* Boston: Houghton Mifflin.

Lund, L., & Wild, C. (1993). *Ten years after a nation at risk.* New York: The Conference Board.

Macaulay, D. (1988). *How things work.* Boston: Houghton Mifflin.

Maccoby, E. E., & Martin, J. (1983). Socialization in the context of family: Parent–child interaction. In P. H. Mussen (Ed.), *Handbook of child psychology: Socialization, personality and social development* (4th ed.) (pp. 1–102). New York: Wiley.

Maslow, A. H. (1970). *Motivation and personality* (Rev. ed). New York: Norton.

Mayberry, M., Knowles, J. G., Ray, B., & Marlow, S. (1995). *Home schooling: Parents as educators.* Thousand Oaks, CA: Corwin.

McBride, B. A. (1989). Interaction, accessibility, and responsibility: A view of father involvement and how to encourage it. *Young Children, 44*(5), 13–19.

McCarthy, A. R. (1992). The American family. In L. Kaplan (Ed.), *Education and the family* (pp. 3–26). Boston: Allyn & Bacon.

McCormick, L., & Holden, R. (1992). Homeless children: A special challenge. *Young Children, 47*(6), 61–67.

McNeil, J. D. (1990). *Curriculum: A comprehensive introduction* (4th ed.). Glenview, IL: Scott, Foresman.

Meadows, S. (1986). *Understanding child development: Psychological perspectives in an interdisciplinary field of inquiry.* London: Hutchinson.

Merenda, D. W. (1989). Partners in education: An old tradition renamed. *Educational Leadership, 47*(2), 4–7.

Meringoff, L. K. (1980). Influence of the medium on children's story apprehension. *Journal of Educational Psychology, 72,* 240–249.

Metz, E. G. (1993). The camouflaged at-risk student: White and wealthy. *Momentum, 24*(2), 40–44.

Miles, J. (1986–1987). Wilderness as a learning place. *Journal of Environmental Education, 18*(2), 33–40.

Miller, A. C. (1987). *Maternal health and infant survival.* Washington, DC: National Center for Clinical Infant Programs.

Miller, M. S. (1991). *The school book: Everything parents should know about their child's education, from preschool through eighth grade.* New York: St. Martin's Press.

Miller, S., & Campbell, R. (1990). Home schooling in the United States and Canada. In A. Pederson & P. O'Mara (Eds.), *Schooling at home: Parents, kids, and learning* (pp. 67–78). Santa Fe, NM: John Muir Publications.

Minuchin, P. P., & Shapiro, E. K. (1983). The school as a context for social development. In P. H. Mussen (Ed.), *Handbook of child psychology: Vol. 4. Socialization, personality, and social development* (pp. 197–274). New York: Wiley.

Moore, G. T. (1985). State of the art in play environment. In J. L. Frost & S. Sunderlin (Eds.), *When children play* (pp. 171–192). Wheaton, MD: Association for Childhood Education International.

Morgenthau, T. (1989, September 11). Children of the underclass. *Newsweek, 114,* 16–24.

Naisbitt, J., & Aburdene, P. (1990). *Megatrends 2000.* New York: William Morrow.

National Association for the Education of Young Children. (1990). NAEYC position statement on media violence in children's lives. *Young Children, 45*(5), 18–21.

National Center for Children in Poverty. (1990). *Five million children: A statistical profile of our poorest young citizens.* New York: School of Public Health, Columbia University.

National Center for Education Statistics. (1992). What young children do at home: Reading and TV-watching are among the most common family activities for 3- to 8-year-olds. *Principal, 72*(2), 21–24.

National Commission of Excellence in Education. (1983). *A nation at risk: The imperative for educational reform.* Washington, DC: U.S. Government Printing Office.

National Commission on Migrant Children. (1992). *Invisible children: A portrait of migrant education in the United States* (Stock No. 022-003-01173-1, Supt. of Documents). Washington, DC: Author.

National Education Goals. (1993). (ED 1.2:G 53/5).

Neill, A. S. (1960). *Summerhill.* New York: Hart.

Nelson, E. (1986). *Home schooling* (Report No. R-86-0003). Washington, DC: Office of Educational Research and Improvement. (ERIC Document Reproduction Service No. ED 282 348)

Neuman, S.B. (1991). *Literacy in the television age.* Norwood, NJ: ABLEX.

Neuman, S. B., & Roskos, K. (1994). Bridging home and school with a culturally responsive approach. *Childhood Education, 70*(4), 210–214.

The new face of America. (1993). *Time, 147*(21), 54–65.

Nichelason, M. G. (1994). *Homeless or hopeless.* Minneapolis, MN: Lerner.

Nielsen Media Research. (1990). *1990 report on television.* New York: A. C. Nielsen Co.

Noddings, N. (1992). *The challenge to care in schools: An alternative approach to education.* New York: Teachers College Press.

Notar, E. E. (1989). Children and TV commercials: Wave after wave of exploitation. *Childhood Education, 66*(2), 66–67.

Notar, E. E. (1992). They come with stories. *Childhood Education, 68*(3), 131–133.

O'Brien, S. J. (1989). Teachers and parents now play on the same team. *Childhood Education, 66*(2), 106–108.

O'Callaghan, J. B. (1993). *School-based collaborations with families.* San Francisco: Jossey-Bass.

O'Hare, W. P. (1992). America's minorities: The demographics of diversity. *Population Bulletin, 47*(4), 2–40.

Olson, M. R., & Haynes, J. A. (1993). Successful single parents. *Families in Society, 74*(5), 259–267.

Opie, I. A., & Opie, P. (1969). *Children's games in street and playground: Chasing, catching, seeking, hunting, racing, duelling, exerting, daring, guessing, acting, pretending.* Oxford: Clarendon.

O'Reilly, R. C., & Green, E. T. (1992). *School law for the 1990s: A handbook* (2nd ed.). New York: Greenwood.

Oregon Department of Education. (1990). *Business–education partnerships in Oregon.* Salem, OR: Author. (ERIC Document Reproduction Service No. 325 971)

An Ounce of Prevention Fund. (1994). *Head start on Head Start: An Ounce of Prevention Fund paper.* Chicago: Author. (ERIC Document Reproduction Service No. ED 368 475)

Owens, K. (1993). *The world of the child.* Englewood Cliffs, NJ: Merrill/Prentice Hall.

Pardeck, J. T. (1990). An analysis of the deep social structure preventing the development of a national policy for children and families in the United States. *Early Child Development and Care, 57*, 23–30.

Parke, R. D. (1990, Fall). *Family–peer systems: In search of a linking process.* Newsletter. Developmental Psychology, American Psychological Association, Division 7.

Patchin, S. H. (1994). Community service for five-year-olds (and laughing all the way). *Young Children, 49*(2), 20–21.

People v. DeJonge, 501 N.W. 2d 127 (Mich., 1993).

Perchemlides v. Frizzle, no. 16641 (Mass. Hampshire County Superior Court, 1978).

Perry, D. G. (1987, Fall). How is aggression learned? *School Safety*, 23–25.

Physicians Task Force on Hunger in America. (1985). *Hunger in America: The growing epidemic.* Middleton, CT: Wesleyan University Press.

Piaget, J. (1967). *Six psychological studies.* New York: Random House.

Polakow, V. (1993). *Lives on the edge: Single mothers and their children in the other America.* Chicago: University of Chicago Press.

Popin, M. (1990). *The active parenting discussion program.* Marietta, GA: Active Parenting.

Postman, N. (1983). Engaging children in the great conversation. *Phi Delta Kappan, 64*(5), 310–317.

Powell, D. R. (1990). Home visiting in the early years: Policy and program design decisions. *Young Children, 45*(6), 65–73.

Priesnitz, H. (1990). First day of school at thirteen. In A. Pedersen & P. O'Mara (Eds.), *Schooling at home: Parents, kids, and learning* (pp. 200–202). Santa Fe, NM: John Muir Publications.

Proctor, P. (1984). Teacher expectations: A model for school improvement. *Elementary School Journal, 84*(4), 469–481.

Quality Education for Minorities Project. (1990). *Education that works: An action plan for the education of minorities.* Cambridge, MA: Quality Education for Minorities Project, Massachussetts Institute of Technology.

Quint, S. (1994). *Schooling homeless children: A working model for America's public schools.* New York: Teachers College Press.

Ramirez-Smith, C. (1995). Stopping the cycle of failure: The Comer model. *Educational Leadership, 52*(5), 14–19.

Raywid, M. A. (1995). The struggles and joys of trail-blazing: A tale of two charter schools. *Phi Delta Kappan, 76*(7), 555–560.

Reid, W. J., & Crisafulli, A. (1990). Marital discord and child behavior problems: A meta-analysis. *Journal of Abnormal Child Psychology, 18*(1), 105–117.

Rice, M. L., Huston, A. C., Truglio, R., & Wright, J. C. (1990). Words from *Sesame Street:* Learning vocabulary while viewing. *Developmental Psychology, 26*(3), 421–428.

Rich, D. (1987). *Teachers and parents: An adult to adult approach.* Washington, DC: National Education Association.

Rich, D. (1992). *Megaskills: In school and life—the best gift you can give your child.* Boston: Houghton Mifflin.

Rich, J. M. (1992). *Foundations of education: Perspectives on American education.* Englewood Cliffs, NJ: Merrill/Prentice Hall.

Richards, M. H., & Duckett, E. (1994). The relationship of maternal employment to early adolescent daily experience with and without parents. *Child Development, 65*(1), 225–236.

Richardson, S., & Zirkel, P. (1991). Home schooling law. In J. A. Van Galen & M. A. Pitman (Eds.), *Home schooling: Political, historical, and pedagogical perspectives* (pp. 159–210). Norwood, NJ: ABLEX.

Riley, R. W. (1995). Reflections on Goals 2000. *Teachers College Record, 96*(3), 380–389.

Rosenthal, R., & Jacobson. (1968). *Pygmalion in the classroom.* New York: Holt, Rinehart & Winston.

Rotter, J. C. (1987). *Parent-teacher conferencing: What research says to the teacher* (2nd ed.). Washington, DC: National Education Association.

Sadker, M., & Sadker, D. (1985). Sexism in the schoolroom of the '80s: Things haven't changed. Boys still get more attention, encouragement and air time than girls do. *Psychology Today, 19*(3), 54–57.

Sadker, M., & Sadker, D. (1991). *Teachers, schools, and society* (2nd ed.). New York: McGraw-Hill.

Sadker, M., & Sadker, D. (1994). *Failing at fairness: How America's schools cheat girls.* New York: Scribner.

Salt, P., Galler, J. R., & Ramsey, F. C. (1988). The influence of early malnutrition on subsequent behavioral development: The effects of maternal depressive symptoms. *Developmental and Behavioral Pediatrics, 9,* 1–5.

Salzstein, H. D. (1976). Social influence and moral development: A perspective on the role of parents and peers. In T. Lickona (Ed.), *Moral development and behavior: Theory, research, and social issues* (pp. 241–252). New York: Holt Rinehart & Winston.

Sameroff, A., Seifer, R., Barocas, R., Zax, M., & Greenspan, S. (1987). Intelligence quotient scores of 4-year-old children: Social–environmental risk factors. *Pediatrics, 79,* 343–350.

Saul, W., & Newman, A. R. (1986). *Science fare: An illustrated guide and catalog of toys, books, and activities for kids.* New York: Harper & Row.

Scarf, M. (1995). *Intimate worlds: Life inside the family.* NY: Random House.

Schiamberg, L. B. (1988). *Child and adolescent development.* Englewood Cliffs, NJ: Merrill/Prentice Hall.

Schlossman, S. (1976). Before Home Start: Notes towards a history of parent education in America, 1897–1929. *Harvard Educational Review, 46*(3), 436–467.

Schorr, L. (1988). *Within our reach: Breaking the cycle of disadvantage.* New York: Anchor.

Schott, J. C. (1989). Holy wars in education. *Educational Leadership, 47*(2), 61–66.

Schwartz, P. (1995, February 16). The silent family: Together, but apart. *The New York Times,* p. C6.

Schweinhart, L. J., & Weikart, D. P. (1980). Young children group: The effects of the Perry Preschool Program on youths through age 15. *Monographs of the High/Scope Educational Research Foundation, 7.*

Schweinhart, L. J., & Weikart, D. P. (1993). Success by empowerment: The High/Scope Perry Preschool study through age 27. *Young Children, 49*(1), 54–58.

Seay, T. A., & Altekruse, M. K. (1979). Verbal and nonverbal behavior in judgments of facilitative conditions. *Journal of Counseling Psychology, 26,* 108–119.

Seefeldt, C., & Barbour, N. (1994). *Early childhood education: An introduction* (3rd ed.). Englewood Cliffs, NJ: Merrill/Prentice Hall.

Shames, S. (1991). *Outside the dream: Child poverty in America.* Washington, DC: Children's Defense Fund.

Shoop, R. J., & Dunklee, D. R. (1992). *School law for the principal: A handbook for practitioners.* Boston: Allyn & Bacon.

Sigel, I. E. (1982). The relationship between parental distancing strategies and the child's cognitive behavior. In L. M. Laosa & I. E. Sigel (Eds.), *Families as learning environments for children* (pp. 107–131). New York: Plenum.

Sigel, I. E., Dreyer, A. S., & McGillicuddy-DeLisi, A. V. (1984). Psychological perspectives of the family. In

R. D. Parke (Ed.), *Review of child development research: Vol. 7. The family* (pp. 42–79). Chicago: University of Chicago Press.

Sigel, I. E., McGillicuddy-DeLisi, A. V., & Goodnow, J. J. (Eds.). (1992). *Parental belief systems: The psychological consequences for children* (2nd ed.). Hillsdale, NJ: Lawrence Erlbaum Associates.

Silber, J. (1989). *Straight shooting: What's wrong with America and how to fix it.* New York: Harper & Row.

Singer, J. L., & Singer, D. G. (1980). *Television, imagination, and aggression: A study of preschoolers.* Hillsdale, NJ: Lawrence Erlbaum Associates.

Singer, J. L., & Singer, D. G. (1990). *The house of make believe: Children's play and the developing imagination.* Cambridge, MA: Harvard University Press.

Smilansky, S., & Shefatya, L. (1990). *Facilitating play: A medium for promoting cognitive socio-emotional and academic development in young children.* Gaithersburg, MD: Psychosocial-Educational Publications.

Smith, M. L. (1990). *Walking the edges: Tracing literacy across three generations.* Unpublished doctoral dissertation, University of Cincinnati, Cincinnati, OH.

Smith, T. B. (1994). *Home-based family literacy mentoring: A guide for Head Start teachers.* (ERIC Document Reproduction Service No. ED 372 290)

Smith, T. B., & Newman, S. (1993). Older adults in early childhood programs: Why and how. *Young Children, 48*(3), 32–35.

Smolowe, J. (1993). Intermarried, with children. *Time, 147*(21), 65–67.

Smrekar, C. E. (1993). Rethinking family–school interactions: A prologue to linking schools and social services. *Education and Urban Society, 25*(2), 175–186.

Spewock, T. S. (1991). Teaching parents of young children through learning packets. *Young Children, 47*(1), 28–30.

Sprafkin, C., Serbin, L. A., Dernier, C., & Connor, J. M. (1983). Sex-differentiated play: Cognitive consequences and early interventions. In M. B. Liss (Ed.), *Social and cognitive skills: Sex roles and children's play* (pp. 168–192). New York: Academic Press.

Stallings, J. (1980). Allocated academic learning time revisited, or beyond time on task. *Educational Researcher, 9*(11), 11–16.

Stein, C. B., Jr. (1986). *Sink or swim: The politics of bilingual education.* New York: Praeger.

Stiggins, R. J. (in press). *Student-Centered Classroom Assessment* (2nd ed.). Englewood Cliffs, NJ: Merrill/Prentice Hall.

Stinnett, N., & DeFrain, J. (1986). *Secrets of strong families.* Boston: Little, Brown.

Studer, J. R. (1993–1994). Listen so that parents will speak. *Childhood Education, 70*(2), 74–76.

Sutherland, Z., & Arbuthnot, M. H. (1991). *Children and books* (8th ed.). New York: HarperCollins.

Swap, S. M. (1993). *Developing home-school partnerships: From concepts to practice.* New York: Teacher's College Press.

Szasz, M. C. (1977). *Education and the American Indian.* Albuquerque, NM: University of New Mexico Press.

Szasz, M. C. (1988). *Indian education in the American colonies, 1607–1783.* Albuquerque, NM: University of New Mexico Press.

Taylor, K. W. (1981). *Parents and children learn together.* New York: Teachers College Press.

Teale, W. H. (1986). Home background and young children's literacy development. In W. H. Teale & E. Sulzby (Eds.), *Emergent literacy: Writing and reading* (pp. 173–206). Norwood, NJ: ABLEX.

Terpstra, M. (1994). A home/school school district partnership. *Educational Leadership, 52*(1), 57–58.

Thompson, S. (1993a). Whole child, whole community. In S. Thompson (Ed.), *Whole child, whole community* (pp. 1–4). Boston: Institute for Responsive Education.

Thompson, S. (Ed.). (1993b). *Whole child, whole community.* Boston: Institute for Responsive Education.

Tiedt, P. L., & Tiedt, I. M. (1989). *Multicultural teaching: A handbook of activities, information and resources* (3rd ed.). Boston: Allyn & Bacon.

Tittle, C. K. (1986). Gender research and education. *American Psychologist, 41*(10), 1161–1168.

Travers, P. D., & Rebore, R. W. (1995). *Foundations of education: Becoming a teacher* (3rd ed.). Boston: Allyn & Bacon.

Truglio, R., Huston, A., & Wright, J. (1988). *The relation between children's print and television use to early reading skills.* Manhattan, KS: Center for Research on the Influences of Television on Children, Department of Human Development, University of Kansas.

Tushnet, N. C. (1993, April). *Educational Partnerships Program as a force for educational change: Findings for a national study.* Paper presented at the meeting of the American Educational Research Association, Atlanta, GA. (ERIC Document Reproduction Service No. ED 360 731)

Uphoff, J. K. (1993). Religious diversity and education. In J. A. Banks & C. A. McGee-Banks (Eds.), *Multicultural education: Issues and perspectives* (2nd ed). (pp. 90–107). Boston: Allyn & Bacon.

U.S. Bureau of the Census. (1991). *Census of Population and Housing Data. CPH-L-80.* Washington, DC: U.S. Government Printing Office.

U.S. Bureau of the Census. (1992). *Current Population Reports. No. 174 and No. 175.* Washington, DC: U.S. Government Printing Office.

U.S. Bureau of the Census. (1993). *Statistical abstract of the United States: 1993* (113th ed.). Washington, DC: U.S. Government Printing Office.

U.S. Bureau of the Census. (1994). *Statistical abstract of the United States: 1994* (114th ed.). Washington, DC: U.S. Government Printing Office.

U.S. Department of Education. (1986). *What works: Research about teaching and learning.* Washington, DC: Author.

U.S. Department of Education. (1991). *America 2000: An education strategy.* Washington, DC: Author.

U.S. Department of Education. (1993). *Goals 2000: Educate America.* Washington, DC: Author.

U.S. Department of Education. (1994). *Strong families, strong schools.* Washington, DC: Author.

Valente, W. D. (1994). *Law in the schools* (3rd ed.). Englewood Cliffs, NJ: Merrill/Prentice Hall.

Van Galen, J. A. (1988). Becoming home schoolers. *Urban Education, 23*(1), 89–106.

Van Galen, J. A., & Pitman, M. A. (1991). *Home schooling: Political, historical, and pedagogical perspectives.* Norwood, NJ: ABLEX.

Voss, M. M. (1993, Dec.). "I just watched": Family influences on one child's learning. *Language Arts, 70,* 632–641.

Wagner, N. J. (1995). *Into the woods.* Unpublished master's thesis, University of Maryland, Baltimore, MD.

Wagstaff, L. H., & Gallagher, K. S. (1990). Schools, families and communities: Idealized images and new realities. In B. Mitchell & L. L. Cunningham (Eds.), *Educational leadership and changing contexts of families, communities, and schools: Eighty-ninth Yearbook of NSSE, Part II* (pp. 91–117). Chicago: National Society for the Study of Education.

Walberg, H. J. (1984). Improving the productivity of America's schools. *Educational Leadership, 41*(8), 19–27.

Walberg, H. J., & Tsai, S. (1985). Correlates of reading achievement and attitude: A national assessment study. *Journal of Educational Research, 78,* 159–167.

Walker, G. H., & Kuerbitz, I. E. (1979). Reading to preschoolers as an aid to successful beginning reading. *Reading Improvement, 16,* 149–154.

Wallace, N. (1990). Home schooling's unique structure. In A. Pedersen & P. O'Mara (Eds.), *Schooling at home: Parents, kids, and learning* (pp. 183–190). Santa Fe, NM: John Muir Publications.

Wallerstein, J. S., Corbin, S. B., & Lewis, J. H. (1988). Children of divorce: A ten-year study. In E. M. Hetherington and J. D. Arasteh (Eds.), *Impact of divorce, single parenting and step parenting on children* (pp. 197–214). Hillsdale, NJ: Lawrence Erlbaum Associates.

Webb, L. D., Metha, A., & Jordan, K. F. (1996). *Foundations of American education* (2nd ed.). Englewood Cliffs, NJ: Merrill/Prentice Hall.

Weber, E. (1969). *The kindergarten.* New York: Teachers College Press.

Webster, D. (n.d.). *The BSD lighthouse project.* Bennington, VT: Bennington School District.

Weikart, D. P., & Schweinhart, L. J. (1991). Disadvantaged children and curriculum effects. In L. Rescorla, M. C. Hyson, & K. Hirsch-Pasek (Eds.), *Academic instruction in early childhood: Challenge or pressure?* (No. 53) (pp. 57–64). San Francisco: Jossey-Bass.

Weikart, D., Bond, J. T., & McNeil, J. (Eds.). (1978). The Ypsilanti Perry Preschool Project: Preschool years and longitudinal results through fourth grade. Monograph of the High/Scope Educational Research Foundation, No. 3. Ypsilanti, MI: High Scope Foundation.

Weinberg, M. (1977). *A chance to learn: A history of race and education in the United States.* New York: Cambridge University Press.

Weitzman, L. J. (1985). *The divorce revolution.* New York: Free Press.

Wells, G. (1986). *The meaning makers: Children learning language and using language to learn.* Portsmouth, NH: Heinemann.

Werner, E. E., & Smith, R. S. (1982). *Vulnerable but invincible: A longitudinal study of resilient children and youth.* New York: McGraw-Hill.

Werner, E. E., & Smith, R. S. (1992). *Overcoming the odds: High risk children from birth to adulthood.* Ithaca: Cornell University Press.

Westinghouse Learning Corporation–Ohio University. (1969). *The Impact of Head Start.* Springfield, VA: Clearinghouse for Federal Scientific and Technical Information, U.S. Department of Commerce.

White, B. L. (1971, October). *Fundamental early environmental influences on the development of competence.* Paper presented at the Third Western Symposium on Learning, Cognitive Learning, Washington State College, Bellingham, WA.

White, B. L., & Watts, J. C. (1973). *Experience and environment: Major influences on the development of the young child* (Vol. 1). Englewood Cliffs, NJ: Prentice Hall.

White, B. P., & Phair, M. A. (1986). "It'll be a challenge!" Managing emotional stress in teaching disabled children. *Young Children, 41*(2), 44–48.

Whitman, W. (1855). *Leaves of grass.* Brooklyn, NY: Andrew & James Rome.

Williams, L. R. (1992). Determining the curriculum. In C. Seefeldt (Ed.), *The early childhood curriculum: A review of current research* (2nd ed.) (pp. 1–15). New York: Teachers College Press.

Williams, P. A., Haertel, E. H., Haertel, G. D., & Walberg, N. J. (1982). The impact of leisure time television on school learning: A research synthesis. *American Educational Research Journal, 19*(1), 19–50.

Wisconsin v. Yoder, 406 U.S. 205 (1972).

Wissbrun, D., & Eckart, J. A. (1992). Hierarchy of parental involvement in schools. In L. Kaplan (Ed.), *Education and the family* (pp. 119–132). Boston: Allyn & Bacon.

Zelizer, V. A. (1985). *Pricing the priceless child: The changing social value of children.* Princeton, NJ: Princeton University Press.

Zinsmeister, K. (1990, June). Growing up scared. *Atlantic Monthly, 265,* 49–66.

Index